Pra

ALL AB

Named one of the 5 Books Not to Miss
by *USA Today*

Listed as one of the 35 Best Books to Give
as Holiday Gifts This Year by *The New York Post*

"Infused with nostalgia and [Mel Brooks's] signature hilarity."

—*Parade*

"In this laugh-a-minute memoir, actor and producer Brooks looks back at his rise through Hollywood, gleefully doling out punch lines along the way. . . . Studded with snickering asides and rapid-fire jokes, Brooks's account of making it in show biz is just as sidesplitting as his movies."

—*Publishers Weekly* (starred review)

"Brooks is legendary in comedy, TV, and film, and his upbeat memoir is just the sort of fun book many readers are seeking."

—*Booklist*

"Worth the wait . . . Brooks has told many of these stories countless times over the years, but they remain as funny and endearing as ever, especially when presented in the full context of his life. It's a story told by an inveterate writer in a wonderfully conversational style, with a hint of childlike wonder at the things he's been able to experience and create. . . . A must-read for fans of comedy, film, and theater."

—*Library Journal* (starred review)

"If you're a Mel Brooks fan, *All About Me!* is the book you've been waiting for."

—*The AV Club*

"Mel Brooks has written about a life that truly epitomizes the American dream. Even at 480 pages, you will be sorry when you reach the end."

—*bookreporter*

"Full of both hilarity and wisdom."

—ADAM GRANT (15 Inspiring Books to Read Over the Holidays)

"This book has everything you would ever want Mel Brooks to tell you, and at 480 pages it is still not enough! Pure joy."

—JUDD APATOW

"Mel Brooks is Mount Hilarious. All any of us can do is look up and feel small and not as funny in comparison."

—MARC MARON

"No one ever made me laugh harder than Mel Brooks. There was no more magical couple than Mel and Anne Bancroft. I treasure every memory with him and with them."

—NORMAN LEAR

"There are people who have great stories and there are people who tell great stories. Mel is that precious combination of a person with amazing stories who happens to be one of the greatest storytellers of all time. Lucky for him? Lucky for us!"

—SARAH SILVERMAN

"If you are holding the great Mel Brooks's memoir and you are wasting time reading this blurb, you're an idiot."

—CONAN O'BRIEN

"This marvelous book by the great man himself will give you a mega-dose of sheer reading pleasure. It's the personal, delightfully revealing life story of a giant comic talent. *All About Me!* delivers a much-needed, therapeutic supply of full-out laughter."

—DICK CAVETT

"*All About Me!* isn't a typical comedy memoir, and why would it be? Mel is a singular talent, still witty, still sharp, and still zinging us after all these years. These stories thread a hilarious narrative that is also profound and touching. Reading this, you'll learn very quickly why Mel Brooks is a king of comedy."

—WANDA SYKES

"Not since the Bible have I read anything so powerful and poignant. And to boot—it's a lot funnier!"

—M. BROOKS

ALL ABOUT ME!

ALL ABOUT ME!

My Remarkable Life in Show Business

Mel Brooks

BALLANTINE BOOKS NEW YORK

2022 Ballantine Books Trade Paperback Edition

Published in the United States by Ballantine Books,
an imprint of Random House, a division of
Penguin Random House LLC, New York.

BALLANTINE is a registered trademark and the colophon is a
trademark of Penguin Random House LLC.

Originally published in hardcover in the United States by Ballantine Books,
an imprint of Random House, a division of
Penguin Random House LLC, in 2021.

ISBN 978-0-593-15913-2
Ebook ISBN 978-0-593-15912-5

Printed in the United States of America on acid-free paper

randomhousebooks.com

2 4 6 8 9 7 5 3 1

"I was so careful.
I picked the wrong play, the wrong director, the wrong cast.
Where did I go right?"

—Max Bialystock, *The Producers*

Preface

The writing of this book serves as a kind of confession.

You, the readers, will be my confidants. I'm going to tell you all my secrets. Things I've never told anybody. Things I don't want anybody to know! I don't want you to breathe a word of what you find out in this book. Keep everything under your hat!

Wait a minute, wait a minute . . . that might not work.

I'm not in a confessional booth, and a lot of you are probably not priests.

This is a book! And this book needs to sell!

So let me revise what I've just told you:

Don't keep it under your hat. Spill the beans! Spread the word. Let the secrets out! Tell all! Tell everybody! Let everybody you know hear all the terrible things I've done. Everything I didn't want the world to know—shout it from the rooftops!

(Because I think I'm gonna need a couple of million confidants to make any money on this book.)

So fasten your seatbelts and hang on for this wild ride that's mostly about my life and career in this crazy thing called show business.

Okay, let's start the adventure!

Mel Brooks

Contents

ALL ABOUT ME!

Chapter 1

Brooklyn

It is 1931, I am five years old, and my older brother Bernie takes me to see a movie called *Frankenstein* at the Republic Movie Theatre. Big mistake! That evening, even though it was a hot summer night, I closed the window next to my little bed. My mother hears it being closed and immediately comes into the bedroom and quickly opens it.

"Mel," she says, "we're on the top floor and it's a hundred degrees in here. It's very hot. We have to keep the window open."

I counter with, "No, we must keep it closed! Because if we keep it open, Frankenstein will come up the fire escape and grab me by the throat and kill me and eat me!"

(Even though it was the doctor who was named Frankenstein, all the kids called the monster Frankenstein because that was the title of the picture.)

My mother, realizing that she could never win by demanding that the window stay open, decides to reason with her five-year-old baby boy. "Mel," she says, "let's say you are right. That Frankenstein wants to come here and kill you and eat you. But let's look at all the trouble he's going to have to get to Brooklyn. First of all, he lives in Transylvania. That's somewhere in Romania. That's in Europe. And that's a long, long ways away. So even if he decides to come here, he has to get a bus or a train or hitchhike to somewhere he can get a boat to go to America. Believe me, nobody is going to pick him up. So let's say he's lucky enough to find a boat that would take him here. Okay, so he is here in New York City, but he really doesn't know how the subways work. When he asks people they just run away! Finally, let's say he figures out it's not the IRT, it's the BMT and he gets to Brooklyn. Then he's got to figure out how to get to 365 South Third Street. Okay, it's going to be a long walk. So let's say he finally gets to Williamsburg and he finally finds our tenement. But remember, all the windows at 365 are going to be wide open and he's had a long journey, so he must be very hungry. So if he has to kill and eat somebody, he probably would go through the first-floor window and eat all the Rothsteins who are living in apartment 1A. And once he's full, there is no reason for him to go all the way up to the fifth floor and eat you."

The story made good sense to me. "Okay," I said, "open the window. I'll take a chance." And that's how my patient, loving mother solved only one of the many problems I would hand her each day.

Since we're talking about me, let me go back to the very beginning. I was born on June 28, 1926. As far as I was concerned, a very good time to be born. Maybe not so good a date for the Archduke Ferdinand of Austria, as it was the twelfth anniversary of his assassination, which kicked off World War I. But in America things were good, we were still at peace and the Great Depression wouldn't start until 1929. I was born in the Williamsburg section of Brooklyn, New York. That's where the Williamsburg Bridge makes its way over to Manhattan. I was the last child born to Kate Kaminsky, whose maiden name was Katie Brookman. A little later on in life when I was fourteen and learning to be a drummer, it occurred to me that if I was going to be in show business, Mel Brookman was a much better stage name than Melvin Kaminsky (which would be a good name for a professor of Russian literature). So with my new stage name decided on I began painting it on my bass drum, but when I got to B-R-O-O-K- there was no room left for M-A-N. I only had room for one letter, so I threw in an S at the end of BROOK.

Hence, Mel Brooks, which has stood me in good stead ever since. But let's get back to Melvin Kaminsky.

Rumor has it that my mother said she already had three boys and the only reason she tried again was in the hopes that this last child would be a girl. The story goes that when the doctor delivered me and said to my mother, "You have a big, beautiful bouncing baby boy!"

My mother replied, "Do you want him?"

But I'm sure she was kidding. (At least I hope so.)

Being the baby of the family was good stuff. Everything went my way. I had three older brothers: Bernie who was four years older, Lenny who was seven years older, and Irving who was ten years older. I remember Bernie telling me one night that Daddy had come home with a little yellow rubber duck in his hand. Bernie was sure the duck was for him, but Daddy went right past his eager face and of course gave it to the baby—me. Bernie never forgave me for that. But my brothers were wonderful; we were like puppies in a cardboard box. We enjoyed one another's company tremendously. Plenty of fights, but plenty of fun. My uncles and aunts also adored me, as I was the youngest. I was always in the air, hurled up and kissed and thrown in the air again. Until I was five, I don't remember my feet touching the ground.

When I was only two years old my father died. Max, like so many others at that time, was swept away by tuberculosis. It wasn't very traumatic to me at that age, but it was to my older brothers. I was probably six years old when I realized that other kids had fathers and I didn't. It was a brushstroke of depression that really never left me, not having a father, another great wellspring source of love that every child is entitled to. My father's absence caused a lingering frustration in my life. I felt cheated because he never got to enjoy being a proud father. It was a shame that he never got to see me succeed in my career.

The eldest of my brothers, Irving, kind of took over as a surrogate dad to us. We didn't have much money, so during the winter,

Irving would find a broken sled that somebody had thrown out and make a big present of it for me. Then he would pull me around the block on it in the snow. I'd say, "One more time, Irv, please!" and even though he had already done it twenty times and his hands were frozen, he still gave me one more ride around the block. Nothing quite like having an older brother.

Even though my brother Bernie wasn't very tall (he was only five feet five), he was a great underhand softball pitcher and a great hitter too. Lenny used to catch for him. Bernie became one of the best-known pitchers in the schoolyard. I was so proud of him. Unfortunately, he peaked at fourteen.

My brother Lenny was especially good to me on Saturday nights. When he left the house, god bless him, he would flip me a half a buck. (A small fortune to a little kid!) For half a buck in Brooklyn in those years I could go out with my friends and get a salami sandwich and a Dr. Brown's Cel-Ray tonic. And then I still had money left over for joining my friends at the movie house for a Saturday night double feature. And after that I still had fifteen cents left so I'd end up in an ice cream parlor and I'd have a frappe—two scoops of vanilla ice cream smothered in chocolate syrup with a cherry on top. Half a buck. It covered all of it!

Lenny also got me hooked on swing music. He was madly in love with Larry Clinton and his vocalist, Bea Wain, and with Shep Fields and his Rippling Rhythm, which sounded like somebody blowing bubbles into a glass of seltzer water. Lenny spent all his money on clothes; especially on a fedora hat he bought from Moe Penn's, a hat store in Williamsburg. For twenty minutes he just worked the brim to get it exactly right. I used to sit on the toilet seat, cover down, and watch Lenny as he adjusted his Moe Penn hat in the medicine chest mirror. He would try the brim up and then shake his head no. Put the brim down front and back and shake his head no. Put the back up, put the brim down in front, and then with a broad smile on his face nod his head yes. He was happy. A private moment that I'll always be grateful to him for allowing me to share.

My brothers were all wonderful. And even though they didn't have a father of their own, they made sure that this little half-orphan, Melvy, who would never get to know his father, was cared for and looked after.

Not by choice, my mother became both parents. After my brothers were old enough to work, Kitty was able to stay home with her youngest son, me, "Melvy." We got to know each other. She was my first comic foil, and enabler, and nurtured my imagination. On a Saturday morning she would give me three empty milk deposit bottles, which, upon return to the grocer, got me three cents each. Nine cents, I was short one penny to get into the movie house for a matinee. And believe it or not, during the Depression sometimes we didn't have that extra penny in the household. So my mother would go next door to borrow a penny from a neighbor so that I could make the dime for the movie ticket.

I couldn't wait for Saturday morning. The movie theaters opened at ten o'clock and we'd all be there. It was the beginning of a lifelong love affair. For one thin dime, you got two feature films, serials, a race, a newsreel, an animated cartoon, and coming attractions. Movies were magic. You stepped out of the real world (which had terrible things in it, like homework) and into a land of happy endings where dreams came true. There was nothing like the movies. My mother would send me to the theater with a salmon and tomato sandwich, wrapped in wax paper—"'cause it's a long day, you know?"

My mother was a true heroine. Losing her husband when she was only thirty, and then having four little kids to raise without a father. She was busy from morning to night: getting breakfast, washing dishes, doing laundry, scrubbing floors, cooking dinner, and finally getting her children to sleep. Everybody assumed my mother had a Yiddish or Jewish accent, probably because of my being the 2000 Year Old Man with Carl Reiner, which I performed with a decidedly Jewish accent. Actually, strangely enough if my mother had any accent at all it was Irish. As a little kid she went to public school in New York City on the Lower East Side and practically all the teachers in the city at that time were Irish. So when she learned how to speak English, she spoke it with a bit of an Irish brogue. Instead of "Thirty-third Street" she'd say, "Tirdy-tird Street." And instead of "Flush the toilet!" She'd say, "Flush the terlet!"

My mother was definitely short. So short in fact that I think she could walk under a coffee table with a high hat on. I loved her to pieces. She was particularly sweet and loving to me, her darling baby boy. I suspect I inherited my love for music from my mother's wake-up songs. She used to wake me at eight o'clock every morning to get me ready for kindergarten. She always was singing along with Bing Crosby, who had a radio broadcast between eight and eight-fifteen every weekday morning. I still remember her sunny voice singing a Crosby hit, "I Found a Million Dollar Baby (in a Five and Ten Cent Store)."

"If you should run into a shower,
Well step inside my cottage door,
And meet the million dollar baby
From the five and ten cent store."

But what I particularly remember was that on cold winter mornings my mother would lay out my school clothes on top of our apartment radiator so they were nice and toasty. Then, she would take the heated clothes and dress me under the covers so that when I popped out of bed I was completely warm. No greater love.

Living in an apartment just below us on the fourth floor was my mother's mother, my grandma Gertrude, and her daughter, my aunt Sadie. Sadie was the youngest of Grandma's children—which began with Uncle Joe; Aunt Jenny; my mom, Kitty; then Aunt Mary; Aunt Dottie; and finally the last unmarried one, Sadie, who was last born and saddled with the job of taking care of her mom, my grandma. Sadie was a terrific sister to my mother. She was always there for her, especially when my father died. She worked in a Garment Center factory on Seventh Avenue, like almost everybody in our building did. But she was not just any ordinary worker; she was a "floor lady" (the male equivalent at the time was a foreman). She was responsible for the output and conditions of all the seamstresses on her floor. Sadie made a fairly good salary in those days, for roughly fifty hours of work a week she got the amazing sum of $30—which, believe it or not, was a lot of money when most workers were getting $18 to $22. When my mother was widowed, Sadie gave her about a third of her income each week. She also provided my mother with a couple of extra dollars a week by bringing home some work for her from her factory. Usually they were big bundles of bathing suit sashes, which were the shoulder straps that crossed at the back of the bathing suits. They were sewn on the back side of the fabric, and my mother was given a steel rod, which she used to reverse the fabric and turn them right side out, nice and shiny. A couple of times a week Sadie would come home with a big bundle of those bathing suit sashes for my mother to turn over. It was laborious work and took her over an hour to do each bundle. I don't know when she went to bed, but she couldn't have gotten more than five or six hours of sleep because she had to be up at six A.M. to prepare breakfast for her four children.

One night, when I got up to pee (the only toilet we had at this time was in the kitchen), while half asleep on my way back to bed, I spotted what I thought was a mound of little diamonds sitting in front of my mother on the kitchen table. I couldn't believe my eyes!

"Mom!" I said. "Diamonds! Look at all those diamonds! I don't even want to know where you got them, all I know is that we're rich!"

She said, "No, no. I'm sorry, Mel. I got them from Aunt Sadie. They're not diamonds. They're called rhinestones. They look like diamonds, but they're not."

I said, "Well, they've got to be worth something, Mom. Look how shiny they are!"

"Yeah . . ." she said, "unfortunately, they're worth less than a penny."

Sadie had provided a little machine for my mother, which clasped the rhinestone with little tin stars with a hoop on the back so that they could be sewn together. Bitterly disappointed that we were poor again, I trudged back to bed.

Although my mother was wonderful, she wasn't always perfect. When I was just old enough to have lost my baby teeth and gotten my second and permanent set of teeth, I began having toothaches. (Probably from Tootsie Rolls, which I adored and chewed nonstop.) After a few nights of listening to moaning about my toothaches, my mother decided to take me to the Bible House to get them taken care of. The Bible House was a children's dental quick fix for the lowest prices in New York. So we went across the Williamsburg Bridge to somewhere on the Lower East Side. The dentist examined my teeth and told my mother that I had two cavities on the upper side of my mouth. Their prices were simple: a dollar for fillings and fifty cents for extractions. Well, you can guess the rest.

My mother promptly had the two troublesome teeth yanked out. I yelled my head off but soon everything was better, no more toothaches. Because of those extractions, later on in life I think I became a poster boy for a new concept in dentistry—implants. To this day many years later, although most of my lower teeth are still mine, fit, and working, a lot of my upper teeth are implants. They're fine, they look and work like teeth are supposed to. I can't really blame my mother for making that foolish choice. If we were going to cast blame, I guess we'd have to blame it on the Depression. Every penny counted, and if truth be told, we didn't have a lot of pennies.

I remember when I was only about five years old we had a fateful family meeting. My mother informed us that our neighbors down the hall, the Applebaums, were moving out of the building. Their soon-to-be-vacant apartment was in the front of the building and had a view of the street. This was in stark contrast to our apartment, which my mother complained had a dismal view of clotheslines strung with freshly washed mattress covers, sheets, pillowcases, etc.—which my mother in a disparaging voice called "wet wash." My mother said, "I'm sick and tired of looking out the windows and seeing nothing but clotheslines full of wet wash and a backyard full of cats."

Her greatest heart's desire was to live in the front of the building to see what was going on in the world. Unfortunately, the Applebaums were paying eighteen dollars a month for that magnificent view of Herstein's drugstore and Feingold's candy store across the street. We were only paying sixteen dollars a month. We didn't have the extra two dollars. What to do, what to do?

Irving immediately said, "We can do it, Mom. I'll find some extra jobs."

Lenny chimed in with, "I know there is a part-time job open at Mercury Messenger and Arnie Miller will lend me his bike."

And Bernie said, "I'll run telephone calls from Herstein's drugstore to everybody in the neighborhood."

I said, "I'll run with you, Bernie!"

(In those days the pharmacist, Herstein, had three telephone booths in his drugstore and people were often called from the tenements to come answer phone calls at his store.)

Somehow between the four of us we would earn the extra two dollars a month. It was a little like a 1930s Clifford Odets play, but believe it or not, like the happy endings in those plays, we did it. We moved into the front apartment, and my mother was in her glory, leaning on a pillow on the windowsill and looking at what was going on in the world beneath her. It was wonderful for my mother, but turned out to be terrible for my brother Bernie . . .

One night, when I was about six years old, I woke up and I desperately had to pee. My brother Bernie was in the bathroom, so I banged on the door and said, "Bernie! I gotta pee! I gotta pee! I gotta pee!"

And through the door I heard, "I'm making! I'm making! I'm making!"

I think making is a lot bigger than peeing. So there's no way

I'm getting in. What are my options? The sink! But I'm too little to reach the sink and I can't find anything to step up on. I also can't find a bucket or anything else like that. I'm really getting desperate. I can't hold it in anymore; I think I'm going to burst. What to do, what to do . . . Ah! I've got it! I see my answer. An open window. So I quickly run over and in a perfect arc I pee right out the front window.

I begin singing an Irving Berlin song, "*Heaven, I'm in heaven . . . and my heart beats so that I can hardly speak . . .*"

Everything was going splendidly until I hear tumult and consternation from down below. What could be going on? So I look out and there on the front stoop below our window is my mother and all our neighbors looking up from the front steps of the building. One of the neighbors points to the window and shouts, "Kitty! It's coming from your window!"

Oh no. Soon after I hear the thumping and bumping of what sounds like a small rhinoceros coming up the tenement stairs. I dive back in my bed and pull the covers over my head. Just as my mother enters our apartment Bernie comes out of the bathroom with a big smile on his face and says, "Hi, Mom!"

Bang! She greets him with a resounding smack that sends him crashing to the floor and screams, "How could you do that? Are you crazy?" I stayed hidden.

My brother Bernie was a real sweetheart of a guy. I didn't confess the truth about this to him until I was nearly sixty-six and he was seventy. But even then, with a faint smile I could see he still resented it.

In those days our neighborhood had an open-window policy that created a sense of community where families looked out for one another, especially one another's kids. Although from the perspective of a free-spirited young kid it also felt like you had dozens of parents who were watching your every move.

The neighborhood was full of kids and we never stopped playing games. Ring-a-levio, Johnny-on-the-pony, kick the can, and, a little later on, stickball and roller hockey. On Saturdays and Sundays I was always too busy to come up for lunch, so my mother would often make a sliced tomato sandwich on a buttered kaiser roll and put it in a paper bag and fling it out the fifth-story window for me to catch and have lunch. I almost never missed, but once when I did, the bag hit the sidewalk and flattened out, drenching the kaiser roll with rich tomato juice from the sliced tomatoes. It was one of the best things that I ever tasted. I loved it. From then on, I always missed it on purpose so the sandwich would flatten out. It was probably the first version of a "pizza" I ever ate.

I've told you about my mother's side of the family, now let me tell you about my father's side. My father's father, Abraham Kaminsky, came from Gdansk (which back then was known as Danzig), a thriving Prussian seaport. He and his brother Bernard were in the herring business. They'd meet the Swedish fishing boats loaded with herring and take the fish to their warehouse where they processed them in big wooden barrels. They made five or six different kinds of cured herring: namely pickled herring, matjes herring, schmaltz herring, rollmop herring, and god-knows-what-else herring.

When they came to America they found a big warehouse on Essex Street in the Lower East Side of Manhattan and continued in their herring trade. My uncle Lee, who was the youngest of ten children that Abraham and Bertha Ruchel produced (and by the way also one of my favorite uncles, more of him later), told me how they set up their business. Putting together their meager savings and a loan from a bank they built a hundred pushcarts. They fitted out the pushcarts with galvanized metal trays that held a block of ice on top of which were scooped-out metal containers that held the herring. They provided wax paper and brown paper bags for the customers. It was a simple but brilliant deal. Each morning they got a hundred pushcart pushers to take the herring out and sell it in Jewish neighborhoods all over Manhattan. At the end of the day the pushcart pushers got fifty percent of the take, and the other fifty percent went to Abraham and Bernard for providing the wherewithal to sell the herring. Sometimes I think that formula would have been good for all kinds of enterprises, but I doubt very much if Henry Ford would have gone for it.

My grandfather Abraham was really a sweet, loving man. The only problem was he hugged and kissed all his grandchildren, and unfortunately, he had a beard made of steel wool and his grandchildren had to suffer those Brillo kisses. It was not a thrilling experience. When my father passed away my grandfather always sent my mother a little money to help us every month. He was a good man.

I think one of the reasons I am a comic is because of my uncle Lee. Very funny, and very peppy, Uncle Lee was a good-looking guy who really loved show business and was a naval lieutenant on a destroyer during WWII. We would all go to my grandfather Abraham's house in Bensonhurst for the Passover seder meal. It was a long table filled with aunts and uncles. Uncle Lee sat right at the bottom because he was one of the youngest, and then next to him were me and my brothers and cousins; we were at the children's table. So my grandfather would read from the prayer book, chanting in Hebrew. My uncle Lee would lean over to the kids' table to translate for us what Grandpa was reciting in Hebrew. But he gave it a twist—he turned into a sportscaster calling a baseball game: "It's a high fly ball heading out to right field! Will it be a Dodger home run? No! The Giants' right fielder Mel Ott leaps into the air and snags it just before it can get into the stands! Crushing the Dodgers' hopes for a chance to even the game and going down to miserable defeat, six to five."

We loved it and always broke into joyous laughter. My grandfather would hear us, and he'd yell, "What's with the laughter down there? The Jews are still in Egypt, what's so funny?"

Uncle Lee also told me a family legend about Grandpa Abraham's uncle Louie Kaminsky from Minsk. I don't know whether it was fact or fiction, but it was pretty funny. It seems that Uncle Louie was some kind of a religious zealot. On Saturdays, he would take stones and bricks and hurl them through the air and break

Me at age eight (center) with my cousin Merrll (left) and my brothers, Bernie, twelve (right), Lenny, sixteen (top left), and Irving, eighteen (top right), on the street in front of my grandpa's house in Bensonhurst, Brooklyn.

every window of every store that was open on Saturday in Minsk. He was always arrested and spent the night in jail.

"Louie," the policemen said, "these stores are not owned by Jews. They're allowed to be open on Saturday."

And Louie countered with, "That doesn't matter. It's Saturday, and on Saturday nothing should be open!"

Even though he knew for the rest of his life he would spend every Saturday night in jail, he still threw the bricks. I've broken a few windows in my life but never on purpose, and I think looking back that there is still a lot of crazy Uncle Louie in me. For instance . . .

Normally at the end of my stand-up performances, I would open the show up for questions from the audience. Sometimes when my response to a question got an enormous laugh I would save that question. One of the questions I saved was: "Mr. Brooks, were you ever arrested?"

My immediate answer was "No!" And then I thought . . . wait a minute.

"Let me amend that. Was I ever arrested? Well . . . nearly."

Here is where the touch of Crazy Uncle Louie in me comes out.

Sometimes on a Sunday afternoon, a couple of us kids would frequent the local Woolworth, which we knew as the five-and-ten because a lot of the items were actually sold for five or ten cents—Hershey bars, little pen-sized flashlights, whistles, yo-yos, etc. We'd often walk up and down the aisles and when the clerks weren't looking we'd try to snatch something. We never called it *stealing*; we used to call it "taking."

"Let's go taking!"

Normally, when no one was looking I could always get a yo-yo or a whistle and slip it into my jacket with no problems. But one Sunday afternoon I tempted fate. There, in a special display of Roy Rogers hats and T-shirts, was a pearl-handled toy replica of a Roy Rogers six-shooter. It was the most thrilling thing I'd ever seen. But how to slip it into my coat? It wasn't a whistle or a yo-yo, not easy. When the clerk at the display turned his head to attend to a customer, I took off my sweater, dropped it on the pistol, and picked it up. I was nearly out the door when hands grabbed me by the scruff of the neck and pulled me back in the store.

A great big man announced, "I'm the manager and I'm sick and tired of you kids stealing!"

And I knew, this was one guy I couldn't con by saying, "just taking."

As the manager marched me up the aisle he said, "I'm gonna call the police and have you arrested! And then I'm gonna call your parents and let them know everything!"

"Please!" I tearfully shouted. "I don't have parents! I just have a mother! My father is dead! Please, give me a break."

The budding actor in me tried his best, but to no avail. The unrelenting manager kept steadfastly marching me toward his office. In a blinding flash an idea popped into my head. I reached into my sweater, pulled out the toy gun, and shouted, "Get back or I'll blow your head off!"

For a moment, it worked. He saw the gun and jumped back. I ran with all my might and got out of the store. I never went back there again, and hoped that he wouldn't remember my face. Chances are he didn't live in our neighborhood but came from Queens or somewhere to work at the store.

I realized then that I could never be half as good as Arsène Lupin, the famous fictional French jewel thief. So right then and there I decided to give up "taking," for good.

When we weren't "taking," my friends and I loved to play stickball. I was a skinny, stringy little kid with endless energy, and I was always running. One day we were playing stickball and I was up at bat. There was a '36 Chevy parked on our street and I took off my brand-new camel's hair Passover holiday sweater, folded it very carefully, and tucked it in that nice niche in the front of the fender right underneath one of the headlights. Then I got a scratch single and a bad throw sent me to second. Suddenly I see this beautiful black '36 Chevy pull away from the curb and take off with my sweater. *Whoosh!* I went after it. "He's out!" they were yelling. "He's out! He left the base!"

But I was gone, the heck with the game. What was that compared with a new holiday sweater? For twenty minutes I chased that car. Somewhere in Flatbush I finally flagged it down and got my sweater back. Jesse Owens could not have made that run any faster, only a ten-year-old boy built like a wire hanger.

When I was about six and my brother Bernie was about ten, we boarded a bus together to go to Camp Sussex. It was a camp in New Jersey that was free for underprivileged children. It was funded by Eddie Cantor, a famous radio, stage, and movie star in those years. It was for kids from ages five to ten, that's why it was just me and Bernie. It was the first time I had ever left home. It was both wonderful and terrible.

When the bus pulled in, I was amazed to see miles and miles of grass and trees and sky. I asked my counselor, "Where are the tenements? Where are the fire escapes? Where are the stores? Where are the cars?" He explained that this was called "the country," and that, believe it or not, there was a lot more of it than the city. I didn't like that a bit. It was pretty hard to swallow. Ever since I was born, all I saw were stoops and streets and stores and buildings. I didn't know about this thing called "the country." It was a little alarming.

But pretty soon I got used to it and discovered the free food—little green apples that grew on an apple tree that you could pick and eat and didn't have to pay for! One afternoon I ate about thirty of them and got the worst bellyache of my life, not to mention the runs. That was about a hundred years ago and I've steadfastly stuck to my vow never to eat another little green apple.

The counselors told us to write to our parents, so it was really the beginning of my career as a writer. With my stubby pencil I used to write letters that went something like this:

Dear Mom,
I miss you. Send me gum. I love you.
Your son,
Mel

Rather primitive. It wasn't much of a letter, and later in life my writing skills improved somewhat. I actually won an Academy Award for writing the original screenplay for *The Producers*. But it was a beginning, and a beginning is a beginning.

I remember always being funny, but the first time was at Camp Sussex. I was about six years old and whatever the counselors said, I would turn it around.

"Put your plates in the garbage and stack the scraps, boys!"

"Stay at the shallow end of the pool until you learn to drown!"

"Who said that? Kaminsky! Grab him! Hold him!" *Slap!*

But the other kids laughed and I was a success. I needed a success. I was short. I was scrawny. I was the last one they picked to be on the team. "Oh, all right, we'll take him. Put him in the outfield."

I would have liked to have been taller, but as I understood it there are only two ways to be taller. One way was to have very tall parents. That would assure that you wouldn't be so short, you would certainly be taller. The other way was a difficult process: large men pulled up on your head and your chin while other large men grabbed your ankles and pulled down with all their might for four hours a day. I thought it through and decided no, I'll stay short. Besides, if they don't set your ankles back again right you walk like Harry Ritz for the rest of your life. (More about the Ritz Brothers later.)

I liked most of our activities at Camp Sussex: playing games like tag and hide and seek, and swimming in the roped-off section of the lake. Every once in a while bullies would pick on me, but my brother Bernie always came to my rescue. He got into many fights, but he never lost. When Bernie was in his late seventies he moved to Las Vegas, and I made sure to go see him at least twice a year. And every time I did we would always sing the song that they used to sing to us right when we got off the Camp Sussex bus.

"We welcome you to Sussex Camp
We're mighty glad you're here
We'll send the air reverberating with a mighty cheer
Rah! Rah!
We'll sing you in
We'll sing you out
With all our praises we will shout
Hail! Hail!
The gang's all here
And you're welcome to Sussex Camp!"

Many years later I got the chance to thank Eddie Cantor for my time at Camp Sussex. I had begun writing for Sid Caesar in 1950 and had reason to attend a big charitable function at Madison Square Garden with him. I saw that one of the stars on the program was Eddie Cantor. I was still rather young and intimidated by all the big stars, but I gathered my courage and knocked on Eddie Cantor's dressing room door. He said come in and I told him that I was one of the writers on *Your Show of Shows* and he exclaimed, "I love that show!"

I told him that when I was a little kid, I went to Camp Sussex and I thanked him for making that happen. Then I added, "By the way, my mother tells me that she knew you when you were both children and played together on Henry Street on the Lower East Side of Manhattan."

"Yes," he said, "I used to play on Henry Street every day when I was a kid. What was your mother's name?"

I said, "Kitty Kaminsky."

He ran it over a few times, "Kitty Kaminsky . . . Kitty Kaminsky . . ." He said, "I hate to tell ya, I knew every kid that I ever played with on Henry Street and I'm sorry, there was no Kitty Kaminsky."

I couldn't believe it. My mother never lied; she didn't know how to lie. Crestfallen I said, "Well, thanks for saying hello" and shook his hand and went to the door. As I started to leave a burst of revelatory thought exploded in my head. "Wait!" I said. "Her name couldn't have been Kitty Kaminsky. She was just a kid. She wasn't married yet. Back then her name was Katie Brookman!"

He jumped out of his chair. "Katie Brookman! I loved her! A little redhead, freckles, blue eyes. Who knows, if Ida didn't marry me I might have married your mother! She was really cute. I could have been your father! Then maybe I wouldn't have had just five girls. I could have had a boy!"

I said, "You could have had four! I have three older brothers."

We both broke into a fit of laughter. He said, "Katie Brookman, wow."

As I left, I never felt so satisfied in my life—my mother hadn't lied.

When I was about eight or nine I learned to roller skate. I was doing fine until one night right after dinner when I was practicing my "spread-eagle turn," a slow arc made by facing your heels together and turning your toes out to move in a smooth half circle. I remember being in the middle of doing one and being very happy with my progress when suddenly I was knocked down to the street and felt the front wheel of a car go over my belly. To this day I remember the great big *ooff!* that came out of my mouth.

I don't know exactly what happened. Obviously I started my turn before I saw the car, and it suddenly appeared out of nowhere and hit me while I was in the middle of making my turn. I guess a little kid's belly is like a rubber balloon, able to be squashed and then popping right back up. The next thing I knew I was in my brother Irving's arms and he was rushing me to the corner drugstore. I remember onlookers blocking his path and Irving shouting at them, "Get out of the way, you stupid son of a bitch!"

I was shocked. I'd never heard my brother Irving curse before!

Soon enough, I was in an ambulance with Irving headed for St. Catherine's Hospital. When I got there they put me on an X-ray table, took a picture, and put me in a hospital bed. The doctor told Irving that miraculously the X-ray showed nothing was wrong with me, but that they would keep me a few days for observation. No bones were broken and my organs seemed to be intact. Like I said, little kids' bellies are made of rubber. And I was very lucky that the car that ran me over was a light model Ford that in the old days used to be called a "Tin Lizzie" or a "Flivver." Thank goodness it wasn't a Buick or a Cadillac, or I wouldn't be telling this story.

St. Catherine's was a Catholic hospital and the nurses were attired in nun's garb. When they put me in my hospital bed a nun who looked not unlike a huge penguin approached me wearing a heavy wooden cross and holding a glass container in her hand and said, "Urinate in this." When she saw the puzzled expression on my face she quickly added, "Make peepee into this." I said, "I'm sorry. I can't." I simply didn't feel like peeing. She said, "If you don't pee, we'll have to shove something up in your peepee to get it out." I quickly shouted, "Gimme that glass thing!"

I was in the hospital for three days, but it wasn't so bad. There was always family around, I had nonstop visits from neighborhood friends and classmates, and somebody even brought me a Whitman's Sampler, a whole box of delicious chocolate-covered candies, which made the whole thing worthwhile. I was the center of a lot of attention, which always felt good.

One of the other things I was interested in as a kid in Brooklyn was building model airplanes. They were mostly constructed with very light strips of material called balsa wood. We had a little club called the Balsa Bugs consisting of myself, Bernie Steinberg, and Tony Galliani. We made all kinds of planes, from WWI biplanes to single-engine light planes called Piper Cubs. They were all propelled by a rubber-band-driven propeller. Frankly, I think we liked sniffing the airplane glue that held them together more than any other part of the process.

Anyway, one Sunday afternoon after we had finished our doodling, Tony Galliani invited me to his home for a Sunday Italian spaghetti and meatballs dinner. Occasionally my mother would make spaghetti for me and my brothers that we thought was okay. It consisted of boiled egg noodles put into a casserole tray then doused with ketchup and baked until it was ready. My mother then cut squares from it and served them to us. It wasn't bad, but (as I was about to find out) it really wasn't spaghetti.

Tony's apartment was redolent with a wonderful aroma of garlic, basil, and oregano. Already things were looking up! His wonderful, welcoming mother served me a great big dish of lightly al dente La Rosa spaghetti and meatballs swimming in a rich sea of tomato sauce and sprinkled with a generous helping of grated Parmesan cheese. What a revelation! It didn't need anything—I salted it with my own tears of joy.

That night when I got back to our apartment I screamed, "I've tasted spaghetti! I know what spaghetti is now, and, Mom, no offense, but you don't make spaghetti."

I didn't want to make a pest of myself, but every once in a while I would beg Tony to invite me to another Sunday afternoon spaghetti and meatballs dinner. Later on in my life, I think one of the reasons I married Anne Bancroft was the fact that her real name was Anne Italiano and, boy, could she make spaghetti.

As a kid, any time I could put five cents together, I would run across the street to Feingold's candy store and get an egg cream. What is an egg cream? It is a delicious chocolate drink that is made with neither eggs nor cream. Why was it called an egg cream? I don't know. For generations, Talmudic scholars have never been able to answer this profound question. Let me describe this nectar of the gods for you: Into what you might know as the typical Coca-Cola glass with the big round bulge at the top, Mr. Feingold would pump about an inch and a half of U-Bet chocolate syrup (if it wasn't U-Bet, it wasn't honest-to-God chocolate syrup) and on top of that he would put about an inch of milk (in those days we only had whole milk), then he'd move it to the soda squirter which had two functions, one was a powerful thin burst of soda, which would mix the chocolate syrup and the milk together, followed by a soft stream of soda, which would bring the heavenly mixture to its frothy top. He stirred it with a long spoon once or twice and then put it on the marble counter with a slight thud. That thud told you everything. It was indeed an egg cream. The trick was to sip it slowly and make it last as long as possible. And at the end, we always pushed the glass back across the counter to Mr. Feingold and said, "There's still a little chocolate syrup at the bottom, could you give it another spritz?" He'd shake his head and sigh, but he always gave us another spritz. Heaven, pure heaven.

I loved my childhood in Brooklyn. Oftentimes, when I'm interviewed, people ask, "What was the happiest time in your life? Was it making your first movie? Was it winning the Academy Award?"

My answer is always, "Being a little kid in Brooklyn. That is . . . until age nine."

They'd say, "So what happened at nine?"

And I'd say, "Homework." Couldn't run to the playground right after school, couldn't meet the guys right after supper for cards and talk, had to do homework. And I realized, uh-oh, the world wanted something back. Homework, what a blight.

One night, I was having a particularly difficult time with my homework. My teacher, Mrs. Khune, wanted us to name at least six signers of the Declaration of Independence. My brother Irving had just come back home after one of his night classes at Brooklyn College. Irving went to Brooklyn College for eight years to become a pharmacist. Simultaneously, he worked eight hours a day at Rosenthal and Slotnicks, in the Garment Center. He felt it was incumbent upon him to be a father figure, and so he helped raise me. He was my inspiration and my guide through life. There was no cursing in my family. If I even said, "bum," Irving would hit me. That night he heard me moaning and groaning over my homework.

"What's the matter?" Irving asked.

I said, "My teacher wants me to name at least six signers of the Declaration of Independence, and all I could think of is Washington!"

He laughed. "By the way," he said, "Washington is *not* one of the signers of the Declaration of Independence."

Oh! I was crushed, that was my big one. "But there was Jefferson, right? And maybe Franklin?"

"Yes," he said. "You're right on those two. Any others?"

"No! Can't think of another one." I moaned.

Irving thought for a bit and then said, "Where do you play punchball?"

I said, "Right around the corner on Hooper Street."

He said, "Hooper! He's a signer. William Hooper. Now, what's your favorite movie house?"

Without hesitation I answered, "The Commodore Theatre!"

"Which is on what street?"

"Rodney Street."

"Rodney! That's another signer. And where's Greenwald's deli?"

"On Hewes! . . . Wait a minute, are you telling me that all the streets in Williamsburg are signers of the Declaration of Independence?"

He smiled. "Well, most of them. Why do you think they call

this place Williamsburg? Because the Declaration of Independence was signed in Colonial Williamsburg! So there's a good chance that a street name in Williamsburg is a signer of the Declaration of Independence."

Wow! I thought. My teacher only wanted six names, but I gave her over twenty by remembering every street in Williamsburg I had ever played on or walked on. It was the first time I got an A on my homework, all thanks to my genius brother Irving.

My elementary school, P.S. 19, was on 323 South Third Street, which was about a ten-minute walk from our building. I was a bright kid and I was bored, so I'd try to yuk it up in school.

When the teacher said, "Melvin, what do you know about Columbus?"

I'd immediately answer, "Columbus Cleaning and Pressing!"

Which happened to be a well-known neighborhood dry-cleaning shop on Fifth and Hooper. I'd get a bad mark, but I didn't care because I got a big laugh. Why was that laugh important? Why was comedy so important to me? Well, as I mentioned earlier, I wasn't very big. Most of the kids in my class were taller than me. I needed a weapon to protect myself. That weapon turned out to be comedy. I became accepted and was allowed to hang around with the bigger kids because I made them laugh. Comedy made me friends, big friends to protect me from bullies. I made them laugh, and you don't hit the kid that makes you laugh.

At eight years old I could reduce my best friend, Eugene Cohen (who later in life became a theatrical publicist and changed his name to Gene Cogan), to uncontrollable hysterics by singing "Puttin' on the Ritz" in the persona of Boris Karloff. We had folie à deux, a mental disorder that two people share at the same time. It got so bad that Eugene couldn't hear that song near a window, because he might roll out and fall to his death. I could send Eugene crashing to the floor by uttering just one word in Boris Karloff's voice. The word was "antipasto" but in Boris Karloff's voice it came out sounding like "antipaTHto?" That would be the end of

Eugene; he'd be on the floor, laughing his head off no matter how much the teacher punished him. He would have to be dragged to the principal's office by his feet, with his head banging on the steps, still laughing!

Because the kids at P.S. 19 (myself included) were generally so unruly, teachers back then had to be strict and sometimes really tough. In math class Mr. Ziff carried a stopwatch on a leather lanyard, like Captain Bligh from *Mutiny on the Bounty*. If he saw you cribbing or even looking at somebody else's paper during a test, you'd get a sharp whack across the hand with that lanyard. If you misbehaved in our English class, Mrs. Hoyt would smack the base of her palm against your forehead very hard, snapping a few small bones in your neck. When you caused trouble in geography for Mrs. Garrison she would twist your ear until you had to go with it or lose the ear. Everybody in her class was either a potential Van Gogh or an acrobat. I learned how to do backflips to save my ear!

In Brooklyn at the time, you went to elementary school, then junior high, then high school. And after that you were probably taken to the Garment Center and they gave you racks of clothing to push around and you did that until you died. Most of the young men in Williamsburg ended up as shipping clerks, older men maybe as cutters, and as slightly older men, pattern makers, one notch above, then going from shoulder or sleeve work to being a buyer, where you wore a suit and met other people for lunch and drank martinis. It seemed like everyone at 365 South Third Street and its immediate surroundings was destined for Seventh Avenue to work in the Garment Center. To cut, work on machines, or, if you had some personality, a salesperson. I think I would have been a great salesperson. But unlike most of the people in the neighborhood, I had no aspirations of being a shipping clerk, cutter, or even a salesman.

To be perfectly honest, I did briefly work in the Garment Center part-time during the summer break to earn some extra money. I ran errands and mopped the floors of a thirty-four-hundred-square-foot factory called the Abilene Blouse & Dress Company. At ten o'clock each morning I'd run across the street to the coffee shop and get a bagel with cream cheese and coffee for the owner, Mr. Sussman.

One day, curiosity got the best of me, and I said to him, "Mr. Sussman, I don't understand what possessed you to name your company, the Abilene Blouse and Dress Company, after a small town in Texas."

He replied, "Texas? What Texas? I named it after my two daughters: Abby and Lena." So much for suppositions.

I remember coming home one day from junior high and my mother greeted me with an application to Haaren High School for a course in aviation mechanics. Mom figured that people who learned a trade could earn a good living. This was especially relevant to us, as we were struggling through the Depression. She filled out all the forms, brought them home, and gave them to me.

"You sign here, Mel."

I said, "Okay, Mom."

I loved airplanes, and thought maybe one day I would get to fly one. When we lived in Brighton Beach my friend Bobby and I used to go to Floyd Bennett Field to see the planes. We were thrilled when the pilot of a red Waco biplane allowed us to sit in the cockpit for a minute. He showed us the stick in the middle, which when pulled back made the plane go up and when shoved forward made the plane go down; the rudder bar, which made the plane turn right or left; and a throttle, which gunned the engine and made the plane go faster or slower. Of course it wasn't as simple as that, but when it came to a little kid's imagination, I was ready to do it tomorrow.

For five dollars he would take you up in the air, circle the beach, Coney Island, and then land. But in those days five bucks to my pal Bobby and me—it might as well have been a million. It was out of the question.

When my brother Irving got home from night school at Brooklyn College, Mom and I proudly showed him the application to Haaren High School. Irving turned to Mom and said, "Your mind and your heart are in the right place, Mom, but this kid is special. He's different. He has something. He's really bright and I think we've got to give him a chance to go somewhere in life. He's not going to be an aviation mechanic. He's going to go to college." And with that he promptly tore up the application and put it in the trash.

I'll forever be grateful to Irving for seeing in me a future with great expectations.

In 1935 I was nine years old. I was outside one day throwing a ball against the front stoop of my tenement when my uncle Joe came by and said, "Mel, I've got two free tickets to a Saturday matinee of a Broadway musical called *Anything Goes*. Would you like to come with me?"

I shouted, "OH YES!" so loudly that I think I heard windows opening all up and down the street to find out what was going on. Uncle Joe knew how much I loved music because every time he came into our apartment he saw me glued to our little Philco radio listening to the songs of the day. Uncle Joe was another one of my favorite uncles, and the only uncle on my mom's side of the family. Everybody else was an aunt. I guess because my mom, his sister, was without a husband, he helped us out every day in every way he could.

Here I am at age sixteen with my mother, Kitty, in Brighton Beach, Brooklyn.

Uncle Joe drove a checkered cab, a great big beast of a machine that rumbled up and down the streets of New York. He said, "Okay, I'll pick you up Saturday at noon to see the show."

Let me add that Joe was the shortest taxi driver in the city. So on Saturday, when I saw a checkered cab coming down the street without a driver, I knew it was Uncle Joe.

Even back then, it was illegal for a New York cab driver to carry a passenger in his car when he had his empty flag up on the taxi meter. So whenever Uncle Joe took me anywhere in his cab, I had to hide on the floor in the back as long as his flag was up. And that's how, on that long-ago Saturday afternoon in 1935, I went to my first Broadway musical, scrunched down in the back of Uncle Joe's bumpy old taxi.

When we were off and rolling I shouted from the floor in the back, "Uncle Joe? How come you got free tickets to *Anything Goes*?" Even though I was just a kid, I knew it was one of the biggest hits on Broadway at the time.

He said, "Al the doorman at the theater is one of my pals and when I pull in for the night, I take him back home to Brooklyn with me—just like you, on the back floor."

I knew when we were crossing over the Williamsburg Bridge to Manhattan because I heard the loud thrumming as the taxi's tires went over the steel grating. We must have been getting closer to Broadway when I saw the top of the Empire State Building as we passed Thirty-fourth street. (I was just a little disappointed not to see King Kong hanging there.) Soon it was the Chrysler Building on Forty-second Street, I knew it was the Chrysler Building because of the big needle at the top. My heart was racing along with the engine of the cab as we approached the Alvin Theatre on Fifty-second Street. (Later, the Alvin Theatre would be renamed the Neil Simon Theatre—named for one of the most famous and prolific comedy playwrights in Broadway history, who also happened to be one of my co-writers on *Your Show of Shows,* starring Sid Caesar and Imogene Coca, and a dear friend. More about him later.)

Uncle Joe parked right outside the theater. It was no problem in those days; his friend Al the doorman had reserved the space. I got so excited when I got out of the cab and saw the marquee: ANYTHING GOES BY COLE PORTER. STARRING ETHEL MERMAN, WITH WILLIAM GAXTON AND VICTOR MOORE. Wow.

When we finally got to our seats all the way up in the last row of the second balcony I got a little dizzy from the height. I should have known that free seats weren't fifth row on the aisle. The house-lights dimmed and from the orchestra pit came the strains of the overture, a mélange of all the famous Cole Porter hits from the show. One great song after another, not only "I Get a Kick Out of You" but also "You'd Be So Easy to Love," "You're the Top," "It's De-Lovely," "All Through the Night," and, of course, the show's wonderful title song, "Anything Goes."

In those days the cast didn't depend on microphones like Broadway shows do today. When Ethel Merman belted out "You're the Top" even though Uncle Joe and I were two miles away in the cheap seats, it was thrilling but maybe a little *too* loud. What a voice! They said she could hold a note longer than the Chase National Bank. I thought she was the greatest thing since chocolate milk. I had goosebumps.

Anything Goes was falling-down funny. When the final curtain fell, I leapt to my feet and cheered my nine-year-old head off clapping my hands till they stung. Way up there at the top of the second balcony, I figured that I was as close to heaven as I'd ever get.

On the way home, still buzzing with the excitement from the show, I made up my mind, and from the floor of the taxi I announced, "Uncle Joe, I am not going to go to work in the Garment Center like everyone else in our neighborhood." I knew I had bigger fish to fry. I said, "I am going into show business and nothing will stop me!" And, strangely enough, nothing did.

I fell in love forever with Broadway musical comedy that afternoon and also began a lifetime of admiration for the music and lyrics of Cole Porter, who, together with Irving Berlin, is still one of my all-time favorite songwriters. Years later, when I discovered to my amazement that Cole Porter wasn't Jewish, I was taken aback for a moment but then quickly forgave him. I remember thinking while lying awake in bed that night after seeing "Anything Goes" that when I grew up I would like to be a Broadway writer. Not only creating the characters and the stories, but maybe also writing the songs. Being a Broadway songwriter, I decided, would be even better than playing shortstop for the Brooklyn Dodgers, which up until then had been my most fantastic dream.

As a family, we were not very religious and did not keep kosher. As a matter of fact, one of my favorite sandwiches was ham and cheese. However, my grandmother, who for a time lived in the same building, was very observant. Thank god for the long hallways in those old railroad apartments. It gave us at least two minutes to clear the kitchen of non-kosher food before my grandmother could get there. She was a pretty good ice box detective, so my mother hid things like ham in a little tray behind the ice.

I grew up in Williamsburg in the 1930s, during the time of the Great Depression. There was just enough money in the majority of households for the basic necessities: rent, food, clothing, etc. When Hanukkah or Christmas came around, kids didn't get a lot of expensive toys. And even though we were Jewish, we enjoyed the Christmas tradition of hanging up our stockings. Four different-sized stockings were hung up on the bookshelf, which we made believe was the fireplace. And every Christmas morning we were surprised and happy that when we reached into our stockings we found the same wonderful Christmas gift: a box of chocolate snaps. I tried to make mine last for a week, but I always failed. In the magazines we saw pictures of wonderful Christmas toys like beautiful shiny red scooters, but they were way out of reach.

But kids in Brooklyn were inventive. There was no lack of ingenuity. We made our own scooters. We called them push-mobiles. A push-mobile consisted of a flat board around three feet long. We took apart a roller skate, strapped the front end to the front of the board and the back end to the rear of the board. On the front of the board we nailed an empty fruit box. The fruit boxes were discarded from the fruit store after the apples or pears or grapes that they previously had contained had been sold. On top of the box, we nailed two handles made of two-inch wooden struts that came from other places, like egg crates. The push-mobile, like a scooter, was propelled by putting your left foot on top of the board and pushing the ground as hard as you could with your right foot. When you gathered enough speed, you put your right foot up on the board behind your left and merrily traveled along. If you were lucky, you found a long hilly street where you didn't have to push at all. You just shoved off, put both feet on the board, and sped down at breakneck speeds like five miles an hour. It was absolutely thrilling! I wonder if I'm the only person still around that remembers the amazing invention of the push-mobile?

We were too poor to afford tickets for High Holiday services (Rosh Hashanah and Yom Kippur), so we hardly ever attended temple. But at age thirteen, like most Jewish boys, I was bar mitzvahed at a tiny synagogue on Keap Street. Learning Hebrew was nigh on impossible, but I got away with the prayers by memorizing the sounds and syllables. The only thing I remember is that when I was finished, all the kids in the synagogue threw hard candies at me to celebrate, some unfortunately finding their mark. I ended up having a black-eye bar mitzvah!

My path to comedy, and eventually to Broadway, started when I became a drummer. Shortly after my bar mitzvah we moved from the Williamsburg section of Brooklyn to the Brighton Beach section. I started high school at Abraham Lincoln. I tried out for the Abraham Lincoln High School band and was assigned second drummer (in case the first drummer couldn't do it).

In the band was a classmate by the name of Mickey Rich, who played the alto sax. I got to know Mickey and we became pretty good friends. One day, I said, "Rich! Rich? You're not related in any way to Buddy Rich, are you?"

He said, "I try not to brag about it but yeah, he's my older brother."

Wow! Buddy Rich! One of the greatest drummers that ever lived.

I said, "I don't believe it."

He said, "Come on. I'll show you his set of drums."

Wow, wow! I lived on Brighton Sixth, only four blocks away from Brighton Court on Brighton Tenth Street, where Mickey and

Buddy lived. We got to Mickey's house and he led me to a kind of den or study and there was this incredible set of pearl-covered Gretsch drums. On the big bass drum were the letters A.S. and up in the left-hand corner was a shield with the smaller letters B.R. Oh my god. I said, "It *is* Buddy Rich! A.S.—that's Artie Shaw!"

I knew that Buddy Rich was the drummer of Artie Shaw's band. I couldn't believe my eyes. For a while I just gazed in wonder at the drum set. A big bass, a snare, a tom-tom, a hi-hat, and a couple big Zildjian cymbals—an actual drum set that Buddy Rich played on!

Later on, I got the courage to ask Mickey if I could sit at the drum set and maybe try to play a little, and he said sure. So one Saturday afternoon when nobody was around but Mickey and me, he let me come over and sit at Buddy Rich's drum set. He put on an Artie Shaw song called "Traffic Jam" that was up-tempo, with Buddy blazing away at the drums. I did my best to imitate his playing.

Suddenly the record went off and from the doorway I heard, "Not good, not too bad." And there was Buddy Rich. He could have been brutal, but he was amused. He taught me how to hold the sticks correctly and emphasized the importance of driving the band with the rhythmic beat of the bass drum. I can still play a little and to this day I'm grateful to Buddy for stressing to me how important rhythm was. I constantly still think in terms of rhythm, which is so important when it comes to comedy timing.

Even as a kid, I loved all movies, black and white, color, what have you. We all had favorite movie stars. When I was little they were mainly cowboys: Hoot Gibson, Ken Maynard, Buck Jones, and Roy Rogers. They never lost a gun battle or a fistfight, and they never fell off their horses. Later in life, I could wax eloquently about masterpieces like Marcel Carné's *Les Enfants du Paradis*, Renoir's *Grand Illusion*, Vittorio De Sica's *The Bicycle Thief*, Akira Kurosawa's *Rashomon*, Orson Welles's *Citizen Kane*. But to tell the truth, I loved the musicals more than anything else. *Shall We Dance*, *Swing Time*, and *Top Hat*. The Fred Astaire and Ginger Rogers movies thrilled me through and through. Dick Powell, Ruby

Keeler, Allan Jones, Betty Grable, Alice Faye, and Borrah Minevitch and his Harmonica Rascals. Nearly all of my films have a musical number in tribute to my affection for the great movie musicals of that era.

Right on the heels of musicals I loved comedies. Charlie Chaplin's *City Lights*, Buster Keaton's *The Navigator*, and of course the Marx Brothers, the Ritz Brothers, and Laurel and Hardy. When I was older and more sophisticated there was Ernst Lubitsch's smart comedies like *Ninotchka*, *The Shop Around the Corner*, and *Design for Living*, Preston Sturges's *The Palm Beach Story* and *Sullivan's Travels*, and the foreign comedy masterpieces such as Monicelli's *Big Deal on Madonna Street*, and Jacques Tati's *Jour de fête*.

I learned about rhythm. Rhythm is the ability to know where the top of the vocality, the vocal message, happens. It's a rim shot, it's a whack, depending on what kind of comedy you're into. The Marx Brothers had that—they were my mentors. After *Top Hat*, *A Night at the Opera* is my favorite movie of all time. It's brilliantly constructed. First, their hearts are in the right place. Groucho, Chico, and Harpo want to give Allan Jones a chance to sing at the opera, because they know what the audience will hear—his gorgeous tenor voice. All hell breaks loose because they are doing what the Marx Brothers do, jamming a hundred people into a ship's tiny stateroom. They are crazy and anarchic, but they still have charm and warmth. They married intellectuality and a brushstroke of wit with their great physical comedy.

The Three Stooges were a brilliant combination of timing and earnestness. They are very serious. Their physical timing was impeccable. They never laugh, or break up, or seem to enjoy the violence they inflict upon one another. They left that for the audience. They showed me that comedy is a juxtaposition of textures. Later in my career I got to do a Stooges-like routine with Rudy De Luca in *Life Stinks* when we slap each other silly.

I also loved the Ritz Brothers. Harry, Jimmy, and Al came from my neighborhood. They were like gods to me. They were big in the thirties and forties. Harry had a physical insanity and freedom that no other performer ever had. He was the master of wild, bizarre walks, facial contortions, and wacky sounds. You could see Harry's influence in Danny Kaye's voices, in Milton Berle's facial expressions, in Jerry Lewis's crazy walk, and especially in Sid Caesar's mannerisms. In my film *Silent Movie*, Sid's in a hospital bed, and he has to swallow a large white pill. He places the pill prominently on his tongue and then Sid takes a big glass of water. He drinks for an entire minute, and swallows and swallows and then he breathes. He opens his mouth, and lo and behold, the big white pill is still there! That's all Harry Ritz.

The Marx Brothers were much more intellectual. They had a sense of character and story. The Ritz Brothers had a sense of the *meshuga*—craziness. They were unfettered by anything normal. I took from both of them, so I suppose I have a combination of the Marx and the Ritz brothers. You might say that I'm an intellectual *meshugenah*.

Charlie Chaplin was the only person who could make you laugh and cry simultaneously. I got to re-create Chaplin's *One A.M.* routine for *Silent Movie*. Like Chaplin in the earlier incarnation, my character Mel Funn, having drunk himself into a stupor, is having difficulty managing the Murphy bed (a bed that folds down out of the wall) in his hotel room. While sitting down on the bed it suddenly folds up into the wall. I fall flat on my backside, much like Chaplin had done more than sixty years earlier.

My soul adored Buster Keaton. He was a master at physical comedy. His scenes were extremely crazy, but he played them with absolute reality. He never winked at the audience. I loved that he could stand in the doorway and have an entire house fall down around him—leaving him unscathed. I loved Laurel and Hardy even more. W. C. Fields was a genius at skit construction. Jack Benny and Fred Allen showed me new kinds of irony. I loved the "Road" pictures with Bob Hope, Bing Crosby, and Dorothy Lamour. I was drawn to teams and siblings. Unconsciously I was a pup in a cardboard box with three other pups, my brothers, and we tumbled about with one another. That's why my films are almost always about at least two guys on a journey. I didn't have to learn about pathos, loyalty, and a family that stuck together in order to weave that into my stories. I was raised and taught by my own childhood.

Comedy was as important—if not *more* important—than music in the neighborhood. Our training began on the street corners. You had to score on the corner. No bullshit routines. No slick laminated crap. It had to be "Lemme tell ya what happened today . . ." You really had to be good on your feet.

"Fat Hymie was hanging from the fire escape. His mother came by. 'Hymie!' she screamed. He let go and fell off the ladder right on his head."

We laughed hard at real stories of tragedy. It had to be real and it had to be funny. Somebody getting hurt was wonderful. Later, as the 2000 Year Old Man with Carl Reiner I explained the difference between comedy and tragedy: If *I* cut my finger, that's tragedy. Comedy is if *you* walk into an open sewer and die.

Comedy is a very powerful component of life. It has the most to say about the human condition because if you laugh you can get by. You can struggle when things are bad if you have a sense of humor. Laughter is a protest scream against death, against the long goodbye. It's a defense against unhappiness and depression.

Words were my equalizer. In our gang, I was the undisputed champ at corner shtick. We drank egg creams, watched girls, and riffed on one another. My wit is often characterized as being Jewish comedy. Occasionally, that's true. But for the most part to characterize my humor as purely Jewish humor is not accurate. It's really New York humor. New York humor is not just Jewish humor. It has a certain rhythm. It has a certain intensity and a certain pulse. Lenny Bruce, Rodney Dangerfield, Jackie Mason, and stand-up comedians like me were not simply Jewish. They were New York—there is a big difference.

My mom got homesick for the old neighborhood and we moved back to Williamsburg to 111 Lee Avenue. I transferred from Abraham Lincoln High School in Coney Island to Eastern District High School in Williamsburg. I was on the senior council and the fencing team. Under "goal" in the yearbook I put "To be President of the U.S." No lack of chutzpah there.

My yearbook photo at Eastern District High School in Brooklyn.

Just to be clear, I never really became president. When I am asked, "Why did you become a comedian?"—there is no way to psychologically explain and say it's this or it's that. A lot of people think that comedy and getting laughs and applause is making up for an unhappy childhood. Au contraire! I think it's just the opposite. All I can say is that in my case comedy was keeping the joy of a happy childhood going strong. I definitely wanted a continuum of the love that I got from my mother, brothers, and aunts and uncles. Laughter is a concrete response to your actions, a way to let you know that people are responding to your efforts. You do get the spotlight when you're the baby of the family. Somewhere around sixteen or seventeen you don't get that anymore. I wasn't getting kissed for just being Melvin anymore. Now I had to go out and earn it. I needed to be kissed for being somebody.

So I sought the spotlight.

Chapter 2

The Mountains

Early on, one of my only connections to show business was an actor, writer, and director by the name of Don Appell. He was one of the few people in the Williamsburg section of Brooklyn that actually was working in show business. My buddy Joe Gevanter wanted to be an actor and I wanted to be a comedian. Somehow, Joe found out that this actor Don Appell lived off Keap Street and was in a Broadway play directed by Orson Welles called *Native Son*, which was playing at the St. James Theatre.

(Strangely enough, many years later, *The Producers* made its debut at the very same theater, the St. James on Forty-fourth Street.)

Anyway, Joe said we should wait for Don Appell at the stoop of his apartment building so that when he got back from the theater, we could ply him with questions about how to break into the business. Starting at eleven P.M. we waited outside his building hoping to get lucky. A week went by, but we never seemed to be there at the right time to catch him. But one night when we were just about to quit and go home, *BAM!* There he was, Don Appell in person, wearing a camel's hair overcoat with a belt and a white fedora. When we approached him, he was surprised, but not particularly angry. The actor's ego in him flowered when Joe and I peppered him with praise and questions. He told us he'd be glad to meet with us and gave us some times and dates when he'd be free. We eagerly met with him every chance we could. Unfortunately, my friend Joe moved away from Williamsburg, so I then became Don Appell's only loyal fan.

Later in life, in addition to being an actor, Don Appell wrote the book for *Milk and Honey,* a hit Broadway musical with songs by Jerry Herman. He also went on to write a successful drama about anti-Semitism called *This, Too, Shall Pass.* He spread his wings into television where he wrote, produced, and directed many productions in both New York and Hollywood.

I couldn't wait to meet up with Don and show him my latest display of comic ideas. Once in a while he laughed out loud when I came up with different concepts for impressions like Susan Cagney, James Cagney's sister. I would be doing Cagney, but with lines like: "Where did I put my curlers? Somebody must have taken them! You dirty rats!" He thought I was pretty good for a fourteen-and-a-half-year-old wannabe.

It turns out that during the summers Don worked in the Borscht Belt as a social director at the Avon Lodge. The Borscht Belt was an affectionate term for the area of the Catskill Mountains about ninety miles north of New York City, which was replete with Jewish summer resorts. It was the starting point for the careers of a lot of Jewish comics. Social directors in the Catskills resorts were responsible for the summer's entertainment. Together with their staff, they'd put on plays, musicals, arrange for afternoon games on the lawn, and make the guests feel like stars when they participated in various talent shows. So in the summer of 1941 Don used his influence to get me a job as a busboy at the Butler Lodge in Hurleyville, New York, with a chance to step in and act as an understudy if somebody in the dramatic society got sick. Wow!

The busboy job was not easy. I was assigned to the sour cream station. I would take a huge stainless steel bowl filled to the brim with sour cream (which weighed about as much as I did) from the kitchen to the dining room and the minute it was empty I'd rush back to the kitchen to fill it up and bring it out again. For some reason, the Jews in the Borscht Belt had this strange affinity for sour cream. They loved it on their blintzes. They loved it on their potato pancakes. They loved it on their chopped crunchy vegetables like radishes, celery, carrots, etc. And if nobody was looking, they gobbled it down all by itself with nothing but a huge tablespoon. Sour cream, unfortunately, was loaded with cholesterol. The normal cholesterol levels for healthy people should be between 150 and 200. I would say the average cholesterol of the sour-cream-loving Jews who came to the Borscht Belt was probably 1500–2000.

Strangely enough that wasn't what killed them. And now—from straight out of my stand-up act—I'll tell you what killed them . . . it was a song called "Dancing in the Dark."

After lunch they would sit and rock on the porch, which for some of the guests was the closest they would get to the "outdoors." They would rock and start singing. The most dangerous thing a Jew could do in the mountains was to sing "Dancing in the Dark." Why "Dancing in the Dark"? Because they never understood the range of that song and would invariably start in the wrong key. The only person capable of really singing that song safely was Bing Crosby. Bing Crosby got it right—but the Jews didn't. For some strange reason the Jews would start singing it in a very high key and never made it to the end of the song.

They would start with:

"Dancing in the dark
Till the tune ends
We're dancing in the dark
And it soon ends . . .
And we can face the music
Together . . ."

When they hit the word "together" it was too high for human ears! If you could reach it only dogs would be able to hear you. And that's what did it—*Bam!* Stroke! They fell right out of their rocking chairs. That's why "Dancing in the Dark" wreaked such havoc on the porch of the Butler Lodge.

(Sorry about slipping back into my act—but I love that bit!)

I loved being in the mountains. When I finished my tour of duty as a busboy I would run to other hotels like Browns, the Nevele, and the most famous of them all, Grossinger's (which I later worked at for one summer), to see their comics perform. Comedians like Henny Youngman, Jan Murray, Mickey Katz, Jackie Vernon, etc. One of my favorites was Myron Cohen. Later in life I stole one of his best jokes (but of course gave him credit!). It goes like this:

> A guy walks into a grocery store and says to the grocer, "I'd like a half a pound of lox, a pint of cream cheese, and . . ."
>
> Then he stops because he's puzzled by the store shelves filled with just boxes and boxes of salt
>
> He says to the grocer, "You've got so many boxes of salt on your shelves. I've never seen so much salt! Excuse me for asking but . . . do you sell a lot of salt?"
>
> The grocer replies, "Meh . . . to tell you the truth if I sell a box of salt a week I'm lucky. I don't sell a lot of salt. But the guy that sells me salt . . . BOY! CAN HE SELL SALT!"

It always gets a big laugh.

One day while working in the mountains I got really lucky. Fate was with me because I found out that one of the actors in the play *Uncle Harry* that was slated to be on that night had stepped into a gopher hole and sprained his ankle and couldn't perform. He was to play the district attorney who questions Uncle Harry. So they called me in to replace him!

When they saw me, the social director said, "He's just a kid! He's much too young looking to be the district attorney."

I immediately sprang forth with the lines that I had quickly mastered:

"There, there," I said. "Harry, have a seat. Here, have a glass of water and tell me in your own words what exactly happened on the night of February the fifteenth . . ."

The social director said, "He knows the lines! Good enough. Make him old."

So they gave me a white wig, a goatee, painted many lines on my face, and shoved a rolled-up towel on my back to make me look old and hunched over.

I said, "Do we really need the towel? I'm playing a district attorney, not Quasimodo."

"Shut up," they replied.

So there it was, at eight o'clock I'd be making my debut as an actor in front of a live audience. I made my way out onstage and sat behind the district attorney's desk. The curtain went up. Uncle Harry entered.

"There, there. Harry, have a seat," I said. Trembling with fear I sallied forth.

"Here," I said. "Have a glass of water and tell me in your own words what exactly happened on the night of February the fifteenth . . ."

Unfortunately, I poured a little too much water in the glass. It slipped out of my hand and crashed in a thousand pieces onto the silver platter on the desk below.

A huge gasp followed by stunned silence filled the auditorium. Everybody was paralyzed. Nobody moved. Harry didn't move. I didn't move. The audience didn't move. The band was frozen. I didn't know what to do. So I decided to spill the beans.

I walked straight down to the footlights, took off my wig and goatee, and said, "Sorry, folks. I'm only fourteen! I've never done this before!"

The audience exploded in a huge roar of laughter. I felt great! I'd found my true profession. I wasn't an actor. I was a comedian.

Unfortunately when the curtain came crashing down the social director was not amused, and he came after me with murder in his eyes. I ran. I ran! I ran past three different hotels until I was sure the social director wasn't going to catch me and kill me. Needless to say I was never again asked to be an actor at the Butler Lodge.

I kept my job as a busboy on the sour cream station and because of the big laugh I had gotten that night, the owner of the hotel asked me to be a "pool tummler." The job was simple; the pool tummler wakes up the Jews when they fall asleep around the pool after lunch. He goes around telling jokes, doing impressions, and keeps them amused. He'll do anything to get the audience on his side. Instead of them drifting off, he keeps them happy and alert and that's the job.

One of the things I did as the pool tummler was to do an act. I wore a derby and an alpaca coat and I would carry two rock-laden cardboard suitcases and go to the edge of the diving board and start yelling: "Business is no good! I don't wanna live!"

I'd then jump off into the pool. My suitcases would take me straight to the bottom and my derby would float on the surface. It always got a huge laugh.

It was impossible to swim to the surface in a pool-drenched alpaca coat. So I was looking up from the bottom of the pool for help from Richard, the good-looking blond gentile lifeguard. I was hoping he would notice me at the bottom and dive down and save me. Unfortunately, he was still holding his stomach and laughing with everybody else at my antics on the end of the diving board. But fate was with me; I'd mouthed the words, "Richard, save me." And he somehow remembered that I was at the bottom of the pool and brought me to the top, struggling for air. For some reason I got even more laughs while gasping for breath.

On my second or third summer back in the Borscht Belt I developed an act mostly made up of a lot of stolen jokes like, "Good evening, ladies and germs! I just flew in from Chicago and boy, are my arms tired. I met a girl in Chicago who was so skinny that when I took her to a restaurant the maître d' said, 'Can I check your umbrella?' "

Eventually I began to flower as a comedy writer when I created some crazy impressions. I would do an impression of James Madison, fourth president of the United States, who was married to Dolley Madison. And I'd do stuff like, "Dolley! Hurry! Set out the fruit salad! Franklin and Jefferson will be here any minute!" And

I knew nobody could quarrel with the historical accuracy of my powerful, stentorian James Madison.

But the Jews were a tough audience. I used to do a "Man of a Thousand Faces." I'd hold up a finger and say "one" and then make a crazy face, with blown-out cheeks and crossed eyes like Harpo Marx. Sometimes they'd wait for a hundred and fifty crazy faces before I got my first laugh.

All of the comics in the Borscht Belt had opening songs. They became your identity songs. Don Appell had one he did: *"My name is Donny; they say I'm funny!"* All the comedians named Jackie had the same identity song. *"They call me Jackie; they say I'm wacky!"*

I came up with a song to introduce myself to the audience. Upon reflection, it's maybe a bit too self-congratulatory.

It goes like this:

Here I am, I'm Melvin Brooks.
I've come to stop the show.
Just a ham who's minus looks,
But in your hearts I'll grow!
I'll tell ya gags, sing ya songs.
Happy little snappy tunes that roll along.
Out of my mind, won't you be kind and
Please love . . . Melvin Brooks!

It always got a big hand.

The Borscht Belt was so important for my training in comedy. I think it was there that I first learned my craft. The audiences were very tough. They didn't give it away. When you got a laugh, you really earned it. Those audiences sharpened your ability to survive and sometimes triumph over disastrous performances.

Let me digress for a moment . . . I have a message for those readers who are setting out to make a career for themselves as writers or comedians. I call it "An Ode to Failure."

Before achieving success in my career, I failed on large scales and small ones. During my time in the Catskills, some jokes worked and some didn't. As a result, you didn't just not do those jokes again, you learned what the audience expects, what they want. And then you have to learn a bigger lesson: Don't give them what they expect! Give them what they don't know and what they don't expect and maybe you'll get an even bigger explosion of laughter.

Failure is vital. It is an incredibly important quotient in the equation of a career. After you wipe away your tears, it's not a bad experience and under the right circumstances it will make you better, both as a person and as an artist.

I think it's important to fail, especially between the ages of twenty and thirty. Success is like sugar. It's too good. It's too sweet. It's too wonderful and it burns up very quickly. Failure is like corned beef hash. It takes a while to eat. It takes a while to digest. But it stays with you. Failure may not feel good when it happens, but it will always sharpen your mind. You'll always ask yourself, "Where did I go wrong? Why didn't this joke or this sketch work?" And there will always be reasons. You can't just say, "Well, it's not funny." You have to ask yourself, "*Why* is it not funny?"

My son Max, who wrote *The Zombie Survival Guide* and *World War Z*, gave the graduation speech at Pitzer College in Claremont, California, where he went for his undergraduate degree. To the graduating class, he said, "Go forth and fail."

He was absolutely on target, because nothing helps you to succeed like failure.

Chapter 3

World War II

By this point I knew I wanted to go into show business, but Hitler had started a war. It was 1943 and my mother had three blue stars hanging in the window, meaning she had three boys in the service—all of my older brothers. Thank god none of them were gold, because a gold star meant that you lost a child in combat.

My brother Bernie was fighting in the South Pacific and eventually became a Japanese code breaker. Lenny was fighting in the Fifteenth Air Force as an engineer gunner on a B-17 Flying Fortress stationed in Foggia, Italy. And Irving was a second lieutenant in the Signal Corps and fighting his way every day across the George Washington Bridge to Fort Monmouth, New Jersey.

Lenny was a true hero. The December 20, 1943, edition of the *New York Herald Tribune* reported:

> **N.Y. Flyer Freezes Hands, Repairs Gun at 32 Below**
>
> **Flesh Sticks to Metal, but He Carries Out Mission**
>
> WASHINGTON, Dec. 19 (AP)—With full knowledge of the consequences, Staff Sergeant Kaminsky, of 111 Lee Avenue, Brooklyn, peeled off his heavy gloves to repair his jammed machine gun in the waist of a Flying Fortress at a height of five miles and in a temperature of 32 degrees below zero dur-

ing a recent mission against an Austrian target, the War Department said today.

Kaminsky's hands froze almost immediately—as he knew they would. His fingers swelled to twice normal size, and the skin of his hands stuck to the steel as he worked. But he repaired the gun and went back into action to help fight off German fighter planes as his Flying Fortress was returning from an attack on the Messerschmitt aircraft factory at Wiener-Neustadt.

Now in a hospital, he is recuperating.

Fortunately, but unfortunately, his hands healed quickly, and he went right back into action. On the day Lenny was supposed to come home, they changed the requirement from twenty-five to fifty missions. On his thirty-sixth mission he was shot down and captured as a prisoner of war. When he bailed out of the plane, he ripped his dog tags off because they read "A- Blood Type, H" and H meant Hebrew. He had heard that Jewish flyers were being sent to concentration camps, which was likely certain death.

When he was arrested on the ground by the Germans, they threw him into a prisoner of war camp and asked, "*Papolsky?*" Meaning, "Are you Polish?"

He said, "Yeah. Yeah. Papolsky."

For nineteen months, he was in a Stalag Luft, an air force prison camp. He got through it, but he never would have made it if the Germans found out that he was Jewish.

We held our breaths for a month and a half until we got word from the Red Cross that he was alive and a prisoner of war. The Red Cross went to prisoners of war and they did a lovely thing, they recorded them saying or singing things and they sent those recordings to their loved ones back home.

Lenny loved to sing so he recorded a song called "Miss You." My mother would put that little cardboard record on every night and cry. Every single night! Finally I said, "Mom, maybe just hold the record? Maybe don't put it on so much? I mean he's alive, but it's depressing hearing him sing every night!"

Even though we loved him dearly, truth is he was slightly off-key.

In early 1944, I was seventeen years old and in my senior year at Eastern District High School in Brooklyn. One day an Army recruiting officer came around and said that if anybody in the senior class scored high enough on an aptitude test they could join the Army Specialized Training Reserve Program. If you were accepted you would receive early graduation from high school and be sent to a college paid for by the government. Then when you turned eighteen and joined the Army you would be in a better position to choose your field of service. This sounded great to me. Besides, I knew I was destined to be drafted anyway.

So I took the test. I think they really wanted everybody they could get. Some of the questions were not too difficult, like "2 + 2 = what?" Needless to say, I passed. I was not in the Army yet; I was in the ASTRP, the Army Specialized Training Reserve Program.

I was sent to college at VMI, the Virginia Military Institute, founded in 1839 and known as the "West Point of the South," for special training. After a long overnight train ride I arrived in Lexington, Virginia, the home of VMI. I was stunned by the setting of the college in the beautiful Shenandoah Valley. I'd never seen a vista like that.

When we got to the campus we were issued military garb. Wow. An Army uniform! I felt like a soldier. Well, *almost* a soldier. For a short time, I was an honorary "rat." That was the affectionate term for freshmen cadets at VMI. It was popularized by the 1938 film *Brother Rat*, starring Eddie Albert, future president Ronald Reagan, and his future wife Jane Wyman.

Being from Brooklyn, VMI took a lot of getting used to. I had never even seen a cheeseburger before, and they had a cola drink that was only popular in the South then called Dr. Pepper. Talk about a little Brooklyn fish out of water!

Even though I think they were speaking English, the language was very different. In restaurants down there, after I ordered, the waitress would often add in a Southern drawl, *"Youwantgrisswiththa?"*

It took me a long time to figure out exactly what they were saying. And what they were saying was, "Do you want grits with that?" It turned out that "grits" were a Southern dish that was a kind of porridge made of ground corn. So my previous answer of "No thanks!" still worked.

Life at VMI was wonderful and terrible. The terrible part was getting up at six a.m. to shave, shower, and have breakfast. And also having to make my own bed with hospital corners. (I won't take the time and trouble to explain what hospital corners are; you'll have to find that out on your own.)

The wonderful part was that the VMI cadets were so welcoming to us, the Army Reserve trainees. They never resented our sharing the school with them. VMI was not just an academic college. Like I said before, it was "the West Point of the South" and truly

Here I am as a soldier cadet at VMI, the Virginia Military Institute.

And here I'm surrounded by my Army VMI buddies; most of them were also from New York and New Jersey.

a great school. So in addition to my academic studies of electrical engineering and learning all about cosines, tangents, slide rules, and such, they also trained you to be a cavalry officer. So I learned to ride a horse and wield a saber—something I had never seen any kid from Brooklyn do.

It was thrilling—if you didn't fall off. To get the horse to really gallop, you'd yell "Yah! Yah!" and at the same time you had to wield your saber and cut little flags off the tips of bamboo poles. I loved it. I felt like Errol Flynn in *They Died with Their Boots On*. I kept telling myself: "Wait till I tell the kids back in Williamsburg what I've been doing. They'll never believe me!"

On Saturday nights there were dances that were called "cotillions." They were held in a large gymnasium at Washington and Lee University, whose campus was connected to VMI's campus. And there were girls at the cotillions. Beautiful Southern belles! Unfortunately, there was no getting close to them while dancing, because they all wore large hoop skirts so whether you wanted to or not, you had to keep your distance.

All in all, my semester at VMI before the Army was a wonderful transition between leaving home and being out in the real world. I loved it, and the gracious Virginians couldn't have been nicer to the brash kid from Brooklyn.

When I turned eighteen, I was officially in the Army. They sent me to Fort Dix in New Jersey, which was an induction center. For some reason, even though I had spent a semester studying electrical engineering at VMI, the Army in its great wisdom decided that I should be in the field artillery. They shipped me out to Fort Sill, Oklahoma, which was the Field Artillery Replacement Training Center. When reduced to its initials, it spells FARTC.

(Which somehow lingered in my unconscious and later made its way into a comedy scene in my film *Blazing Saddles*. Waste not, want not.)

Fort Sill is in the southwest corner of Oklahoma. It's cold, it's flat, and it's windy. If you ever have a chance, don't go there. If you're not in the field artillery, I don't know why you would go there. It's not an ideal spot for a fun weekend. It was a very long train ride to get there. We arrived around two in the morning and they fed us because we really hadn't eaten in close to twenty-four hours and we were starving. I remember the mashed potatoes were terrible. They were gray, watery, woody, and splintery.

I said, "These are the worst mashed potatoes I've ever eaten in my life!"

My friend Sonny turned to me and said, "That's because they're not mashed potatoes. They're called turnips. We're eating mashed turnips."

I said, "Oh. Thank god!" Because I'd been about to give up mashed potatoes for the rest of my life, but after experiencing them I could very easily give up mashed turnips for the rest of my life. And to this day I don't think I've ever knowingly eaten a turnip—mashed or not—ever again.

Having gone to VMI, basic training at Fort Sill wasn't that difficult. I had already learned how to do close-order drills, and basic training was more of the same, perhaps with more intensity. It's lots of drilling. You learn how to carry a rifle, how to drill with a rifle, and how to shoot a rifle. The rifles we trained with were not the M1 Garand that was actually used in combat, but an earlier model called the Springfield. It was a single bolt-action rifle that had quite a kick when fired. A tip from one of the sergeants on the rifle range saved my shoulder from being bruised from that kick. He told me to fold a towel over my shoulder before shooting and it worked. By the way, I was very good at the shooting part and it earned me my first little badge as an expert marksman.

We'd go on long marches with only ten-minute breaks. Five-, ten-, and occasionally sometimes even long exhausting twenty-mile hikes. That was tough. Then there'd be the infiltration course. It was like graduation, where they tested your skills and used live ammunition while you kept your head down and crawled on your elbows and your knees. That was scary.

The good part was that I was trained as a radio operator. That was going to be my job when I went overseas with a field artillery unit. I was so happy to be picked for a job that was not right next to the cannons, because they made a loud bang. However, for the first two weeks we had to be given some basic instructions on how to be part of a field artillery cannon crew. So for two weeks I was going to have to endure the incredibly loud explosions that the 105- and 155-millimeter Howitzers made. But I was lucky: One of the noncoms (non-commissioned officers) teaching us how to load, elevate, and fire the cannons gave me a great piece of advice.

He said, "Listen, buddy, the earplugs they give you really don't work. What ya gotta do is break a cigarette in half, roll the ends tight, and shove them in your ears. That's your best protection from the sound."

And he was right! I got through those two weeks without breaking an eardrum.

Funny little anecdote: When I was getting my insurance physical for my first film, *The Producers*, the nurse who was looking into my ears said, "Mr. Brooks, I've seen a lot of inner ears in my life, but I've never seen any so yellow! Did you have jaundice or some disease or anything when you were a kid?"

I said, "No, no. That yellow is not a disease. It's called Camels. When I was in basic training in the Army, I shoved Camel cigarettes in my ears to shut out the noise, and believe it or not, they really worked!"

I was discharged in 1946 and this was in 1966. Twenty years later my ears were still bright yellow from the Camels. Well, I guess that's a small price to pay for not losing my hearing.

The regular Army was an education. A really rough education. I'd never gone to the toilet before with sixteen other guys sitting next to me. I would go crazy waiting for the latrine to be free of people so I could rush in, do my stuff, and rush out. It took a lot of getting used to.

And then there was chow time. Breakfast in the mess hall was an experience. First of all, you got on line. Everything in the Army is first you get on line. I looked over at the breakfast setup. There were huge grills on top of which was a sight I've never seen before in my life—it was amazing and a little scary. On top of one of the huge grills there were about a hundred eggs all cooking sunny-side up. You said give me two, three, four, whatever. You had to be careful about how much you took, because of the huge sign above the cooking area that read TAKE ALL YOU WANT, BUT EAT ALL YOU TAKE. So I never took more than two eggs, because I might want something else like oatmeal, cornflakes, or bacon. Not that anybody really watched how much you took and how much you left.

Sitting with twelve other guys having breakfast was another new experience. Everything was "Pass the butter! Pass the milk! Pass the sugar! Pass the jam!" There was a strict code. When somebody said, "Pass the jam," you weren't allowed to stop the jam and put any on your own plate. That was called shortcutting and was not allowed. You had to pass the jam to the person who said, "Pass the jam" even though the jam looked good and you wanted to take a little on the way, you didn't. It was forbidden. The mess hall was good-natured but incredibly noisy and busy. It took some getting used to.

One morning at breakfast as I went through the chow line they put something strange on my plate. I brought it back to my table and said to one of the GIs, "What is this?"

He said, "It's called shit on a shingle!"

"Shit on a shingle?" I said.

"Yeah, but actually it's chipped beef and cream gravy on toast."

I watched the other guys at my table, they were eating it and they didn't seem upset. So I tried it. It was weird; I couldn't make sense out of the taste. But I was eighteen and always crazy hungry. So I ate it. It wasn't good; it wasn't bad. It was food and it was filling. Later on, I kind of got used to it and came to like it. It was just good old Army chow. But I'll never forget the first time I stared down at the confused mess on my plate and heard the expression "shit on a shingle."

When we were on bivouac (a temporary campsite away from the barracks), we were on the chow line with our mess kits. Mess kits were two small oval aluminum trays with indentations for food and an aluminum knife, fork, and spoon attached. You waited on line with your mess kit and they'd throw some beef stew in one of the indentations. Then came the mashed potatoes, and even though there were other indentations for the mashed potatoes they always threw it right on top of the stew. Then—you won't believe this—for dessert there were usually sliced peaches. Which of course, you expected they would put into in one of the remaining empty places in the mess kit. But what did they do? You've got it! They hurled it right on top of your mashed potatoes and your beef stew. They simply didn't care. And we were starving so we gobbled it down.

(And for some reason, to this day I'm vaguely nostalgic for some sliced peaches on top of my beef bourguignon.)

After chow you waited on line once again to clean your mess kit. First you swirled them around in a garbage can bubbling with hot soapy water. Then you moved them to the next garbage can of rinse water, still filled with the remnants of soap. And then the last garbage can with clear hot water. That did the job. It never occurred to me to ask my sergeants and officers: Why do we have to do all this stuff? Isn't there a better way? Couldn't we have a little more time for reading a book we liked, or maybe taking a nap once in a while? And then I realized: That's why the Army likes eighteen-year-olds. No questions asked. You do what you're told. Maybe that's why I never thought seriously about reenlisting.

In addition to our military training at Fort Sill we were taught how to drive, which leads to a funny but pretty scary story. (Funny for you, scary for me.) I learned how to drive on a two-and-a-half ton 6x6 big Army truck. As opposed to the automatic cars of today, it was an old-fashioned stick shift. There was a lot of what was called "double-clutching," meaning that in order to go from one gear to another you couldn't just use your clutch once, but twice. It was not easy, but finally I learned how to drive it.

Obviously I finally learned to drive at Fort Sill or they wouldn't have let me get behind the wheel of this jeep.

Even though I learned how to drive it, I really didn't know exactly how to turn it. It seems that when you're driving a truck and you're going to make a turn, you move out a little so that the back wheels of the truck follow the front wheels with plenty of nice room to complete the turn. So here I am, coming to a right turn around the headquarters building of the camp. Without thinking, I turn the wheel sharply to make the turn. The front of the truck is fine. The back of the truck—not so fine. It takes off the entire corner of the bungalow headquarters building. When I felt the jolt and heard the crash I stopped and looked back. There was a corporal, sitting at his typewriter at his headquarters desk looking around at the sudden revelation of blue skies above him and wondering where his walls went.

I shouted back at him, "Sorry! Sorry!"

He yelled back, "I don't think *sorry* is going to do it!"

He was right. Right after I got the truck back to the motor pool, I got a visit from our first sergeant.

He said, "How do you like the Army?"

I said, "What do you mean?"

He said, "Well, I hope you like it because you're going to be in it for the rest of your life! You caused about ten thousand dollars' worth of military damage, and at a private's salary I figure you could get it paid for in about a hundred years."

He was joking but I didn't know it, and my heart and my spirit sank down to my boots. A hundred years! I didn't think I could make it. Anyway, I didn't pay for that accident with time or with money. But I did a lot of extra guard duty and a lot of KP, which are initials for "Kitchen Police," meaning peeling tons of potatoes and scrubbing out big pans to the point of exhaustion.

To this day, while I no longer drive a 6x6 truck, I still always move my vehicle out just a little wider than most when I'm making a turn, just in case a first sergeant shows up.

Every once in a while at Fort Sill, I would be struck with bouts of homesickness. Especially when I heard Bing Crosby on the radio. He would sing songs like "Moonlight Becomes You," a sweet tune by Jimmy Van Heusen and Johnny Burke that I remembered from a wonderful picture called *Road to Morocco* with Bing and Bob Hope and always their same love interest, Dorothy Lamour. I would think of my mother, singing along with Bing and dressing me in the morning under the covers when I was a little kid. I missed my brothers, I missed my friends in Williamsburg, and I even missed my strict teachers. I missed things like penny candy, egg creams, and charlotte russes. For those of you who are not worldly, a charlotte russe is a little round circle of yellow cake in a cardboard container liberally filled with a swirl of thick, sweet whipped cream and topped with a maraschino cherry. When I was on those long twenty-mile hikes at Fort Sill— Oh! How I would long for the good old days of egg creams and charlotte russes.

My Williamsburg pals (left to right): Bernie "Flappy" Rothman, Eddie Albert, and me in Brooklyn before I boarded a troopship to Europe.

When I finished basic training at Fort Sill, I was shipped back to Fort Dix for overseas assignment. I was lucky to get a weekend in New York so I could see my mom, my grandma, my aunts and uncles, and the few friends that were also in the service but hadn't shipped out yet. I stuffed as much of my mom's delicious food as possible down my gullet, because I knew I'd be on Army chow for the foreseeable future. She made me things I loved like matzo ball soup, potato pancakes, and stuffed cabbage—things I knew were hardly ever served on an Army chow line.

At the Bridge Plaza in Brooklyn, mimicking General MacArthur.

And then one night, I think it was around February 15 or 16, 1945, together with three or four hundred other guys I boarded a troop transport at the Brooklyn Navy Yard. The ship was called the *Sea Owl* and I was told it was a liberty ship. Regrettably, we were not lucky enough to get a voyage on a victory ship, which had more stabilizers and more spacious accommodations. I remember going down below to the third or fourth deck and I was greeted with the sight of rows and rows of stacked metal bunks. Each row was six beds high. It looked like hundreds of bunks. Unfortunately, in my row I got the third one, which was right square in the middle of the stack with what looked like a two-hundred-pound GI above me.

Things were fine until the ship got to the open sea. Nobody told me about the North Atlantic in February. Huge waves slammed us from side to side, and then like a corkscrew moved us way up and plunged us way down. And I realized there was no way to stop it.

Soon the throwing up began. It quickly became a cacophony of puking that never stopped.

Happily, I found out the next day that there was a ship's newspaper and volunteered to write a column for it. They graciously accepted and, taking the title from Eleanor Roosevelt's daily column called "My Day," I called my column "My Floating Day." Here's a gander at what went on day and night on the troopship *Sea Owl* fighting the waves and the weather on its way across the North Atlantic to war:

My Floating Day

The shrill blast of a whistle tore me from my girlfriend's arms and opened my eyes to another day on the ocean. I crawled out of my bunk and put on my shoes. I went to the latrine to wash. All they offered to wash with was salt water. Using salt water you can't get enough lather to shave the hair on a flea's leg.

I ate chow, but my breakfast was not a military secret for long. The gentle, exotic sway of the boat continued. Soon I made a spectacular dash to the latrine, where the menu underwent a full-field layout.

After a police detail I was unchained and allowed on deck with the others. I really enjoy being on deck. The air was fresh and once in a while a refreshing spray of salt water slapped you in the face like an insulted girl. It was real democracy; once I even talked to a Real First Sergeant. I felt so big I bowed only twice when I left him.

After lolling on deck we're called to chow. They chuckled, punched our TS cards, and another meal trickled down to my yawning stomach.

In the evening, the ship changed from a troop transport to one of the largest gambling houses afloat. There were so many card games you had to be an athlete to get back to your bunk. The boys were really dice happy.

I was strong and brave for about eight days, but then I could no longer take sleeping down in the incredible stench that permeated the lower deck. The journey would normally take no more than five or six days by ship today, but not only were we weathering a stormy North Atlantic in late February, we were also zigzagging every few miles to avoid German U-boats. It also occurred to me that even though the sinkings of Allied ships were getting dramatically lower in early 1945, there was still the bad luck chance of a U-boat deciding to sink our troopship. So I decided to take my chances sleeping on the top deck. With twenty dollars, I bribed a merchant marine sailor to let me put my sleeping bag under a lifeboat, and he was nice enough to give me some all-weather tarps to cover me against the sea spray. It was rough up on deck, but so much better both smell-wise and torpedo-wise than sleeping down below.

Fortunately, I only had to do it for two nights, for on the third night, there it was, the rugged coast of France. Soon we were moored at the port of Le Havre. Even though we were finally on solid land, the earth still seemed to move under my feet with every step. I'm grateful to this day to the Salvation Army that met the troopships when they arrived in Europe and served donuts and hot coffee. Nothing ever tasted so good!

So even though I was sent overseas as a radio operator in the field artillery, once again the Army decided that I should be something else. This time it was a combat engineer. The Army moved men to various units as needed. I was transferred with some of my other shipmates to the 1104th Engineer Combat Battalion. We were put on long troop transport vehicles and sent to Normandy for combat engineer training. It was a long trip, made even longer by the fact that I was going crazy.

Every sign I saw was in French. Instead of a grocery store it was *épicerie*. Instead of a bakery it was *boulangerie*. Instead of a laundry it was *blanchisserie*. And the street signs were never streets, but always *rues*.

I said to my buddy, "If I don't see something in English soon, I'm gonna blow my top!"

He said, "Well, get ready to blow your top because we're in France, pal, and they have a habit of making all their signs in French."

Small groups of men left the truck and were deposited at different villages. Eight men including me got off at a little farmhouse with a sign on the entrance that said MON REPOS. It occurred to me that Mon Repos was a rather grandiose name for maybe the summer home of a retired nobleman. "My repose" is very fancy indeed.

Mon Repos in Normandy, where I was stationed in February 1945.

But it turned out to be just a simple little country farmhouse with this grand name. It was in the village of Saint-Aubin-sur-Scie. The village was near a larger town called Offranville, not far from the fairly big and busy port of Dieppe on the English Channel.

We were quartered in the main farmhouse, and the family that owned and occupied the farm was in a smaller house on the property. It wasn't such a bad deal. They had cows so there was fresh milk and they provided most of the charcuterie for the village. Charcuterie is cured meats like sausage, salami, ham, etc. So like I said, the eats were good. We were not dependent on Army chow. The farmer and his family were very gracious. There was a little kid on a tricycle named Henri; he got to be my pal and kept looking for me. Maybe it was because I gave him chewing gum and chocolate. He'd shout my name, "Private Mel, Private Mel!"

Back at Mon Repos in Normandy with the screenwriters of Brooksfilms production of The Elephant Man, *Eric Bergren (right) and Christopher De Vore (left).*

There is more to this story than just being a soldier learning how to be a combat engineer in a little farmhouse in Normandy. Because, if I may digress, some thirty-five years later I had created a company called Brooksfilms and we were busy with David Lynch at the helm making a film called *The Elephant Man. The Elephant Man* screenplay was written by Eric Bergren and Christopher De Vore, based on the book by Frederick Treves. I was in England, where the sets were in the last stages of construction at Shepperton Studios. It would be ten days or so before we were to start shooting, so I had a brilliant idea. Eric and Chris had done such a wonderful job on the screenplay, and I was thinking of what I could do to give them a little extra something. And then it hit me. *Bang!* Why not go back to that little village of Saint-Aubin sur-Scie and show them Mon Repos, the little farmhouse that I had trained in? The writers loved the idea of the trip. So before you could turn around we were on a ferry, then on a train to Paris, and from our hotel in Paris we hired a car for the journey to Normandy.

After a couple of hours we arrived. I got chills seeing that same little sign, MON REPOS, as we entered the property. The farmhouse had been repainted and a few things changed, but it was mostly just like I remembered as a kid in uniform back then. I knocked on the door. It opened to reveal a huge man sporting a big black beard framed in the doorway. I said in halting French, "*J'étais un soldat en quarante-cinq stationné ici dans cette chambre à l'étage.*" In English, "I was a soldier back in forty-five stationed here in that bedroom upstairs." His eyes widened, he swallowed hard and shouted, "*Mon dieu!* Private Mel?"

And I replied, "Petit Henri?" He crushed me in his big bearlike arms. Little Henri was no longer petite.

It was one of the best afternoons I've ever spent. Henri showed us around. He took me to the little apple tree on the property that I used to eat green apples from (forgetting my vow at Camp Sussex never to eat little green apples again). It was now a huge tree sporting hundreds of apples. He fêted us with all kinds of *charcuterie* and *fromage* (which they were still making) and topped it all off with a toast with the great French apple brandy that Normandy is known for, calvados.

Okay, digression over. Back to being a soldier learning how to be a combat engineer.

We were taught to safely unearth land mines. Some of them were big and some of them were smaller. The big ones were called Teller mines. They are either named after a guy named Teller, or *Teller* could be a big dinner plate in German. Either way, they carried a lot of explosives in them. You would have to probe the earth lightly with your bayonet and if you heard *Tink! Tink! Tink!* you knew there was something dangerous underneath. You had to be very careful. So you would clear away the dirt and then ask the help of the one guy in your platoon who was an expert at defusing mines—who really knew what and where all the wires were. He would take out a whisk broom and lightly dust away the earth surrounding the mine and proceed to disengage the fuse. I couldn't really see exactly what he was doing, because we were a good twenty yards away hunkered down beneath our steel helmets. Lucky for me, our expert always defused them without a mistake.

Other land mines were trickier. They were set up with trip wires. Soldiers could be walking, hit the trip wire near them, and then you'd hear a click and an S-mine, a canister filled with all kinds of shrapnel that we nicknamed a "Bouncing Betty," bounced up about chest high and for a radius of twenty feet, destroyed anything around it. If you heard that click, you knew that the mine was in the air, and you hit the ground as quickly as you could and buried your face in the earth because it exploded in a conical manner, so as close as you could get to the ground, the safer you were. Running was not an option.

We were also taught to search and clear unoccupied houses of booby traps. What's a booby trap? Well, for instance, if you were sitting on the john and pulled the chain behind you sometimes instead of the flushing sound you might hear a loud explosion and find yourself flying through the air. Which would mean that a booby trap was positioned in the water closet above the toilet. So before troops could occupy a domicile we had to be very sure it was cleared of booby traps.

Being a combat engineer was not easy, but one of the nice advantages was you didn't have to carry an M1 Garand rifle, which was pretty heavy. You were supplied with an M1 carbine, which was a much lighter rifle and gave your shoulder a wonderful rest.

In addition to clearing mines, combat engineers were taught to build makeshift structures to span small rivers or creeks. They were called Bailey bridges. It's like a giant erector set. It's constructed on one side of a river or a creek, and then it's swung over the water and drops down on the other side. They were light, practical, and strong enough to support the weight of 6x6 trucks or even a Grant or a Sherman tank.

One night, while assembling a Bailey bridge I thought I heard Germans singing on the other side of the river. The *ja, ja* at the end of each phrase was a dead giveaway. I thought the sound of the singing was terrible, and I decided to teach them what real singing sounded like. So I picked up a big bullhorn, went to the bank of the river, and started singing à la Al Jolson:

"Toot Toot Tootsie goodbye.
Toot Toot Tootsie, don't cry.
That little choo-choo train
That takes me
Away from you, no words can tell how sad it makes me."

When I finished the song, I thought I heard coming from the other side of the river (where the Germans were) a round of applause and, *"Sehr gut! Sehr gut!"* ("Very good!") Maybe it was my imagination, but anyway it makes for a good story.

When our training in Normandy was over we boarded more 6x6 trucks and made our way through Belgium down to Alsace-Lorraine. I was lucky to get through Belgium on my way to Germany a couple of months after the Battle of the Bulge. Had I been born six months earlier, I probably would have been fighting in that and who knows what would have happened? Anyway, luck was with me and the Germans were finally in retreat and life got a little better and a little safer.

We were stationed in Saarbrücken, which was right on the border of France and Germany. Even though the war was still on, there was a French-German restaurateur who kept his restaurant open. It was a blessing in disguise. You could actually get Alsatian dishes. So instead of Army chow my buddies and I would get to eat onion soup, bratwurst, sauerkraut, German potato salad, and French bread. And to drink there was either German beer or French wine! It was a lucky little island of gastronomic happiness. As I said, it was right on the border between France and Germany. There was a huge period painting hanging over the fireplace of the restaurant and it was double-sided. Depending on which side was winning, the painting would either display a picture of the kaiser on one side or, on the other side, Napoleon. We were lucky to get the Napoleon side.

The 1104th combat battalion was attached to the Seventh Army, and, like I said before, the Germans were retreating. Our job was to use our combat engineer training in land mine and booby trap detection to clear the dwellings in newly captured territories. It was hard work, not to mention scary work, but we went over everything with a fine-toothed comb. To this day, even though I'm not a soldier and I'm not in Germany and I'm not in a war, if I enter a toilet with a pull chain behind the commode I have a tendency to stand on the bathroom seat and peer into the tank above to see if there is a booby trap . . . which hardly makes any sense in a restaurant in New York. Needless to say, I never saw any—but I still breathe a sigh of relief every time I look in and just see water.

One day I was out on patrol with my platoon and we found a case of German Mauser rifles near an old railway siding. They were beautiful sharpshooting rifles with bolt action. Sure enough, there was a box of ammunition right next to them. So we had a contest. There were these white ceramic insulation things up on the telephone poles, and any man who shot one down won a dollar from each of the others. I was pretty good at that, and I'd made about twenty-one dollars when suddenly we got a strange call on our command car radio: "Get back to the base immediately!"

When we arrived back to our base there was a lot going on. Platoons of men were moving rapidly all over the place. My company commander told us that Army communications had been severed. It seems that some telephone and telegraph wires had been destroyed. Uh-oh!

I quickly realized that we were the destroyers. Those white ceramic insulators were the wrong things to make a target-practice game of. So knowing that we were really not in danger, I gallantly offered to take my men out again and search for the enemy snipers that had sabotaged the phone lines. My company commander gave me permission and sent us off with a salute that connoted something like, "You men are a brave bunch." We never let on.

It was the beginning of May 1945, and it looked like the war in Europe was rapidly coming to a close. My unit was stationed in a little German town called Baumholder, in the southwest part of Germany. We occupied a small German schoolhouse. There was a fellow soldier with me named Richard Goldman, who later became a well-known tax lawyer. He had been with me on the boat coming over, with me when we were transferred from the artillery to the combat engineers, and generally slogged through the mud by my side as we tried to stay alive during the war. Richard was very smart. A lot smarter than I was. Because on V-E Day, that glorious day that the war ended in Europe, he marched me down to the cellar of the schoolhouse and showed me some K rations and a bottle of wine that he had procured for us to eat and drink.

I said, "Dick, what's this all about?"

He said, "Even though the shooting ended today, tomorrow is the official announcement of V-E Day. Everyone will go crazy. They will be joyously firing their weapons into the air. No one in that state of euphoria will realize that what goes up must come down, and the bullets will surely come raining down on what's below. So that's why we are going to spend the next twenty-four hours in this cellar, trading the joy of victory for the tired cliché of just staying alive."

So thanks to the savvy thinking of Richard Goldman, I'm still here.

The war was over, but I didn't go back to America immediately. We were part of the Army of Occupation. It was much safer, but kind of dull. Once in a while a USO show would come through our vicinity and we would be part of a large Army audience to see the show. One afternoon, I couldn't believe it! One of the shows that was coming to perform was the Bob Hope show with Frances Langford and Jerry Colonna. I snaked my way down to the first row. Bob Hope was great. I never laughed so hard in my life.

When the show was over and he was leaving the stage something possessed me. I had a pencil and paper in my hand and thought that if I didn't get his autograph, I would die. I rushed to the edge of the stage. Just as he was about to exit, I grabbed the cuff of his pants, and wouldn't let go. It was funny for a minute, but then when I wouldn't let go, he actually got a little scared and was glad to sign his name for me just to escape. I don't know what happened to that autograph. I'm sorry I lost it. It meant a lot.

Okay, get ready for another digression. It's many years later and I've just finished performing on *The Johnny Carson Show*. Needless to say, I was great. As I was marching back to my dressing room at NBC I heard a familiar voice say, "Hey, kid. That was pretty funny."

Could it be? Yes! It was. It was Bob Hope. He had just seen the show. I turned to him and said, "Mr. Hope! I can't tell you what hearing words like that from you means to me."

He said, "Put it there, pal,"—shaking my hand—"it's a pleasure to meet you."

I said, "Bob, this is not the first time we've actually met. Right after the war ended you were doing a USO show somewhere in Germany and when you were just about to exit the stage a crazy soldier grabbed the cuff of your pants and wouldn't let you go until you signed his autograph."

"Oh my god! I remember that crazy soldier!"

"Bob, that crazy soldier was me!"

"Wow, I don't know what to say. Thanks for your service."

"Thanks for your autograph!" We both laughed. Life is funny.

Okay, back to Europe. One day, a lieutenant from Special Services who was touring Army installations in our area said, "Is there anybody in this unit who can sing? Dance? Tell a joke or play an instrument?"

I immediately raised my hand.

He said, "What can you do?"

I said, "All of the above! I can sing, dance, tell jokes, and play the drums."

I told him all about what I had done in civilian life back in the Borscht Belt, etc. He asked my CO if he could borrow me for a few weeks. So I joined his Special Services unit and became one of the comics in a variety show touring different Army camps. Needless to say, I was an exceptional addition to his staff. As a result, the lieutenant asked my CO if he could permanently transfer me to Special Services. Permission was granted, and I was now an entertainer once again.

I reported to Special Services in Wiesbaden, Germany. I was made acting corporal and put in charge of the entertainment at noncom and officers' clubs. It was a great gig. I got a big beautiful twelve-cylinder Mercedes. (Which, by the way, they told me was one of Von Rundstedt's cars.) And believe it or not, a gorgeous

A Star Is Born . . . . ?

DETERMINATION . . . .

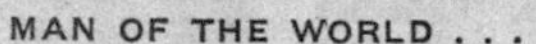

MAN OF THE WORLD . . . .

HAPPINESS . . . .

CONFUSION . . . .

POST Photos by Cpl. Louis Forgione Charles Haas

Here are just four reasons why First Sergeants get that way—This character is known in the Army as Pvt. Melvin Kaminsky, and to be expected, he hails from Brooklyn. Head of the entertainment crew for Special Services, Kaminsky is very much in demand as an M.C. His stage name is Melvyn Brooks. His last appearance before entering the Army was in the play, "Bright Boy", so he says, and he adds: "I had three lines in that show, was on the stage about two minutes, what a part!" A member of the Combat Engineers before coming to Dix, Kaminsky expects to be discharged in June.

From the Army newspaper Stars and Stripes*—the beginnings of a wacky comedian.*

blond fiddle player who was also a driver to be my chauffeur. Her name was Helga. Quite often I would say, "Helga! Pull over and play Brahms's lullaby!"

Things were really looking up. We made trips followed by a big 6x6 Army truck to German cities like Cologne and Dusseldorf and would load up with wine, beer, and cognac to distribute to the clubs.

(By the way, I used Dusseldorf as one of my lyrics in my song "Springtime for Hitler." To wit: *I was born in Dusseldorf und that is why they call me Rolf!*)

I was busy putting together German civilian talent with American GIs who could sing, dance, and play instruments for variety shows that I would MC. I loved the job, and to add to my good feelings, I got a letter from my brother Lenny. He was liberated from his German prison camp and was on his way back home. Believe it or not, I was almost disappointed when I was told my time in Europe was up and I would be going back to the USA.

The journey back to America in April 1946 was a lot faster and safer than the journey to Europe. We were on the *Queen Elizabeth*, a big and beautiful boat and slightly different from the *Sea Owl*. By the way, here's a little history lesson: The *Queen Elizabeth* and the *Queen Mary* were both used as troop transports during the war. Their high speeds allowed them to outrun hazards, principally German U-boats, usually allowing them to travel outside a convoy. During her war service as a troopship, *Queen Elizabeth* carried more than 750,000 troops, and she also sailed some 500,000 miles. It was seven or eight in the morning when we entered New York Harbor. At the sight of the Statue of Liberty smiling down at us, many a GI broke into tears. I think I was one of them.

I was sent to Fort Dix for a month or two before processing my reentry into civilian life. I did some camp shows with Special Services while there. I exercised my songwriting skills by writing parodies. For instance, instead of Cole Porter's "Begin the Beguine,"

Back together with my brothers on the roof of 111 Lee Avenue in Brooklyn. Irving (far right) and I (far left) are still in uniform, but Bernie (next to me) and Lenny (next to Irving) had been honorably discharged and wear shiny gold lapel buttons sporting a proud eagle, sometimes referred to as "the Ruptured Duck."

we'd sing, "When we begin to clean the latrine." And for "The Boogie Woogie Bugle Boy of Company B" we rolled up our pants legs and became the Andrews Sisters.

When I was at Fort Dix, I got a phone call from my brother Irving saying that he was going to be there the next week for his own processing and discharge. Wow, my brother Irving! I was told which bus he would be on and when he got off the bus, I spotted him immediately. I grabbed him and we fell to the ground in a heap, rolling around in happiness. Two MPs jumped on me and pulled me off him. It seems that corporals are not allowed to tackle first lieutenants. My brother quickly explained that we were brothers and had not seen each other for a long time. They let me go.

I was discharged—honorably, I might add—in June of 1946. Being a civilian once again was wonderful and terrible. I didn't have to eat in a mess hall anymore; I could eat Chinese, Italian, or deli anytime I wanted to. But what to wear? In the Army it was easy. You put on the same clothes every day. But I had actually grown about an inch and put on about twenty pounds while I was overseas, so I had to get a whole new wardrobe. My favorite wing-tipped black-and-white shoes were heartbreakingly too small to wear anymore. I had grown up.

The Army didn't rob me of my youth; but actually, come to think of it, they really gave me quite an education. If you don't get killed in the Army you can learn a lot. You learn how to stand on your own two feet.

Chapter 4

Television—The Sid Caesar Years

In 1947 I answered an ad in *The Show Business Daily,* which at the time was a broadsheet newspaper featuring auditions and casting calls for Broadway shows and other theatrical productions in New York City. "Wanted: Production Assistant for Benjamin Kutcher Productions." His office was on Forty-eighth between Broadway and Eighth Avenue. I knocked on the door and went in. It was a typical down-on-their-heels Broadway producer's office, replete with shabby furniture and featuring a big half moon window looking down on Forty-eighth Street.

Unfortunately, I'd caught Mr. Kutcher taking down his underwear and socks from a hastily strung clothesline stretched across his office.

He shouted at me, "Don't you wait for a 'Come in!' before you come in?"

"I'm sorry! I'm so sorry," I said; I was flustered and didn't know what to do. So I said, "I'll go out and come in again!"

And I went back out and knocked on the door. He got even by making me wait awhile before he said, "Come in." I came back in and he pointed to a chair and said, "Sit."

I didn't know it then, but this was the birth of *The Producers,* and Benjamin Kutcher was Max Bialystock.

He said, "Okay, tell me . . . what did you see when you entered the office the first time? What was I doing?"

I thought quickly. If I said, "Taking down your underwear and your socks from a clothesline" I knew I'd be in trouble. So I said, "Nothing! I saw nothing."

"Good." He said, "You're a liar. That's a good beginning."

In a short time, he told me of his adventures as a producer on Broadway. He'd never had an actual hit. But somehow, he made enough money to stay in business. Like many other producers, he always raised a little more money than the budget called for, just in case of unforeseen troubles.

Somewhere in the back of my mind was the phrase "You could make more money with a flop than you could with a hit." Without my realizing it, *The Producers* was actually taking shape somewhere in the deep recesses of my mind.

My first job was to place show cards in store windows that told of the appearance of Mexican born singer and actor Tito Guízar, who was doing a one-man show at Town Hall in a few weeks. In addition to putting on plays, variety shows, musicals, etc., Mr. Kutcher also presented single performers in one-man shows.

Kutcher was smart. He said, "If they say no, give them a couple of passes to the show."

They all said no, and pretty soon, I was out of passes. So I went back, got more passes, and dutifully covered the neighborhood with the rest of the Tito Guízar cards.

Mr. Kutcher raised most of his money from a bevy of backers consisting of elderly women that he would flatter to pieces. I don't think that he ever went as far as Bialystock in *The Producers*, who when asked what the name of the play was would answer, "Cash. The name of the play is Cash. Make it out to Cash." That was my own invention.

Sometime later that year Mr. Kutcher bought the rights to a play called *Separate Rooms*. It was written by a well-known actor, Alan Dinehart, and was originally performed by Alan Dinehart and Lyle Talbot. It was an old chestnut, a backstage comedy that appeared at the Plymouth Theatre for almost a year in 1940–41. It was fraught with a lot of bad jokes. My job was to help put a cast together and take the show on the road. I decided to give myself a part in the play, which was okay with Mr. Kutcher, and we debuted the road company of *Separate Rooms* at the Mechanic St. School theater in Red Bank, New Jersey. (By the way, Red Bank is famous for being the birthplace of the talented swing band giant Count Basie.)

The part I had chosen for myself in the show was that of Scoop Davis, the press agent for the play within the play in this backstage comedy. I think I chose it for my opening line. All the other actors are onstage, anxiously waiting for me to come in with the reviews.

As I hit the lights they ask: "Well? Well!"

I shout, "Not to worry, not to worry. It's a hit! It's the greatest thing since pay toilets."

I got my reward: a great big laugh.

I worked for Benjamin Kutcher Productions for almost a year. I still remember an unforgettable image of him wearing his navy blue double-breasted coat, a white silk scarf, and on his head was perched a well-worn dusty gray homburg hat. He wore spats and was always sporting a black walking stick with a fake gold tip. What a guy. Thinking back, I was probably the precursor of Leo Bloom—*The Producers* naïve accountant who just dreams of being in show business.

Sometime in late 1947 I reconnected with Don Appell. He called to tell me that one of his discoveries when he was a social director at the Avon Lodge, a guy by the name of Sid Caesar, was actually going to be opening at the Copacabana as the leading comic. He asked me to join him on opening night to catch Sid's act. As we were headed to the Copacabana, Don told me that back in the Borscht Belt Sid was actually a saxophone player in the band, but Don had caught him telling jokes and breaking everybody up so he pulled him out of the band and decided to make him a comic in his variety shows. Don told me that even though he was a wonderful saxophone player, he was an even better comedian and that he always scored. He also told me that Sid was in the Coast Guard during the war and was the starring comic in a film about the Coast Guard called *Tars and Spars*. (Which I got to see later, and was very impressed with Sid's performance.)

When we arrived at the Copacabana, Sid had arranged a front-row table for Don so we got to see his performance unimpeded by other people's heads. Needless to say, Sid's performance was absolutely terrific. His comedy was completely different. He had an amazing range of talent. In his monologue that night, he did a satire of a war picture playing both the good-looking American pilot and the evil-looking German pilot. And the sounds he made were amazing; the plane's engines, the machine guns, and the hero's dialogue as well as the villain's guttural crazy German. In addition to that he played a sad pinball machine that was sick and tired of getting hit by heavy metal balls. Once again, the sounds he made were incredible. I don't remember laughing so much in my life.

We went backstage at the Copa, and I met the guy that I was to spend nearly the next decade of my life writing jokes for. We bonded immediately. Sid's comedy was not a bunch of one-liners, but a satire of the human race. He loved that my comedy also had to do with people and their stories, not a series of punch lines. And I loved his comic take on everything in the world. We were instantly on the same page.

Sid invited me to come backstage and hang out with him at his next gig, which was in the stage show at the Roxy Theatre. In those days, movie houses on Broadway featured, in addition to the film itself, a stage show, which followed the movie and was replete with a big band, singing, dancing, and a comic. Sid told me he would be the comic in the stage show following the showing of a new film, called *Forever Amber*. He said, "It's a silly costume movie. It'll probably last about two weeks."

He was dead wrong about *Forever Amber*. It set a house record at the Roxy and months later, the Linda Darnell and Cornel Wilde period piece was still running and I was still going backstage to hang out with him. It was good and bad. Good because a lot of people got to experience the comic genius of Sid Caesar, and bad because he was going nuts doing five shows a day all featuring the same material. He begged me to come see him as much as possible, probably because I always came up with some new situations and comic avenues for him to pursue. As a result, we became close friends.

Funny things happened during my visits to the Roxy that I would later use in my own stand-up comedy. There was a drummer in the Roxy band that I bonded with, as I was also a drummer. His name was Al, and he was blessed and cursed with a stammer when he spoke, which he brilliantly used to get laughs. One of his surefire laugh makers was "M-M-M-Mel, c-c-call m-m-me." Then there was a long pause and he said, "If n-n-nobody answers . . ." another pause, ". . . it's m-me!" It was the kind of comedy from real life that was so much better than tired stand-up jokes.

One day, Sid told me that he had gotten a call from a guy by the name of Max Liebman, who had seen *Tars and Spars* and thought he was terrific and wanted him to star in a new variety show that he was producing for television. Max Liebman was well known for his stewardship of the entertainment at a resort hotel in the Poconos called Tamiment. Out of Tamiment came a Broadway show called *The Straw Hat Revue*, which starred Imogene Coca—who Max brilliantly decided should co-star with Sid Caesar in his new TV show. Max had an eagle eye for talent and was gifted in his picking of unknowns who would become stars. He discovered Danny Kaye, and also Sylvia Fine, a great comedy writer who would later become Mrs. Danny Kaye. Sid was very excited about doing the TV show. It was going to be called *The Admiral Broadway Revue*. In those days both radio and television often had the sponsor's name in the title of the show. Popular examples included *The Maxwell House Hour*, *Texaco Star Theatre*, and *The Kraft Music Hall* starring Bing Crosby. Admiral was a well-known company that made television sets. Max brought his Tamiment writing team to *The Admiral Broadway Revue*—Mel Tolkin and Lucille Kallen. Mel, together with Lucille Kallen, had written wonderful material for Max's Tamiment shows. Later Mel Tolkin was to become the head writer of the famous Saturday night blockbuster called *Your Show of Shows*.

At the time, Mel and Lucille were the only billed writers on *The Admiral Broadway Revue*. Sid immediately said to me, "I want you to be my own writer, no matter what." He offered me forty dollars a week out of his own pocket. I think I said yes before he even finished talking.

He invited me to a rehearsal of the first *Admiral* show, which was at the International Theatre on Columbus Circle. I got to the stage-door entrance and announced my name and told them I had been invited by Sid Caesar, the star of the show. They promptly threw me out.

Unfortunately, Sid's manager was in charge of the list of Sid's backstage guests. He had seen me with Sid and thought that I was just a hanger-on, a pest, and told them, "No dice, don't let him in."

Undeterred, I immediately found out where Sid's dressing room window was and shouted up to the open window, "Sid! Sid! It's Mel! Mel! Sid! Sid! It's Mel! Mel!"

Luckily, he heard me and stuck his head out the window. "Mel! Mel! What are you doing down there? Why aren't you in the theater?"

I said, "They won't let me in!"

Sid said, "Go back to the stage door."

Dutifully, I ran around back to the stage door and I waited for Sid to appear. He did, and gave heated instructions to everybody that I was his writer and I was to be admitted to every place that he was performing. They apologized and said they were told by his manager that I was just a pest. I came up to Sid's dressing room with him and he said, "Wait here."

I could hear him just outside the door, dressing down his manager. "I can always get another manager," he shouted, "but good writers are hard to find. Besides, he's my pal."

I can't tell you how good that made me feel.

I never got credited as a writer on *The Admiral Broadway Revue*, but Sid was happy to keep paying me out of his own pocket because he valued my contributions. I told him that I needed a little more money, as I was living in a hovel in Greenwich Village. He went to visit my place, which was a cellar on Horatio Street outfitted with a bed, a chair, a toilet, a stove, and a small refrigerator. He said, "Mel, you don't live in a hovel. You live *under* a hovel."

Sid increased my pay to fifty dollars a week. I helped write his monologues on the show and also contributed some jokes to pep up his part in the sketches. Making Sid Caesar laugh was one of the great joys of my life. He was not only one of the greatest performers in history; he was also one of the best audiences.

The Admiral Broadway Revue ran only nineteen weeks, from January 28 to June 3, 1949, and was not renewed. I was perplexed. I knew the show, which appeared on two networks at the same time—NBC channel 4 and DuMont channel 5—was getting very good ratings and was really popular. And then I discovered the reason. The show was so popular that Admiral could not keep up with the demand for television sets that the program generated. When the show first began, Admiral had been producing fifty to a hundred sets a week, and selling the same number. The popularity of the show caused business to pick up, and within months orders skyrocketed to five thousand sets a *day*. They were way beyond what they could produce. The company was faced with a choice: It could continue to sponsor the show, or it could take that money and build a new factory. They chose the latter. Bizarrely enough, *The Admiral Broadway Revue* was and is probably the only show in history to be canceled because it was too successful.

Advertising executive and future NBC president, Sylvester "Pat" Weaver, had the idea that people would stay home on Saturday nights if they got the same quality of entertainment at home on TV that they could get by going out to a movie. To that end, he created a two-and-a-half-hour special variety show called *Saturday Night Revue*. The first hour, from eight to nine P.M., was *The Jack*

Carter Show, coming from Chicago. Then the next hour and a half from nine to ten-thirty P.M. would be *Your Show of Shows*, coming from New York and starring Sid Caesar and Imogene Coca. *The Jack Carter Show* didn't last very long, but *Your Show of Shows* was an instant hit, and became a standalone ninety-minute show. It was one of the five top-rated shows of the season. It turns out that Pat Weaver, who went on to create *Today* and *The Tonight Show*, was absolutely right. Sixty million Americans were ready to stay home and be entertained by ninety minutes of live television every week for thirty-nine weeks a year. The show was so popular that Broadway show receipts were down on Saturday nights, and so were restaurant and taxicab profits. A group of Broadway movie-house owners went to an NBC executive and begged him to use his influence to get *Your Show of Shows* rescheduled for a time slot during the week. Maybe a dead night, like Monday? But it never happened.

Your Show of Shows was conceived and produced by Max Liebman, who had previously produced *The Admiral Broadway Revue*. It was an amazing concept, a new Broadway revue broadcast live every week for thirty-nine weeks. It had singing, dancing, opera, ballet, comedy, pantomime, and a new guest star every week. The show was a great success.

I knew that I was not a favorite of Max Liebman. He thought I was too self-assured, cocky, and brash. And he wasn't wrong when he said I was "very disruptive." For instance, quite often during a dance rehearsal, I couldn't resist the shiny wooden floors. I would run like mad and slide all across the floor between the dance director and the chorus. When I hit the far wall I'd yell, "SAFE!" Everybody laughed, except Max Liebman. Sometimes Max was so angry that he would take a lit cigar from his mouth and hurl it at me. Sometimes, he blew on them to make them hotter. Thank god he always missed.

I had just found out that Sid and Max were going to meet with Pat Weaver, now the head of NBC, and General David Sarnoff, the

Writing session on the first Your Show of Shows *in 1950 with (left to right) Sid Caesar, Mel Tolkin, Lucille Kallen, and me.*

head of the parent company, RCA. Sarnoff formed the entire Radio Corporation of America. I knew they would be talking about *Your Show of Shows,* and somehow, I felt I should be part of that meeting. I begged Max to let me come to the meeting. "I won't make a noise, I'll sit in the corner," I promised.

Not surprisingly (and not politely) he said no. And not surprisingly, I was not taking no for an answer. Every once in a while I would suffer an attack of outright no-holds-barred madness. This was one of them.

I went nuts. I ran around the rehearsal area, which had a lot of props. I saw a straw boater hat and then I grabbed a white duster coat (a long coat that people wore to drive cars in 1893) that Carl used to wear sometimes in sketches. I put on the hat, coat, and a pair of goggles, and I burst into the meeting! I jumped up on the long conference table and yelled: "Lindy landed! He's in Paris, he made it!" And I hurled my hat out the open window.

They quickly threw me out. Sarnoff and Weaver were puzzled, Max was mortified, but Sid collapsed in laughter.

Two years later, I was working at the top floor of the RCA building and General Sarnoff walked past me with another executive. He nodded at me. And then at the end of the corridor I heard him say to the other executive in a loud whisper: "Lindy landed!"

He never forgot what happened. And I'm sure neither did whoever was walking on the street in Rockefeller Center when the straw hat landed.

I took a big chance in demanding that I no longer just be Sid's boy, but rather a real, full-fledged member of the writing team with credit, etc. There was a stormy argument between Sid and Max when Sid proposed this, but Sid won and Max reluctantly gave me credit on *Your Show of Shows* as "Additional Material by Mel Brooks" onscreen. Not to mention, a hundred and fifty dollars a week which would be paid by the show and no longer by Sid. When Sid slapped me on the back and told me all this, I nearly fainted. Wow! My name was going to be on the show, and I was going to be making more money than my three older brothers' salaries put together. Sometimes dreams really do come true.

I had never actually thought of myself as a writer until 1950, when I first saw my name on the credits of *Your Show of Shows*. I got scared. I said to myself, "I'm not a writer, I'm a talker." I wished they'd change my billing on the show to "Additional Talking by Mel Brooks," so I wouldn't feel so intimidated. But I worked hard and conquered my fear of the empty page, which is the journey that all writers have to make. I worked my ass off thinking and writing day and night. I was lucky that Mel Tolkin and Lucille Kallen (who had followed Max Liebman to *Your Show of Shows* from *The Admiral Broadway Revue*) welcomed me aboard. They couldn't have been kinder and more helpful.

As well as contributing to the guest stars' sketches, my special writing province turned out to be Sid's monologues and a new feature of the variety show in which Sid played a series of characters that were interviewed by a reporter every week. My first contribution was an interview sketch where he played "Jungle Boy," a Tarzan-like character wearing a loincloth and carrying a big club, who somehow managed to survive in urban New York City. It went like this . . .

REPORTER: Where are you from, sir?
JUNGLE BOY: Jungle.
REPORTER: Sir, how do you survive in New York City? . . . What do you eat?
JUNGLE BOY: Pigeon.
REPORTER: Don't the pigeons object?
JUNGLE BOY: Only for a minute.
REPORTER: What are you afraid of?
JUNGLE BOY: Buick.
REPORTER: You're afraid of a Buick?
JUNGLE BOY: Buick. Buick big. Buick yellow. Buick have big shiny teeth. Wait for eyes to go dark. I sneak up on sleeping Buick, punch in grille hard. Buick die!

It got huge laughs, and Sid was effusive in his thanks for my helping make "Jungle Boy" work.

Originally, the comedy interviews were conducted by one of the leading singers on the show, Tom Avera. Tom was doing a very good job for a singer, but he wasn't what Sid needed. Sid was looking for a real second banana that could also do double-talk for the foreign movie satires that we had begun to write. Sid was a genius at mimicking foreign languages. Luck was with us. On a TV show called *The Fifty-Fourth Street Revue* we discovered Carl Reiner, a tall, good-looking, fast-talking comedy find. He was added to the top-drawer talent that already included Sid and Imogene Coca, and was talented enough to keep up with Sid's brilliant French, Italian, German, and Japanese crazy double-talk. What a find!

(Small digression here, you're going to hear a lot about Carl

Reiner in the future. He became my partner in the 2000 Year Old Man, and has become my very best friend for too many decades to count.)

Carl met and interviewed a series of comedy characters played by Sid. The most consistently funny one that always worked was "the German Professor," a know-it-all scholar dressed in an old-fashioned swallowtail coat, wide tie, the yellow W. C. Fields vest with the roll collar, baggy striped pants, and a broken-down top hat. He was an expert on everything. I remember helping Sid get big laughs on an interview with the German Professor as a world-famous expert on mountain climbing.

CARL: Professor, what do you do if when you're climbing a mountain your rope breaks?

SID: [as the professor, in a German accent] When your rope breaks you immediately start screaming, and keep screaming all the way down until you hit the ground.

CARL: How does that help you?

SID: Actually, it doesn't help you at all. But it helps the people on the ground know where to find you.

The German Professor solidified my role as a valued contributor to the show. Writing the show was wonderful and terrible. The wonderful part was hearing the laughs that my jokes and sketches got from the live audience. The terrible part was I'd stay up until two or three in the morning trying to think of characters and situations that we could use on the show, which led to quite often being late for the writing sessions with Sid, Carl, and the other writers. They started at ten a.m. and I'd get in at eleven a.m. I would call the Carnegie Deli for my bagel, cream cheese, and coffee so it was waiting for me when I got there. One of the secretaries usually paid the dollar and a half, and I would reimburse them when I got there. The bagel and coffee came to about a dollar, but I always gave the delivery guy a fifty-cent tip.

One morning after being warned by Sid not to be late again, I came in my usual one hour late and gave the secretary a dollar fifty.

She said, "Sorry, Mel. It's not a dollar and fifty cents today, it's twenty-one dollars."

"What! Twenty-one dollars? For a bagel and coffee?" I exclaimed.

Holding back a laugh, she said, "Yes, twenty-one dollars. Mr. Caesar paid for your bagel and coffee, and he tipped the delivery guy twenty bucks. I think he wanted to send you a message about being late every day."

For a while after that, I was always on time.

Let me jump away for a minute and tell you a little story about my very first appearance on television. Even though I had been a performer in the Borscht Belt and then in the Army, I felt that I couldn't compete onstage with the likes of a Sid Caesar, an Imogene Coca, and a Carl Reiner, and was more than happy to contribute my talents just as a comedy writer. Carl Reiner was with the William Morris Agency and his agent was Harry Kalcheim of the (at the time) well-known William Morris Kalcheim brothers—Nat and Harry Kalcheim. Harry thought I was funny and always prodded me to grab a small part on the show. I always resisted saying, "The comedy is in good hands with Sid, Imogene, and Carl."

But one day, he told me that there was a small comedy part open on the *Texaco Star Theatre* hosted by Milton Berle. It was the part of a dopey stooge for Sid Stone, the famous *Texaco Star Theatre* pitchman. He was the guy who said, "You say you're not satisfied? You say you want more? Tell you what I'm gonna do!" He'd slap his hands together and open his little suitcase and make his sidewalk pitch. On this particular show, I was a window washer.

Sid Stone said, "I've got a great job for you. It's the Empire State Building!"

"Too many windows," I said. "And besides I don't like to work way up high. I'm afraid."

"What are you afraid of? Falling?" Sid said.

"No. Pigeons," I said. "Pigeons, they live up there."

Anyway, it got a few laughs. The amazing thing was, when I got back to Williamsburg to visit family and friends, I was an instant celebrity. Everybody in Brooklyn had seen me on the *Texaco Star Theatre* as the window washer on the Sid Stone spot. I was actually signing autographs!

Anyway, back to *Your Show of Shows*. My one and only personal appearance on the show was completely offscreen and turned out to be a near disaster. Let me explain . . . In the sketch there is a darkened bedroom and we see a woman asleep in bed and Sid stealthily opens the drawer next to her bed and takes out a letter that can prove his innocence. Slowly he backs out of the room. In the semi-dark we see a cat asleep on the rug, its tail fully extended. Sid, continuing to back up, doesn't know the cat is behind him. When he's nearly out of the bedroom he is supposed to step on the cat's tail and all hell breaks loose. The cat is supposed to let forth with a great big cat yowl—I was playing the cat. It seems that the soundman was informed by more than one person that nobody made a better cat sound than Mel Brooks. So he asked me to audition, and I did. He said, "That's the best cat sound I've ever heard in my life. I'm not going to use my cat sounds, you're it."

He didn't know, and neither did I, that standing there at the microphone I would get "sound fright." Realizing that my cat sound would be heard by millions of people my mouth dried up, and when it came time to make the cat sound all I did was make big dry wheezes. Finally, I got it together and came up with the best cat sound I ever made. Sid jumped at the sound—along with everybody else in the audience. It was my first and last live performance on *Your Show of Shows*.

To fill out the comedy sketches on the show we needed another actor—a third banana. So Howard Morris was hired not only for his ability to do foreign double-talk with Sid and Carl, in addition to his comic acting skills, but also because Sid said, "I need somebody I can pick up by the lapels and shove my nose into his face."

I said, "I know the guy! He's Howie Morris and he's funny and weighs about a hundred pounds."

Sid auditioned him by picking him up, shouting into his face, and then putting him back down. "You've got the job," he said.

Howie Morris was a bright comedy addition to Sid, Imogene, and Carl. I remember one of my most successful sketches consisted of a takeoff on an old Emil Jannings German film called *The Last Laugh*. Sid is being dressed as a German general by Howie Morris. They both spray the scene with meticulous phony-baloney German double-talk. For instance, Howie spits on the brass buttons of the general, and then brushes them clean.

Sid shouts in fake German, *"Vas ist los bist du mishuga? Spritzin auf ein General?"*

Howie replies apologetically, *"No, no, Herr General. Ich habe nisht geshpritz auf ein General. Ich habe geshpritz auf dem buttons!"*

Big laughs! When Sid is fully dressed, he marches in all his splendor—brass buttons, epaulets, medals, etc.—through the revolving doors of the hotel. When he reaches the sidewalk he pulls out a whistle and blows it loudly. As a cab pulls up he opens the door for a couple to enter and we realize that he's not a general, he's just the doorman. Thanks to the talents of Sid and Howie, the sketch really worked.

About Howie Morris, let me say this—I loved him. He became a dear friend. But before he actually knew me well, I decided to rob him. Let me explain . . .

I figure nature made two different types. One type was little birds, pigeons, white mice, etc. They were victims. They were called prey, and Howie was one of them. The other type nature made was wolves, bears, lions, etc. They were called wild beasts, and I was one of them.

One night, when Howie and I were walking down a street in

Greenwich Village called MacDougal Alley it was quiet and nobody was around. It occurred to me that this would be a perfect place to rob someone. So I slammed Howie against the alley wall and said, "Give me everything in your pockets and your watch and your ring!"

Howie said in a half laugh, "You're kidding, right?"

I just growled. He decided to take the safer course and gave me everything, including his watch and wedding ring. And then I said, "Run!" And he ran home.

The next day, I got a call from Sid. He said Howie had just called him and said that I robbed him.

I said, "It was a crazy joke! It was a perfect place to rob somebody . . . so I robbed Howie. Please go along with it for a while."

Sid chuckled and said, "Sure, why not."

When I saw Howie, I acted perfectly normal, like nothing had happened.

Howie said, "About last night . . ."

And I said, "What about last night?" And crossed my eyes slightly.

Howie said, "Nothing! Nothing! Forget it."

I let it go for about a week and then I said, "Howie! It's all coming back to me . . . Did I rob you last week in MacDougal Alley?"

He said, "Yeah, and I really could use my wallet and my car keys back."

I gave him everything back including his watch and his wedding band and apologized and said, "As you know, I'm in analysis and every once in a while I'm overcome with things I can't control."

About a year later Howie and I were out to lunch together and we had rented a boat to paddle around the Central Park Lake. As we rowed under a bridge, it was suddenly dark and quiet and a perfect place to rob someone. So I slapped him in the face and shouted, "Give me everything in your pockets, and get out of the boat!"

Without a moment's hesitation, he emptied everything he had in his pockets, and once again gave me his watch and his wedding ring, and then stepped out of the boat into waist-high water and waded to shore.

I didn't wait more than a few days this time to return everything, along with another apology.

"It's okay," he said. "I understand." He thought for a minute and then added, "How often you think you're gonna do that thing?"

I laughed, hugged him, and said, "I think the joke is over."

To begin with, *Your Show of Shows* was written by Mel Tolkin, Lucille Kallen, and me. Sid often sat in on the writing sessions. Unlike other variety show stars, who didn't respect the writers and would send back scripts with comments like "This stinks!" scribbled on the cover, Sid really cared about the quality of the writing and would sit in the writers' room and work with us from time to time. He wanted to be there for each premise, each line, and each note. He knew what he wanted out of the writers and the scripts. Mel, Lucille, me, and occasionally Sid, first worked in a writers' room that was also the chorus dressing room at the City Center. We were creating comedy amid racks of socks, underwear, Roman togas, and Japanese kimonos. After we became a hit, we could afford better office space. Max Liebman took offices at the City Center and we wrote the show in Max's L-shaped office in Suite 6-M. The writers' room was now fancy enough to have a couch and two chairs! Later on, Carl Reiner would often sit in with us too, throwing in really valuable ideas. In the writers' room, we were less concerned (and to be fair, in some instances not concerned at all) about one another's feelings and more about the best show we could produce. Sixty million people were watching the show every week and we had to come up with an original script of at least six comedy sketches every week for thirty-nine weeks a year. That was pressure. You could yell and scream at someone in a writing session, and an hour later you'd be having lunch together, laughing as if the contentious session had never happened. Writing an hour and a half show each week for thirty-nine weeks a year is absolutely impossible! But somehow we did it, and most of the stuff was damn good.

The writers' room started me on my noble quest to always get to the "ultimate punch line," the cosmic joke that all the other jokes came out of. The goal was to go as far as you can go, as deep as you can go. One of the most difficult things to do in comedy is to come up with a good ending to a scene or a sketch. The real struggle is to take a premise, the center of it, and nurture it and blossom it into a punch line. We managed to do it each week because it was life or death. We fought like beasts in that room. Our backs were up against the wall. Between Sid and Max, we knew if a joke worked. We were told if an ending to a sketch wasn't great, and we'd have to rewrite it. It's almost impossible to create a great ending to a sketch. We pulled it off at least half the time.

We wrote things that made us laugh, not what we thought would get a laugh from the audience. But stuff that really made us collapse and grab our bellies, that knocked us down on the floor and made us spit and laugh so we couldn't breathe—that's what went into the script. We wrote sketches with beginnings, middles, and endings—little playlets. It was a different kind of comedy, not just one-liners. Everything we wrote was based on truth. We commented on what was happening in the world at the time.

For instance, in the early fifties new apartment buildings were going up with lower ceilings and thinner walls. Landlords were getting ever more greedy. So we wrote a sketch with Sid as a guy who couldn't sleep because the sound and light of the neighbor's television came right through his walls. So he broke his lease by simply walking through the walls of ten different apartments. The sketch worked, giving us some hope that we were on the right track.

There was a lot of anger behind the comedy. There were a lot of jokes about death and murder, dirty language, quarrels, conflict, a lot of yelling. Sid punched the wall so much it was bent. We'd throw pencils in frustration at the acoustical ceiling, where they would get stuck. Sometimes the screaming and fighting in the writers' room would get so bad I felt like I was back at Fort Sill in basic training on the infiltration course with live machine gun bullets flying over my head! It was all creative anger, intense competitiveness, all trying to please Sid. We cared passionately about what we were doing and who we were working for. We were responsible for entertaining millions of people on live television every week. There were no second chances. The pressure was not just to be good, but to be outstanding.

There was no sneaking in of script ideas to Sid. It was all done by committee, and all ideas were equally considered. We never really passed judgment until something was tried on its feet. We'd do it as a skit. I would play Sid. Sometimes Lucille would play Imogene, sometimes Carl. Sometimes Imogene would be there to play herself. I was always performing in the room. I could go from playing a rabbinical student in one minute, and then in the next I'd be Moby Dick thrashing about on the floor with six harpoons sticking out of my back. We yelled out ideas, competing for Sid's attention and approval. Sid was not tyrannical, but he would occasionally have fits of anger. He once lifted a huge desk and banged it to the floor to punctuate his anger, yelling: "Joke no good!" Mel Tolkin quietly offered, "Sid, don't worry. We're not married to it," all in a voice meant to calm Sid down. Another time, the wall phone in the office rang during an idea exchange and disrupted the creative flow. So Sid ripped it out of the wall and threw it into the hallway. Other than emergencies, there were no more calls during working hours.

Our head writer, Mel Tolkin, was a veritable font of worldly information and taught me so much. I relied on him often for advice. An émigré from Russia as a child, he retained more than a bit of an accent. Sometimes he sounded like Bert Gordon, who played "the Mad Russian" on *The Eddie Cantor Show*. He introduced me to all the great Russian writers. Not only the ones I knew like Tolstoy or Dostoyevsky, but geniuses like Nikolay Gogol, Vladimir Nabokov, Aleksandr Pushkin, and Leonid Andreyev.

(Later, I myself discovered two newer Russian writers called Ilf and Petrov, who wrote a book called *The Twelve Chairs,* which I adapted into a screenplay and it became my second film. More on that later.)

Mel Tolkin could be funny on paper and—without knowing it—also funny in real life. Example: Every spring the restaurant across from our office and writers' room on Fifty-seventh Street, Longchamps, featured an item called "spring lamb." All the writers together with Sid, Carl, and Max dutifully went across the street to go get our spring lamb. It was a big item. We all ordered it.

As I'm finishing my entree, Mel Tolkin says to me, "Mel, would you mind very much if I had a bite of your spring lamb?"

"Mel," I said, "you just finished a whole portion yourself."

And he said, "Yes, that is absolutely true, but to be perfectly honest I must tell you that I ate it so quickly I really didn't taste it."

Talk about real-life humor!

Tolkin wrote some great stuff, but once in a while he had some silly jokes like, "She married a station beneath her! She got off at One-hundred-and-twenty-fifth Street and he got off at One-hundred-and-tenth!" We all forgave him.

Some time after that first season, I began getting anxiety attacks. I was worried about not being able to come up with the volume of material needed to do show after show, or that what I did come up with wouldn't be funny enough. I started vomiting between parked cars. I couldn't figure out why. Mel Tolkin knew everything, so I asked him, "Mel, why am I vomiting between parked cars?"

He said, "You need to talk to a psychoanalyst. He'll be able to help you."

Mel sent me to his analyst, Dr. Rubin. In those days, it was twenty-five dollars for a fifty-minute session. He was too busy to take me on as a patient so he sent me to a psychoanalyst on Central Park West named Clement Staff, who was analyzed by Theodore Reik, who in turn was actually analyzed by the world-famous Sigmund Freud. So theoretically I was getting psychotherapy right from the horse's tail!

I was in therapy on and off for three years. During my sessions, I would go from weeping softly to shouting defiantly. After a while, the therapy opened me up. Instead of continuing to vomit in between parked cars, I found the courage to ask for a raise and, equally important, a real writing credit on the show. I went from "Additional Material by" to "Staff Writer" and a generous raise in salary to boot.

I had become a full member of the writing staff, but I was still learning my craft every day from Tolkin and Kallen. Lucille Kallen was brilliant at writing the domestic sketches. She was responsible for writing a lot of the comedy for Imogene Coca. She also was great at contributing to the guest stars' sketches. The show featured as guest stars the famous film and theater stars of that time, including Charlton Heston, Geraldine Page, Rex Harrison, Madeline Carroll, Douglas Fairbanks, Jr., Pearl Bailey, Melvyn Douglas, and many others. Some of them took to television and were good, and some of them were god-awful. (But I won't name names.)

Like I said before, my forte was Sid's monologues as well as the German Professor, and later on, the foreign movie satires. It was presumptuous of us to write these foreign movie sketches. After all, how many people out of the millions watching the show at that time had actually seen a foreign movie? They only played in a few big cities in a handful of movie houses. But somehow, they worked. The double-talk in Italian or French and then suddenly a punch line in English always got a big laugh. Sid was absolutely remarkable in his ability to do foreign double-talk. The funniest may have been our sketches based on the Kurosawa Japanese films like *Rashomon*. It was amazing that Imogene, Carl, and Howie were able to keep up with him.

It was a pretty classy show. In addition to the comedy, Max Liebman booked a variety of musical performances. *Your Show of Shows* presented arias from famous operas like *La Bohème* with stars like Marguerite Piazza as Mimi singing *"Sì, mi chiamano Mimì"* and Robert Merrill singing Marcello, the male lead. There were also musical guest stars such as world-famous cellist Gregor Piatigorsky and pianist Earl Wild. Stars that could easily have been performing at the Metropolitan Opera House or Carnegie Hall, but *Your Show of Shows* was bringing them into people's living rooms. In addition to that, Max discovered wonderful dance teams like Mata and Hari, the Hamilton Trio, and Fosse and Niles—the Fosse being the great Bob Fosse who later became a legendary choreographer and director.

Max believed his vision made the show successful. He thought that the musical numbers were driving the show, but he was wrong. It was a case of the musical tail that was wagging the comedy dog. People were tuning in to see the comedy much more than the elaborate musical numbers. More people wanted to laugh than wanted to hear fifteen choruses of an operetta or a classical aria.

The only time music and comedy were in conflict was when musical numbers ran long, and Max directed us to cut the comedy sketches, which were easier to edit right beforehand than the musical pieces because they would have to be rearranged and reorchestrated and that took much too much time. The comedy cuts would always have to be made at the last minute, on Saturday afternoon after the dress rehearsal. Sid would get the writers together, and it was painful. We all loved our favorite jokes and didn't want to lose them. To get a minute and twenty seconds out of a sketch, you had to cut out a whole section, not just a line. So we would compromise. We generally looked for the weakest sketch and cut from there, but nobody liked the process. We could never take comedy sketches past five or eight minutes, because of Max's preference for the musical numbers.

Presenting *Your Show of Shows* was a herculean task. The weekly script, with music, dancing, and six original comedy spots, had to be finished by Wednesday to air on Saturday night. Time needed to be allotted for the mimeograph machines to crank out duplicate scripts for orchestration, props, scenery, costumes, makeup, and sound effects to be readied by performance time. Not to mention the fact that we first had to work on the actual show run-throughs, rewriting, blocking, and rehearsals.

Thursday was the most creative day of the week and also the most stressful. Nothing was complete yet. We had the page, now we had to get it on the stage. We all got together in a big rehearsal room and put the whole show up on the stage, taking the ideas and fleshing them out. We'd add things to the script, cut things out, and make changes on the spot. It was also at this time that I was getting my first experiences as a director when Max Liebman asked me to help out by putting the comedy sketches on their feet and running them a couple of times.

We gave the sketches room to breathe. As soon as Sid, Imogene, Carl, and Howie were comfortable with the script, there would be a loose blocking. They would then rehearse all the places they'd have to hit onstage. There were black lines, blue lines, red lines, yellow lines, green lines, purple lines, which all corresponded to different scenes, where the scenery had to be put and where the camera had to focus.

By the time we got to the live show on Saturday night, we had been through four rehearsals. The first time there was a loose blocking, which was followed by a tighter blocking. Friday was a complete run-through with a few stops for the technical people. The cameramen studied the shots; the costumes and props were tested and altered as necessary. On Saturday we'd have a full-dress rehearsal, and then we'd go out live at nine o'clock that night.

We never thought about the following week's show. We were still writing the current week's installment right up to curtain time! The writers were there, watching, making suggestions, and contributing additional dialogue. We stayed there right through the actual live broadcast, watching from the green room and often making changes right up through to the time the sketch was performed live. We were an extremely dedicated and passionate group.

Believe it or not, even with all that tireless preparation mistakes and blunders still sometimes happened during the live performance. For instance, on one show, Sid's dresser got the running order of the sketches mixed up. Sid entered a board-meeting sketch, filled with men in business suits, wearing a Roman costume topped with a Roman helmet and carrying a sword. Everybody was shocked, but Sid carried it off brilliantly. "Sorry I'm late," Sid said, "but I just came from an all-night costume party. Let's get on with the business."

Amazing! We were absolutely petrified and then incredibly relieved. We all collapsed in a heap of hysterical laughter.

Another time was when we satirized the movie *High Noon* in which Gary Cooper has to face the bad guys all alone after the townspeople desert him. Sid was playing the Gary Cooper sheriff character, and we made a lot of the townspeople deputy sheriffs. To punctuate their quitting, they pinned their badges on Sid's chest over his own badge. Sid was supposed to have a sponge inside his shirt to protect him from the pins. But in his haste, the dresser forgot to put the sponge in during the quick change. We were amazed at how realistically Sid yowled when one by one they pinned the badges on him.

Sid and Imogene were great at going with the flow, but once in a while, it got to be a bit much. The audience never knew if anything was wrong. For instance, we were doing a satire on *From Here to Eternity,* which became "From Here to Obscurity." Sid and Imogene were in the classic Burt Lancaster and Deborah Kerr scene where they are falling in love on the beach while the waves break over them. Off camera, there were five or six stagehands with big buckets of water hurling them at Sid and Imogene. I don't know how they did it, they were practically drowning, spitting water like human fountains all over the place. But they never broke up and the audience laughed their heads off, never knowing what Sid and Imogene were going through.

Sid had an incessant nervous cough. It was nothing more than that. But he learned to use it to his advantage. He had an enormous amount of material to memorize and the cough gave him momentary pause to remember exactly where a line or situation fit. Occasionally, I would even write in the cough to give him time to swallow what was coming. He got a kick out of seeing "cough, cough" in the script.

And to be perfectly truthful, not all the jokes worked. I had an idea for an interview with the German Professor in a zoo. He is walking by the reptile house and he hears a tapping on the window. It's a snake tapping his teeth against the glass, trying to get his attention.

"What's the matter with you?" the professor asks.

The snake says, "You gotta get me out of here. It's dangerous!"

The professor says, "Why?"

The snake replies, "I'm surrounded by snakes!"

"I have bad news for you," the professor says. "You'll have to stay. You're a snake too."

That joke didn't get any laughs. Complete silence.

"Mel," Sid said, "I will see you after the show."

From that point on, whenever someone in the writers' room

Carl Reiner trying futilely to separate Howie Morris from Sid Caesar's leg in the classic sketch "This Is Your Story."

suggested that we use an unpopular joke we'd say, "You want to do the snake joke again?"

We got to do a few live shows at the Center Theatre, the sister theater to Radio City. The five-thousand-seat theater had its own amazing energy. It was there that we did probably the funniest sketch ever done on television. It was the now celebrated takeoff of *This Is Your Life*. In the sketch that we wrote, Carl Reiner as the host of "This Is Your Story" comes down into the audience, walks up the aisle, and when he reaches the row that Sid is sitting in, he smiles. Sid thinks he is picking the guy sitting next to him to be in the show, and chuckles at what's going to happen. But when Carl points directly at Sid and says, "Al Duncey, this is your story!" Sid passes out.

When Carl takes him by the arm, Sid wakes up, and instead of sticking to the script, which has Carl leading him to the stage, Sid shows the genius that made him immortal. He swats Carl with his raincoat, driving him back, and decides to improvise—telling us in pantomime that he is not going up there on that stage no matter what. Carl, thinking on his feet, grabs a couple of ushers and says, "Let's get him up there!" When the ushers go for Sid, he once again smashes them back with his raincoat and runs up the aisle. Thank god we had a guy with a handheld camera who followed him on his mad chase all over the Center Theatre. It was amazing. Nobody knew what was happening, but it was absolutely hilarious!

Finally, all the ushers in the theater tackle him and carry Sid to the stage. He relents, and reluctantly becomes part of the show. Now, the parade of relatives begins. The funniest and most memorable is Howie Morris playing Sid's "Uncle Goopy." They hug each other ceaselessly, crying tears of joy to be together again. When Carl finally gets control of the show for a moment, he takes Sid downstage to introduce a new relative. But Howie will have none of it. He leaps onto Sid's leg and never lets go. Sid carries him around as if Howie was always part of his leg. Occasionally, Carl is able to tear him off Sid's leg and carry him back to his seat, but only for a second. Before you can count to three, he is back on Sid's leg. The sketch is exploding with hilarious improvisations between Howie, Sid, and Carl. The laughter was nonstop; you couldn't catch your breath.

Sid Caesar was a crazy comic genius, but occasionally he was also just crazy. Let me take you back to Chicago in 1950. It was just after the first season of *Your Show of Shows* and Sid had a two-week engagement at the Empire Room at the Palmer House Hotel. He took me along to punch up his act and as good company. Things were going swell for a while, but then doing his act twice a night finally started to get to him. After the show, he'd go up to his room and to help him relax, he'd drink a half a bottle of vodka and light up a cigar.

"Give me some new material!" he would shout. "I'm sick and tired of doing the same stuff every night!"

The hotel suite was filled with cigar smoke and it was hard to breathe. One night I asked Sid to open the hotel window, which was jammed shut. I tried with all my might to open it but it wouldn't budge. So I said, "Please, Sid, I can't breathe in here. I need some air! Please open the window."

Sid went over to the window, and with one hand yanked it wide open. (He was very strong.) Then, with a crazy look in his eye, he said, "So you want some air? I'll get you plenty of air."

He picked me up by my collar and my belt and hung me out the window! There was State Street directly below me! I could see the traffic so clearly; I knew which taxis were empty by the lights on the top.

Sid said, "Got enough air?"

In a very calm voice I said, "Oh yes. Plenty! I've had enough."

I was very calm. I didn't want to make him any more crazy than he already was.

He brought me inside, sat me in a chair, and said, "Let's go to work."

Out of sheer panic, I think I must have written twenty new jokes that night. And I never again asked him to open a window.

One night, we were driving in a rented car with Sid at the wheel. Out of nowhere, a Chicago taxi appeared, and Sid avoided crashing fully into it, but the fenders of the two cars touched slightly. When they came to a stop the cabdriver rolled down his window and shouted, "What's the matter with you? Why don't you learn to drive, you stupid son of a bitch!"

Sid immediately got out of the car. I ran around and grabbed him and said, "Sid, please! Forget it! We're in Chicago! We don't know anybody here. Let it go! Let it go!"

But there was no stopping him. I knew trouble was brewing.

When Sid walked over to the taxi, the cabdriver, who saw how big he was, immediately rolled up his window. But Sid, undeterred, spoke to him in a rather pleasant voice through the little triangular clipper window that allowed air to circulate.

He said, "Excuse me, I'm not mad—I just have one question . . ."

The cabdriver looked at him strangely and said, "What?"

Sid said, "The question is very simple. I just want to know, do you remember being born?"

The cabdriver again said, in a slightly louder voice, "What? What the hell are you talking about!"

Sid said, in a strange calm-crazy manner, "Well, you obviously can't remember being born. So I'm going to help you by reenacting your birth."

He reached in and grabbed the cabdriver by his black leather bow tie and began shoving his head through the little clipper window. I had to bite Sid's hand before he let go, otherwise he would have pulled all of that taxi driver through the little window and turned him into one long taxi-driver snake! We got back in the car and drove away. Sid seemed satisfied.

Another testimony to Sid's incredible strength was one day when we were going to lunch at Al & Dick's restaurant—a smart

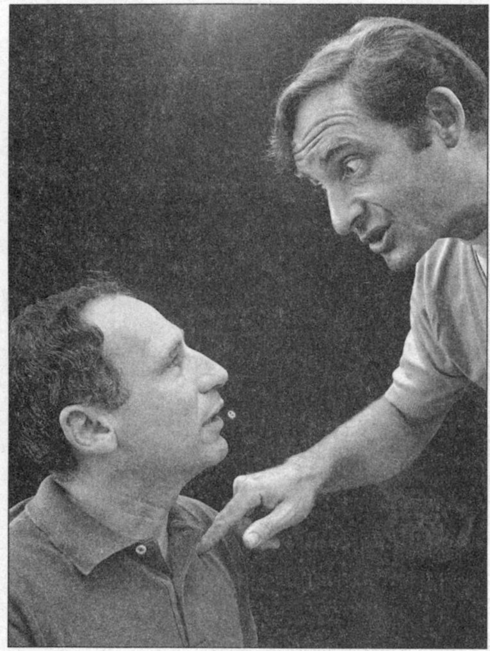

Sid Caesar sparing my life.

eatery on Fifty-fourth Street. We called in advance, which allowed for somebody to go outside and reserve a space in front of the restaurant for Sid's car. They usually did, but that day when we arrived, a yellow Volkswagen Beetle was parked there. Sid surveyed the situation and quietly went to work. He put his hands under the bumper at the back of the Volkswagen and with one heave lifted the back of the car onto the sidewalk. He walked around to the front, grabbed the bumper, and did the same. He then parked in the space that was now free. We walked around the Volkswagen, now parked on the sidewalk, and went into the restaurant for lunch.

There were lingering thoughts in my head. What would people think to see a Volkswagen on the sidewalk in the front of the restaurant? Even more interesting, what would the driver who had parked the Volkswagen think when he saw his car on the sidewalk? I thought, I guess he'll have to drive on the sidewalk until he hits the street again so he can go about his business.

No doubt about it—Sid was really strong. I was taking my life in my own hands one day when Sid and I were having an argument about a sketch I wrote that he wanted to cut. I was adamant and demanded that the sketch stay in. To emphasize my feelings, I took the two fingers of my right hand and I savagely poked them into his shoulder. A giant mistake. Sid looked at me strangely, and I realized what I had done. I waited for what could be the end of me.

Sid just smiled, and in a crazy Russian accent said, "I let you live."

Believe me, I never poked him again.

Around this time, I got an offer from a producer to write a sketch for a new Broadway revue called *Curtain Going Up*. Even though I was incredibly busy with *Your Show of Shows* I couldn't say no—Broadway was always my ultimate dream. I sat down and wrote a takeoff on *Death of a Salesman,* stealing a title from a beloved Russian author, Ivan Turgenev—*Fathers and Sons*. I called it "Of Fathers and Sons." It was a ten-minute satiric sketch having fun with the characters in Arthur Miller's *Death of a Salesman*. Unfortunately, *Curtain Going Up* came crashing down during its out-of-town tryout in Philadelphia and never made it to New York.

However, luck was with me. Another revue was trying out in Philadelphia at the same time as *Curtain Going Up*. It was called *New Faces of 1952*. The producer, Leonard Sillman, and the creator and star, Ronny Graham, saw my sketch and loved it and wanted it for their revue. In addition to Ronny Graham, appearing in *New Faces* were future stars like Eartha Kitt, Carol Lawrence, Robert Clary, Alice Ghostley, and Paul Lynde.

Alice Ghostley was cast in my sketch as Willy Loman's long-suffering wife. The Willy Loman role was played by the incredibly gifted Paul Lynde. The son was my creation. He was neither Biff nor Happy. He was a strange, strange child played by Ronny Graham. Ronny was hilarious.

The sketch begins with Paul Lynde telling his wife: "Alice, I don't know. I'm no good anymore. I can't do it. I was the best pickpocket in Philadelphia, the best! So smooth, nobody even knew things were missing for days. I can't do it anymore. Too many cops. My hands sweat and I can't do it."

She says, "Sure you can, Harry. Come on. I'll make some spaghetti. You'll have a glass of wine. You can do it."

He says, "Oh, well, maybe. Where's my boy? Where's the light of my life? Where's my son?"

And in comes Ronny Graham. And he's carrying a bat and tossing a ball. His father, a petty crook, was dreaming that one day his son would follow in his footsteps and become a world-renowned criminal. Paul says to Ronny, "What are you doing? He's supposed to be learning how to pick pockets. What are you doing? What's with the bat and ball?" And then Paul says, "Show me your report card." Ronny stalls, and finally reluctantly gives it up. Paul reads it hoping to see bad marks like F's and D's. Instead, it's a bunch of A's. Paul exits the stage while heartbreakingly moaning, "A. A. A. A!"

After a long pause, Alice Ghostley brought the house down with, "You're killing that man." It was a laugh that went on forever.

The show came to New York and opened on Broadway at the Royale Theatre. It was an instant hit. It got very good reviews and my sketch was singled out by the famous *New York Times* theater critic Brooks Atkinson. I couldn't believe it! I was actually a writer on Broadway.

Ronny and I went on to become frequent collaborators and lifelong friends. Even though I was in the funny business, nobody made me laugh like Ronny Graham. For instance, there was always a line of autograph seekers at the stage door of the Royale Theatre where *New Faces* was holding forth. Ronny was always the last one to leave the theater. I don't know why, but by the time he opened the stage door the crowd had left. It didn't mean a thing to Ronny. He made believe he was besieged by screaming autograph hunters. He would push his way through the imaginary throng screaming, "Please! This is too much! Let me breathe! I'm an ordinary human being just like you! Please let me through."

Even though I was the only person there, he never stopped performing. I would collapse with laughter.

Ronny and I wrote crazy songs together. We gave movies that didn't have title songs their own music and lyrics. Like, "*The Crea-*

ture from the Black Lagoon . . . Has Stolen My Heart." And "*War and Peace . . . I'll Take Peace.*"

Later, we wrote a wonderful song that I'm still trying to find a place for called "Retreat." It's an ode to cowardice.

Here's a sample:

Retreat, retreat!
Drop your sword and run.
Our foe is near, our choice is clear,
Get outta here, Hooray for fear,
We're done.
Run away, Run away,
If you run away you'll live to run away another day!

I never got it into a show but it's a winner whenever I sing it in front of an audience.

During the summer breaks in production on *Your Show of Shows*, we would all do our own thing. My reputation as a comedy writer was spreading. I got a call from Freddy Kohlmar, a film producer at Columbia Pictures in Hollywood. He had produced some well-known pictures such as *Kiss of Death* (1947) starring Victor Mature and Richard Widmark, and *The Ghost and Mrs. Muir* (1947) starring Gene Tierney and Rex Harrison. He called with an incredible opportunity: He wanted me to do the screenplay for a well-known Rodgers and Hart Broadway hit called *Pal Joey*. He offered to fly me out to L.A. and pay me a thousand dollars a week for eight weeks. I was so dumbstruck, for a moment I couldn't answer. On the other end of the phone I heard, "Well, well . . . are you coming?"

I finally found my voice and said, "Turn around, I'm there!"

It was the first time I'd been to California. Having been born and raised in Brooklyn in the jungle of tenements, I'd never seen anything like it. I was stunned by the beauty of the place. Palm trees! Endless blue skies! The Pacific Ocean! It was paradise. And to boot, there were orange trees—thousands of orange trees with big juicy oranges that sometimes hung into the street from people's backyards. Since they were in the street, I figured they were public property. So every day I'd pick some and happily munch on an orange or two on my way to work.

I had a big office all to myself on the third floor of the Columbia Pictures building on Gower Street in Hollywood. I went to work diligently writing the screenplay of *Pal Joey*, but only two weeks into the script, Jerry Wald, the head of production at Columbia Pictures, called and said, "We can't get Sinatra to play Joey. He's too busy. So Columbia wants to keep it on the shelf for a while. But I have another project for you. It's called *Apple Annie*."

So I started work on *Apple Annie*, the story of a poor little old lady who sold apples on the street corner, but in letters to her son back East she pretended to be a wealthy dowager throwing lavish parties every night. But the son was coming out to visit her and soon the game would be up, unless she could find a way to fool him. So with the aid of a gang of less-than-honest bookies, gamblers, etc. they would manage to help her pull it off.

(By the way, many years later *Apple Annie* turned into a movie called *Pocketful of Miracles* [1961] with a wonderful performance by Bette Davis.)

I was lucky my next-door office neighbor was a guy by the name of Alfred Hayes, who had written a novel with a beautiful love story about a GI and an Italian girl called *The Girl on the Via Flaminia*. He was also from New York, so we hit it off. Alfred was actually born in the Jewish neighborhood of London called Whitechapel and came to New York when he was only three. We had lunch every day and traded stories about growing up in New York City.

One day, when we came back from lunch Alfred noticed that his name was not on his door. I said, "Maybe it's on the floor?" The nameplates could be slid in and out from the slots on the doors. So we looked around for it, but we couldn't find it. Alfred called downstairs to report that his name was not on his door, and he couldn't find it. The explanation was simple and terrible. They told him thank you for services rendered, but he was no longer needed at Columbia Pictures.

He said, "I guess that's the way they fire you. They just slide your name off the door!"

That night, I was so angry I couldn't sleep. I decided I had to do something about how Alfred was treated. I got up real early and snuck into the building with the janitorial staff at six a.m. I went to the third floor. I took every name from its slot on the door. I went down to the first floor. I took every nameplate from the first floor and put them in the empty slots of the third floor. And then I went to the second floor and swapped those out too. In a fit of outraged insanity, I changed the name on every door at Columbia Pictures! Then I went back up to my office, put my feet on my desk, and fell asleep.

After an hour or two I was awakened by an incredible din in the halls outside my office. It seemed that people were upset. All of Columbia Pictures was flooded with angry agents and lawyers.

I was happy. I had gotten even.

Unfortunately, around four o'clock that same day there was a tap on my door. Jerry Wald stuck his head in and said, "Mel . . . you were seen."

I said, "What?"

He said, "Yes, somebody saw you change all the names and Harry Cohn wants to see you in his office."

Ten minutes later I was on the red carpet in the office of the head of Columbia Pictures, Harry Cohn. (Strangely enough, his office carpet was actually red.)

He was not happy.

Freddy Kohlmar and Jerry Wald pleaded my case. They said things like:

"He's a crazy kid! He does crazy things!"

"But he's good! He's funny! He's writing for us."

"He's gonna make us money! Don't fire him, Harry."

Cohn, his face boiling with rage, shouted, "I don't want him fired! I don't want him fired. I want him KILLED!"

And I knew that he probably knew exactly the guys who could do it.

But thanks to Freddy and Jerry, I got off with just a blast of angry invective. After my tour of duty at Columbia was over, I was happy to head home to New York. My first foray into movies was an unmitigated disaster. Oh, so happy to be back to the safety of television and the talent of Sid Caesar.

But Hollywood was not wasted on me. I realized there was a big difference between movies and television. As a writer, a movie afforded you all the time you needed to develop characters, story, and a satisfying *denouement*. Television gave you no time at all. I also realized that films lasted a long time—sometimes forever. But television was forgotten the week after it aired. I brought this new understanding home to Sid Caesar.

We had done two seasons, actually three seasons, if you count *The Admiral Broadway Revue* and two of *Your Show of Shows*. Sid was one of, if not the hottest comedian in America. We were among the highest-rated shows on TV and we were doing an hour and a half show thirty-nine times a year. Amazing by today's or any other standards.

So I asked Sid to have dinner with me—just he and I alone.

He answered with, "What is it? You're not going to quit, are you? If it's a matter of money I could get you a raise."

I said, "No, no. Not going to quit. It's not a matter of money, it's a matter of survival."

So that night we had dinner. He had his usual two-inch steak, baked potato, asparagus, etc. I was nervous and not too hungry, so I just had (in a salute to him) a Caesar salad. And I said, "Sid, I know your renewal contract is coming up. I don't want you to sign it . . . I want you to quit. I want you to quit this show, this highly successful, top-rated show."

"What are you, crazy?" He laughed.

"I want you to quit. I want us to get on a plane and fly to Hollywood. I want us to make movies. Movies last. It's fifty years later but we still see Harold Lloyd hanging from that clock in *Safety Last!* We still see Charlie Chaplin eating his shoe in *The Gold Rush*. Movies are forever, but no matter how brilliant you are on television it's forgotten a week later. On TV it's all a thing called kinescope—I don't know what it is. I don't know what we're being captured on. It could be cellophane! It could be cotton! We come and we go. We explode every week, we do a show and in an hour it's forgotten. You're forgotten and you're a genius. You're brilliant. You're funnier than big Hollywood comedy stars like Danny Kaye and Red Skelton. You're funnier than anybody in Hollywood. You'll be a revelation to the world! Now, they only know you on television and they're crazy about you. If you do movies, they'll be crazy about you in Sweden, in France, in Moldavia. And you're handsome! You could carry a picture. You'll be the funniest leading man that ever lived! And we'll take our time. It's not like we're going out there looking for a job. They want you. You're already a star. We'll move your face from a little TV set to the big screen."

He was blinking a lot, and I knew that the more he blinked the more he was getting it. He said, "I'm not going to give you an answer now, but you're making a lot of sense and I'm really gonna think about it."

He didn't say a word about it the next day, or for that matter he didn't say a word about it for the next two weeks. I was scared. I was puzzled. I didn't know what to think. And then, finally, he chased everybody out of his office and sat me down. He said, "Mel, you're probably right. It might be wise to leave at the top of your game in television and get into movies where your career could last a lot longer. But I couldn't do it. I signed with the network to do the show for the next three years. I'll tell ya why. When I told Max Liebman that I was thinking of quitting and going to Hollywood and gave him all your good reasoning why I should, he said, 'You may be right or you may be wrong. Let me talk to NBC.' "

Last-minute rehearsal rewrite session with (left to right) writers Danny Simon, Joe Stein, me, Neil Simon, Tony Webster, Mel Tolkin, Sid Caesar, and NBC executive Hal Janis.

It was the end of 1952 and Sid was earning about five thousand dollars a week, a gargantuan sum for that time. When Max Liebman told the head of NBC that Sid was thinking of not renewing, that he was thinking of going to Hollywood and making movies . . . they made him an offer he couldn't refuse. They didn't want, under any circumstances, to lose their time slot and its incredibly lucrative sponsorship. So they offered him an unprecedented raise in salary. He would go from five thousand dollars a show to twenty-five thousand dollars. Which came out to a million dollars a year.

He said, "Mel, I just couldn't say no."

I never brought it up again, and we went into our next seasons with flags flying.

In 1954 NBC split *Your Show of Shows* up into three different entities. Max Liebman went on to produce musical specials, which were called "Spectaculars." Imogene Coca got her own show, a sitcom, and Sid went on to do three more seasons in a new incarnation called *Caesar's Hour*, an hour-long version that had much more comedy than the ninety-minute *Your Show of Shows*. Mel Tolkin, Carl Reiner, and Howie Morris went with Sid. Lucille Kallen went with Imogene.

After the first couple of seasons on *Your Show of Shows*, the comedy writing demands had become too great for just Mel Tolkin, Lucille Kallen, and me, so we added the Simon brothers writing team—Danny and his kid brother, "Doc" Simon. The "Doc" being Neil Simon, who later would go on to be one of the most celebrated comedy playwrights on Broadway. Neil taught me that every second counts in comedy writing. Both Danny and Neil were like that. They took advantage of every second and every joke at their disposal. Neil never forgot a joke. He said that he never forgot anything that he ever heard that had made somebody laugh, whether he wrote it down or not. That's the type of memory he had. He didn't need to steal jokes; he was so damn talented.

When *Your Show of Shows* morphed into *Caesar's Hour*, the writing staff grew even larger, adding the talents of the likes of Larry Gelbart, Joe Stein, and Mike Stewart. All of whom would go on to great success: Larry Gelbart, who created one of television's most celebrated series, *M*A*S*H*; Joe Stein, who wrote *Enter Laughing* and *Fiddler on the Roof* for Broadway; and Mike Stewart, who later created the books for great Broadway musicals like *Bye Bye Birdie*, *Hello Dolly*, and *42nd Street*. Though we had lost Lucille and Imogene to their new show, we gained another great female comedy writer, Selma Diamond, and the beautiful and talented Nanette Fabray was Sid's new leading lady on *Caesar's Hour*. We had a bigger budget, real offices in the Milgrim Building in midtown Manhattan, and our own theater at the Century on Eighth Avenue. Writing comedy with all those truly gifted comedy writers on *Caesar's Hour* was like the thrill of jamming with great musicians. We made great comedy music in that room. But Sid would take it and bend it through the prism of his heart, his crazy mind, and what evolved would be beyond our wildest expectations. He always took our material to a higher level.

Doc Simon was incredibly funny but very shy. Carl Reiner knew this and would sit next to him in the writers' room and quite often Doc would whisper his contributions into Carl's ear. Then Carl would leap to his feet and say, "Doc's got it!" And another great Neil Simon joke was born.

Larry Gelbart and Doc Simon both really enjoyed my comic spontaneity, and we'd often have lunch together. One day we were walking up Fifty-seventh Street and coming down toward us were three nuns. They immediately knew I couldn't resist.

Larry said, "Mel, leave it alone."

Doc said, "Mel, whatever you were gonna do—don't do it."

I answered, "Not to worry, not to worry." . . . But I was lying.

As the nuns approached, I shouted: "Get out of those costumes! The sketch is OUT!"

Both Larry and Doc collapsed in laughter and hit the sidewalk. They were my best audience.

On another occasion after lunch we were on Sixth Avenue and there in a store window were a hundred little toy microscopes selling for ninety-nine cents each. I walked into the store, Larry and Doc followed.

I said to the store owner, "I'm Dr. Melvin Brooks, head of the Johns Hopkins School of Medicine." Larry and Doc stifled their laughter, wondering where I was going with this.

I continued, "At Johns Hopkins I am working on multi-celled anomalies and need a very strong and powerful microscope to detect cellular differences. Will those microscopes in the window do the job?"

The shop owner shrugged and said, "Yes, they're very good." Again Doc and Larry, unable to contain themselves, screamed in laughter and hit the floor. They never stopped telling the microscope story.

At the 1957 Emmy Awards ceremony, Sid, Carl, Nanette, and Pat Carroll all won Emmys and the show won for best series of one hour or more, but *The Phil Silvers Show* beat out *Caesar's Hour* for best comedy writing. I leapt up onto the table and screamed, "Coleman Jacoby and Arnie Rosen won an Emmy for comedy writing and Mel Brooks didn't! That writers like that can win the award and geniuses like me would be denied? Nietzsche was right! There is no god! There is no god!"

They were good writers. But we were great writers. We were the best comedy writers that ever wrote for television. And they still won the Emmy! I went backstage and found a pair of scissors in the wardrobe room. I cut up my tuxedo. I cut my bow tie first. Then I cut my jacket into little black shiny confetti. Then I took my trou-

Me desperately selling Sid a joke with fellow writers Woody Allen and Mel Tolkin looking on.

sers off and proceeded to cut them up too. I was just in my shorts. I was almost naked in front of everybody when I said, "I'm never wearing a tuxedo again!" Somebody put a sheet around me, and put some ice on my head, and took me home. I might have been a little drunk.

The pressures and grind of a weekly live network television show took its toll on Sid. On set he was alert and prepared. Off camera, he was drinking more and more to cope with the pressure. He would spend Sundays, our only day off, in the shower for hours, trying to decompress.

The writers, his friends, were extremely protective of him. What is now known as "the Coleslaw Episode" occurred on a Wednesday night during the run of *Caesar's Hour.* A sketch unexpectedly fell apart and we had to write an entirely new sketch in a single day. Sid, Carl, and the other writers and I went to dinner at a nearby

Going back to Europe to write for Sid Caesar's BBC show, this time crossing the Atlantic without a rifle and a helmet.

restaurant. "First we'll have a drink," Sid said, "then we'll eat, and then we'll work."

What Sid didn't tell us was that he'd been taking a strong sedative at the time.

When the waiter came to take the food order after our drinks, Sid said, "I'll have fillet of sole . . ." and promptly slumped forward, face-first, into a bowl of coleslaw.

The writers laughed at first, thinking it was a joke. When we realized that Sid had passed out, Carl told us that we had to pretend that this was a skit or else the incident would be in all the morning tabloids.

I stood over Sid with a knife in my hand and said: "So, Inspector, this undoubtedly is the murder weapon."

Larry Gelbart responded, "Let us pray," and they all put their heads down on the table.

This kind of improvisation went on for forty-five minutes, with Sid out cold. We periodically checked to make sure he was still breathing. Finally, as the waiter brought the check to the table, Sid's head popped up and he said, ". . . and shoestring potatoes," picking up exactly where he had left off when he went down into the coleslaw.

After *Caesar's Hour* ended in 1957, we did several special hour-long variety shows starring Sid. On those, we got the assistance of a brilliant young writer called Woody Allen. Woody got into the swing of the writers' room very easily right from the start. He didn't just write funny jokes, he wrote characters, behavior, funny situations. Quite often after a hard writing session, I had to walk it off. That is, instead of taking a cab home I would walk. It was a long walk from Rockefeller Center all the way up to Fifth Avenue and Eighty-seventh Street (where I lived at the time), and Woody would generously offer to accompany me. I don't know whether it was just for the good talk, or if he thought at least he'd be there to call 911 if I collapsed. I appreciate the memory of his friendship and entertaining chatter on those long walks home.

In addition to those specials, I also got to continue to write for Sid on his new series *Sid Caesar Invites You . . .*, which we got to do both on United States TV and were invited to do across the pond for the BBC.

Near the end of Sid's epic nine- or ten-year run on television, our ratings were dropping fast. I don't know of any other comedian, including Charlie Chaplin, who could have done nearly ten years of live television. Sid was one of the greatest comedy artists that was ever born into this world. But over a period of years, television ground him into sausages—one sausage a week, until finally there wasn't much of the muse left. The decline was affecting all of us. I wasn't sleeping much, and I was angry and ill-tempered most of the time. In 1958 and '59 the show was losing its top status and we were falling behind in the ratings to, believe it or not, Lawrence Welk, with his bubbly dance music. We were all working day and night to keep the show on the air. My nerves began to fray and I was always in a bad mood. I must have been absolute hell to live with, that's probably what led to the end of my first marriage. It was one of the worst periods of my life.

I think there is a saying that goes like this: It's a stormy wind that doesn't blow somebody some good. So even though the marriage didn't work out and in the later years was beset with stormy times, the good part of the wind that blew me some good was my three children from that marriage. Stefanie, Nicholas, and Edward were always a source of comfort and happiness. No matter how life was treating me, they were always there for me with their love and affection. A real blessing.

When Eddie was just a little kid, maybe eight or nine, Carl Reiner was making a movie called *Where's Poppa?* In one of the hilariously funny scenes of that movie, Ron Leibman is forbidden to leave the house by his wife. When she blocks the door he says to her, "Get away from that door, or I'm gonna choke your child!" And to prove his resolve he grabs his little boy and begins choking him. My son Eddie was that little boy. Eddie was playing it so real, with incredible gagging sounds, that as I watched I actually was

From Carl Reiner's hilarious movie Where's Poppa?
Here is my ten-year-old son, Edward Brooks, in his acting debut.
He was so good, I was afraid that actor Ron Leibman
was actually choking him!

terrified that he might really be choking him! Anyway, he didn't and the scene got nonstop laughter. Eddie went on to grow up, get married, and have a child of his own. My wonderful granddaughter Samantha, who turned out to be beautiful, incredibly smart, and really talented. He was and has always been an exceptionally loving and really great father in his own right.

Nicholas went on to somewhat follow in my own footsteps. He wrote and directed a wonderful film called *Sam*, a romantic comedy in which the character he created, Sam, drinks a magic potion and suddenly turns into "Samantha" and drives his best friend crazy trying to convince him that underneath Samantha he's really still Sam. I know what it takes to write and direct a movie; it's a herculean task. So I am so proud of Nicky for all the great work he did in fashioning his terrific film.

My daughter, Stefanie, was smart and funny from the day

she was born. I'll never forget the night we threw a party for our friends, and three-year-old Steffie entered the room dressed as a fairy-tale princess. The living room was crowded and when Carl Reiner spotted her coming into the room he said, "Oh, look at the beautiful little princess!" Steffie looked around the room and came back with, "*Yeth*, and the beautiful little *printhess* has nowhere to sit."

At three years old she broke up a whole living room full of pretty sophisticated people.

I am so lucky to have my children in my life. Every week I can count on a call from them to check in on their doddering old dad.

So Sid Caesar's magical ten-year reign on TV had finally come to an end. Later on in my movie career, whenever there was a special character that needed a bit of genius, I always cast Sid. Like the caveman in my *History of the World, Part I*. He's the very first artist in history. When he finishes his magical cave painting another caveman (the first critic in the world) comes up and studies it thoughtfully. He makes up his mind and proceeds to urinate all over it. The look on Sid's face took the moment to another level.

(I'm sure that didn't keep me in good stead with critics. Every time I got a bad review, I was sure they were thinking of that cave scene.)

During the last few years of Sid's life we spent many great dinner parties together. Every other Friday, Sid and I would spend a couple of hours together, riffing and laughing. Sid was my mentor and my lifelong friend. We remained connected and close until his passing in 2014. That magical spark never disappeared.

I have said this many times, and I still believe it: If there was no Sid Caesar, there would never have been a Mel Brooks.

Chapter 5

Carl Reiner and the 2000 Year Old Man

So back to 1960, I go from a highly paid TV writer to a highly unpaid, unemployed TV writer. I'm saved from utter destitution and sleeping on a park bench by the one and only Carl Reiner.

Carl Reiner was always a big fan of my crazy, spontaneous comedy improvisations. One of his favorites was my impression of a Jewish pirate. I'd say, "I'm very depressed. The price of sailcloth has gone up to eight and a half doubloons a yard. I can't afford to set sail anymore. It's been weeks since I pillaged or raped!"

Carl loved it, and made me do the Jewish pirate at every party we were at together.

The 2000 Year Old Man was born one day when Carl walked into the *Caesar's Hour* writers' room during a lunch break. He was carrying a strange gadget.

I said, "What is that?"

He explained, "It's a wire recorder. You talk into the mic, and it captures your voice and plays it back." (I think it preceded the tape recorder.)

He plopped down on the couch next to me and then, as was his wont, he surprised me with, "Here next to me is a man who was actually at the scene of the crucifixion two thousand years ago! Isn't that true, sir?"

I immediately sprung forth with, "Ohhh boy."

Carl said, "You were there! Did you know Jesus?"

I said, "Thin lad, right? Wore sandals? Hung around with

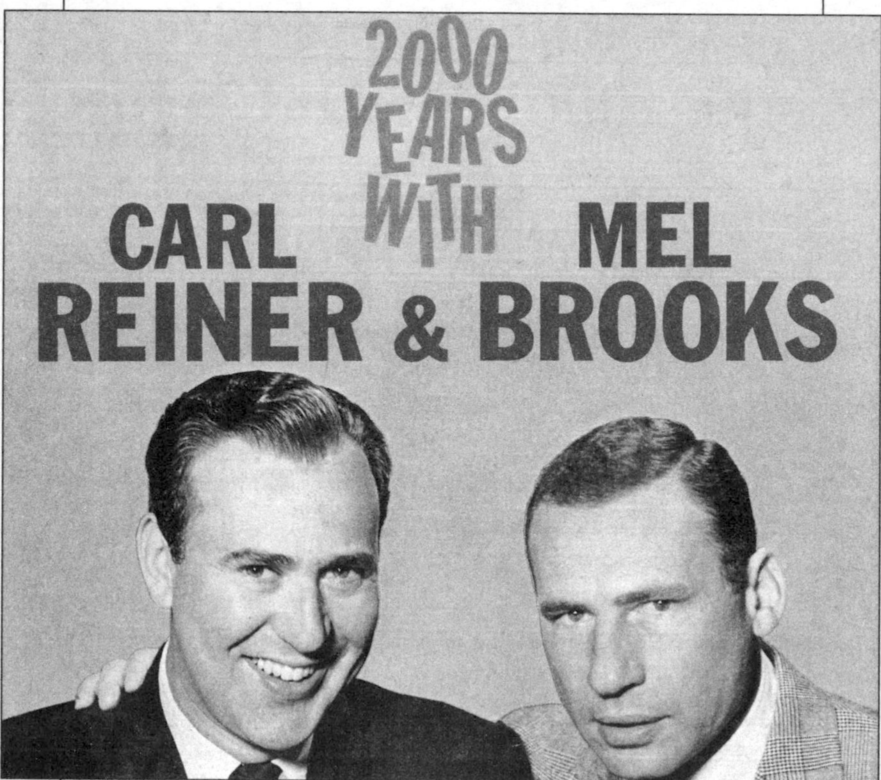
2000
YEARS
WITH
CARL
REINER
&
MEL
BROOKS

twelve other guys? They always came into my store. Never bought anything. They just asked for water."

Needless to say, everybody in the room broke up.

Carl, never one to give you a break to think, charged ahead:

CARL: Well, sir, I must say that you really don't look two thousand years old.

MEL: I take care of myself. I eat right. I never touch fried food.

CARL: But I think we'd all believe it more if you had some way to authenticate it. Do you have a birth certificate?

MEL: We didn't have that two thousand years ago. We didn't have nothing. We didn't have ballpoint pens. We weren't even up to ink, darling. We were primitive. We were . . . atavistic. What is the word I'm searching for? . . . I got it. Dumb! We were very dumb.

From that moment on, Carl never stopped besieging me with questions. He made me a Texan psychoanalyst, a cockney filmmaker, a best friend of Da Vinci, the boyfriend of Joan of Arc—he was relentless. But the character that always worked and became a real fountain of knowledge and humor was the 2000 Year Old Man. It never missed.

If you knew Carl you didn't just like Carl, you loved Carl. There simply was no like. There was just love. To be clear: Carl Reiner isn't the best friend I ever had—he's the best friend *anyone* ever had.

Carl came to *Your Show of Shows* and thought I was really talented. He supported me at every turn. Carl was a little older and had been on Broadway, starring in a wonderful post-war musical about soldiers reentering civilian life by Harold Rome with a book by Arnold Auerbach called *Call Me Mister*. I was leaning on him for the first two years of *Your Show of Shows* until I felt I could hold my own and had my own sense of confidence.

If I said I was the best, he said, "You are."

For the first portion of my life Carl was my rock. Christ said,

"On this rock I will found my church." On this Jew from the Bronx, Carl Reiner, I founded *my* church.

Carl was a natural comedian, impresario, and nurturer of talent. He would study any room he was in, stealthily case it like a creative cat burglar, mine it for ideas, talent, and potential laughter. He was going to figure out how to make you laugh, you just didn't know it yet. And you weren't just going to laugh—you were going to be an active participant in the party. His raison d'être was to bring out the best in you, whoever you were, especially if you were his partner. He did that with Sid Caesar, then me, Dick Van Dyke, Steve Martin, and many others.

If you don't have anyone in your life like Carl Reiner, stop reading this right now and go find someone!

Carl was an immediate and intuitive foil and partner, feeding off my energy and adding to it. I once took Scotch tape and attached my nose to my cheek, my lower lip to my chin, and an eyebrow to my forehead. I looked cruelly disfigured.

I burst into the writers' room, and Carl immediately nurtured the bit:

CARL: How did it happen? Who did that to you?

MEL: The Nazis! They did it to me. Threw me in a ditch and did it!

CARL: You mean they beat you? Disfigured you?

MEL: Oh no. They took Scotch tape and stuck it all over my face.

Carl broke up and hit the floor, clutching his belly and laughing like crazy. For me that was a home run. Anytime I could make Carl laugh, I knew I had a winner.

But back to the 2000 Year Old Man, for the next few years, any time there was a lull in the writers' room, a party, a dinner—absolutely anywhere, Carl began interviewing me. Not only about the biblical days, but under the premise that this man knew everybody and everything.

CARL: Did you know the Apostles?

MEL: I knew them well.

CARL: Can you tell us about them? Who they were?

MEL: There was Ben, Murray, Al, Richie, Sol, Abe . . .

CARL: No, no. That's not the Apostles.

MEL: Wait. You're right. That's the William Morris Agency!

Like all classic comedy straight men, Carl would provide the framework and atmosphere and cautiously redirect and set me up with his questions and reactions. I would not only take the comedy bait, but also provide additional setups for Carl as straight man to use for more options. In every classic comedy duo, from Laurel and Hardy to Abbott and Costello to Martin and Lewis, in order for the exchange to work, the quality of the straight man had to be as dynamic as that of the funny guy. Carl was the best at this.

I could use a single question as a springboard to unplanned exposition and tangents that would be as much of a surprise to Carl as they were to the audience. Carl was a gifted partner: While he deferred the punch lines to me, he knew me well enough to follow along and cross paths enough to set me up for more opportunities. He also knew he could throw me a complete curveball and I'd swing for the fences. We were a great ad-libbed high-wire act, and like the best high-wire acts, ours was dependent upon complete trust and respect for each other.

Carl once said, "A brilliant mind in panic is a wonderful thing to behold."

I was at my best when I was backed into a corner. Like a cornered rat I had to somehow jump out of it. I would never surrender. Carl knew he would never get the same answer twice, and I loved to surprise him.

CARL: Who is the favorite of all your girlfriends of all time?

MEL: Shirley.

CARL: What was so special about Shirley?

MEL: Her friend Leila.

Carl hit the floor.

A few years later, Broadway producer Joe Fields threw a party in Hollywood and every major star was invited to come hear us perform this bit. Without bragging (or maybe *with* bragging), we were sensational. The laughs were nonstop and came like cannon fire.

Edward G. Robinson came up to us afterward and said, "Make a play out of it. I want to play that thousand-year-old man!"

Then George Burns came over and asked, "Is there an album?" And when we said no, he said, "Well, you better put it on an album otherwise I'm gonna steal it."

At that same party was Steve Allen, the first host of *The Tonight Show*. He said to us, "Fellas, you've got to put this on a record."

And we said, "No, no. This is just for us, for our own amusement. Not for the public."

And he said, "I'll tell you what. I'll get a studio. You go in, do your thing, and in the end if you don't like it you can throw it in the garbage and get rid of it."

Needless to say, we didn't throw it in the garbage.

At first, we said no. I didn't want to. This was for friends. I thought some of it may be too inside, and I was afraid some of the pieces might be offensive to Jews and Catholics and provide some stimulus for anti-Semitism. The material was never designed for a national audience. I thought it might be too hip, but Steve convinced us that the Sid Caesar shows had elevated the comedy consciousness of the country.

Steve didn't want to be a partner; he just wanted to get it out there. He was the kind of guy who liked everybody to hear fun. He loved to present fun for people, laughter. He gave us free recording time at a studio that he co-owned, World Pacific. We recorded for over two hours. It was all ad-libbed. I didn't know what Carl was going to ask.

In fact, when we made the album, I said to Carl: "Don't tell me anything, nothing in advance, just hit me with questions and when I can't come up with a good answer, cut it. When I come up with a great answer, keep it in."

Carl and me performing the 2000 Year Old Man sketch on The Andy Williams Show.

And that's the way we did it. We cut that first album down to forty-seven minutes and it became *2000 Years with Carl Reiner and Mel Brooks,* released in 1961.

Steve Allen was kind enough to write the liner notes for the album, and this is how he introduced me:

> But who, you ask, is Mel Brooks? He probably often wonders, himself. Whoever he is he is very funny. And like Carl, he spent ten years with Sid Caesar. But not on camera. Mel is basically a writer; if this album becomes a stepping-stone to a performing career no one, I am sure, will be more surprised than Mr. Brooks.
>
> . . . And thereby hangs an interesting psychological tale. My wife has a theory that there is often a similarity in either appearance, personality, or philosophy between the comedian and the person who works for him. Her hypothesis is certainly confirmed in the case of Brooks and Caesar. Their styles, as you will discover in listening to this collection of ad-libbed routines, are remarkably similar. The two men, it

> seems, have had a pronounced effect on each other. Their approaches to humor are similar. But to hell with analysis. Let's just enjoy. Bear in mind when listening to these routines that they are ad-libbed and that they are never the same twice.

The record was a big hit and we were asked to appear on some important variety shows on TV like *The Ed Sullivan Show*, Steve Allen's show, and *The Hollywood Palace*. We started out just sitting next to each other on stools, almost as if we were performing for radio. Later my character began wearing a kind of 2000 Year Old Man costume replete with a cape and walking stick.

But making the records was so much better. When we were asked to do television show appearances together even though we got big laughs it was never the same. It wasn't as much fun because we already knew what jokes we were going to do. I was not surprised by Carl's questions and he was not surprised by my answers. It was simply not the same joy as doing the 2000 Year Old Man all ad-libbed. The free-form nature of the longer performance pieces allowed a creative exchange that generated far more spontaneous magic.

Part of my motive for doing the 2000 Year Old Man was to preserve the Yiddish dialect and the sounds that I grew up with. I was doing my grandparents. My father's father and mother, and my mother's father, and their friends. I loved them. Hearing those voices always made me feel safe. The 2000 Year Old Man is a feisty fellow, a tough guy, and a survivor. He's the Eastern European immigrant Jew, pronouncing himself forcefully, struggling to make it in America. He's got to know all the answers, because it's about survival. He's a no-nonsense, no-bullshit guy. He tells a lot of human truths, whether he knows them or not. Like the German Professor from the Sid Caesar shows, it's not lying . . . it's self-promotion! He doesn't give you any bad advice. In his exaggeration and fabrication there's always a little truth.

I always thought a rich lie is better than a poor truth:

CARL: Sir, sir, I read somewhere that you lived in Boston during the American Revolution. Did you know Paul Revere?

MEL: An anti-Semite bastard!

CARL: You didn't like Paul Revere?

MEL: I hated Paul Revere.

CARL: No, no, no. He was a hero! How could you call him an anti-Semite?

MEL: He had fear that we were going to go in the neighborhood and move in. "They're coming, they're coming. The Yiddish are coming!" All night he was yelling!

CARL: Were you living in that neighborhood at that time?

MEL: I was there. I heard him yelling.

CARL: No, he was yelling, "The British are coming."

MEL: Oy, my god.

CARL: You were wrong!

MEL: Ooh, I'm going to have to send his wife a note.

CARL: You've maligned the man for all these years!

MEL: I didn't know. And I didn't go to his funeral. Oh my god.

CARL: Two hundred years you have maligned the man . . .

MEL: I'm glad we spoke. I'd better ask you about some more of these people.

Even though the Caesar show was over, and we each had our own projects, Carl and I always got back together from time to time to make another 2000 Year Old Man record. And we'd often hit pay dirt.

I remember on one of the records we got a terrific laugh with a bit about Shakespeare:

CARL: Did you know Shakespeare? He was reputed to be a great writer. He wrote thirty-seven of the greatest plays ever written.

MEL: Thirty-eight.

CARL: Thirty-eight? Only thirty-seven are listed.

MEL: One bombed!

CARL: Actually, it's never been recorded. What was it?

MEL: Unfortunately, I had money in that play.

CARL: You invested in a Shakespearean play that was a failure?

MEL: He said would you put money in it. I read it up and I said to him, this is a beauty.

CARL: What was the name of it?

MEL: *Queen Alexandra and Murray.*

CARL: I never heard of it. Did it ever see the light of day?

MEL: It closed in Egypt!

That was one of the few times that Carl really broke up. Here are a couple of my other favorites:

CARL: I want to talk about the impact of the Ten Commandments.

MEL: There were more. But they weren't important.

CARL: Can you tell me one?

MEL: Certainly, "thou shalt not squint."

CARL: Do you remember the very first book you ever read?

MEL: The first book. You don't forget the first book.

CARL: You remember what it was?

MEL: I was a child. It was a simple book in the ancient Hebrew. It was called *Zaichem, Rochem, Bruchem.*

CARL: And that translates into?

MEL: *See Moses Run.*

CARL: Do you remember the story?

MEL: It was a page-turner.

CARL: Of all the discoveries of all time, what would you consider the greatest? Would you say it was the wheel, the lever, fire?

MEL: Fire. Fire. Far and away, fire. Fire was the hottest thing going. Fire, you can't beat fire.

CARL: Really?

MEL: Fire used to warm us and light up our caves so we wouldn't walk into a wall, so we wouldn't marry our brother Bernie.

CARL: That's right.

MEL: That's Satan's hell, fire. And cooking, oh, you can't beat fire.

CARL: When did they first learn to cook with fire?

MEL: It was an accident. There was an accident. A chicken.

CARL: What?

MEL: Chicken walked into the fire by mistake and over. And it was over. Burnt up.

CARL: What? That chicken?

MEL: Yes. We kept them around the cave as pets.

CARL: I see.

MEL: So we took it out to give it a funeral, you know, bury it, because it was our pet and we all went . . . hey, that smells good. So we ate them up and since then we've been eating chickens.

CARL: You know, I've heard this story, but I've heard that the animal that wandered into the fire accidentally was a pig.

MEL: Not in my cave.

Speaking of caves, there was another one that always got a big response.

CARL: How about an anthem?

MEL: We had a national anthem!

CARL: What was the anthem?

MEL: Well, you see it was very fragmented. Fragments.

CARL: Yes.

MEL: It wasn't a nation, it was caves. Each cave . . .

CARL: Was a nation?

MEL: Each cave had a national anthem!

CARL: So do you remember the national anthem of your cave?

MEL: I certainly do. I'll never forget. You don't forget a national anthem in a minute.

CARL: Well, let me hear it, sir!

MEL: [singing] "Let 'em all go to hell except Cave Seventy-six!"

The 2000 Year Old Man also led me to one of my favorite stories to tell onstage. It goes a little something like this . . .

I was working in Hollywood at Universal Studios for a producer named Marvin Schwartz. He had several projects in the idea stage for me to help him develop.

I noticed a sign on the next bungalow read GRANART.

I asked Marvin, "What's Granart?"

He said, "That's Cary Grant's company."

I got so excited. "Does he ever show up?" I asked.

Marvin said, "Yes. He comes to the office all the time."

One day I was walking to lunch and I heard a voice behind me: "Mel Brooks, Mel Brooks!"

I turned around. Oh my god! It was Cary Grant.

He's talking to me. I heard my name! I said to myself, "My name is Mel Brooks!" So I turned around and said, "Cary Grant!"

He said, "Yes! I'm Cary Grant."

I said, "Well, I don't know if you're Cary Grant or not, but that's the best impression of Cary Grant I've ever heard!"

He laughed and I said, "You shouldn't talk to me. I'm nothing! I'm a . . . I'm a figment of your imagination! You're a great big star. I'm a little Jew from Brooklyn. Don't even look at me!"

He said, "I spent a thousand dollars yesterday buying your *2000 Year Old Man* record. I've sent your records to all my friends, it's the funniest damn record I've ever heard in my life!"

I couldn't believe it. Praise like that from Cary Grant!

"Where are you going?" he said.

"I'm going to the commissary," I said.

"Okay, come on. I'll buy your lunch."

To which I said, "All right, Cary Grant!"

So we go to the commissary together. I walk past my friend Murray who worked for Lou Wasserman and I said, "Murray, me and Cary Grant are going to lunch!"

Murray was impressed.

We sit down and Cary orders dry toast, two boiled eggs, and a cup of tea. I order a tuna fish sandwich on rye. We eat. And we start talking about different things.

He asks, "What's your favorite color?"

I said, "Blue. What's your favorite color?"

He said, "Yellow."

Okay, fine, great! We finish lunch, and we go back. He goes to Granart. I go to Schwartz.

Next day. Ring! "Is Mel Brooks there?"

Yeah, he's there. "It's Cary Grant."

Carl and me, back to back, laughing it up.

"Cary Grant, for me?"

"Are we going to lunch?"

"Yes, Cary! I'll meet you right outside."

"Okay, buddy!"

Cary Grant and I are walking to lunch.

I said, "How you doing? What's your favorite car?"

He said, "Rolls-Royce. What's yours?"

I said, "I like a '38 Buick." We talk about clothes. He likes double-breasted, I like single-breasted. We talk shoes. He likes brown, maroon, or black. I like black-and-white wing tips. We can't get enough of each other. We continue our small talk. "I like a red tie, you like a blue tie, isn't that great?" I like his hair; he has no comment on mine. We arrive at the commissary. He has boiled eggs; I have a tuna fish sandwich. We finish lunch. He goes back to Granart. I go back to Schwartz. Fine.

The next two days? Ring! "Mel? It's Cary."

"Lunch?"

"You got it!"

By this time we meet outside and we're skipping to the lunchroom; we're so happy to be together. But the conversation is getting sparse. I don't really know what to say anymore at lunch. I'm getting a little worried.

The next day, Friday, the phone rings . . .

"Hello, is Mel Brooks there?"

And I said, "If it's Cary Grant—I'm not in!"

That is the story I tell onstage and it really garners big laughs, but the truth is in real life our conversations were a lot more in-depth. Cary told me about his struggles with the studios, he wanted to be doing more important serious films and not just light comedies. But the studios system wouldn't allow it as long as the light comedies were making them big money. I remember seeing a few of his serious films and we talked about *Penny Serenade* (1941) and *None but the Lonely Heart* (1944). I told him they were both wonderful and his performances in them were incredibly moving. He really appreciated the compliment and explained that unfortunately neither film did that well at the box office. So unless he could raise his own money, he was stuck with what the studio offered him. He was intelligent, sensitive, and I really treasured his company and friendship.

In a strange way, I always felt that Carl was the unsung hero of our 2000 Year Old Man act. He took me to places I never imagined. He had a genius for asking questions that were unanswerable, and I was always delighted to reward him with a crazy answer that he never saw coming.

Many years later one of the last things I got to do with Carl was a voiceover for Pixar's *Toy Story 4* (2019). I have a suspicion that they designed the characters for us, because their names were "Melephant Brooks" and "Carl Reinerocerous." Once again just like way back then, when we were recording *The 2000 Year Old Man,* we sat next to each other in front of microphones and worked hard to break each other up.

I really enjoy doing voiceovers for animated projects. In 2003 I was offered a voiceover part playing a funny sheep in a really creative animated children's series called *Jakers!* on PBS. I took the job because I realized it would be a while before my grandchildren could see all of my movies, but I knew they would enjoy hearing Grandpa's voice as Wiley, the adorable wiseacre sheep. It turned out I had a natural talent for voiceover acting, something I hadn't explored that much earlier in my career. Doing voiceovers was so much fun that it led to me helping create several other animated characters in the years that followed *Jakers!* I voiced Bigweld, the idolized famous inventor and owner of Bigweld Industries in *Robots* (2005). That movie also featured the voices of such talents as Robin Williams, Ewan McGregor, and Halle Berry. The very funny Adam Sandler asked me to play his character Dracula's vampire father, Vlad, in the *Hotel Transylvania* movies, which were a lot of fun to record. Vlad is over a thousand years old and pretty disappointed with his son Dracula's chosen career, so he has cute lines like: "So you run a hotel now? From prince of darkness to king of room service . . ."

One of my most famous voiceover roles was actually not in an animated movie at all, but as "Mr. Toilet Man" in my friend Amy Heckerling's comedy *Look Who's Talking Too* (1990). I would only play a part with a name like that for a truly dear friend!

But Carl Reiner was a lot more to me than just my straight man and partner on the 2000 Year Old Man. He was my best friend in the world, and I loved him. We spent many years and had many great times together.

He also went on to become a wonderful movie director. When I asked him what prompted him to direct, he said that he'd written a movie that wasn't directed to his liking. When two actors have a scene together and one hits the joke, you don't cut to the guy who's said the joke. It was cut up so badly that he said, "I'm going to have to protect my movies by directing my own!"

And that's when he directed his first movie: *Enter Laughing.* Many iconic comedy classics followed, like *The Jerk*, *Where's Poppa?*, and *All of Me*. Whatever Carl turned his hand to was always top-drawer.

I've worked with many great people in my life, but there will never be another Carl Reiner.

Chapter 6

Johnny Carson and *The Tonight Show*

Getting back to 1960, my only income was from the *2000 Year Old Man* record and a couple of TV appearances. One of those appearances was actually historic. I was on the very first *Tonight Show Starring Johnny Carson* on October 1, 1962, along with Groucho Marx, Joan Crawford, Rudy Vallee, and Tony Bennett. It was the first appearance in a long association with Johnny Carson that really helped me to become a famous comedy name.

In the various decades since I appeared on that night, I tried unsuccessfully to find that very first Carson show. I've been told that it was either lost somewhere or got taped over. Maybe at that time, nobody expected the show to be as important and memorable as it later became? So perhaps, as they used to often do on live TV at the time, they reused the tape and something else was taped over it? Another explanation was a suggestion from a studio engineer who told me that he thought the first show was in black and white, and after that all the others were in color. So maybe they just discarded that one episode because of the black-and-white issue? Who knows? I really never got a definitive explanation for it being missing, however it seems someone in the control room or maybe even the audience had an audio copy of the show, so at least I was able to listen to it again.

Johnny Carson was a great audience for me. He loved my comic inventions, and sometimes would literally fall off his desk chair

Singing up a storm on the October 1, 1962, debut of The Tonight Show Starring Johnny Carson.

while laughing uncontrollably. I once told Johnny that I collected wines and had a wonderful wine cellar, which led him to suggest one of the funniest things I ever did on his show—a wine-tasting bit.

I was blindfolded, and Johnny poured me a glass of wine. I tasted it and said, "No doubt about it. This is one of the greatest red wines ever made. It's unmistakably Chateau Lafite-Rothschild 1961."

He said, "I'm sorry, no."

I said, "Of course. How stupid of me! It's the other Rothschild classic—Chateau Mouton."

He said, "No."

I said, "I can't believe it. Wait a minute . . ." I took another sip and said, "Ahh! I've got it. It's the great 1955 Chateau Latour."

He said, "No."

I struggled for a while and then asked, ". . . Is it a white wine?"

The studio audience burst into an enormous laugh.

Johnny, holding back his own laughter, said, "No, I'm sorry. It's not a white wine."

I took another sip and said, "What's the matter with me! How could I not know it? It's beer! It's a Budweiser beer!"

The audience erupted again, and Johnny nearly collapsed. He managed to say, "No, no. It's not beer."

I said, "My taste has gone crazy! What's wrong with me? Wait! I know—it's not even a liquid, it's a solid! It's Chiclets, right?"

The audience exploded and Johnny hit the floor. He couldn't get control of himself for five minutes. It was so funny that even I broke up.

The Johnny Carson Show was one of the best venues for me, not only for selling my movies but just for flat out enjoying the company of the great Johnny Carson.

I was kind of scraping the bottom of the barrel, earnings-wise, when I got an offer from Jerry Lewis to work on a new screenplay with him. It was called *The Ladies Man* and was all about the janitor of a hotel for young ladies in Hollywood.

Working with Jerry was both wonderful and terrible. He was really gifted and funny as hell. That was the wonderful part. The terrible part was writing with him. He was not easy to work with and quite often we'd get into a terrible spat. Finally, it became impossible, so eventually either I quit, or he fired me—I'm not sure which.

He sent me the final draft of the screenplay, which he had finished writing with Bill Richmond, who was a great drummer and, for a drummer, a pretty damn good writer. It contained only two scenes that I had originally written for Jerry. One was dusting a butterfly case, and when he opens the case all the butterflies fly away. The other was going through a car wash in a convertible, and absentmindedly hitting the button that opens the top. Both were funny and worked, but not enough for me to want my name on the script.

So I submitted my draft of what I did with Jerry and the final draft with just my two contributions to the Writers Guild. Normally, the job of the Writers Guild is to make sure you got credit on the screen, but in this case, I wanted them to keep my name *off* the screen. I told them I didn't feel that I had enough input on the final to have my name on the screenplay. It was a tough fight but finally they agreed, so I got no credit for that movie. Which was fine by me. Despite this, through the years I stayed in touch with Jerry as a friend and we'd occasionally get together and have some wonderful laughs.

Chapter 7

The Chinese Gourmet Society

So there I was, once again still basically not employed. The William Morris office got me a couple of TV specials to help me pay the rent. One of them was writing *The Victor Borge Show*. So funny, so talented. That was a great experience.

It was a difficult period of my life, but good friends and good food will get you through the roughest times. One of my good friends then was Irving "Speed" Vogel, whom I first met on Fire Island. He was a wonderful guy. Speed ran a textile factory and then quit everything to be a direct metal sculptor. He produced wonderful pieces.

Speed introduced me to Ngoot Lee, who was a brilliant calligrapher and furniture designer who worked for Bloomingdale's. He would set up some of their furniture displays and do framed calligraphy on the walls. Ngoot was a great cook himself, but he always knew where the best restaurants in Chinatown were. So Speed asked Ngoot to take us to a Chinese restaurant that he thought was really good. That was the beginning of a nine-year tradition of Tuesday nights in Chinatown. We called ourselves the "Chinese Gourmet Society."

We had strict eating rules at the Chinese Gourmet Society. You were not allowed to eat two mouthfuls of fish, meat, or chicken without an intermediate mouthful of rice. Otherwise, you would be consuming only the expensive food. The check and tip, and the parking fees, if any, were equally divided among the members. It was compulsory, if you were in New York, not working nights, and in reasonable health, to be present at every Chinese Gourmet Society meeting.

We added to the group. First was Georgie Mandel, a really talented writer whose books included *The Wax Boom*. He was hit by a German sniper in World War II and had a metal plate in his head, but it never stopped him from being a gifted writer. We also added two other really celebrated writers, Joseph Heller and Mario Puzo. As I got to know Joe and Mario, we would trade many stories, and laughs.

Joe Heller, who wrote *Catch-22* and became one of the most influential writers of the twentieth century, was the funniest of the bunch. He always insisted on serving the food.

He would say, "Let me serve; let me be the server."

They'd bring crab and black bean sauce and rice. He'd fill up his plate and pick the best pieces of crab, the middle sections, and then he'd take the rest of it with the claws and everything and give it to me and say, "Here, now you be the server."

It always got a laugh.

Mario Puzo (the future author of *The Godfather*) was by far the best eater. In all of our stomachs is a thing called the vagus nerve, which tells us when we are full and to stop eating. For some reason, Mario was not blessed with a vagus nerve. He could eat until the cows came home, and if one of them was unlucky enough to stumble into his apartment, he'd eat it! Normally, when people leave a Chinese restaurant, they often take with them some cardboard containers of leftovers. Thanks to Mario, we never had any leftovers.

I don't know if it's true, but there is a great story about Mario and food. He lived in Bay Shore, Long Island, where he would write deep into the night in his attic office. Often around midnight, hunger pangs would strike. He'd go all the way down to the kitchen and make himself his favorite sandwich, a Dagwood. If you're familiar with the old comic strip *Blondie*, her husband, Dagwood, was famous for making a multilayered Dagwood sandwich. It consisted of different luncheon meats, cheeses, tomato, pickles, relish, olives, etc. It was a foot high. It seems that one night, Mario was beginning to climb the stairs to his attic while carrying his beloved Dagwood sandwich when one of his slippers . . . slipped. He tumbled down the stairs and ended up on the floor of the living room. His leg hurt a lot, so he thought maybe it was broken. The telephone was about six feet away, and with a good crawl he could get there and call a hospital. However, six feet in the *other* direction lay Mario's Dagwood sandwich, which had landed remarkably intact . . . and was staring at him. What to do, what to do? So pain or not, he crawled on his elbows, like an infantryman under fire, over to his beloved sandwich. He ate it with relish and then proceeded to crawl all the way back to the telephone to call the hospital and report his broken leg.

Like I said, I don't know if it's true, but it's a great story.

We were also joined by another friend of Speed's and mine from Fire Island, Julie Green, who was a diamond merchant. He was incredibly well read and very bright and good company. Julie had read and loved a book called *The Little Golden Calf*. He then read an earlier book by the same writers, Ilya Ilf and Yevgeni Petrov; it was called *The Twelve Chairs*. He loved it even more than *The Little Golden Calf*.

He gave it to me to read and said, "I think this probably could make a good movie."

So I read it, and I loved it, and he was right—eventually I made it into my second movie.

(More on that later.)

I loved all those dinners. My friends were a source of stability and inspiration and got me through those rough times.

Chapter 8

Kismet—Meeting Anne Bancroft

It's 1961 and I was working with Charles Strouse (who we all called Buddy) and Lee Adams on a Broadway show called *All American.* Buddy and Lee had just had a huge hit with *Bye Bye Birdie* and I was brought on to write the book for their new musical project.

One day when we were in the middle of writing, Buddy said to me: "Mel. Come with me. I have to go to a Perry Como show rehearsal at the Ziegfeld Theatre because I'm going to be playing the piano for Anne Bancroft. We're rehearsing for a performance she is going to do at the Actors Studio later this week and I have to find the right key for 'Just You Wait Henry Higgins.' After I get the key, we'll go back to work at my place."

So I tagged along. When we get to the Ziegfeld Theatre they're doing a dress rehearsal. After a few minutes the guest star, Anne Bancroft, takes the stage.

I'd never seen anything like it. She was wearing a stunning white dress and she was singing in a sultry voice a Gertrude Niesen favorite, "I Wanna Get Married." She was just incredibly beautiful.

When the song was over, I leapt to my feet, applauded madly, and shouted, "Anne Bancroft! I love you!"

She laughed and shouted back, "Who the hell are you?"

I said, "I'm Mel Brooks! Nobody you've ever heard of!"

She said, "Wrong! I've got your *2000 Year Old Man* record with Carl Reiner. It's great."

That was the beginning.

After Buddy got the key for their song he said, "Let's go back to my place."

And I said, "Forget it. I think I'm in love."

I went backstage to see Anne. We started talking, and we never stopped.

I asked her, "What are you doing after this? Let's go out for coffee."

She said, "I'm sorry I have an appointment. I have to see my agent Bernie Seligman at the William Morris office."

I said, "Bernie Seligman? I have to see him too! I promised to get back to him two weeks ago."

That was the beginning of a string of lies that I never stopped telling, just to be wherever she was.

I said, "Let's share a cab."

When we hit the street I whistled for a taxi. She was really impressed with my whistle.

She said, "That's the best taxi whistle I've ever heard."

True or not, it struck a chord. That was February 5, 1961. A date I'll never forget.

Every night that week I checked on where she would be. I found out who her friends were, and I called them. For some reason they trusted me and actually told me her whereabouts.

I'd show up at a restaurant she was at or a nightclub or I'd even wangle my way into a big party if she was going to be there. By the end of the week I said to her, "It's amazing! We're always showing up at the same places! It's kismet!"

She laughed and shouted back, "It's not kismet. You're stalking me! If you wanna see me why don't you be brave and ask me for a date?"

So I did. She said yes, and I saw her almost every night.

She loved foreign movies; I loved foreign movies. She loved Chinese food; I loved Chinese food. Which leads me to a pretty funny story. Like I said, we saw each other almost every night and after a while I told her that we couldn't go to fancy places because I was

Anne and me sharing a moment.

simply not earning a lot of money at that time. As a matter of fact, even though I was writing a show for Broadway, you don't see any money for that until the show actually opens.

So one night when we went to a Chinese restaurant I was running low on cash. In those days, one of the least expensive dinners out was at a Chinese restaurant. Knowing my financial situation, when the check arrived Anne slipped me a twenty-dollar bill under the table. The check came to about eleven or twelve bucks. I gave the waiter the twenty dollars and said expansively, "Keep the change."

When we got outside, Anne hauled off and smacked me!

"What?" I said. "What!"

"Listen, *big shot*, don't leave such a big tip with *my* money!"

She could hit pretty hard, so I never did that again.

Even though she was already a very successful actress and used to going to the best places, she'd join me anywhere that I could afford. I remember one night she said, "Don't worry. I believe in you. You're talented. You're gonna go places . . . you won't always be poor."

Like I said, this was not a great time for me as far as making money was concerned. I took almost any job I could get. One of the more interesting ones was doing the voiceover for a commercial for Bic Banana, which was the name of their new pen. It went like this:

> "Don't write with a peach. If you write with a peach, you'll get a very wet letter. Don't write with a prune. Words will come out wrinkled and dopey. Let's face it, the only fruit you can write with is a banana. The Bic Banana. A fine line marker. Not to be confused with a ballpoint. Writing a letter to your son, right? Right. Usually I write, "Dear son, how are you? I'm fine." Write that same letter with a Bic Banana and you'll get: "Dear Sonny, I miss your face, Mom." See what a nice letter it writes? And it comes in colors. Most fruits only come in one color except grapes, which come in two colors and of course, pits and pitless. Look, if you've got to write with a fruit, write with a Bic Banana! It's only twenty-nine cents. Your best buy in writing fruit. The Bic Banana. A different way to write!"

Commercials were a lifesaver. The next one I did was a lot of fun. It was a Ballantine Beer commercial with Dick Cavett. I did a takeoff on my 2000 Year Old Man, called the 2500 Year Old Brewmaster, and Dick interviewed me. We really hit it off well; we had great chemistry between us.

Many years later, Dick and I recorded a wonderful conversation we had onstage that became a really funny HBO special called *Mel Brooks and Dick Cavett Together Again* (2011). I always looked forward to working with Dick Cavett, he is so bright and funny and a real pleasure to work with.

Still needing money to date Anne Bancroft in style, I did any project big or small that came my way. *The Critic*, a short animated film, was the brainchild of Ernie Pintoff, who was a cartoonist extraordinaire. He was a brilliant talent at both stills and animation, including *New Yorker* magazine cartoons. He had an idea. He wanted to do a takeoff on Norman McLaren, who was a Canadian animator and cartoonist who did avant-garde creations. Ernie thought that my interpretation of it with an English accent could be a clever idea.

But I said, "Wait a minute, what if I'm an old Jew who wanders into a movie house, and in between a double feature accidentally sees Norman McLaren's very avant garde cartoon? And I try to make some sense of it?"

I said, "You do the animation and just let me ad-lib."

So he did a kind of Norman McLaren, Picasso-ish, Braque-ish animated short. And I, as a little old Jewish man, recorded the voiceover, trying to make sense out of it.

It was downright hilarious. I said things like:

"This is cute, what the hell is it? I know what it is. It's garbage, that's what it is."

"It must be some symbolism. It must be symbolic of . . . junk!"

"I didn't come pay two dollars in a movie to see cockroaches."

"I don't know much about psychoanalysis, but I'd say this is a dirty picture."

People had never seen anything like it.

The Critic debuted at the Sutton Theatre, a well-known art house on Third Avenue and Fifty-seventh Street. The audience loved it. It was about three and a half minutes long and they laughed uproariously from start to finish.

And miraculously enough, it went on to win the Academy Award for Best Short Subject (Cartoon) that year.

Chapter 9

Get Smart

Anne and I were seeing each other every day and every night. I knew I wanted to marry her, but couldn't think seriously about it because I was not earning enough money to support her. Not only in the style to which she was accustomed, but frankly, in any style.

And then in 1964—a stroke of luck!

I was called by one of the partners of a successful showbiz company called Talent Associates. His name was Danny Melnick. He ran the company with David Susskind, the well-known host of *The David Susskind Show*. I went to their offices on Madison Avenue and Fiftieth Street in the Newsweek Building. They said, "We need a show and we want you to write it. Inspector Clouseau and James Bond are the biggest things in the world now. Got any ideas?"

They then asked if I would like to write it with anybody. They suggested a list of names. One of the names on the list was Buck Henry. I liked Buck Henry a lot, and admired his talent. He would later go on to write *The Graduate* and *Heaven Can Wait*.

He could also shoot pool, and Talent Associates had taken out their conference room table and replaced it with a pool table. What a perfect partner.

This was the year of the secret agent, both in film and television. Sean Connery was James Bond in the recent megahit *Goldfinger*, and Robert Vaughn and David McCallum were in *The Man from U.N.C.L.E.*

I wanted to do a crazy, unreal comic-strip kind of piece about something besides a family. No one had ever done a show about a CIA agent who was also an imbecile. I decided to be the first. I called it *Get Smart*, based on the leading character's name, Maxwell Smart.

Buck was very intelligent and extremely witty. The more we worked on the pilot, the funnier and more insightful we got. Another stroke of luck was getting Alfa-Betty Olsen, a friend of mine at the time, to be our recording secretary. She nailed down every thought and every crazy joke and brushstroke of madness we threw out. Nothing escaped her.

(Later, when I was doing *The Producers* she became my right-hand gal and was invaluable in the forging of that script.)

It took Buck and me about three and a half months to write the pilot script. We could have done it in a couple of weeks, but we loved playing pool. We would also play against the various guests who would visit the offices. If we thought we could beat them we'd place bets and we'd make a little money on the side. Every once in a while, Peter Falk would stop by. He was a pool shark. He would always beat us and take our money. I think Peter Falk had one real eye and one glass eye, and having one eye was probably better for shooting pool than having two.

The only person we wanted to beat and never could was David Susskind. He was a terrible pool player, but he was our boss—so we'd always lose. Who needed that trouble?

Maxwell Smart needed to be stupid and innocent, but also a noble and heroic character. Don Adams was absolutely perfect in the leading role. I knew I was going to name the main character Max, because at that point I had named *all* of my main characters Max. *The Producers* had Max Bialystock. My father's name was Max, his grandfather's name was Max, and later I named my youngest son Max. It made sense to use Smart as a second name because of the cliché "get smart." As in "don't get too smart," and "wise up." Also, everybody was chasing Maxwell Smart. Ergo, *Get Smart*. And it worked, and it still works.

Max was Secret Agent 86. I came up with using the number 86 because when I worked as a busboy whenever we were out of anything that was ordered, somebody in the kitchen would yell, "Eighty-six on the rye bread; eighty-six on the cream cheese, and eighty-six pickled herring."

Which was restaurant shorthand for "we're out of it." At critical moments in the story, sometimes Max was completely out of brains. So I thought that "86" was an apt number for him.

Max worked for a fictional government spy agency called CONTROL, and its ever-present archenemy was KAOS, an evil organization determined to rule the world. Max had a remarkable lack of insight, but since he was our hero, he would always win—despite his inefficiency. Buck and I saw Max as earnest and innocent. He was noble and he believed in justice. He was incorruptible, so the naïveté worked for him. He was always wrong, but always came out on top. He never played the joke and never shared with the audience that he was aware that what he was doing was funny. It was very real, character-driven comedy.

Buck and I created a lot of signature pieces and gadgets. Spies who would hide in lockers in the bus station. Sunglasses that became binoculars. Cuff links that had mirrors so you could see behind you. The "Inflato-coat," a trench coat that inflated, lifting the wearer off the ground, as well as a coat with fake arms so that Max could easily escape being restrained.

Like I said before, Buck was absolutely brilliant. He came up with "the Cone of Silence." The Cone of Silence was a Plexiglas dome that would descend from the ceiling over the Chief and Max to keep their top-secret conversations from being overheard. There was only one small problem with it . . . they couldn't hear each other.

I created the shoe-phone that Max used to field calls. One day, every phone in my office started ringing. I took off my shoe and pretended to answer it. I thought the most bizarre place to put a secret telephone would be in the heel of your shoe, and I thought we could have a lot of fun with that. If you got a very important call, you had to stop and take off your shoe. One wrong step and the phone breaks. For years afterward, Don couldn't eat in restaurants without grateful patrons taking off their shoes and saluting him with them like they were toasting him with wine.

I didn't realize it, but I might have just created the first cellphone. Had I patented it, I probably would've made so much money that I wouldn't have had to write this book.

A lot of comedy business came from Don Adams. He created "Would You Believe?" which was a sequence of exaggerations that kept getting smaller and smaller.

MAXWELL SMART: And I happen to know that at this very minute, seven Coast Guard cutters are converging on this boat. Would you believe it, seven?

MR. BIG: I find that pretty hard to believe.

MAXWELL SMART: Would you believe six?

MR. BIG: I don't think so.

MAXWELL SMART: How about two cops in a rowboat?

It originally was part of Don Adams's stage act as a stand-up comedian. His act was based in part on an imitation of William Powell, who was a famous movie star. Powell played Nick Charles, who played against Myrna Loy's Nora in the successful *Thin Man* series. Don wrote a routine that was based on the end of every *Thin Man* movie, where the murder suspects were all gathered in a room and Nick would walk around and sum up the facts and expose the murderer in a very dynamic way. Prior to *Get Smart*, Don played Byron Glick, the house detective at a New York hotel where Bill Dana played bellhop Jose Jimenez on *The Bill Dana Show*. The jet energy, the motor behind *Get Smart*, was Don. He really believed in what he was doing. He was indefatigable.

We were also very lucky to get Barbara Feldon, a former model, to play Max's partner, the beautiful Agent 99 (we refused to give her a name). We cast Barbara early on. She was smart, good-looking, and could handle the subtle comedic material. Barbara and Don liked each other personally from the start. Agent 99 was an important foil. She legitimized Max. She was the wise and common-sensical George Burns to Max's naïve Gracie Allen. Agent 99 was the sane one. Very beautiful and very feminine, so you could see why Max would put up with being always corrected by her, which would have been humiliating to a lesser man:

MAX: Looks like I've messed everything up.
99: Don't feel badly, Max. You've messed things up before and you'll mess things up again.
MAX: You're just saying that to make me feel good.

We were also fortunate to get Ed Platt, a serious and talented actor, to play the Chief of CONTROL. He was another great foil for Max:

CHIEF: Are you thinking what I'm thinking?
MAX: No, Chief. I'm thinking what *I'm* thinking.

The Chief was stability. In a gang comedy, you need someone to do the reaction takes. When someone does something funny, the audience doesn't laugh unless another character on the screen does the "take." The Chief couldn't believe what Max was saying, and then he would shake his head and continue to deal with this idiot.

CHIEF: Max, I don't know what I'm going to do about you. You bungle assignment after assignment.
MAX: I resent that, Chief.
CHIEF: Do you deny it?
MAX: No, but I resent it.

We spent a lot more money on production as a single-camera show than other three-camera in-studio situation comedies. We were actually making a mini movie every week. We shot on location. It would have been a lot easier to set up three TV cameras and shoot it like *I Love Lucy*. But it wouldn't have captured the great production quality that *Get Smart* showed every week.

We rehearsed for two weeks. I told everybody: "Get everything out in terms of ideas and suggestions during rehearsals. Let's not waste time and ad-lib during the actual shooting."

That axiomatic way of rehearsing stayed with me through all of my movies: fun, insanity, creativity, total chaos during rehearsal, but total discipline during shooting.

Our producer was Jay Sandrich, who had worked on *The Andy Griffith Show* and then later on *The Mary Tyler Moore Show*. His father, Mark Sandrich, worked at RKO Studios and directed great movie musicals including *Shall We Dance*, with Fred Astaire and Ginger Rogers, and *Holiday Inn*, with Bing Crosby and Fred Astaire.

Leonard Stern, who had worked for Jackie Gleason, Phil Silvers, and Steve Allen, was brought in as our show runner. He came up with the opening and closing sequences that framed the show and became a visual signature and great way to remember it. The entrance to the secret headquarters of CONTROL is a long corridor, divided by a series of steel doors. An agent dials a number in a phone booth, and a trap door opens and drops him into headquarters. He came up with the closing sequence as well and kept coming up with great innovations.

The pilot episode opens with a voiceover narration:

> This is Washington, D.C. Somewhere in this city is the headquarters of a top-secret organization known as CONTROL. Its business is counterespionage. This is Symphony Hall in Washington. Somewhere in this audience is one of CONTROL's top employees, a man who lives a life of danger and intrigue. A man who's been carefully trained never to disclose the fact that he is a secret agent.

The concert is interrupted by a phone ringing, as Maxwell Smart, Secret Agent 86, excuses himself amid the confused and disturbed patrons to answer his shoe-phone.

That was the first time that a phone rang in an audience during a public event. We were prescient. We knew that one day the audience would abound with shoe-phones interrupting public gatherings, or as they are now called, cellphones.

Originally, we did the pilot for ABC, which we shot in black and white. When they saw it, they said, "We pass." I don't know whether it was that they thought the production budget would be too high, or if they simply didn't go for it.

That turned out to be lucky for us because we had some really good friends at NBC. I ran into Grant Tinker, who was running NBC at the time, at the Beverly Hills Hotel. He asked, "Do you have anything that fell on the floor from the Sid Caesar shows that you didn't use? We're always looking for new funny shows."

I said, "It so happens that we have a brand-new funny show that's just been passed on by ABC."

He said, "Great! I'd love to see it!"

Without wasting a moment, we sent the pilot over to Grant Tinker's team and they loved what we had done and bought the show immediately.

The same thing happened to me almost ten years later with Columbia Pictures and *Young Frankenstein*. They were tough on the budget, and when I told them I wanted to shoot it in black and white they went crazy and said, "Never!" We then took it to Alan Ladd, Jr., at Twentieth Century Fox. The rest is not only history; it's also explained in a later chapter.

For the first season of *Get Smart*, a few teams of writers were hired, all of whom were friends of ours. Buck was the script supervisor. There were three people responsible for the quality of the show: Don, Buck, and Lenny Stern.

We added some terrific characters and actors later. Hymie the Robot was played by Dick Gautier. I had first seen Dick in *Bye Bye Birdie*. His timing was impeccable. I loved him so much that when I did *When Things Were Rotten*, the television show based on the legend of Robin Hood, I immediately thought of Dick to play

Robin Hood. Bernie Kopell was cast as KAOS agent Baron Von Siegfried, who was Max and 99's frequent nemesis and a brilliant addition to the show.

After the first season NBC sadly informed us that the ratings didn't warrant its being picked up for another season. They had made several new pilots and tried them out that summer, thinking that one of them would be a good replacement for *Get Smart*. Once again luck was with us; the new pilots didn't test well. "The powers that were" at NBC decided to give *Get Smart* a shot at another season.

From there on, it took off. Sometimes, getting the audience into the habit of watching a new show is just as important as its quality.

As I look back at *Get Smart*, if I had to do it again now, I would have maybe trimmed a few jokes, but would have basically kept it the same. It holds up because we were having fun with inept idiots. Inept idiots will always be fun. I'm very proud of the bold wit we laced through the pilot script and the other scripts I wrote. We never condescended to the lowest common denominator with the goal of getting the best ratings—the standard network concept of the lower the brain level of the script, the more people were going to watch it. We never gave in to that. Buck and I decided that it was only what made us laugh, and that would also make the world laugh.

In the end, I think we were right.

What *Get Smart*'s success meant for me personally was that at last I was getting a steady paycheck. So on August 5, 1964, I was able to marry Anne and pay the bills. I was not only able to take her out to dinner, but now she didn't have to slip me money under the table anymore to pay the check—I could actually pay for it.

We went down to city hall in lower Manhattan to get married by a justice of the peace. We were in such a hurry that I forgot two things: one, a ring and two, a witness! We were lucky on the ring, Anne happened to be wearing hoop earrings and she took them off

Here we are, newly married and standing in front of our first home together in Greenwich Village.

and we used one of them for the ring. But a witness, where would I get a witness? There was a couple at city hall that had just been married, so we asked to borrow their witness. They called over this kid named Samuel Boone.

And I walked up to him and said, "Sam, we don't have a best man or anything. Could you stand up for us?"

He said, "Yeah. Sure." And then he said, "But I want to warn you. Let me tell you about the clerk who is gonna marry you. He just married my friends, and he has a really crazy voice. We had a tough time not breaking up when we heard that loopy voice."

I said, "Well, we're in show business. We can deal with that, whatever it is."

So we get in front of this clerk and the kid was right. The clerk had the wackiest voice I had ever heard. He started with, "Dooo youuuu Anna Marie Louise Italianoooo . . ."

And already we were in big trouble. For the rest of the ceremony Anne and I never looked at each other, because if we did, we knew we'd crash to the floor laughing. Somehow, we got through the ceremony. All's well that ends well.

We took a cab back home to the village kissing each other and both kissing the earring that had become our wedding ring.

Chapter 10

The Producers

Once *Get Smart* sold to NBC, I didn't have to worry as much about making a living and instead, I could think about what I really wanted to do. I knew that I wanted to write a play on Broadway, all about a play on Broadway.

Like I said earlier, the main character in *The Producers*, Max Bialystock, had been forming in my subconscious ever since I worked for that larger-than-life Broadway producer Benjamin Kutcher, when I got back from the war in the late forties. The thrust of the plot was bold and simple: You could make more money with a flop than you could with a hit.

I wrote a brief synopsis of a three-act play called *Springtime for Hitler*. Why *Springtime for Hitler*? Well, I knew I needed a terrible play for the producers to achieve their goal of a play that would close on opening night. Remember—you could make more money with a flop than you could with a hit.

So I was blessed with an inspiration: How about a musical called *Springtime for Hitler—A Gay Romp with Adolf and Eva at Berchtesgaden*? That would surely send the opening-night audience fleeing the theater before the first act was over, and certainly garner the worst notices the critics had ever bestowed on a Broadway play.

The story line went like this: Bialystock and Bloom, my producers, would find the worst play ever written, which led me to create Franz Liebkind, not only one of the worst writers that ever wielded a pen, but also a regenerate dyed-in-the-wool Nazi. He was madly in love with his Führer, Adolf Hitler, and always wore a World War II German helmet splattered with pigeon droppings.

The next step would be to find the worst director who ever directed a play on Broadway. Thus assuring our crooked heroes the worst production ever produced on Broadway. And to top it all off, the very worst actors to ever set foot on a Broadway stage. (I knew I could find those characters; there were always plenty of very good and bad actors around.)

Then, taking a page out of the past, Bialystock would entertain a collection of little old ladies who would be happy to invest in his play for a few kisses and a little flattery.

I sent the outline of *Springtime for Hitler* to several Broadway producers to see if anyone was interested and excited enough to actually produce it. The most interesting response I got was from Kermit Bloomgarden, who had produced Arthur Miller's *Death of a Salesman*, one of the most memorable plays ever on Broadway. He was kind enough to invite me to lunch, where he told me, "This is a great idea, but you have too many characters in too many scenes. One of the unwritten rules of getting your money back on Broadway is no more than one set and five characters. We try to stick to that. You have about thirty-five characters in thirty-five sets. It is not a play. What it *is*, is a movie. Write it as a screenplay and you've got a chance for success."

He made a lot of sense.

So I immediately began writing it as a movie. He was right. I could see it, scene after scene. I could almost hear the dialogue.

It went something like this:

BLOOM

Amazing. It's absolutely amazing.
But under the right circumstances, a producer could make more money with a flop than he could with a hit.

QUICK CUT TO BIALYSTOCK'S SLEEPING FACE.
HIS EYES POP OPEN.
CUT BACK TO BLOOM.

BLOOM

Yes. Yes. It's quite possible.
If he were certain the show would fail, a man could make a fortune.

BIALYSTOCK

Yes?

BLOOM

Yes, what?

BIALYSTOCK

What you were saying. Keep talking.

BLOOM

What was I saying?

BIALYSTOCK

You were saying that under the right circumstances, a producer could make more money with a flop than he could with a hit.

BLOOM

Yes, it's quite possible.

BIALYSTOCK

You keep saying that, but you don't tell me how.
How could a producer make more money with a flop than with a hit?

BLOOM

It's simply a matter of creative accounting.
Let us assume, just for the moment, that you are a dishonest man.

BIALYSTOCK

Assume away!

The wonderfully talented Alfa-Betty Olsen (who had helped Buck and me work on the pilot of *Get Smart*) once again assisted me in translating my play outline into a screenplay, and with her invaluable help, I set sail.

While I was writing the screenplay, I hit a stone wall. I would need a production number so awful that it would send the first-night audience flying out of the theater. I had a great title; a big musical celebration of the Third Reich called "Springtime for Hitler." But who could write the song? I mentioned my dilemma to Anne.

"I know who could write it," she said.

"Who?" I asked.

"You," she said. "You're musical. You're a good singer. You never stop singing around the house! And besides, you're a born songwriter. No one else could write 'Springtime for Hitler' but you. So here's a pad and a pencil. Go into the next room, and I bet within an hour you'll come out with the beginning of a song."

I did exactly what she said. I took a pad, a pencil, and went into the next room. And one hour and one month later, came out with "Springtime for Hitler." I had come up with not only the lyrics but also the tune, which I'd heard in my head, picked out on a piano, and then sung into a tape recorder. A full 32-bar song that a musicologist friend of mine then transcribed into actual notes on actual music paper, a method of composing I've since used for all of my songs.

(After all, I went to VMI, not Juilliard.)

I loved music to death, but I never thought that I could write music itself from a blank page, that I could compose a song. I developed my method right then, which was, and still is, that the songs are written for characters within a story. I just don't sit down and write like other composers who write a love song. For me it always comes from the story or the characters. So for this story, I came up with the most offensive song in the world that would have Jews looking for the exit doors.

Here's a sample:

Germany was having trouble
What a sad, sad story
Needed a new leader

To restore its former glory
Where, oh where was he?
Where could that man be?
We looked around
And then we found
The man for you and me
And now it's
Springtime for Hitler and Germany
Deutschland is happy and gay
We're marching to a faster pace
Look out
Here comes the master race!

I had every faith in the fact that when the audience saw this Nazi spectacle the producers' dreams of a big flop would come true.

Music infuses a film with the correct emotion that you need in the scene. You shade your film with the right colors while directing, but music is especially important. I needed another song at the end of the screenplay because even though crime never pays and our heroes are put in jail, they are undaunted in their zeal to produce another flop. So they come up with a new musical called *Prisoners of Love,* and once again raise more money than they need from convicts, guards, and even the warden to put it on. Once I had written "Springtime for Hitler," "Prisoners of Love" came easily and I said to myself, "Maybe in addition to being a writer, director, and an actor, I'm also a songwriter?"

I can't tell you how thrilled I was to see the first copies of the sheet music of my songs and the credit in the upper-right-hand corner: "Words & Music by Mel Brooks."

When the script was finished, someone I knew said, "I've got a friend who just produced *The Eleanor Roosevelt Story* and won an Academy Award for it."

"Yes," I said. "But this is about Hitler. I don't think we should go to that guy."

"No, go!" he insisted. "He's good. He works with a company called UMC, owned by Louis Wolfson, who's very rich and he has racehorses in Florida. They've got a lot of money."

"Okay," I agreed. "Let's see this guy. What's his name?"

"Sidney Glazier."

I went up to Sidney Glazier's office; he was eating a tuna fish sandwich and drinking coffee from a big cardboard cup. I congratulated him on *The Eleanor Roosevelt Story*. I started to prepare him, "This is kind of a crazy comedy, I'm not sure you want to be—"

"I love your stuff," he cut me off. "I was the biggest fan of *Your Show of Shows* and Sid Caesar. Do me a favor—I don't like reading. I read if I have to, but can you just tell me the story?"

So I began talking to him about Bialystock and Bloom. I described the blue blanket scene, in which Bialystock takes away Bloom's little blue security blanket and Bloom becomes wildly hysterical. Sidney was in the middle of tuna fish and coffee and he exploded with laughter. Tuna fish and coffee all over the place, but he couldn't stop laughing. When I finally finished telling him the story of the movie, he stood up from his desk and said, "I love it! I'm gonna get this movie made."

It takes nine months to make a baby, which is exactly how long it took to make *my* baby. Sidney and I took *Springtime for Hitler* to every studio. We came close to real interest from Universal, but with one small caveat. They thought Hitler was just too offensive. They suggested Springtime for Mussolini. Mussolini was a much more acceptable dictator. I think they just didn't get it.

The only studio head who seriously considered it was Joseph E. Levine of Embassy Pictures (which eventually became AVCO Embassy). Joe started as an exhibitor in Boston, owning theaters and showing movies, and he'd already been successful producing and distributing kind of spaghetti Westerns. At that time, he had made movies like *Hercules Unchained* (1959), and because it did so well he was thinking of a sequel called *Hercules Caught and Chained Again*.

They were called "Sword and Sandal" pictures and a lot of people went to see them. But he didn't stop there, and later in his career he also went on to make really good movies like *The Lion in Winter (1968)*, *A Bridge Too Far (1977)*, *The Graduate (1967)*, and my film *The Producers*.

Sidney and I met with Mr. Levine in his spacious, well-appointed office. When we entered the room, he gave us each an apple from a big bowl of them on his desk.

"Golden Delicious," he said. "They're thirty-five cents apiece. I only get the best."

He might not have been well read, but he was well versed in what he thought was good commercial material and he really liked my script.

While we were eating our Golden Delicious apples he said, "What do you think it'll cost?"

"About a million dollars," Sidney replied. "But don't worry, I can raise half of it. If you can come up with half a million, we can make the movie for a million bucks, with a forty-day shooting schedule."

He agreed to do it. His first question was, "Who's going to direct?"

My quick response was, "I'll direct."

He logically responded, "Have you directed before?"

I told him that I directed in the Catskills and I also directed the floor comedy on *Your Show of Shows*, basically a segment producer. I had also directed a play in Red Bank, New Jersey.

But I hadn't yet directed a film.

"So what makes you think you can direct a film?" he asked.

"Because I'm the writer. I created it," I confidently responded. "All those little scenes that I wrote, they're in my head already. I can see them. It'll save us a fortune! I don't have to search for the setups and the lighting because I know what it should look like in advance. If you get another director, he won't have those scenes in his head already; he'll have to make them up."

He said, "Nobody's ever said that; that's pretty smart. All right. If you don't ask for too much, you can be the director."

And then he said, "As you know, my background is in exhibition. I own theaters in Boston, New York, and Chicago. I know a lot of exhibitors. After reading your script I tried your title, *Springtime for Hitler* on all of them. I got a resounding no. They said they would never put 'HITLER' on their marquees. So you've gotta come up with another title."

I instantly said, "Okay!"

If that was his only objection, I wasn't going to stand in the way of writing and directing my first film because of a title. I immediately came up with, "How about *The Producers*? Bialystock and Bloom are anything but producers. It's ironic."

He said, "Great! I love it. Just one more thing . . . go out and direct something. A commercial, anything. Just so you have a little more directing experience under your belt."

"Fine," I said. "Done!"

We shook hands all around; it was a great day.

To make Joe feel more comfortable I reached out to a friend named Steve Frankfurt, who was a genius who worked at Young & Rubicam, the advertising agency.

I asked him, "What have you got that I can direct?"

And he got me two commercials for Frito-Lay. I went to New Jersey and directed these crazy commercials. I learned a little about how to deal with a camera, a set, and a crew. I got exactly what I should have gotten out of it: fourteen hundred dollars for the commercials, a huge free box of Frito-Lay chips, and the beginning of a career as a film director.

I never thought about being a director. I thought I'd be very happy as a writer and comedian. On *Your Show of Shows* I had watched some very good directors work. But sometimes they chose a close-up or something that to me was very bizarre. I would say, Go to the recipient of the joke! Don't zoom in on the guy telling the joke—which seemed natural to them, but was all wrong to me.

Many writers become directors initially to protect their own work and then they fall in love with directing as an art form. While the writer is the proprietor of the vision, the director becomes the author of the film, because the director crafts the style, feelings, and casting. But the director will never get the writer's initial look and progressions. So I decided to become a writer/director to protect my vision.

I always considered myself, first and foremost, a writer. As much as I respect directing, I will always respect writing more. Anne and I once had a fight. She was preparing for a movie and said, "This scene! I can't. I can't get a handle on this character. I'm going crazy. It's impossible! I can't. It's hard!"

I took a blank piece of paper and I said, "You know what's even harder? Writing. Look!" I tapped the blank page. "That's writing. The blank piece of paper. You have to fill it! Fill it with thoughts, with characters, with ideas. Fill it with continuity, with a beginning, a middle, and an end! And you have to make it memorable!"

Even before I wrote the screenplay, I wrote a description of my leading characters:

Max Bialystock: A Seedy Producer in His Middle Fifties.

Max Bialystock is a living crescendo of flesh and noise. Bialystock is not an ordinary man. He is a FORCE—a massive cyclone of furious energy, bellowing, threatening, weeping, cajoling, and generally bullying his way through life.

Bialystock is extravagantly alive. He is dramatically sensitive to all that surrounds him. A perfect seedless grape starts him pirouetting through the air in a wild ballet of joy. A beautiful spring day sends him to the ground in a dead faint. The smell of fresh rye bread makes him bang his head against the wall in a fit of ecstasy.

There is nothing small about Max Bialystock. He talks big, he eats big, he drinks big, and he lives big. Not only doth his cup runneth over but it spilleth all over the floor.

Leo Bloom: A Timid Accountant in His Early Forties.

Leo Bloom is a well-mannered, curly-haired, blue-eyed, forty-two-year-old walking anxiety attack. Leo Bloom and Pinocchio would probably have been very good friends. Both of them desperately want to become real live boys.

Franz Liebkind: A Bad Playwright in His Late Forties Who Speaks with a Thick German Accent.

Franz Liebkind is crazy. He always wears a German helmet. When Germany lost the war Liebkind immigrated to South America hoping to find Hitler. (He had it from very good sources that the Führer was working as a headwaiter in Buenos Aires.) After a fruitless search and several embarrassing incidents (twice he was arrested for following headwaiters home), he moved to New York where our heroes find him.

I stole the name Leo Bloom from *Ulysses*. I don't know what it meant to James Joyce, but to me Leo Bloom always meant a vulnerable Jew with curly hair. In the course of any narrative, the major characters have to metamorphose. They have to go through an experience that forces them to learn something and change. So Leo was going to change; he was going from a little nobody to a big somebody. He was actually going to bloom. Hence, Leo's last name: Bloom.

He would start out as a little man who salutes whatever society teaches him to salute. But in Leo Bloom's heart, there was a much more complicated and protean creature. The guy he'd never dare to be, because he ain't gonna take them chances. He was going to

Here I am cradled in the arms of the great Zero Mostel on the set of The Producers.

play it straight and trudge right to his grave . . . until he ran into Max Bialystock.

Bialystock is a Broadway producer who's so broke he's wearing a cardboard belt. He makes love to little old ladies on their way to the cemetery. They stop off to have quick affairs on the cracked leather couch in his office, which charms them so much that they write out checks for his current production, usually named *CASH*. Compared with Bloom, Bialystock is the id. Bite, kiss, take, grab, lavish, urinate—whatever you can do that's physical, he will do.

When Bloom first meets him, he's appalled. But then they get embroiled in each other's lives and they catalyze each other. Bialystock has a profound effect on Bloom. So much so that this innocent young guy comes up with the idea of making a fortune by producing a surefire flop. On the other hand, Bloom evokes the first sparks of decency and humanity in Bialystock. It was a nice give-and-take.

It seems that in a lot of my movies there is a recurring philosophical dilemma about money versus love. I often have the characters decide that love and friendship are better than riches. Max and Leo end up getting arrested and in court during their trial, Leo confesses how much Max means to him and how happy they are to have found each other. Leo was just a caterpillar who would never become a butterfly until Max became his catalyst. And Max was just a crook that didn't care about people, art, or theater until Leo awakened in him a dormant feeling of brotherly love that connected him with the passion and glory of what he was actually doing: producing a Broadway show.

As far as casting was concerned, there was nobody else in the world to play Max Bialystock but Zero Mostel. Even as I was writing the screenplay, I always saw Zero as Max. Zero was a bit of a genius. He never hid anything; he let it all hang out. He was incredibly talented. Zero won Tony Awards for Eugene Ionesco's *Rhinoceros* in 1961 and Stephen Sondheim's *A Funny Thing Happened on the Way to the Forum* in 1963, and also originated the role of Tevye in *Fiddler on the Roof* on Broadway, winning the Tony for that role in 1965. He had energy, brains, power, and he immediately understood who his character was at all times.

If I couldn't get Zero Mostel to play Max Bialystock, I don't think I would have done the film.

. . . Leo Bloom was a whole other story.

I first met Gene Wilder in 1963 when he was in a production of the Bertolt Brecht play *Mother Courage and Her Children,* starring

Anne. When I saw the play, this particular actor playing the chaplain caught my eye. He had something. There was a radiant innocence in his performance. Like Chaplin, he could be sad and funny almost at the same time. I asked Anne about him. She thought he was one of the best actors in the play.

I would go to the Martin Beck Theatre almost every night to pick up Anne and grab a bite to eat. I asked her to introduce me to Gene. When I met him, I immediately was thinking, *Leo Bloom, Leo Bloom*. I asked him to come out with us a couple of nights so I could get to know him. He would ask me for advice on how to play his role in the play—he was disturbed by all the laughs he got when he wasn't asking for them. I told him, "Look in the mirror. Blame it on God."

The more I got to know him, the more I thought, *I'm not wrong*. He was definitely a consideration for Bialystock's partner in crime, Leo Bloom.

When the play's closing notice went up, Anne and I invited Gene to spend a weekend with us on Fire Island. I had thirty pages of the screenplay finished. After dinner, I read the first three scenes of *Springtime for Hitler*, almost verbatim as they eventually appeared onscreen, and told Gene that I definitely had him in mind to be my Leo Bloom. He was absolutely thrilled. He loved the character, he loved the script, and he was flattered and honored that I would choose him.

I told Gene not to take anything on Broadway or Off Broadway or anywhere else without checking with me first. He said, "You'll never get it made. This is too crazy, too wild. And besides, we're too close to what's happened. The world isn't ready for a comedy featuring Adolf Hitler. Maybe in ten years."

I said, "Never mind. If I ever raise the money, you're gonna be Leo Bloom."

He smiled and said, "I'm really touched and flattered, but it's too good. Nothing really good ever gets made."

Thank god, for once in his life he was wrong.

When Joseph E. Levine came up with the money and I knew we were actually going to make the movie, one of my first stops was the Broadhurst Theatre backstage. Gene was replacing Alan Arkin in the lead role of Murray Schisgal's play *LUV*.

I entered his dressing room when he was taking off his makeup. He was startled to see me.

"What? What?" he exclaimed.

I flung the script for *The Producers* down on his makeup table and said, "We got the money, we're going to make it, and you're Leo Bloom."

At first, he couldn't speak, and then he burst into tears and couldn't stop crying.

"I can't use you if you keep crying!" I told him. I held him in my arms until he relaxed and then I said, "Just one small favor . . . Zero Mostel, who is playing Bialystock, has casting approval in his contract and he wanted to make sure he would work with whoever was going to be playing Leo Bloom."

Gene said, "Of course. I'd love to meet him."

I was a little nervous, but I didn't have to be. When Zero met Gene he immediately took to him. As a matter of fact, he frightened Gene a little when he swooped him up in his arms and kissed him on the lips screaming, "You're my Leo Bloom!"

Zero was crazy—good crazy.

For Franz Liebkind, I had originally considered a young actor named Dustin Hoffman. He wasn't famous yet. He actually lived on my block in Greenwich Village on Eleventh Street, between Fifth and Sixth avenues. My lawyer, Alan U. Schwartz (who has been my lawyer all my life in showbiz), told me that he was a brilliant stage actor. Dustin read Franz Liebkind for me, and he was absolutely spot-on. He got the craziness and the love of Hitler right from the start, and his German accent was pretty damn good. But life is funny and, like the cliché says, often stranger than fiction.

One night at about two in the morning I was awakened by pebbles being tossed against my bedroom window. I opened my

Zero Mostel as Max Bialystock desperately begging Gene Wilder as Leo Bloom to launch their criminal scheme.

window to see what was going on. When I did I got hit with a few. There, down on the street, was Dustin Hoffman. Before I could say "What the hell are you doing?" he shouted, "Come down! We have to talk."

I threw on some clothes, came down, and we sat on my stoop.

Dustin said, "You won't believe this. I just got a call from Mike Nichols in L.A. He wants me to fly out tomorrow to do a screen test."

I said, "For what? Mike Nichols is in Hollywood doing *The Graduate* with my wife, Annie."

He said, "Yes. That's it, that's it! He wants to audition me for the part of Benjamin Braddock."

I said, "This can't be happening! But anyway, I'm not worried. No offense, but you're not the handsomest guy in town. The minute they see you they'll send you flying back into my arms and back into *The Producers*."

Boy, was I wrong.

Two days later he called to tell me he got the part. He had already signed a contract with me, so I could have bollixed up everything by legally stopping him, but I let him go and wished him luck. I added one small caveat: "You're going to be playing opposite my wife—don't fool around."

Now, what to do, what to do? I needed a new Franz Liebkind. So for the next week I auditioned about a dozen actors for the role. Some of them near misses, but nobody perfect. And then, Kenny Mars came through the door wearing a pigeon-splattered German helmet.

Sometimes in show business, something bad happens but then you take a good bounce. Let me explain . . . I lost Dustin Hoffman, who probably would have been a wonderful Franz Liebkind. But because of it I took that good bounce and got Kenny Mars, who would turn out to be a truly memorable Franz Liebkind.

I'll never forget the laugh he got when he was ranting about what a bad painter Winston Churchill was: "Churchill! With his cigars. With his brandy. And his rotten painting, rotten! Hitler, there was a painter. He could paint an entire apartment in one afternoon! Two coats!"

Nobody could have delivered those lines as sensationally as Kenny Mars.

I was then blessed with a remarkably funny duo—Christopher Hewett as the hilarious Roger De Bris, the world's worst director, and playing his "roommate," the over-the-top Carmen Ghia, was Andreas Voutsinas. In my back pocket I already had the wildly funny Dick Shawn in mind to play LSD—Lorenzo St. DuBois, our hippie Hitler. His Eva Braun turned out to be Renee Taylor, who came to the part with an original idea: Eva Braun would come from the Bronx. And Lee Meredith was the icing on the cake as Bialystock and Bloom's beautiful and sexy secretary, Ulla.

Bloom says, "A secretary who can't type?"

And Max lecherously replies, "Not important."

On the first day of shooting, everybody was nervous—a crazy story and a director who had never directed a movie before at the helm.

After the assistant director said, "Quiet on the set!"

I began directing by shouting "Cut!" Everybody broke up. I said, "Oh! That's right. First I say '*action*,' and then I say '*cut.*' " But it worked. Everybody on the set relaxed. Even I relaxed. And then we began shooting.

My heart took wing when I saw how beautifully Zero and Gene seamlessly melded into Bialystock and Bloom. I was thrilled when they were doing this scene, where Bialystock shows Bloom the unbelievable script:

BIALYSTOCK

Smell it. See it. Touch it.

BLOOM

What is it?

BIALYSTOCK

What is it. We've struck gold.
Not fool's gold, but real gold.
The mother lode. The mother lode.
The mother of them all. Kiss it.

BLOOM

[brightening]

You found a flop!

BIALYSTOCK

A flop, that's putting it mildly.
We found a disaster! A catastrophe! An outrage!
A guaranteed-to-close-in-one-night beauty!

BLOOM

Let's see it.

BIALYSTOCK

This is freedom from want forever. This is a house in the country. This is a Rolls-Royce and a Bentley. This is wine, women, and song and women.

BLOOM

SPRINGTIME FOR HITLER,
A Gay Romp with Adolf and Eva in Berchtesgaden.
Fantastic!

BIALYSTOCK

It's practically a love letter to Hitler!

BLOOM

[*ecstatic*]

This won't run a week!

BIALYSTOCK

Run a week? Are you kidding?
This play has got to close on page four.

We started filming on May 22, 1967. Most of filming went well, but in the making of every movie there are always a couple of unforeseen rough spots.

Like when we were at the Playhouse Theatre on Forty-eighth Street to film our big production number, "Springtime for Hitler." We were blessed with the talents of our choreographer, Alan Johnson. One of the big numbers in every burlesque show is a parade of girls coming down the steps to the rhythm of a tenor singing "A Pretty Girl Is Like a Melody." Alan did the same thing, only he dressed the girls in German clichés: German helmets, bratwurst, pretzels, and beer. As "Springtime for Hitler" reached its musical climax, I had an overhead camera shoot the chorus forming a huge swastika slowly rotating in the magical tempo of Ravel's "Boléro."

That was the first unforeseen rough spot I had to get over. It seemed that Joseph E. Levine, who'd been invited to watch the filming of the number, furiously objected to the big swastika climax. He said it had to go or he'd stop the production.

I said, "Joe, don't worry about it. It's out."

This was the beginning of a pattern for me . . . lying to the studio at every turn. On every movie I've done since then, I've often lied when the studio objected to something by saying, "It's out!"

But of course, never taking it out. It was always in. (Thank god, they never remembered.)

Another rough spot was that we were running out of time one day and I had scheduled the blue blanket hysterical scene in which Gene Wilder goes berserk. I knew I had to get it done because we were changing the set the next day and I would be out of the office set. We had rehearsed the scene and Gene was exhausted.

When I told him we had to shoot it right then he said, "I can't. Please, Mel, let's do it tomorrow when I'll have enough energy to do it right."

I said, "Gene, we're in trouble. We've got to do it right now. Tomorrow we're in a different set." I asked him, "What can I do to help you?"

He said, "Get me Hershey bars. I need quick energy."

I said, "With or without almonds?"

He said, "Without, without! The nuts might get stuck in my throat."

Faster than you could say "abracadabra," we got him two Hershey bars (without almonds). He ate them, drank a glass of water, and dove into the scene. He was magnificent.

To prove I'm not lying, get a copy of *The Producers* and watch the blue blanket scene. It was hysterically funny then and it will be hysterically funny forever.

One day we were on a tenement roof somewhere on the Lower East Side filming the scene where Bialystock and Bloom meet Franz Liebkind and his pigeons. We broke for lunch and Gene, Zero, Kenny, and I went to a diner nearby to grab something to eat. When we entered, the noisy diner suddenly fell silent. And I thought, *What's going on?*

And then as we walked to a booth in the back I realized they were all staring at Kenny Mars, who was still in costume. He was wearing his German helmet and a swastika armband!

I said, "Kenny, quick! Take off the helmet and the swastika before something happens."

And when he did, everything relaxed. I had gotten so used to living with German helmets and swastikas I completely forgot that we were in New York and not Berlin during World War II. That was a near miss!

One day I said, "Take a half an hour, everybody. Lunch is on me." I ran out and I got maybe thirty sandwiches and thirty coffees in a big cardboard box for the cast and crew. When I got back to the studio, there was a different receptionist at the front desk. A temp.

I'm carrying the sandwiches and she says, "They are shooting a movie in there. The red light is on, you can't go in."

I said, "I have to go in. I'm the director of the movie."

She said, "Excuse me?"

I said, "No, I really am. I'm the director!"

She said, "Oh, you're the director. Can I have a sandwich, Mr. Director?"

Finally, Mike Hertzberg, my assistant director (who would also later produce *Blazing Saddles*), came out and said, "What's going on here?"

I said, "She won't let me in. She doesn't believe I'm the director."

Mike said, "He's the director! He's the director!" and then opened the door for me to go in.

As I passed her she gave a sheepish grin and whispered, "I'm sorry, so sorry, you don't look like a director!"

"Thank you," I said.

To this day, I often wonder what a director should look like.

It's at the Lincoln Center fountain that Leo Bloom caves in and risks everything to join Max Bialystock in their mad scheme to produce the catastrophic Broadway flop that would make them rich. The dialogue goes like this:

BLOOM

If we get caught, we'll go to prison.

BIALYSTOCK

You think you're not in prison now?
Living in a gray little room. Going to a gray little job.
Leading a gray little life.

BLOOM

You're right. I'm a nothing.
I spend my life counting other people's money—
people I'm smarter than, better than. Where's my share?
Where's Leo Bloom's share? I want, I want,
I want everything I've ever seen in the movies!

BIALYSTOCK

Leo, say you'll join me!
Nothing can stop us.

BLOOM

I'll do it! By god, I'll do it!

The black marble base that surrounded the fountain was awash with puddles of water because when we booked the night shoot at Lincoln Center I met the engineer who was in charge of the fountain and I said to him, "On a given signal, could the fountain go really high to celebrate a special moment in the movie?"

He said, "Mr. Brooks, the fountain normally goes up to ten or twelve feet, but if necessary, I can get it up to twenty-five."

"Great," I said. "When I give you the signal, push it up to twenty-five!"

I was going to have them skip with joy all around the fountain celebrating their new enterprise, but I was afraid that the water from the fountain that was spilling over onto the ledge would make their skipping dangerous. Especially for Zero, who had a bad leg. So I gave Zero a carton of ice cream and had Bloom skip around the fountain and every time he passed Bialystock, Max would shove a spoonful of ice cream into his mouth.

This on-location night shoot turned out to be the very last scene we would be shooting. The last shot would be pointed up at Bialystock and Bloom with the white foaming waters of the glorious Lincoln Center fountain shooting up twenty-five feet in the air behind them, and the night sky above. I began to get worried because the sky was turning slightly lighter with each hour that we were filming. But luck was with us, and when I called "CUT! It's a wrap!" the crew, the actors, everybody, burst into a great big cheer. We did it. We made *The Producers*.

The Producers took eight weeks to film and cost $941,000. I brought it in at $35k under budget. Under budget—a phenomenon that stayed with me throughout my film career.

Joseph E. Levine saw the rough cut and had several changes he wanted to be made. But my brilliant lawyer snuck a little paragraph into the contract that read "The director, Mel Brooks, will receive final cut of the film."

That means that nobody, including the studio, is allowed to change the final version of the movie. My ultimate protection, no one could change the movie but me. All thanks to my aforementioned lawyer, Alan U. Schwartz, whom I met after *Your Show of Shows* was finished and he did my contracts for pickup jobs like the Victor Borge and Andy Williams shows. We hit it off immediately; I loved my lawyer, and he was so supportive, cheering me up in those dark days of scattered employment, trying to keep my nose above water.

When I asked him, "What the hell is the U for in Alan U. Schwartz?"

He said with a big smile on his face, "It stands for United States Supreme Court Justice."

That's obviously a figment of his imagination. I think it stands for nothing. He probably just shoved it in there because he thought it looked more impressive to be a lawyer with a middle initial.

I'd often go to lunch at a place called Chock full o' Nuts. New York was sprinkled with them. There was one near Greenbaum, Wolff, and Ernst where Alan U. Schwartz was a fledgling lawyer. Chock full o' Nuts had great sandwiches—chicken salad, tuna salad, cream cheese and walnut on raisin bread. Not to mention their famous Chock full o' Nuts coffee. I'd often bring an extra sandwich and coffee up for Alan U. Schwartz.

Sometimes I'd get there before him and go to his office and misbehave. He caught me once when the phone rang and I answered, "Greenbaum, Wolff, and Ernst, what can't we do for you? . . . I'm sorry, lady, we're not ambulance chasers! We're a classy firm that only handles big cases!"

He heard me as he was coming up the hall, but instead of being angry he burst into laughter. Alan has been my lawyer ever since. He went on to do great things and represent other well-known clients like famed playwright Tennessee Williams, of *A Streetcar Named Desire*; Peter Shaffer, who wrote great plays like *Amadeus* and *Equus;* and also the incredibly gifted Truman Capote. That "final cut" clause that he snuck into my first movie has stayed with me in every movie contract since then. I will forever be grateful. To this day Alan is still a very dear and close friend.

We had a pre-release sneak-preview screening of *The Producers* at the Cherry Hill Cinema in Cherry Hill, New Jersey, right near the Pennsylvania border. Joe Levine was there with three or four associates in distribution. I was there with Alfa-Betty Olsen and her husband, David Miller, who by the way was a terrific actor and played Joseph Goebbels in the Hitler scenes in the movie.

When Dick Shawn as Hitler asks him, "Hey, baby. What's happenin'?" David as Goebbels answers, "I just laid the morning propaganda forecast on the people."

Hitler: "You're puttin' me on. What did they say?"

Goebbels: "I told the people we invaded England!"

Hitler: "Hey, that's a groove, daddy. How'd we come out?"

Goebbels: "We beat 'em, baby!"

Hitler: "Groovy!"

We cut to Franz Liebkind in the first-night audience. "What is dis 'baby'? The Führer has never said 'baby.' I did not write babies."

A woman sitting next to him shushes him. Kenny Mars as Liebkind angrily responds, "You shut up! You are the audience! I am the playwright! I outrank you!"

But back to the Cherry Hill Cinema and our sneak preview. It was a thousand-seat theater but besides Levine's group and Alfa-Betty, David and me, and a shopping-bag lady in the first row, practically nobody showed up. Embassy hadn't spent any money to promote the screening.

Joe Levine watched a few scenes and left in a hurry.

He told Sidney Glazier, "I don't want to spend good money after bad to open this movie. I think it may be a big mistake."

God bless Sidney Glazier, who said to Joe, "You gotta open it. We made it. If you don't open it, I'll open it. You've got to spend some money and you've got to open it. It's not *Hercules,* we know. You can't go by Cherry Hill, New Jersey; there's a big audience out there waiting to see this."

And so Joe, against his better judgment, opened the movie.

Joe got us the Fine Arts Theatre in New York on Fifty-eighth Street, a really terrific independent art house theater. On opening day in early March 1968, I got there at ten o'clock in the morning and, believe it or not, there were lines around the block.

I was stunned—but there may have been a reason for that surprising phenomenon.

It turns out that Peter Sellers had by accident seen a pre-release screening of *The Producers*. This is the story: Peter Sellers was in the middle of making a movie called *I Love You Alice B. Toklas* and every Saturday night he would gather some of the cast and crew and the screenwriters of the film and rent the Aidikoff screening room in Hollywood and have a movie night. One of the screenwriters (who later became a dear friend of mine) was the writer/director Paul Mazursky. Paul told me that they were supposed to see one of Fellini's early films called *I Vitelloni* and were eagerly looking forward to it. But the projectionist, Charles Aidikoff himself, who was running the screening, said that he had looked everywhere but couldn't find the movie.

Peter Sellers said, "Well, do you have anything else for us to see? Anything!"

Aidikoff said, "I have a pre-release copy of a Mel Brooks movie that Embassy is supposed to release next month, but I was told not to let anyone see it. So I can't run it."

"Run that Mel Brooks movie or I'll kill you!" said Peter.

"Okay, Mr. Sellers, here goes," replied Aidikoff.

Paul Mazursky said that the movie was a flat-out hilarious success. Peter never stopped laughing.

That night when the movie was over, Peter Sellers called and woke up Joseph E. Levine and said, "I'm sorry to wake you up, Joe, I know it's two or three in the morning in New York, but I want to tell you I just saw *The Producers* and I want you to know how incredibly funny and marvelous it is."

Joe said something back about a limited release, and Peter said, "No! No! You're wrong! Open it everywhere! Make a thousand prints! Flood every screen in America! It's a great, great comedy."

I don't know what Joe said back, but I know what Peter did. He was so enamored with the movie that he personally paid for a big industry ad in *Variety* that read:

> Last night I saw the ultimate film. . . . "The Producers," or as it was originally titled "Springtime for Hitler." Brilliantly

> written and directed by Mel Brooks, it is the essence of all great comedy combined in a single motion picture. Without any doubt, Mel Brooks displays true genius in weaving together tragedy-comedy, comedy-tragedy, pity, fear, hysteria, schizophrenic-inspired madness and a largess of lunacy of sheer magic. The casting was perfect. Those of us who have seen the film and understand it have experienced a phenomenon which occurs only once in a life span.

Obviously, the ad had found its way to New York, and hence the lines around the block.

My spirits soared, but they came crashing down again when I read *The New York Times* review the next day. The *Times* critic Renata Adler took the picture apart—she lambasted it, saying, "But there is just enough talent and energy to keep this blackest of collegiate humors comic. Barely." And "'The Producers' leaves one alternately picking up one's coat to leave and sitting back to laugh." Not a review that would send you running to the movie theater.

I sat up with Anne all night after that review came out, saying: "Well, I can always go back to television. I guess they don't want me in movies."

I talked about giving up show business and going back to college. I'd major in organic chemistry, become a pharmacist, and open a little drugstore back in Brooklyn, at the corner of South Third and Hooper.

And then, my spirits were lifted when *Look* magazine's review came out. It was by Gene Shalit. I'll never forget his review. He wrote, "*The Producers*—No one will be seated during the last 88 minutes . . . they'll all be on the floor, laughing!"

So I decided to stay in movieland.

The Producers was my first skirmish with Adolf Hitler (not counting my adventures in World War II). Most people got the joke. They loved it. They knew what I was doing. I did get almost a hundred letters from rabbis, students, scholars, and representatives of Jewish organizations who were very angry with me. I wrote back to every single one and tried to explain to them that the way you bring down Hitler and his ideology is not by getting on a soapbox with him, but if you can reduce him to something laughable, you win. That's my job.

I also never asked the audience for sympathy. I never begged the audience for anything. They paid their money and they deserve a show, a good show. And my job is, in the end, for them to leave the theater saying, "I had a good time." And for the most part, they were rewarded.

Let me tell you a little side story here about a foreign release of *The Producers*. It did fairly well in Europe, especially in Sweden. I had become friends with a Swedish journalist and film reviewer named Björn Fremer. Björn asked my permission to use an alternate title in his review, instead of calling it *Producenterna* ("The Producers") he wanted to use my original title, *Springtime for Hitler—Det våras för Hitler*. It caught on, and the marquee in every theater in Sweden playing *The Producers* displayed my original title, *Springtime for Hitler*. It worked! *Det våras för Hitler* was a big hit. So much so that the Swedish film distributors decided to put a new title with *Det våras för . . .* ("Springtime for . . .") in front of all my subsequent films that played in Sweden. For instance, instead of *Blazing Saddles* it was *Det våras för Sherriffen*, "Springtime for the Sheriff," and instead of *Young Frankenstein* it was *Det våras för Frankenstein,* "Springtime for Frankenstein." And so it went, every one of my movies that ever played in Sweden had a "springtime" in front of it. I both blamed it on and profusely thanked Björn Fremer and his Swedish film journalist cohorts for all that Swedish success.

One morning I was at my desk writing, working on my next script, *The Twelve Chairs,* and the phone rang. I answered, and it sounded like my friend Speed Vogel. The voice said: "I just want you to know, Mr. Brooks, you've been nominated for an Academy Award in the category of Original Screenplay."

I said, "Okay, Speed. Not funny! Up yours!" and I hung up.

I later learned that it actually wasn't Speed Vogel. I'd given the "up yours!" to a legitimate member of the Academy of Motion Picture Arts and Sciences.

I called the guy from the Academy back and I apologized and told him I thought it was a put-on. And he said, "You're forgiven. Congratulations on the nomination. By the way, that's the way you talk to your friends?"

Anyway, it was true. An Academy Award nomination for Original Screenplay.

I couldn't believe it!

It was thrilling to get the nomination, but I never thought I had a chance. I was up against Gillo Pontecorvo's *The Battle of Algiers*, one of the greatest movies of all time; Stanley Kubrick's masterpiece *2001: A Space Odyssey;* John Cassavette's innovative and brilliant *Faces;* and *Hot Millions,* the really funny caper movie that Peter Ustinov wrote and starred in. I wasn't being modest when I thought that the odds of my winning the Academy Award for Original Screenplay against that daunting competition were about a hundred to one. I was up against some of the best pictures ever made.

But the Academy thought that *The Producers* was so original that it deserved the award for Best Original Screenplay. And who was I to argue with them?

So there I was at the Oscars on April 14, 1969, at the Dorothy Chandler Pavilion in Los Angeles, California. Frank Sinatra and Don Rickles presented the award. After their fun banter, Frank Sinatra opened the envelope and called out my name. In some kind of a daze, I made my way onto the stage. And this is what I actually said:

> "I didn't trust myself so I wrote a couple of things: I want to thank the Academy of Arts, Sciences and Money for this wonderful award.

I was so excited I almost forgot to take the statue with me!

"Well, I'll just say what's in my heart. Ba-bump! Ba-bump! Ba-bump! Ba-bump!

"But seriously, I'd like to thank Sidney Glazier, the producer of *The Producers* for producing *The Producers.* Joseph E. Levine and his wife, Rosalie, for distributing the film.

"I'd also like to thank Zero Mostel, I'd also like to thank Gene Wilder, I'd also like to thank Gene Wilder. I'd also like to thank Gene Wilder. Thank you very much!"

The camera cut to Gene, who was in the audience, and had burst into tears once again.

By the way, I thought you might be interested in a letter that Gene Wilder wrote to Jerome Robbins, who was the director of *Mother Courage*, the Bertolt Brecht play he appeared in with Anne before *The Producers*.

> Dear Jerry:
>
> When we worked together it was the best of times and the worst of times. But I'm more grateful to you now than I ever could have conceived I would be.
>
> I'll tell you why:
>
> 1. If you hadn't miscast me in *Mother Courage*, I wouldn't have met Anne Bancroft.
>
> 2. If I hadn't met Anne Bancroft, I wouldn't have met Mel Brooks.
>
> 3. If I hadn't met Mel Brooks, I would probably be a patient in some neuropsychiatric hospital today, looking through the bars of a physical therapy window as I made wallets.

Let me tell you a story about where that beautiful golden Oscar that I won for *The Producers* ended up. So because I had been making pretty good money for a few years, I told my brothers I would take over all the expenses that my mother (now living with her sister, my aunt Sadie) incurred. They had moved from New York down to Florida. They were living in Hallandale Beach in a big, beautiful apartment overlooking the ocean. When I asked my mother for the new address she said, "Everybody knows the building, it's called The Presidential."

I said, "The Presidential what?" I knew that grammatically "presidential" had to modify something—The Presidential Apartments, The Presidential Arms, The Presidential Suites. Something!

She said no, she insisted it was just "The Presidential" and I didn't want to argue with her. So I took my wife and my Oscar down to Florida for a visit. When we pulled up to the building, I was astonished to see that she was absolutely right. It didn't modify a damn thing! It was just The Presidential!

The reason I brought my Oscar was because my mother kept all of my awards. It seems she had a regular Friday afternoon tea and cookie session with everybody in the building and their friends who wanted to come tour her apartment and see her famous son's awards decorating the top of her TV set. I knew the Oscar would have pride of place in that collection.

Funnily enough, Anne's awards also adorned the top of her mother's TV set in Yonkers. Most of the awards that we both won, she won first. But where other couples, especially actors and artists, would be naturally competitive, she was never anything but supportive. She knew how to take care of people, especially people she loved. In addition to her Best Actress Oscar for *The Miracle Worker*, she won two Tony Awards, one for the Broadway version of *The Miracle Worker* and the other for her Broadway debut, also written by William Gibson, *Two for the Seesaw,* opposite Henry Fonda; as well as two Emmy Awards, one for a show called *Annie, the Women in the Life of a Man,* which I co-wrote and guest-starred in. She was one of a very few to have earned Hollywood's acting-award triple crown—the Oscar, Emmy, and Tony awards.

While Anne and I were visiting my mother in Florida, I rented a Lincoln Town Car to drive around. One day I pulled up outside of The Presidential in it to pick up my mom and Aunt Sadie for dinner. When I got out of the car a guy in a chauffer's cap threw a question at me. He said, "Who ya got?"

I didn't know what he was talking about . . . and then I realized that I was parked next to another black Lincoln Town Car that was clearly for hire. He repeated his question. He said, "Who ya got? Who ya driving?"

I said, "Oh! Mel Brooks. I'm driving Mel Brooks." I didn't want to lie to him.

He said, "Mel Brooks? Wow. Is he a good tipper?"

I said, "The best!"

Chapter 11

The Twelve Chairs

Like I mentioned before, the book *The Twelve Chairs* was written by two crazy and wonderful Russian writers who were trying to make sense out of czarist Russia morphing into this phenomenon called the Soviet Union.

My education vis-à-vis Russian writers came from the wonderful head writer of *Your Show of Shows*, Mel Tolkin. His family emigrated from Russia to Canada when he was young, and being a born intellectual, he was well steeped in his Russian literature. Which he generously passed on to me. He said to me, "You're an animal from Brooklyn, but I think you have the beginnings of something called a mind."

He gave me a copy of Nikolai Gogol's *Dead Souls*.

Dead Souls was a revelation.

Gogol had two amazing sides to him. One was human, simple, and heartfelt. He had tremendous understanding of the human condition. And the other side was absolute madness. Just madness! Insanity. He would write about a nose that could speak. Gogol was not bound by the rules of reality, and yet he understood how the heart beats, why it beats. What death is. What love is. It's like he stuck a pen in his heart, and it didn't even go through his mind on its way to the page. He was my favorite.

Ilya Ilf and Yevgeny Petrov were two Russians who were best known for writing three books together: *The Twelve Chairs* (1928, known in a British translation as *Diamonds to Sit On*); *The Little Golden Calf* (1931), a tale of the tribulations of a Soviet millionaire who is afraid to spend any money lest he be discovered by the police; and *One-Storied America* (1936, known in a British translation as *Little Golden America*), an account of the two writers' adventures in the land of Wall Street, the Empire State Building, cars, and aspiring capitalists.

The Twelve Chairs, their first glorious novel, was given to me by Julie Green, a charter member of our Chinese Gourmet Society. He said, "Mel, this is a wonderful adventure. Really. It might even make a good movie."

As far as I was concerned, he was dead on—I was sure it would make a good movie. What a story! The plot of *The Twelve Chairs* really appealed to me.

It takes place in Russia soon after the revolution. In czarist Russia, there was a rigid class system. At the top were the aristocrats, the upper class—royalty, nobility, and the clergy. Following that came the middle class of professionals, merchants, and bureaucrats. Then came the working class—factory workers, soldiers, sailors, etc. And last, at the bottom were the peasants or the serfs. After the revolution, the aristocrats, royalty, and the peerage had to give up their big fine houses and their silverware and all the other trappings of their wealth. In one of those grand houses lived Vorobyaninov. There was a dining room, with beautiful chairs from London covered in gold cloth brocade. Vorobyaninov is flattened out. He's no longer an aristocrat. He's no longer a count. He's just a plain clerical worker—very sad.

On her deathbed, his mother-in-law shares a secret: She hid her diamonds in one of the family's chairs that subsequently was appropriated by the Soviet authorities.

"How could you do such a thing? Why didn't you give them to me?" he asks.

"Why should I have given them to you when you had already squandered away half my daughter's estate with your parties and your horses!" she replies.

Vorobyaninov explodes. He shouts at her, "Well, why didn't you take them out? Why did you leave them there?"

"I didn't have time," she says. "You remember how quickly we had to flee? They were left in the chair."

Vorobyaninov moans, "Fifty thousand rubles' worth of jewelry stuffed in a chair! Heaven knows who may sit on that chair. If it's still a chair, it may be firewood by now!"

She says, "I know I did wrong. Please forgive me!"

Vorobyaninov relents and hugs her face in forgiveness, completely forgetting that he still has his clerk's rubber stamp in his hand. When he removes his hands, we see the words "Cancelled—August 17, 1927" stamped on her cheek.

From there the plot of *The Twelve Chairs* is very straightforward. Vorobyaninov is joined by a young crook named Ostap Bender with whom he forms a partnership, and together they proceed to search for these chairs. The partners have a competitor in a Russian Orthodox priest who has also learned of the secret of the diamonds in a chair from the confession of his dying parishioner, Vorobyaninov's mother-in-law. The competing treasure hunters travel throughout Russia desperately looking for the chairs, which enables the authors to show us glimpses of little towns, and big cities like Moscow, and also to have the three central characters meet a wide variety of people: Soviet bureaucrats, newspapermen, survivors of the prerevolutionary propertied classes, provincials, and Muscovites.

Could I write this movie? I said yes. It's all about greed or love. My kind of movie.

Once again, my wonderful girl Friday, Alfa-Betty Olsen, was sitting at the typewriter and cheering me on. I would say things like, "Can I do this? Is it too crazy?"

And she'd say, "No! Never too crazy for you."

When I finished a rough draft of the screenplay, I showed it to Sidney Glazier, the producer of *The Producers*. He said, "Why not? It's a wonderful adventure and it's hilarious. We took a chance on *The Producers*, and we came out on top. So let's do it!"

One of my first challenges was the title song. The film needed a song that captured the vast emotional upheaval of Russia during that stressful period. It had to be both funny and moving. I knew I could do funny, but I questioned whether I could write the song that I knew the opening of the film needed. Once again, Anne stepped into the breach.

"Nobody else could write that song but you. Besides, your mother was born in Kiev. You are a Russian! It's in your blood. So a good part of you is definitely a Russian peasant."

"I beg to differ!" I said. "I was never a peasant. Maybe not an aristocrat, but I was never a peasant."

But she was, as usual, absolutely right. No one could write, "Hope for the Best, Expect the Worst" but me: a Russian peasant.

Here's a sample:

Hope for the best, expect the worst
Some drink champagne, some die of thirst
No way of knowing which way it's going
Hope for the best, expect the worst!

I am especially proud of the lyrics I wrote for the release, or interlude, of the song.

It went like this:

I knew a man who saved a fortune that was splendid
Then he died the day he'd planned to go and spend it
Shouting "Live while you're alive! No one will survive!"
Life is sorrow—here today and gone tomorrow

Forgive me patting myself on the back, but I felt it fit the spirit of the film perfectly. I heard a Hungarian folk song one afternoon and based the melody on that. I later found out that Brahms had based a piece on the very same tune. One day a guy came up to me and accused me of plagiarizing from Brahms. "No, no," I re-

That's me as Tikon, a Russian peasant, holding my broom.

sponded. "Both Brahms and I stole it from some long-gone Hungarian tunesmith."

One of the great things about doing *The Twelve Chairs* was once again working with film composer John Morris. He did a wonderful job on my first film, *The Producers*. His arrangement of "Springtime for Hitler" was absolutely perfect and he used my melody as the basis for his score of the film. So here we are again, and I've given him "Hope for the Best, Expect the Worst" as a musical structure for the score of *The Twelve Chairs*. In addition to that whimsical arrangement, John also had the opportunity to display his extraordinary range as a composer of sensitive and haunting lyricism. He came up with his own beautiful melody called "Vorobyaninov's Theme," which carried Vorobyaninov and Ostap through their journey across the mountains, streams, villages, and fields of Russia.

Me with Ron Moody as Vorobyaninov and Frank Langella as Ostap Bender; they were pummeling me with questions, both desperate to find out where the twelve chairs went.

I got pretty lucky with the casting of the film. For Vorobyaninov, the aristocrat who has fallen on hard times, I got the remarkably talented Ron Moody, who was so splendid in the part of Fagin in the wonderful film adaptation of the Broadway musical *Oliver!* I knew he would be perfect. He had an angry, soulfully expressive face that made you feel exactly what he was feeling.

For the role of his partner, Ostap Bender, the young con man who joins him in his search for the chairs, Anne suggested a young promising actor that she had worked with doing summer theater in Stockbridge—Frank Langella.

For the part of the crazy Russian priest, I was blessed with the talents of the one and only Dom DeLuise—a gift from the comic gods! One of the funniest actors who ever walked the planet, Dom would bless the movie with an occasional funny ad-lib. For instance, there's a scene with Dom running away with one of the chairs on his head. Vorobyaninov spots him out of the corner of his eye and gives chase. They struggle over the chair and together they rip out the seat, spraying the contents everywhere only to discover that nothing is hidden in the bottom—no jewels. Ron Moody as Vorobyaninov fixes Dom with a contemptuous look and says, "You're a priest. You took a dying woman's last confession for personal gain! You're not worth spitting on!"

And that would have been the end of the scene, except that Dom impetuously ad-libbed, "Well, you are!" Then he spits in Vorobyaninov's face and runs away shouting, "Finders keepers!"

Thanks to Dom, it was hilarious.

The Twelve Chairs was my first time working with Dom DeLuise, but from then on whenever I had a character in a movie that could possibly be played by Dom, I always gave him the part. Later, he together with Marty Feldman and myself made a great threesome for *Silent Movie* (but more about that to come).

When Anne wrote and directed her first movie, *Fatso* (1980), she picked Dom to be her leading man to carry the picture. And boy, did he carry it. In my opinion, it was an Oscar-worthy performance. It's a terrific film, and Anne was also sensational in it as his sister. *Fatso* was the first film produced by a new company I created

Here I am with the one and only Dom DeLuise, who plays Father Fyodor, the villainous Russian priest.

And here is my Russian history lesson in one street sign.

called Brooksfilms. But I'm getting ahead of myself, I'll tell you all about Brooksfilms later.

For a small part in *The Twelve Chairs* I also once again cast as a Russian theatrical company manager the talents of Andreas Voutsinas, who was so wonderful as Carmen Ghia in *The Producers*. I gave him a great line; it goes like this: "I hate people I don't like."

Andreas, who was Greek, would often say things in English that were twisted. Like for example, in talking about how and why you chose people for various roles when you were casting he said, "Or you got it or you ain't."

Simple, primitive but absolutely true. When looking for the right person for the right role Andreas's words would always pop into my head. Those words helped me with every movie I ever made. "Or you got it or you ain't."

I wasn't my first choice for the role of Tikon, who is Vorobyaninov's loyal and devoted servant. There was a very good British actor from London that I was going to pay a couple of hundred pounds to come to Yugoslavia and play Tikon. But he got sick, so he couldn't do it.

And I thought, *What the hell?* Like Anne said, I look like a Russian. My mother was born in Kiev! So, I took the part and saved the couple hundred pounds. Once I knew I was playing Tikon, I made sure that some of his dialogue was really entertaining. "Comrade. Everybody calls me comrade. Everybody in the new Soviet Union is a comrade. People you don't know, strangers, everybody says comrade . . . Oh, how I miss Russia!"

And when Ostap asks Tikon, "What goes on in this house?"

I respond, "Mostly dying. It's an old-age home for very old ladies. They tippy-toe in, they have a little bowl of porridge, and *pfft*! That's it!"

I think I was good. I actually got some compliments from Pauline Kael, a well-known critic, for having a wonderful Russian accent. So that was another good bounce for me. It also started me on the road to being an actor in my own films, which I had never thought about before.

Let me honestly say that making a movie in Yugoslavia was both a wonderful and terrible experience. I'd say eighty-twenty. Twenty wonderful . . . you can figure out the rest.

If you're going to shoot a movie in Yugoslavia (which by the way is no longer called Yugoslavia, but it's a lot easier for me to just say Yugoslavia), here is some advice: Don't take a horse and wagon with you. They have plenty of those. As a matter of fact, as far as transportation was concerned, we couldn't really go anywhere on Saturday night because Tito had the car. The one and only car in Yugoslavia at the time, a '52 green Dodge. (I may be exaggerating, but not by much.)

The first thing they told us was that the water was undrinkable. The only safe thing to drink was a Yugoslavian bottled water "kisela voda," a mild laxative. So I would suggest if you're going to make a movie in Yugoslavia, don't forget to bring a lot of toilet paper and a few hundred-watt bulbs. Because when night fell, I think the entire city was lit by two or three thirty-watt bulbs.

Shooting a film in Yugoslavia, where at that time maybe one out of twenty spoke something resembling English, was not an easy task. Here's an example, I needed only one line in English from a Yugoslavian actor who would be playing a museum guard.

When I said, "Who can speak English?" One of the Yugoslavian extras stuck his hand in the air. I said, "Can you speak English?"

He said, "Yes, sir. Yes, sir."

"Here." And I gave him a bell. I said, "Okay, when I say 'Action!' you will ring the bell and say, 'Closing time! Closing time!' Can you do that?"

Once again, he said, "Yes, sir. Yes, sir."

Little did I know that the only English he actually knew were the words "Yes, sir. Yes, sir."

Because when I said "Action!" he rang the bell and instead of saying "Closing time! Closing time!" he said, "Clogy bibe! Clogy bibe!"

"Cut and print it," I said.

I figured I didn't have time to find another Yugoslavian to play the guard, and it was the last shot of the day. I thought I could always get somebody to dub it in English during the post-production. I don't think I ever did, and I think to this day if you pay close attention to the museum guard as he passes a small group of the twelve chairs you will hear him say, "Clogy bibe! Clogy bibe!"

I went all over Yugoslavia mimicking Russia. Having seen pictures of Moscow, I was able to duplicate those same architectural features in Belgrade. It really worked. I created a street sign that I thought should have been posted somewhere in Russia at that time. The oldest part of the sign is faded and overgrown by ivy and used to read CZAR NICHOLAS AVENUE. Underneath it is a newer sign that reads MARX, ENGELS, LENIN & TROTSKY ST.—but Trotsky is crossed out. It's my own private joke, in one single street sign I covered the entire history of the Russian revolution.

Part of the reason we chose to shoot in Yugoslavia was that I got a great deal in terms of our production budget. In film production, "above the line" costs refer to the separation of production costs between script and story writers, producers, directors, actors, and casting; and "below the line" is the rest of the crew, or production team. Our below the line was $450,000 for everything—the crew, the cameras, the trucks, the equipment, the lights, the scenery, and the costumes. And I was blessed with a wonderful Yugoslavian crew. They were efficient, technically up to snuff, and had a great work ethic. I had little or no trouble with them except for one day . . .

Like I said, the Yugoslavian crew were good-natured and helpful, but you had to be careful. And on this one day I wasn't.

We were shooting in Dubrovnik, a beautiful city on the Adriatic Sea. We kept missing a group shot either because of the camera position or the wrong lens or something. We were losing the light and I got crazy. In a fit of pique, I hurled my director's chair into the Adriatic.

Suddenly, from the crew all around me angry voices were heard and clenched fists were raised. Absolutely all work stopped. I turned to my cinematographer, Djordje Nikolic, and asked, "Djordje, what the hell is going on?"

He said, "The crew is very upset. It seems you have thrown the people's chair into the sea."

"It wasn't the people's; it was my director's chair!"

"Yes," he said. "But it was provided to you by the people."

In a much lower voice, he whispered in my ear, "Mel, you're in a communist country. *Everything* here belongs to the people."

I said, "Djordje, please tell them I'm sorry. Tell them I apologize profoundly for throwing the people's chair into the sea. I will never do anything like that again."

He told them that, and they broke into applause. Djordje suggested we all have a drink to celebrate our restored friendship. We poured Vinjak (a powerful Yugoslavian brandy) into shot glasses and toasted one another, embraced one another, and that was the end of work for that day—we were all drunk as skunks. But we ended the day on a good note.

Another benefit I got out of making *The Twelve Chairs* was that I saw places and met people and learned things that I probably never would have if I didn't make a movie in Yugoslavia. Most Americans, when they go overseas to Europe they may visit "important" cities like London, Paris, and Rome. Very rarely would they sidetrack to places on the other side of the Adriatic like Yugoslavia or Albania. It really expanded my knowledge of the world.

I even learned a little of their language. For instance, within Yugoslavia there were differences in language for even simple words like "bread." In Serbian bread is *gleb*. However when I went to Dubrovnik, which is in Croatia, the Croatian word for bread is *kruch*. It also helps to learn simple words like "please," which is *molim* in both languages. In America, before we say "Action!" when shooting a movie we sometimes say "Roll 'em!"

So when I was in Yugoslavia, to the delight of the crew, before I said "Action!" I would yell, "Roll 'em, *molim*!"

There were other phrases like "give me more" or "give me less" that were very important when ordering dinner. For more you'd say *više* and for less it's *manje*. But I think the most important word that I learned above all was *polako*, which probably saved my life every time I took a taxi. The minute you got into a Yugoslavian taxicab, the driver would floor it and you'd be flying at eighty miles an hour in a tin can with wheels.

I'd often shout at the driver at the top of my voice, "*POLAKO*! *Molim*! *Polako*!"

Which means, "SLOWLY! Please! Slowly!"

And sometimes, they would actually listen and slow down.

I am particularly proud of one shot in the film that I personally captured. It's Ostap and Vorobyaninov trudging their way across Russia on their quest to find the chairs. I was belly-down in a Serbian potato field, and as the sun was setting like a big fried egg through the bare trees, I captured the poignant quality of the film in this magical image. When it appears in the film, we hear in the background John Morris's beautiful, eloquent, and haunting theme. It ended up being one of my favorite moments in the film.

There's a strange similarity in character development between *The Producers* and *The Twelve Chairs*. It seems that in the beginning, the leading characters in both movies really don't care for each other. They're complete opposites. I mean Vorobyaninov, who was born an aristocrat, looks at Ostap Bender as just a street boy—nothing but a scoundrel, a thief. And in *The Producers*, Bialystock looks at Leo Bloom like he's just an amateur and an idiot. And little by little, they get to change each other until in the end they get very close, almost like brothers. And maybe since I am one of four brothers, I was attracted to both stories because they had some underlying emotional connections of what brothers often feel for one another.

The Twelve Chairs cost nine hundred thousand dollars to make and I'm not sure, but through the years I think it just about broke even. The picture did pretty well in New York, where people went to art house theaters to see special little movies like *The Twelve Chairs*. But it never made it across the George Washington Bridge.

In between the release of *The Twelve Chairs* and my next movie, an exciting event took place. Anne and I had been married for a little over seven years and we were trying to have a child but weren't having any luck. Then one night when I got home to our townhouse in Greenwich Village on Eleventh Street, Anne was on the stairway leading from the parlor floor to the bedrooms, and when she heard the door open, she stopped and waited for me to come up the stairs. When I was halfway up the first landing, she stuck her head out, looked down at me, and said, "Mel?"

I said, "Yeah?"

With a warm glow on her face she said, "I'm pregnant."

Wow, I couldn't believe it! We hugged and kissed and cried—we were in heaven.

It was an easy pregnancy until the last month, when things got a little dicey. She was told not to do anything strenuous, and to stay in bed most of the time. So we dutifully listened, and thank god things went well. She splendidly gave birth to a beautiful seven-pound, nine-ounce baby boy we named Maximilian, after my father.

Soon after, we packed up Max and made the big move to California. We realized that was where our work was, and that's where we should be. We found a little house on Rising Glen in Hollywood and settled down. We missed New York a lot, because that's where our roots were: me in Brooklyn and Anne in the Bronx. But we were both busy with our careers and our new baby boy.

Max was a great kid. He liked to wear a little hat with the brim turned up. For a while when I saw him in that hat, I called him "Chick" because I thought he looked like a reporter, and that was usually a reporter's name in an old black-and-white movie. He smiled every time I said it, so I was thinking of changing his name from Max to Chick, but then I had a burst of sanity and left it alone. Our neighbors on Rising Glen had a beautiful German shepherd named Jenny. And Jenny would often stick her nose through the fence that separated our backyards and lick Max's face, which prompted Max to yell: "Jenny loves me! Jenny loves me!"

I didn't want to break his heart by telling him that Jenny really loved the peanut butter and jelly that he left all around his mouth when he last ate!

To this day, I get letters from people who have just seen *The Twelve Chairs* for the first time on television somewhere and they are always moved and delighted by the film. I'm so glad I made it, because I think it's one of the best things I've ever done.

Chapter 12

Blazing Saddles

In terms of my career, by 1971, I had the artist part figured out. I had two Oscars and lots of critical acclaim.

The *starving* artist part was starting to get to me.

I had worked for close to two years on both *The Producers* and *The Twelve Chairs* and only made fifty thousand dollars for each film to write, direct, and act. I had my doubts about making a living in the movie business. I still hadn't had a real commercial hit. *The Producers* and *The Twelve Chairs* together didn't make me enough money to buy a new car.

Then came David Begelman.

David Begelman and Freddie Fields, two very successful talent agents, had joined forces to create CMA, Creative Management Associates, which at that time represented me.

So one day, when I was back in New York, walking down Fifty-seventh Street right after a rainstorm and watching the rainwater travel down the gutter to the sewer, and I heard a voice behind me say, "Hiya, Mel. What are you doing, looking for change?"

I turned to see David Begelman, the bright, good-natured bon vivant co-head of the newly formed CMA smiling behind me.

He was a big fan; he loved my movies and knew that I wasn't in the chips. He said, "Join me for lunch?"

I said, "Absolutely." I knew he would take me to a good place for lunch because he dressed well, drove a Rolls-Royce, and generally lived in style.

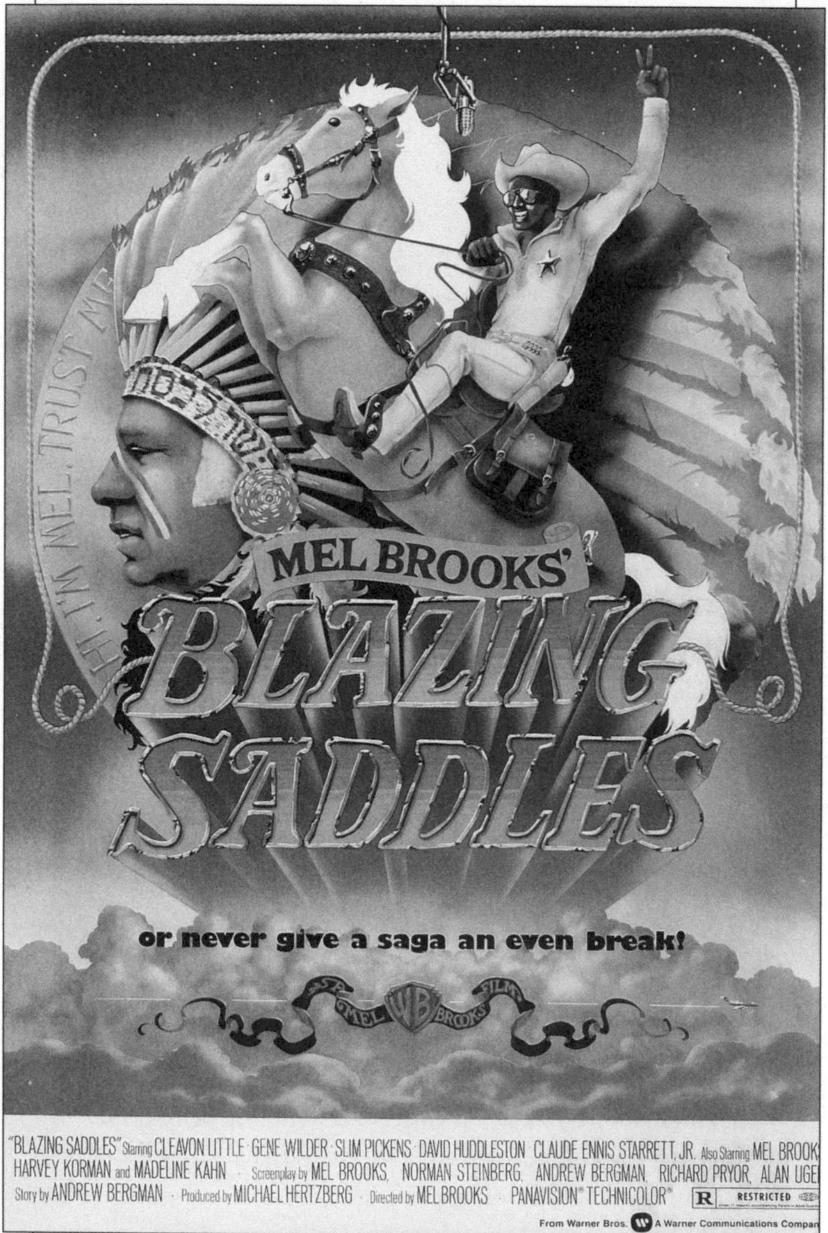

HI, I'M MEL. TRUST ME

MEL BROOKS'

BLAZING SADDLES

or never give a saga an even break!

SR MEL WB BROOKS FILMS

"BLAZING SADDLES" Starring CLEAVON LITTLE · GENE WILDER · SLIM PICKENS · DAVID HUDDLESTON · CLAUDE ENNIS STARRETT, JR. Also Starring MEL BROOK
HARVEY KORMAN and MADELINE KAHN · Screenplay by MEL BROOKS, NORMAN STEINBERG, ANDREW BERGMAN, RICHARD PRYOR, ALAN UGE
Story by ANDREW BERGMAN · Produced by MICHAEL HERTZBERG · Directed by MEL BROOKS · PANAVISION® TECHNICOLOR®

R RESTRICTED

From Warner Bros.  A Warner Communications Compan

I wasn't wrong. He took me to the splendid dining room in the Sherry-Netherland hotel. I had eggs Benedict with very good coffee.

Strangely enough he said, "I have a call in to you today that you haven't returned."

"I'll probably get it when I get home tonight. What's it about?"

"It's about a rough draft of a movie that I just read. A movie that you were born to make. It's all over the place, but there's some wonderful stuff in it and I know that if you put your crazy talented mind to it, it would be sensational."

I said, "You know, David, I only write and direct my own stuff. I don't do anybody else's ideas. Ideas just have to come to me and I have to fashion them in my own way. I'm not really for hire."

He said, "But, Mel, this could well be a very big commercial film. I think I could get you a hundred thousand dollars to write and direct it."

"Wait, David," I said. "Let me rethink my last sentence . . . given the right circumstances, I might be for hire!"

So he took me back to his office at CMA. David Begelman was a real individual in every way, and you could tell this by one glance around his office. It was decorated in red. Everything was red. Different shades of red. Pink ceiling, maroon walls, and a bright red carpet on the floor. His desk was red. His telephone was red. His coffee table was red.

"David," I said. "I'm sure I'm not the first to ask this . . . but why so much red? Why is everything in your office *so* red?"

He smiled and said, "It's not my fault. I gave the decorator 'carte rouge.'"

What a guy.

He handed me this rough draft of a screenplay called *Tex X* and said, "Take it to the office next door, read it, come back, and we'll talk."

Tex X was written by Andrew Bergman, who was not only a talented writer, but who also went on to become a wonderful director. The script was, in fact, crazy! It was a Western poking fun at Westerns. The dialogue was 1974, and the setting was 1874. It was right up my alley. I loved it. I knew it was the beginning of something that could be very, very good.

I told David, “I think I could do something with this. But it’s gonna be a lot of work. I want to work with Andrew Bergman, the original writer. There are still probably a lot of good ideas that he has in his head.”

Usually a new writer/director would throw out the first writer who had too much to say about it because it was his baby. I never felt that way. I just wanted to work with good people.

I also told David, “I’d like to go back to what I know and use a gang of comedy writers.”

It’s a style of writing comedy that always worked for me and that I was comfortable with, the kind of give-and-take that happened in the writers’ room on the Sid Caesar shows. David agreed and I was hired. I got fifty thousand for writing and fifty thousand for directing. Wow!

The first person I asked for besides Andy Bergman was Richard Pryor. Since this story was about a Black sheriff in a white Western town, I knew I needed Richard Pryor to be one of the writers. He was a friend and a brilliant comedian who hadn’t really broken out yet. Richard was not only a gifted writer, but in my opinion there was no better stand-up comic that ever lived. Comics could be either wine or water, and Richard was a fine wine. Nobody could tell stories about family with such vigor, passion, and insanity and comedy like Richard Pryor. His comedy came from the humanity that he had experienced. There was something so profoundly and infinitely soulful, sweet, and moving about Richard. He never lied. His monologues were explanations of his life and his adventures. It was memory- and character-driven comedy. That’s why, like I said, he was the best stand-up comic that ever lived and a perfect writer for this movie.

I collected Andrew Bergman and Richard Pryor, and then I collected Norman Steinberg. Norman used to annoy me every day. He'd come to the Chock full o' Nuts where I'd be having a chicken salad sandwich, he'd put on my coat for me and say: "Mr. Brooks, Mr. Brooks! Help me! I'm a lawyer. I don't want to be a lawyer; I want to be a comedy writer!"

He gave me a few sketches that were surprisingly funny and the fact that he was a lawyer who wanted to give up his career to be a comedy writer struck home. He also told me that he had been writing with a dentist named Alan Uger. And I just loved the idea of having a comedy writing team that included a lawyer and a dentist. They were just so wrong, that they were absolutely right.

So of course, I hired them!

The five of us met every day to write, and my only rule was on the wall in big print:

FIRST, WE LAUGH.

None of us had ever lived in the West. None of us knew anything about Western films, except that as kids we loved them. Every morning we had bagels and Nova Scotia lox from Zabar's for breakfast and started writing. We washed down breakfast with many cups of coffee. Most of us put sugar in our coffee, except for Richard, who occasionally laced his coffee with a shot of Rémy Martin, a very fine French brandy. Once in a while when writing late into the night Richard or Alan Uger would peel off, leaving Norman, Andy, and me to grab a cab and go to Chinatown for a midnight meal. Those were great nights, sometimes rewarding us with fresh ideas.

When you parody something, you move the truth sideways. With *Blazing Saddles*, we moved the truth out onto the street. I told the writers: "Write anything you want. We will never be heard from again. We will all be in jail for making this movie."

When it came to working on the script, there was never a subject I thought was off-limits or untouchable. If we thought of something, if it even entered our minds, no matter how bizarre or how crazy or dirty or wild or savage or not socially acceptable . . . we would still do it. Because if it came into our minds, it was worth exploring. The tone I set for the writing team was the freedom that comes from having nothing to lose. In the writing of *Blazing Saddles,* we had absolutely no restrictions on any and all subjects.

The plot was familiar to Western fans: In the 1874 Old West, a crooked politician, Hedley Lamarr, "attorney general, assistant to the governor, and state procurer," is working for the governor, William J. Lepetomane, "a silver-haired, silver-tongued moron." They are trying to run the citizens out of the town of Rock Ridge to get the land on the cheap so they can profit off the incoming transcontinental railroad.

Hedley Lamarr muses to himself, "Unfortunately, there is one thing that stands between me and that property—the rightful owners."

To placate the Rock Ridge citizens' demand for a sheriff, Lamarr has a stroke of brilliance: He will send them as their new lawman a Black sheriff, assuming that once the townspeople get a look at their new sheriff they will pack up and leave town. But somehow "Black Bart" wins them over and with the help of an ex-alcoholic gunslinger, the Waco Kid, turns the tables on Lamarr and saves the day.

That was a good simple standard plot. We decided to twist it, turn it, and stand it on its ear. We threw crazy comedy bits into the mix. In one scene Bart becomes Bugs Bunny. We just stole it, but it was a Warner Bros. cartoon, and since we were also a Warner Bros. picture, we knew we could get away with it. I also included the "we don't need no stinkin' badges" reference from the Humphrey Bogart and John Huston film *The Treasure of the Sierra Madre*—also a Warner Bros. film.

Sheriff Bart's entrance was spectacular. Instead of background music we used *foreground* music. We started the scene with the

Here in the middle of the prairie, the great Count Basie plays his famous rendition of "April in Paris" to bring on new sheriff Cleavon Little, seen in the distance riding into Rock Ridge.

great Count Basie and his orchestra playing his famous hit song "April in Paris" in the middle of the prairie. I was sure the audience would wonder, "How did Count Basie and his orchestra end up in the middle of the Mojave Desert?" Into the shot rides Sheriff Bart dressed in his cool, with-it Gucci outfit and saddlebags. On the page it was daring, but on the screen it was spectacular. I don't think anyone had ever done anything like that before.

One of the reasons that I was attracted to *Blazing Saddles* was that even though it was a wild comedy, it had a great engine beneath the comedy that was driving it. If I ever taught comedy or comedy movies to film students, I would tell them crazy comedy alone doesn't work. If you want a comedy to last, there's a secret you must follow: You have to have an engine driving it. In *Blazing Saddles*, there's a very serious backstory. Racial prejudice is the engine that really drives the film and helps to make it work.

Here's an example, where the Waco Kid is consoling the Black sheriff who has just been crushed by a racial insult:

> WACO KID: What did you expect? "Welcome, sonny"? "Make yourself at home." "Marry my daughter"? You've got to remember these are just simple farmers. These are people of the land. The common clay of the new West. You know . . . Morons.

It turns a bitter heartache into a great laugh.

I've also always been hard on language. Language has rhythm that I respect. When I was a kid all I ever wanted to be was a drummer, and a lot of that filtered down into my use of language. I mean there's a phenomenon called a rim shot. The sound is produced by simultaneously hitting the rim and head of a drum with a drumstick. As far as I'm concerned, a joke has to end with a rim shot. For example, character names. Lili Von Shtupp—that's a rim shot. Even if the audience doesn't understand the subtext, they get the rhythm. I also decided to name every citizen in Rock Ridge "Johnson." I figured why waste time coming up with last names? Johnson covers it. There will never be a better Western name than Johnson. Our Johnsons included Van Johnson, named after the actor; Olsen Johnson after the famous vaudeville team; Samuel Johnson, the famed English writer; and finally Howard Johnson after the twenty-eight-flavor ice cream and hotel chain.

Six months after our first writing session, we had a rough draft called *Black Bart*. We thought that was appropriate because the sheriff was Black, and Black Bart was a well-known Western name because there was actually an American outlaw with that nickname in the Old West who left poetic messages behind after his robberies. *Black Bart* was a good title, but it wasn't crazy enough. It didn't tell you anything about the nature of the picture. Then one day I was taking a shower, my hair was full of soap and maybe I cleaned my brain because it hit me: *Blazing Saddles*. Two Western clichés, "blazing" and "saddles." No one had ever put them together, and for good reason: They simply don't go together. However, they cry "Crazy Western!" and that's what we were making, a crazy Western. That title tells you everything.

So *Blazing Saddles* it was.

Making a satiric comedy serves two audiences equally and simultaneously: the audience that gets every film reference and all of the subtext, and the other audience that has never seen or heard of any related film. I wanted *Blazing Saddles* to work on its own. What I mean by that is even if you'd never seen a Western before you'd still get it. I try to lace my movies with cultural references, but I've always been careful that they're not weighed down by anything too arcane or inaccessible. I never came with any prerequisites. The only requirement for a Mel Brooks film is that you come in ready to laugh.

So with the rough draft done, I took Andrew Bergman and Norman Steinberg with me to Hollywood, and we continued polishing the script there.

Then we started casting. It was daunting.

Of course, we wanted Richard Pryor to play the Black sheriff, but Warner Bros. said no. They were afraid of his erratic behavior. No matter how much I begged and pleaded, Warner Bros. always gave me a firm no.

So who could we get to play the Black sheriff? A search that ended by me taking another great bounce. Instead of my first choice for Black Bart, I found somebody who was made for the role, born to play it. A Broadway actor who was handsome, sophisticated, and winning. The truly talented Cleavon Little. After he read one page of dialogue I grabbed him, embraced him, and I said, "Cleavon, don't ask for too much money and you've got the part!"

We both knew that a good thing had happened. Even Richard

On the set of Blazing Saddles, *not making the mistake of giving Cleavon direction that he didn't need.*

Pryor agreed wholeheartedly that Cleavon was the perfect choice for the role.

For the part of the Marlene Dietrich–type character there was only one person in the world who could do it. Remember when I said if I didn't get Zero Mostel I wouldn't have done *The Producers*? The same thing almost held true here. If I couldn't get Madeline Kahn to play Lili Von Shtupp, I simply didn't know what I'd do.

I first saw Madeline Kahn in her stunning Broadway debut in Leonard Sillman's *New Faces of 1968* and had followed her career ever since. I saw her in Peter Bogdanovich's wonderful films *What's Up, Doc?* and *Paper Moon*. She was one of the most gifted people—her timing, her voice, her attitude. The camera was in love with her, and if she'd wanted to, she could have been a legitimate Metropolitan Opera singer. She had the pipes! The richest, deepest vibrato. She could sing anything. The only thing that held Madeline back was a psychological defect called modesty.

When it came to Madeline playing Lili, I only had one caveat. Like I said before, Lili Von Shtupp is a satiric version of Marlene Dietrich in *Destry Rides Again.* She straddles a chair onstage and sings "See What the Boys in the Back Room Will Have" in that husky, sultry, slightly off-key Dietrich voice. I knew that Madeline could do a perfect replica of Marlene Dietrich's distinctive voice, so the only question mark was Dietrich's famous black-stocking-clad legs.

Madeline Kahn as Lili Von Shtupp, doing her great Marlene Dietrich impression—right down to those famous legs.

When Madeline came to audition for the part, I asked her to raise her skirt a little so I could see her legs. She said, "Oh, it's gonna be one of those auditions, eh?"

"No, no!" I said. "You got me all wrong! I need an impression of Marlene Dietrich in *Destry Rides Again.* Remember she sings while straddling a chair and displaying those world-famous legs?"

"Ahhh," she said. "I get it."

So she grabbed a chair and straddled it—showing off her perfectly Dietrich-esque gams.

Without hesitation I yelled, "Madeline, you got the part!"

When Madeline sang the song "I'm Tired," she was so amazing that she even hummed off-key, which is very hard to do. When you're a good singer you're glued to the middle of the note and it is very difficult to sing just slightly off-key. I learned that Madeline could do anything.

So far things on the casting side were going well. Now, I needed the bad guy. A slick-talking evil schemer who would manipulate a brainless booby of a governor, played brilliantly by yours truly. I found my Hedley Lamarr on *The Carol Burnett Show*. He was the ever popular and talented laugh maker Harvey Korman. He had a kind of classy Shakespearean tone added to his delivery which really worked for the character.

Here's an example:

> HEDLEY LAMARR: Men, you are about to embark on a great crusade . . . to stamp out runaway decency in the West. Now you will only be risking your lives . . . whilst I will be risking an almost certain Academy Award nomination . . . for Best Supporting Actor.

I have to give myself an extra pat on the back for casting Harvey; he was just a brilliant choice to play Hedley Lamarr. I loved his perfect imitation of Laurence Olivier as Henry the Fifth sending his troops off to do battle when he sends his horde of bad guys off to destroy Rock Ridge proclaiming in an Olivier-esque vocal crescendo, "Now go do that voodoo that you do so wellllll!"

As Hedley Lamarr's big dumb stupid foreman, Taggart, I got one of the best Western comedy actors that ever lived, the immortal Slim Pickens—the guy who rides Stanley Kubrick's atom bomb down to earth in *Dr. Strangelove*. He was a staple of Westerns for decades and he brought so much history to the role.

I remember one day when we were out shooting on location, I said to him, "Slim, you've made a thousand movies. I've only made two. Give me some advice."

He said, "Well, Mel, whenever you get a chance—sit down. Directing takes a lot out of you and you're too busy to notice how tired you are."

He was absolutely right.

For the part of Mongo we needed a big scary brute. No one in Hollywood fit the part, so we looked to professional football, and we were lucky to get Alex Karras, who had played for the Detroit Lions. He wasn't really an actor, but he fit the part like a glove. (A big glove.) He has one of the funniest lines in the movie: "Mongo only pawn . . . in game of life."

Like I said before, everyone in Rock Ridge was named Johnson. And for the Johnsons we got an assortment of wonderfully talented actors. David Huddleston played Olsen Johnson, John Hillerman played Howard Johnson, George Furth played Van Johnson, Richard Collier played Dr. Sam Johnson, and Jack Starrett played Gabby Johnson, who by the way did a terrific impression of Gabby Hayes, a well-known frizzle-bearded nonsense-spewing Western character actor. And we took advantage of that when after Gabby spews his incomprehensible words of wisdom in church, David Huddleston stands up and says:

> OLSEN JOHNSON: Now who can argue with that? I think we're all indebted to Gabby Johnson for clearly stating what needed to be said. I'm particularly glad that these lovely children were here today to hear that speech. Not only was it authentic frontier gibberish, it expressed a courage little seen in this day and age.

Our schoolmarm, Harriett Johnson, was played by Carol Arthur, who in real life happened to be Dom DeLuise's lovely wife. Dom himself does a cameo in the film as Buddy Bizarre, the famous Hollywood dance director who hilariously presides over our big production song-and-dance number, "The French Mistake."

And to top it off, the last but not least Johnson was our wacky reverend, the great Liam Dunn. I found the gloriously funny Liam Dunn when he played the judge in *What's Up, Doc?* Liam Dunn was actually a casting agent. I didn't know who he was, but I loved his delivery and made a mental note to remember him. No one could have read this sermon like Liam Dunn:

> REV. JOHNSON: Now I don't have to tell you good folks what's been happening in our beloved little town. Sheriff murdered, crops burned, stores looted, people stampeded, and cattle raped. The time has come to act, and act fast. . . . I'm leaving.

The only trouble we had was that while filming that scene the extras in the church kept breaking up every time Liam did his sermon. I begged them, "Please! Don't laugh! If you laugh, I can't use the scene! So please, if you can, swallow your laughter."

By take nine, they were able to contain themselves.

My biggest problem was finding the Waco Kid. For the Waco Kid I wanted to cast either a well-known Western hero or a well-known alcoholic—or if I was lucky, maybe a combination of both.

One day, when I was having lunch in the Warner Bros. commissary, I saw at a table across the room the one and only John Wayne.

Wow! I thought, what a stroke of fortune it would be to get John Wayne to play the Waco Kid. So I held my breath, walked over to his table, and introduced myself.

I said, "Mr. Wayne, you don't know me. My name is Mel Brooks and I'm making a picture here at Warner Bros."

He said, "I know you. You're Mel Brooks. You made *The Producers*! It's one of my favorite comedies. So what are you making now?"

"I'm making a Western like there's never been a Western before. It breaks all the rules—except for one: The good guys come out on top. And I'd like you to be one of the good guys."

He said, "Send it over to my office. I promise I'll read it tonight. Meet me at the same table tomorrow at the same time."

Wow! I did just as he said and could hardly sleep that night. Wow, could John Wayne possibly be the Waco Kid?

I met him at exactly the same table at the same time the next day. He had the script in his hand, and he said, "Mel, this is one of the craziest and funniest things I have ever read. But I can't do it. It's just too dirty. My fans will accept almost anything, but they won't take dirty. They're not that kind of audience. So like I said, I can't do it. But I'll tell you this: When it opens, I'll be the first in line to see it."

I thanked him profusely and went forward with my search for the Waco Kid. So I couldn't get my Western hero, but maybe I could get my alcoholic?

I reached out to Gig Young, who was normally a light comedy actor. For example, his delicious performance in Joe Bologna and Renee Taylor's *Lovers and Other Strangers*. But he was also devastatingly emotional as the alcoholic lead in *They Shoot Horses, Don't They?* with Jane Fonda, for which he won the Oscar for Best Supporting Actor. He was a remarkably good actor, and I knew he could be the Waco Kid because he had comedy in his background and was capable of rich drama. But I was still cautious about the alcohol business, because he had a reputation of hitting the bottle now and then. But his agent assured me he'd been on the wagon for more than a year and was totally trustworthy when it came to showing up sober. Good enough for me—I hired him.

Wait a minute . . . We all know that Gig Young is not the Waco Kid. That memorable role is played by the great Gene Wilder.

What is Mel talking about? Let Mel explain.

For some reason, our first day of shooting was scheduled on a Friday. The first scene was a simple introductory meeting between the new sheriff and the Waco Kid. Gig Young as the Waco Kid was hung upside down from his bunk in the jail cell of the sheriff's office. He is trying to recover from a bad hangover.

Cleavon as the sheriff asks him, "Are we awake?"

And upon seeing the Black sheriff he's supposed to respond, "We're not sure, are we Black?"

Instead Gig replies, "We're not sure, are we bla . . . are we bla—BLA?"

I turned to my assistant and whispered, "Wow, look what we're getting. He's so real."

And then the shit hit the fan. Instead of finishing the line, Gig started spewing green vomit all over the jail cell. It was like Mount Vesuvius erupting in green.

I said, "This is a little *too* real. Call an ambulance."

Obviously, Gig was not a recovering alcoholic, recovering had played no part in it. He was still in a lot of trouble. The ambulance came and took him to a local hospital. The doctor who was attending him called me and said he had the d.t.'s (delirium tremens, severe alcohol withdrawal) and was much too sick to perform for the next few months.

It was a Friday night, and I knew what I had to do to save the picture: I called Gene Wilder. Through tears I told him what had happened and begged him to save me.

He said, "I don't know whether to laugh or cry, but I'll be on a plane tomorrow morning."

It was the weekend, and the studio was closed, but they opened up a few departments for me. Someone from wardrobe helped him with a costume. We went through props and he chose a pair of six-shooters. We drove out to the WB ranch, and he picked out a horse. And then he picked out a white cowboy hat and I said, "No, you're not the sheriff. You're the sheriff's buddy."

So he picked out a dark cowboy hat, which suited him perfectly. By the end of that day Gene Wilder had become the Waco Kid.

And believe it or not on that Monday (without losing a day of shooting) he was there, hanging upside down in the jail cell and redoing the same scene that Gig Young had attempted on Friday.

Gene was absolutely perfect and I asked myself: Why hadn't I cast him in the first place? It was because I was suffering the same prejudice everybody had about serious actors and comedy. Either

From their first scene together, Cleavon and Gene bonded immediately.

they can do one or the other. Originally, I didn't want the Waco Kid to be funny. I wanted the Black sheriff to be funny, but I wanted the Waco Kid to be serious. I wanted him to carry some of the more emotional qualities of the film. I was dead wrong, but I didn't know it yet. I hadn't realized if you can find a funny actor who can be serious, then you've got heaven. That day I learned the lesson. A really good actor can do both. Hence, Gene Wilder.

We shot for ten weeks, half on a Western set at Warner Bros., and the other half on location in the Antelope Valley in California. At Warner Bros. I met John Calley, the head of production. He was an invaluable aide in fashioning the movie. I'd often come to him and ask something like, "John, is it too crazy to beat up an old lady in a Western bar fight?"

And he gave me this memorable piece of advice that stayed with me all through my career: "Mel, if you're gonna step up to the bell—ring it!"

There was a scene that I was kind of afraid of putting in the movie. That's not like me, but this particular scene was really testing the fates. What I'm referring to is the campfire scene, in which, like they do in every Western, the cowhands sit around a campfire drinking black coffee from tin mugs while they scrape a pile of beans off a tin plate. But you never hear a sound. You never hear the utter reality of breaking wind across the prairie. I had to risk my life and tell the truth. Surely there had to be one little sound from all those beans. But I decided to let the audience hear the real McCoy, no matter what it would cost me.

I remembered John Calley's motto: "If you're gonna step up to the bell—ring it!"

And boy did I ring it. The air was filled with the unmistakable sounds of nonstop flatulence. It was the greatest farting scene in cinematic history.

I may have been risking my career, but what good is a career if you don't risk it from time to time?

The most fun was shooting the Lili Von Shtupp saloon number. I spent several nights writing "I'm Tired," the song that Madeline Kahn sings. I took special care to write lyrics that would blend with our Dietrich-esque Lili Von Shtupp's slightly off-key notes. "I'm Tired" is a salute to world-weary women everywhere, who give in to the inability of men to make love properly. Madeline loved it, and her performance was absolutely out of this world. We were lucky to get Alan Johnson, who had choreographed "Springtime for Hitler," to do the crazy Teutonic dance steps for us. I was hoping the audience would agree with me after they saw pointy-helmeted Germans singing and dancing in a Western saloon—that this picture was downright crazy!

(Did I tell you that Madeline was incredible? I probably did but I'm saying it again. Madeline was incredible.)

I think *Blazing Saddles* was a giant step forward for me as a director. There was a part of me that I hadn't used before: anarchy. As a director, *Blazing Saddles* was the beginning of my complete disregard for reality. It was the first time I really broke the fourth wall. I pulled the camera back on a fight in a Western town, to reveal to the audience that what they were watching was on a fake Western street in a big place called Warner Bros. Studios. Then I proceeded to zoom in to one of the Warner Bros. stages to reveal Dom DeLuise as a Busby Berkeley–era dance director filming a big studio production number with a chorus of performers in top hat, white tie, and tails singing "The French Mistake."

Suddenly, one of the walls on the stage collapses and cowboys and horses from the Western set come crashing through. A big crazy fight ensues between chorus boys and cowboys.

Dom DeLuise as Buddy Bizarre and Slim Pickens as Taggart face off in the fight. When Dom shouts, "This is a closed set!" Slim responds, "Piss on you. I'm working for Mel Brooks!"

It's a fierce fight, but once in a while, instead of fighting, some of the cowboys and the chorus boys make up and leave together. If that wasn't enough, the camera is then suddenly outside the front gate of Warner Bros. Studios, as Harvey Korman, still in costume as Hedley Lamarr, with his face covered with whipped cream pie from a great salute to pie fights, hails a cab and says to the driver, "Drive me off this picture!"

As the cab speeds away, we see Cleavon on his palomino horse come riding through the gate and gallop after him. The finale of the picture takes place at the famous Grauman's Chinese Theatre in Hollywood. Hedley Lamarr and the Black sheriff face off in a gunfight, and of course . . . the good guy wins. As Hedley Lamarr hits the ground, he notices one of the most famous hands-and-footprints squares in the concrete sidewalk, it reads: DOUGLAS FAIRBANKS. Harvey leaves us with this last line:

HEDLEY LAMARR: "How did he do such fantastic stunts with such little feet?"

By the way, many years later when I was asked to put my own hands and feet in that famous sidewalk cement, I decided that I had been well behaved for such a long time . . . that I needed to be mischievous again! I arranged to have the prop masters from *The Walking Dead* TV series build me a sixth finger on my left hand. I wanted one of the hundreds of tourists that would visit the Chinese Theatre sidewalk that day to shout, "Hey! Did you know that Mel Brooks had SIX fingers on his left hand!"

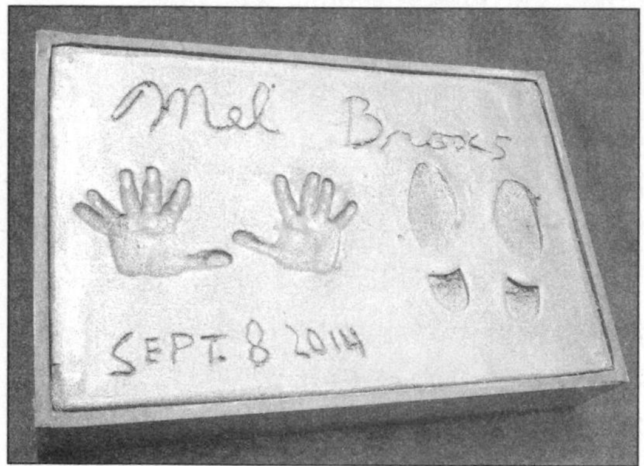

Count 'em: 1, 2, 3, 4, 5, 6.

We pulled it off, and the prosthetic looked so real that I decided to wear my sixth finger on Conan O'Brien's show that same night. Nobody from his production team told Conan about it, so that when I revealed it in the middle of our interview, he went absolutely bananas!

But back to the ending of *Blazing Saddles*, Cleavon and Gene as Bart and the Waco Kid watch the end of our movie inside the Chinese Theatre with popcorn in hand. From the sheriff and the Waco Kid sitting in the theater we cut back to the Western town. The sheriff is back on his palomino, slowly riding out of town. He stops when he sees the Waco Kid, strangely enough still munching on the popcorn from the movie theater.

WACO KID: Where you headed, cowboy?
BART: Nowhere special.

WACO KID: Nowhere special . . . I've always wanted to go there.

BART: Come on.

The two ride off, and then a little later they exchange their horses for a fancy black limousine, which takes them off into a big beautiful Western sunset.

Other directors may have broken the fourth wall, but I think in *Blazing Saddles* I shattered it.

Once again, the great John Morris came on board to score the film. We had a shorthand at this point. I wrote "I'm Tired" for Lili Von Shtüpp and he orchestrated it in single instruments like they did in Berlin in 1920. I thought I'd hear it in a normal orchestration, but he got the incredible Berliner Ensemble feeling like Bertolt Brecht and Kurt Weill's *The Threepenny Opera*. It was just amazing.

John Morris and I collaborated on the title song for the film, "Blazing Saddles." It was a musical parody of every Western title song ever written. The lyrics went like this:

He rode a blazing saddle
He wore a shining star
His job to offer battle
To bad men near and far
He conquered fear and he conquered hate
He turned our night into day
He made his blazing saddle
A torch to light the way

We needed a Frankie Laine–type to sing the song. Frankie was the go-to guy for Western themes from the late 1940s through the 1960s, including *Mule Train*, *Rawhide*, *3:10 to Yuma*, and *Gunfight at the OK Corral*. Nobody could sing a whip-cracking Western song like the great Frankie Laine. So I said, "Why not just ask Frankie Laine himself?"

And so, we did! To my amazement after he finished a beautiful heartrending rendition of “Blazing Saddles” he told me, “I really love that song.”

God bless him! I told him how great he was and thanked him from the bottom of my heart. Frankie’s performance not only made the song and the opening work, but believe it or not, it resulted in one of three Oscar nominations for the film, the first was for Best Song, the second for Best Film Editing, and the third was for Madeline Kahn’s great interpretation of Lili Von Shtupp. I was really very pleased, because I wasn’t sure the Academy was hip enough to recognize the layers and the depth of her brilliant work in that role.

Madeline became part of a great stock company that I was unknowingly putting together for future films. Like writer/director Preston Sturges did in the 1940s, I was starting to gather brilliant performers who I could call on to do almost anything. There was Madeline, Gene Wilder, Harvey Korman, Dom DeLuise, and soon I would add the great Marty Feldman and Cloris Leachman—but more on that later.

My anarchy vis-à-vis *Blazing Saddles* didn’t stop with filming; it carried on to the first screening of *Blazing Saddles* at the Avco Embassy theater on Wilshire Boulevard in Los Angeles. I had the lobby filled with live cattle, mooing and doing what live cattle do. It was terrible and wonderful. The theater was packed. There wasn’t a seat to be had. The audience loved it—they went bananas! It was one of the greatest nights of my life. To work so hard on a film for so long and to be rewarded with nonstop riotous laughter is the greatest payment in the world. It was an incredible screening right from the first Frankie Laine rendition of the title song to the limo driving our heroes off into the sunset. It was, as they say in *Variety*, “A LAFF RIOT.”

My worries about whether or not audiences would get and embrace *Blazing Saddles* went out the window that night. Everything worked . . . except for one slight hitch.

The head of Warner Bros., who hadn't seen any of the footage before, grabbed me on the way out of the screening. He pulled me into the manager's office at the Avco Embassy theater and I grabbed John Calley to come with me for moral support. He handed me a yellow legal pad and a pencil and said, "Take notes! Farting scene, out."

I said, "Farting scene, out."

He said, "No punching a horse. Cannot punch a horse."

I said, "How stupid of me. How silly! Can't hit a horse. Mongo punching horse, out."

It went on and on.

He said, "N-word. Cannot say that word."

I said, "N-word, out."

He continued: "No scenes with the secretary. No boobs."

The greatest thing in *Blazing Saddles* was Madeline Kahn singing "I'm Tired." He said: "Too dirty. Take the song out."

I said, " 'I'm Tired,' out."

I'm taking all of these notes. He's running a film studio, he should realize that if I had listened to every single thing that he wanted me to cut we'd have the shortest movie in the history of film. I sat down after he left, tore the page of notes off the yellow legal pad, crumpled it up, and tossed it in the wastepaper basket.

John Calley said, "Well filed."

I never changed a thing. Like I've said before, as far as movie executives are concerned, always agree with them, but never do a thing they say. When the good reviews, and more important for the front office, the money started rolling in, I never heard a bad word from the head of the studio again.

Blazing Saddles opened in stages. It opened in a limited run in February of 1974, and it must have played in only about a hundred theaters nationwide, but to very successful numbers, pretty good reviews, and, most important, very good word of mouth.

Instead of their normal summer fare, Warner Bros. expanded *Blazing Saddles* into a wide release. Apparently, the exhibitors had been clamoring for it. They made a lot more prints and that summer it really exploded. Whatever I had done before—*Blazing Saddles* was forty times bigger. It was supposed to run through June and July, but instead it went all the way through Labor Day. A lot of the theaters wouldn't take it out. (In those days that was a long time for a movie to run!) There was concern among some critics that the outrageousness of *Blazing Saddles* would destroy the Western as a film genre. Not only were they wrong, at the time it became the second-highest-grossing Western, after *Butch Cassidy and the Sundance Kid*.

Finally, after two good pictures I had managed to make not only another good picture but, to boot, my first big hit.

Chapter 13

Young Frankenstein

One day on the Western town set of *Blazing Saddles*, when we broke for lunch I noticed Gene Wilder leaning against the sheriff's office and scribbling something on a pad propped up on his knees.

I said, "Gene, how 'bout lunch?"

He said, "In a minute, I have to finish a thought I have."

I said, "What are you writing there?"

He handed me the pad and at the top it had the words " '*Young Frankenstein*.' "

I repeated, " '*Young Frankenstein*,' what is that?"

He said, "I have this idea for a movie about Baron Frankenstein's grandson. He's an uptight scientist who doesn't believe any of that nonsense about bringing the dead back to life. Even though he is clinically a scientist, he is as crazy as any Frankenstein. It's in his heart. It's in his blood. It's in the marrow of his bones . . . only he doesn't know it yet."

"Sounds interesting," I said. "What is your dream for this movie?"

He said, "My dream is for you to write it with me and direct the movie."

I said, "You got any money on you?"

"I have fifty-seven dollars," Gene said.

(This is true.)

A
MEL BROOKS
FILM
YOUNG
FRANKENSTEIN
starring
"YOUNG FRANKENSTEIN" GENE WILDER · PETER BOYLE · MARTY FELDMAN
CLORIS LEACHMAN costarring TERI GARR also starring KENNETH MARS and MADELINE KAHN
produced by
MICHAEL GRUSKOFF
directed by
MEL BROOKS
screen story and screenplay by
GENE WILDER and MEL BROOKS
based on characters in the novel "Frankenstein" by MARY W. SHELLEY
music by JOHN MORRIS
PRINTS BY DE LUXE®
PG PARENTAL GUIDANCE SUGGESTED
20th CENTURY FOX

"It's a beginning," I said. "I'll take it. I'll take it as a down payment on writing *Young Frankenstein* with you. And if I like what we've done, I'll direct it."

That was the beginning.

That night, I went over to Gene's bungalow, at the Hotel Bel-Air, to discuss the concept. We stayed up until the early hours of the morning talking about the story line over Earl Grey tea and English digestive biscuits. We talked about being very faithful to the tempo and the look of James Whale's marvelous black-and-white films, *Frankenstein* from 1931 and *Bride of Frankenstein* from 1935.

James Whale's talent was in how he told the *Frankenstein* story visually. Gene and I watched Whale's movies together multiple times. We saw how he took his time. Whale wanted everything to be deep, dark, and somber. He had worked in the theater before he started in film, which is where he met Colin Clive, the actor who plays the insane Dr. Frankenstein. When Whale's *Frankenstein* came out, it was a smash hit, and catapulted Boris Karloff, who played the monster, to stardom. Whale got pigeonholed as a horror director and would go on to direct *The Old Dark House* (1932), *The Invisible Man* (1933), and *The Bride of Frankenstein,* which we later referenced liberally. Whale knew exactly how to scare the hell out of you, but he was also a great artist who was not appreciated for those talents as much as he should have been. We decided to base the look and spirit of *Young Frankenstein* on the James Whale classics.

Gene and I quickly got into a rhythm of working together. Each night after I finished in the editing room on *Blazing Saddles* and had dinner, I'd go to Gene's hotel. At the beginning we concentrated on satirizing and saluting the James Whale films, but later we expanded it into our own story line. We knew exactly where we were going. Gene wrote everything in pencil on his yellow legal pads, which my secretary typed up the next day.

Gene said I taught him the most important lesson he ever learned about screenwriting: "The first draft is just concepts. Then you take a sledgehammer and knock the pillars of the story line as hard as you can. If they hold up, you keep it in. If they start to crumble, you have to rewrite, because the structure is everything."

Gene and I never stopped writing *Young Frankenstein*. We wrote and rewrote, then wrote and rewrote, then wrote and rewrote once again. We always went back to a scene until we were more or less satisfied.

In addition to James Whale's films, we also relied on Mary Wollstonecraft Shelley's *Frankenstein; or, The Modern Prometheus,* published in 1818, for inspiration. Gene and I had both read Mary Shelley's book when we sat down to write this script. Only nineteen when she wrote *Frankenstein;* she was on a summer holiday in Switzerland with her future husband, the poet Percy Bysshe Shelley, and his friend and fellow poet Lord Byron. They were part of a famous group of writers who gave birth to a literary period known as the Romantic Age. Legend has it that they had a contest to see who could write the scariest ghost story. We never found out what Shelley or Byron wrote, but the teenaged Mary's tale lives on to this day. She ended up penning what would become one of the first true works of science fiction and the ultimate story about men playing god.

The concept that has made Frankenstein's monster such an enduring character in film and literature is that at its core he is a deformed creature who has love in his heart, wants to be loved, but is misunderstood. Even though we were doing a crazy comedy, those important qualities were still there. That was no doubt key to the success and longevity of the film.

You never know where and how a stroke of luck is going to cross your path. For instance, we thought about casting even before the script was halfway finished. Right from the beginning we knew that Gene had to be "Dr. Fronkensteen." But who would play the monster, and who would end up playing the weird, funny, humpbacked Igor?

One day Mike Medavoy, who would eventually be running Tri-Star Pictures but was Gene's agent at the time, called Gene and said, "I know you're working with Mel on that Frankenstein picture, is there anything in it for Peter Boyle and Marty Feldman?"

Gene said, "What made you think of that combination?"

Mike replied, "Because I'm not only your agent, I also now handle Peter Boyle and Marty Feldman."

Gene said, "Wow. As a matter of fact, as it happens, I think I do . . ."

And believe it or not, that's how we got Peter Boyle to be our incredible monster and Marty Feldman to be our unforgettable Igor. Talk about a stroke of luck!

God put Marty Feldman together. We had nothing to do with it. I met Marty in England, where he had a television show called *The Marty Feldman Comedy Machine*, which my friend and former Sid Caesar writers' room partner Larry Gelbart was writing. I fell in love with Marty instantly and when Mike Medavoy suggested him, I knew he would be absolutely perfect for Igor.

As everybody who has seen *Young Frankenstein* knows, Marty Feldman has bulging eyes. It's a condition called "Graves' ophthalmopathy" in which his eyes protrude and he more or less sees out the sides of his face like a horse, rather than straight ahead.

I tell this joke about Marty in my stand-up routine: "Anytime I wanted to hide from Marty Feldman I'd put the tip of my nose against his . . . and he couldn't see me!"

I was so lucky to get him to play the role of the mad humpbacked Igor. Marty came up with the funniest retort in the movie.

When Gene says, "You know I don't mean to embarrass you but I'm a rather brilliant surgeon, perhaps I could help you with that hump."

Marty came back with: "What hump?"

It was dynamite.

I first saw Peter Boyle in the movie *Joe*, a tough political story in which he was wonderful in his portrayal of a terrible person. In *Young Frankenstein,* the monster is scary and miserable, but there is a sweet child in him. Gene said, "Peter can do both."

Peter was a consummate artist, and the beauty of him came through, his soul shone through. He bestowed an absolute magnificence on the creature.

We knew *Young Frankenstein* had to be in black and white if we were going to salute those great Universal Pictures that James Whale made in the 1930s, and we thought we needed at least two million dollars to do it (which was the going price to make a modest film in those days). When the script was finished, our producer Michael Gruskoff along with Gene and I went to a meeting to sell it to Columbia Pictures.

Now remember, as we were walking into this meeting *Blazing Saddles* hadn't been released yet, so my reputation as a hit-producing moneymaker was not yet established. Still, the Columbia executives liked the script. They wanted to make it, but the most they would come up with was a million and a half.

(Had they known at the time about the future box office of *Blazing Saddles* they wouldn't have quibbled about a half a million bucks.)

We needed two million, so Mike got them to split the difference and they said yes to 1.75 million dollars. We shook hands all around and said, "It's a deal."

On the way out, I turned back and said, "Oh, by the way, we're going to make it in black and white."

Then I closed the door.

A thundering herd of studio executives chased us down the hall from the meeting room.

They were screaming, "No, no! Wait, come back! No black and white! No black and white! Peru just got color! Everything is in color! Nobody makes movies in black and white anymore!"

The thing about satire is the walls, the floors, the costumes; everything surrounding the comedy has to be real. If we were going to satirize the classic 1930s Universal Frankenstein pictures, our film had to be in black and white.

The Columbia guys offered a compromise: "Shoot it in color, and we'll diffuse it and take the color out for the U.S., but in the rest of the world it would have color."

I knew they were lying. Studios have a way of promising the world and giving you zero. I said no, because I knew they'd somehow trick us and release it in color anyway.

I said, "There's a stock called Agfa. It's a German black-and-white film. It's true, rich, thick black and white. That's the only film stock I'll make it on."

The Columbia guys said, "We're sorry. If it's not in color, that's going to break the deal."

Mike, Gene, and I bravely yelled back, "Then break it!"

On that very same afternoon our producer, Mike Gruskoff, said, "My friend Laddie has just become part of the new leadership at Twentieth Century Fox."

Alan Ladd, Jr.—Laddie to his friends—was the son of the terrific forties film star Alan Ladd, who had played some memorable roles such as the lead in *This Gun for Hire* (1942) and the famous title role in *Shane* (1953). Laddie and Mike had been agents together and they were still good buddies.

Mike ran the script over to Laddie's house that night and Laddie later told me that he read it twice from eleven P.M. until one in the morning. He just couldn't put it down. He really loved it.

We all hit it off at our first meeting because the first thing Laddie said was, "You're absolutely right. It should be made in black and white."

I knew right then and there that I had finally met a studio chief that I could really trust.

He had a lot of faith in me. He said, "Use Stage Five at Fox; it's enormous, it's gorgeous, and it's yours. And don't worry about the money. Whatever you need to make it, you've got it."

What a guy! He authorized a budget of 2.4 million dollars.

I didn't know it then, but I had a new long-term creative home at Fox. During the filming of *Young Frankenstein*, *Blazing Saddles* became an enormous hit, and I was ardently wooed by several big studios, but my heart was now pledged to Laddie and Twentieth Century Fox because he had taken a chance on me. He had picked up *Young Frankenstein* without even knowing that *Blazing Saddles* would be a massive hit. So I later signed a three-picture deal with him at Fox. It's many years later, and at this writing, he's still one of my dearest friends.

But back to *Young Frankenstein* . . .

Once again, I got Kenny Mars, who played the crazy German playwright Franz Liebkind in *The Producers,* to be the crazy German policeman Inspector Kemp in *Young Frankenstein*. Any time I needed a crazy German, I knew I could count on Kenny Mars to be there. He came up with a wonderful suggestion: He would put his character's monocle over his black eye patch, thereby making it completely useless.

For Castle Frankenstein's loony housekeeper, Frau Blücher, we got the truly gifted Cloris Leachman, who had won a Best Supporting Actress Oscar for her brilliant performance in Peter Bogdanovitch's *The Last Picture Show* (1971). She could do anything, drama or comedy. She turned in one of the funniest performances of anybody in the film. I told her as a film model for her performance we decided she would be a Teutonic Judith Anderson replete with a mole on her cheek à la the cold and domineering Mrs. Danvers in Hitchcock's *Rebecca* (1940). We added the touch that every time her name is mentioned the horses would whinny and rear up in fear in the background. There was a General Blücher who was the Prussian victor at the Battle of Waterloo, and I just liked the sound of that name. The horses whinny because Frau Blücher is ominous. Even they know how crazy she is. Someone told me, I think incorrectly, that the German word *Blücher* means "glue" and that when the horses heard the name Blücher they were terrified that they'd end up in a glue factory.

For Dr. Frankenstein's attractive lab assistant, Inga, we got the beautiful and talented Teri Garr. She came up with a wonderfully unique version of a German accent. I knew Teri would be sensational when she was reading the line where Frau Blücher is removing the big steel restraints that keep the monster on the laboratory table.

Teri was supposed to come down the steps and say, "No, no, you mustn't."

In Teri's audition, with great fear in her voice she said, "No, no, you *mozzn't*!"

Giving it just the right Transylvanian touch.

One of my favorite scenes was Teri's unassuming, blushing take when Gene looks at the front door of the castle and sees these incredible iron rings.

When Marty bangs them against the giant door, Gene says: "My god, what knockers!"

And Teri replies, "*Vy* thank you, Doctor."

Teri's performance was spot-on.

To complete the trio of hilarious women in *Young Frankenstein*, we again employed the services of the great Madeline Kahn. Gene and I wrote the role of the snooty Park Avenue socialite Elizabeth with Madeline in mind. We liked the idea that "Dr. Fronkensteen" had a fiancée that was more interested in diamond earrings than reanimated dead tissue.

It was my idea that when Elizabeth is seduced by the monster instead of screaming in terror she bursts into song, singing, *"Ah, sweet mystery of life, at last I've found you!"*

Obviously, she likes the guy. After Elizabeth falls in love with the monster, we modeled her look after Elsa Lanchester's character in *The Bride of Frankenstein,* right down to the bizarre hairdo with white streaks up the sides.

And talk about luck—Gene Wilder used to play tennis every Saturday with another Gene, called Gene Hackman. One Saturday Hackman asked Wilder what he was working on. Wilder explained the premise of *Young Frankenstein.*

Hackman said, "Is there anything in it for me? I'm dying to do some comedy."

Wilder said, "As a matter of fact, there is."

And he explained the role of the blind man.

He said, "It's just a cameo, but if you really wanted to do it, I'm sure Mel would—"

Hackman cut him off. "It's perfect! Count me in."

When Gene Wilder told me about his conversation, I was over the moon. I knew what a consummate actor Hackman was, as he had just won an Oscar for his memorable performance as "Popeye" Doyle in *The French Connection* (1971). We could never have paid Gene Hackman his current salary in those days. He was gracious, did the movie anyway as a favor, and took minor billing.

He was so wonderful as the lonely blind hermit. He almost destroys the monster with his kindness. In the original film the creature is drawn by violin music in the woods and encounters a kind blind hermit, who shows him hospitality and lets him spend the night. In our version the blind man's attempts at hospitality result in hot soup in the monster's crotch and the monster's thumb lit on fire. Peter's creature runs out and Gene Hackman gets one of the biggest laughs in the movie with his superbly delivered, "Where are you going? I was gonna make espresso!"

When people saw *Young Frankenstein* in the theater, nobody knew the blind man was Gene Hackman until they saw his name at the end of the credits. The monk's costume and the beard made him unrecognizable. His line readings were hysterical, but he never pushed it. He got it just right. I will always be eternally grateful to Gene Hackman for that gift of a performance.

Gene Wilder had only one favor to ask of me before we began filming the movie. With a big smile on his face he said, "I'll do it as long as you're not in it. I don't want you to act in it."

I said, "Why?"

He said, "Because I don't want a minute of your concentration to be split between your acting and your directing."

"Done," I said. We shook on it.

I had three weeks of rehearsals before we began shooting. I like rehearsals, because it gives the actors an opportunity to get comfortable with one another.

I told the cast, "We're making a riotous comedy here but you don't know it. At times it's gotta be touching and at other times really scary. And it's got to be very real—no heightened acting. When it's funny, your character doesn't know it's funny. You're just doing your job. The *audience* knows when it's funny. But you don't. So don't you ever play funny."

When writing for other comedians, someone once told me, "I want to make it my own."

I'd say, "Look, the jokes are written. The relationships are written. First, do it as written. Later you can make it your own."

A lot of people don't realize that without a valley, there is no peak. Without information, there is no joke. You've got to set things up. With my *Young Frankenstein* cast, this was never an issue. These were actors who respected what was on the page and yet knew how to improvise. It was the best of both worlds. During those three weeks I had a wonderful feeling that the picture was going to work because the actors blended with one another so beautifully.

Laddie was right, Stage Five at Fox was enormous and could house all the castle interiors we needed for filming. Our production designer, Dale Hennesey, had just done *Dirty Harry* (1971) and two Woody Allen films. His Frankenstein's castle looked like it was made of sweating stone, like it was in the mountains where a mist had settled on the surface, leaving it all wet. It was fifteen thousand square feet and thirty-five feet high. When he constructed the laboratory, it was even grander than James Whale's set. Set decorator Robert De Vestel complemented each set with period chandeliers, drapes, tapestries, pewter platters, goblets, candelabras, and ancient stone stairs and floors. In the laboratory set he filled in all the little empty spaces with turn-of-the-century test tubes, beakers, and Bunsen burners.

We were so lucky that the laboratory equipment that was actually used on the original Universal *Frankenstein* film was still around. It was stored in the garage of the incredibly talented Kenneth Strickfaden, who had designed all that unforgettable laboratory machinery for the 1931 film. These were the contraptions that made the scary lightning zaps and conferred the entire set with a pulsating eerie glow. We visited him at his garage in Santa Monica

On set directing Peter Boyle as the hulking monster with his iconic zipper neck.

and he dusted off each piece and miraculously it all still worked! Being able to once again use those original set pieces really lent an air of authenticity to the look of the film. Hats off to the remarkable Kenneth Strickfaden!

We used more special effects on this film than I had ever used before. To get that low-hanging fog we relied on tons of dry ice. The fireplaces had concrete logs so they wouldn't set the set on fire, and we used silk strips of fabric fluttering in front of lamps out of frame to create the effect of flickering firelight on the walls.

Our costume designer was the prolific and talented Dorothy Jeakins. She had costumed such diverse films as *The Sound of Music* (1965), *True Grit* (1969), *The Night of the Iguana* (1964), *The Music Man* (1962), *Elmer Gantry* (1960), *South Pacific* (1958), and many others. She could do anything. She was one of the best costume designers that ever worked in Hollywood.

When we met and sat down to talk about the look of the costumes she asked, "For the villagers, do you want Alsatian? German? Bavarian? Transylvanian? Bohemian?"

I was amazed at her knowledge of all the subtle differences in different periods of turn-of-the century costumes. I said, "Dorothy, you're the expert—it's your choice."

Gene chose to be in the lab coat for most of the movie and for his street clothes he picked out an old-fashioned, salt-and-pepper English jacket with a belt in the back. He knew Freddie Frankenstein's style. He chose to wear a Ronald Coleman–type mustache. I said no, and then we shot two scenes, one with it and one without it. He was absolutely right. The mustache added great bearing and character. Gene was never more handsome than when he played young Dr. Frankenstein. He was also never more insane. The funny-looking Gene Wilder that I had originally met suddenly became a true leading man, albeit slightly crazy.

The artisans we had were thrilled to be working on a black-and-white picture. Our makeup creator, William Tuttle, had done the makeup for *Singin' in the Rain* (1952), *North by Northwest*

On the set of Young Frankenstein *framing a dramatic shot of Peter Boyle as the monster.*

(1959), and *The Twilight Zone*. He was a master. When I told Bill that we'd be making the film in black and white, he hugged me! He put his head right against my face and said, "I was going to tell you that if you made it in color, the monster would be blue-green. He would look silly. But in black and white, the makeup will look incredible."

He showed me three or four different monster faces. I said to Bill, "I know the monster has to be dangerous looking, but at times he should also be beautiful and angelic."

William Tuttle was a bit of a genius; when I told him we had to find some new way of fastening the monster's head to his neck because I didn't want to use the iconic bolts and have any copyright issues with the original Frankenstein, he came up with a stroke of genius—a zipper!

Every day Bill kept Peter Boyle in the makeup chair for more than four hours to complete his transformation into the monster. But it was worth every minute. Peter stopped complaining the minute he saw the incredible result at the dailies. We further exaggerated Peter's stature by putting him in six-inch platform boots and padding his costume to add heft. He was indeed a big and scary but beautiful monster.

It had been a long time since black and white was standard cinematography, so I wondered if there was a cameraman still around who could work in this format. After an exhaustive search I came up with the right choice—Gerald Hirschfeld. He was a master cinematographer and well versed in the art of filming in black and white. He carefully studied James Whale's famous *Frankenstein* and *The Bride of Frankenstein* to try and match their style.

After the first few days I said, "It's good, Jerry. But I need something extra. I can't even explain it. We're making a satire. So it has to have a little more than we're getting."

Jerry said, "Leave it to me."

Jerry got it just right. Perfection, and a little satiric. It was just a touch brighter than normal. It was perfectly sculptured black-and-white satiric photography with high-contrast backlighting that made the characters stand out. It was "James Whale, plus." I couldn't have been happier.

Throughout filming, I had only one disagreement with Jerry Hirschfeld. It was over a slow move in to a close-up on Gene Wilder's face in the laboratory.

Jerry said, "I gotta do it over again. There was a noticeable shake in the camera as we moved in for the close-up."

I said, "I want that! That's good!"

He looked at me like I was crazy.

Then I explained, "It's called cinematic verisimilitude. It's mimicking exactly the period photography in the original *Frankenstein*. James Whale didn't have his camera on big rubber wheels gliding over a plywood floor. All his slow-moving shots were made on a slightly bumpy studio floor. And a lot of them had that exact little shake in them."

It gave it that 1931 quality that I was dying to get in the film. I loved that little shake!

Jerry broke into a broad smile and said, "Okay, if that's what you want—you got it. We have all the little shake you'll ever need."

One of the problems I had on set was constantly reshooting because of laughing from the crew. So one day I went out and bought a hundred white handkerchiefs. I handed them out and said to the crew, "If you feel like laughing, don't! Stick this handkerchief in your mouth."

I turned around once in the middle of shooting a scene and saw a sea of white handkerchiefs in everybody's mouths.

I thought, *I've got a big hit here. This movie is going to be hilarious.*

There's only one true test of a comedy, and that's outright laughter. I don't care how beautiful the lighting is, how superlative the script is, how wonderful the performances are. If you're making a comedy and the audience isn't falling down, holding their bellies, screaming with laughter, you've probably got a failure.

First laughter and then everything else.

(Shame on me, but it's true.)

One of the white-handkerchief-in-the-mouth scenes actually got me. I was struggling not to break into laughter. I didn't have a white handkerchief to shove in my mouth—I'd given them all out and didn't save one for myself . . . and I really needed it!

The offending scene was the one in which Gene, Teri, and Marty are at the dinner table. Dr. Frankenstein is in the depths of depression over his failure to bring the monster back to life.

Teri says, "You haven't even touched your food."

Gene responds by sticking his hands into his beef stew and boiled potatoes and saying, "There! Now I've touched it. Happy?"

Marty, trying to lighten the mood, blurts out, "You know, I'll never forget my old dad, when these things would happen to him, the things he'd say to me."

Gene and Teri are patiently waiting to hear what Marty's dad used to tell him, and finally Gene asks, "What did he say?"

Marty replies, "What the hell are you doing in the *baffroom* day and night! Why don't you get out of there and give someone else a *chawnce*!" Then he takes a big bite of his boiled potato and just chews.

Somehow, I held it together, and after I said cut, we all collapsed in a heap on the floor and exploded into nonstop laughter. That was a near miss.

For our locations for the movie we used the back lot of MGM, which gave us two wonderful outdoor sets. One was the quaint Bavarian village, replete with authentic winding cobblestone streets, and the other the graveyard where we find and dig up the huge body that becomes Frankenstein's monster. It was during that scene that we came up with the great line in which Gene (covered with mud and dirt from the digging) says:

DR. FRANKENSTEIN: What a filthy job.
IGOR: Could be worse.
DR. FRANKENSTEIN: How?
IGOR: Could be raining.

It immediately starts pouring, and as they are drenched with rain Dr. Frankenstein fixes Igor with a look that is unforgettable.

I loved working with Gene. He had incredible range as an actor, especially in the scene where he goes into the dark cell where the monster is chained to a huge chair. He comes in so sure of himself; just before he goes into the monster's cell he says, "No matter what you hear in there, no matter how cruelly I beg you, no matter how terribly I may scream, do not open this door . . ."

He's so in charge. So smart. He tiptoes in and when the monster wakes up and growls at him, he goes from this commanding doctor into a terrified frightened little child. From self-assurance and perfect command to a scared kid banging on the door and screaming, "Let me out. Let me out of here. Get me the hell out of here! What's the matter with you people! I was joking! Don't you know a joke when you hear one? HAHAHAHA! JESUS CHRIST GET ME OUT OF HERE!"

Talk about range! He went all the way emotionally from A to Z. I loved sitting in a theater, watching that scene, as the audience exploded into gales of laughter all around me.

The "walk this way" scene in *Young Frankenstein* was a salute to the vaudeville shtick in which one comic says to the other "walk this way" meaning "follow me!" But instead of just following him the second banana imitates his comical walk.

So when Marty says to Gene, "Walk this way!" Gene starts to just follow him, but Marty stops him and says, "No, walk *this* way." And Gene catches on and does Marty's crazy vaudeville stooped walk. Thank god once again for white handkerchiefs in the mouth!

("Walk this way" started on *Young Frankenstein,* but for some reason I stuck that iconic bit into many of my later movies.)

One of my favorite moments in *Young Frankenstein* was where Freddie, Inga, and Igor discover that the strange music emanating from the bowels of the castle that led them to the laboratory was being played on the violin by none other than Frau Blücher.

FREDERICK: Then it was you all the time!
FRAU BLÜCHER: Yes!
FREDERICK: You played that music in the middle of the night!
FRAU BLÜCHER: Yes!
FREDERICK: . . . to get us into the laboratory!
FRAU BLÜCHER: Yes!
FREDERICK: That was your cigar smoldering in the ashtray!
FRAU BLÜCHER: Yes!

FREDERICK: And it was you who left my grandfather's book out for me to find!

FRAU BLÜCHER: Yes!

FREDERICK: So that I would . . .

FRAU BLÜCHER: Yes!

FREDERICK: Then you and Victor were . . .

FRAU BLÜCHER: YES! YES! SAY IT! . . . HE VAS MY BOY-FRIEND!

It wasn't just that I was blessed with an amazingly talented group of actors on *Young Frankenstein*—that alone never guarantees success. As clichéd as it sounds, there was an indefinable chemistry on the set, a magic in the way the ensemble of gifted misfits worked together.

It all started with Gene, who *was* Dr. Frankenstein. He completely understood his character. He was that guy. Gene intuited all my directions. Sometimes all I needed from Gene was either for him to be softer when he was screaming or louder when he whispered, but I never had to give him emotional directions because he knew them already. I think he was truly Promethean in that role. There was madness in his eyes and fire in his performance.

Gene and I got along swimmingly during filming, aside from one big fight. It was about the scene where he and the monster sing and dance to "Puttin' on the Ritz." It was Gene's idea, and I told him I thought it

Cloris Leachman as the unforgettable Frau Blücher. (Horses whinny!)

Staging Madeline Kahn's surprise entrance on the set of Young Frankenstein.

was a great idea and very funny, but it was too far out. I was afraid it might have made the screenplay border on being unbelievable. I insisted that it was too silly and would tear the continuity of the movie to pieces.

Gene disagreed. He said, "It's amazing! It's proof of how incredible Frankenstein's creation is."

We fought and we fought. Our tempers rose and we almost got into a fistfight over it. Then Gene calmed me down and he said, "Okay. Do me a favor. Film it and we'll take a look at it. If it doesn't work, I promise we'll throw it out."

I said, "Okay, I'll film it. We'll test screen it, and if enough people agree with me that it's too silly, then we'll take it out."

I filmed it, and after the reaction at our first test screening I turned to Gene and said, "Gene, you were absolutely right. Not only does it work, but it may be one of the best things in the whole movie."

Gene Wilder as Dr. Frankenstein and Peter Boyle as the monster doing their unforgettable showstopper, "Puttin' on the Riiiiiitz."

I have never been so wrong in my life. I think I ate more humble pie on that day than ever before. Gene was right because it took the movie to another level. We left satire and made it our own. It was new, different, crazy, and had the audience laughing out of control.

On the final day of shooting, after we shot the last scene and everybody had left, Gene sat down on the edge of the bed we used in the scene with him and Teri.

He said, "I've got some more ideas for some other scenes for the movie."

I said, "Gene, it's over. We shot it out. It's got a beginning, middle, and end. Perfect!"

Gene buried his face in his hands and said, "Mel, I don't want to go home. I want to stay here. This is the happiest time of my life."

It really was. I loved everybody who worked on that film, both cast and crew. When we finished shooting, we were all emotional. It was hard to let it go. I knew what Gene was feeling because the movie we had just finished was not only funny; it was also sweet and sad. I think it's easier to make people cry than laugh. Laughter is the true test of your talent. Of course, there are cheap jokes and then there are the more exquisite jokes. A story-point laugh is worth its weight in gold. People can laugh wildly at a movie and then come out and say it wasn't any good, it was cheap laughter.

In *The Twelve Chairs* I served audiences Russian soul food and got big laughs. In *Blazing Saddles* I made a conscious effort to attack racial prejudice while still garnering monumental belly laughs. If the story line doesn't work, the laughs won't work. But I was still mostly going for humor. *Young Frankenstein* was my first attempt at fifty-fifty, laughs and story. It's a love story, and like *The Producers*, it's an emotional give-and-take. After watching *Young Frankenstein* I wanted you to feel emotionally satisfied and have deep affection for the characters and, like us, maybe not want to leave the theater at all.

But I was lucky, because for me the job wasn't over.

I had met John Howard when he was my editor on *Blazing Saddles*. It was a great collaboration and I immediately hired him to work with me on *Young Frankenstein* as well. John Howard was so confident, and he had the right to be. Prior to making *Blazing Saddles*, he edited *Butch Cassidy and the Sundance Kid* (1969). I used him on every movie I could. Normally an editor provides the director with his own "rough cut" of the movie and then the director works with him on a "final cut." John knew not to cut a single frame of the movie without me being there. I wanted both of us to vote on every scene right from the beginning.

(And on the rare occasion that he didn't vote with me, I went with my vote because I'm the director.)

By the time I was in the editing room on *Young Frankenstein*, *Blazing Saddles* had come out and become a huge success. As a result, Laddie and the studio completely trusted me and left me to edit without the interference that most directors get from heads of studios during post-production.

The first cut we put together for a test screening was two hours and twenty-two minutes long. That was pretty long for one of my films. *The Producers* was only eighty-eight minutes. While *Young Frankenstein* ran long, I didn't want to leave out anything that might possibly catch fire with an audience. I screened it at the Little Theater on the Twentieth Century Fox lot for people who worked on the lot. The theater was packed, and we didn't get all the laughs we were aiming for. It went well, but not well enough for me. It was just too long.

When the picture was over, I got up in front of the audience and said, "Ladies and gentlemen, you have just seen a two-hour-and-twenty-two-minute failure. In less than three weeks from today, I want you back here to see a ninety-five-minute smash hit movie. I want every one of you back!"

Editing was both easy and difficult. Easy because when something was supposed to get a laugh and it didn't, I simply cut it. Difficult because I was in love with too many moments and had to cut them for the good of the overall film. Sometimes, you have to kill your darlings.

I worked diligently almost day and night, editing like crazy. In keeping with James Whale, I went back to old-fashioned 1930s editing techniques—the iris outs, the spins, and the wipes. Not only did they lend the film a feeling of authenticity to Whale's era, they also helped me move seamlessly between comedy and art. Sometimes I didn't take a scene out, I just shaved it down to where it was valuable. And sometimes scenes weren't cut, they were just rearranged. There is a lot you can change without reshooting. Hundreds of little pieces of film can be arranged in hundreds of different ways.

Of course, it was more than three weeks later when I reassembled most of that same audience at the Little Theater. It was actually closer to three months later. But I had a cut that was pretty damn good and wanted to show it. It went like gangbusters! Every single scene in the picture worked. The audience not only laughed their heads off, but there was a palpable feeling of sweet sadness when the film ended.

My composer, John Morris, and I were re-teamed for our now fourth film together. I told John to give me a theme that would define the emotion of the film. He came up with a melody that was absolutely beyond my wildest dreams. It's the "Transylvanian Lullaby," and it captured the soul of the monster. John Morris conducted the orchestra recording the score, and when they played the music under the opening title, his "Transylvanian Lullaby," the first violinist Jerry Vinci played an incredibly beautiful obbligato (a counter melody) against the theme. I have to admit, it brought tears to my eyes.

Twentieth Century Fox thought December 1974 was a good time to release the film. We would be piggybacking off the success of *Blazing Saddles*. When Fox told us we would open on December 15 and be up against *The Towering Inferno*, which opened on December 14, and *The Godfather: Part II*, which opened on December 20, it sent shivers down my spine.

But there was no need to worry. The picture was great, our reviews were great, and the audience came out to see it in droves. The studio thought they were maybe going to get in trouble with the big theater chains because *Young Frankenstein* was in black and white. But as Gertrude Stein would say, a good picture is a good picture is a good picture.

For our ads, we once again grabbed the talents of Anthony Goldschmidt and his longtime artistic collaborator John Alvin, who had done the arresting poster for *Blazing Saddles*. They came up with a remarkable poster featuring Gene Wilder as a wild-eyed Dr. Frankenstein and the monster sporting a top hat.

One day I was driving down Sunset Boulevard in Hollywood when I passed a tall structure with a magnificent expanse of blank space on the side. I thought, *What a great place to put up a huge movie poster.* It turned out that the structure was the Playboy Building. So I called the late Hugh Hefner and he graciously allowed us to paint the entire side of the Playboy Building on the Sunset Strip as a billboard for *Young Frankenstein*. It was five thousand six hundred square feet, took eighty-six thousand gallons of paint, and was lit up by fourteen huge klieg lights. It was remarkable; it took your breath away. Every time I drove past, I was in seventh heaven.

This was one of the first times somebody used the entire side of a building as a billboard. Nothing like that had ever been done before, and the only complaint we got was that it slowed down the traffic on Sunset Boulevard!

The reviews for *Young Frankenstein* were wonderful. I was thrilled with Charles Champlin's review in the *Los Angeles Times*:

> The movie may be slapstick, but it is not slapdash. It has been conceived and completed as a coherent whole, done in luminously perfect black and white. Everything, most particularly the music, is poignantly faithful to the spirit of old times. . . . There are Vaudeville jokes that may well be older than Mary Wollstonecraft Shelley herself . . . but they are

Our huge, magnificent Young Frankenstein *poster painted on the side of the Playboy Building on Sunset Boulevard.*

> spaced along a carefully developed story line which is executed by a team of hugely talented comic actors rather than one-lining comics.

Young Frankenstein was a certified hit at the box office and was also released in twenty-one other countries. Not only were we happy for ourselves, but for Laddie as well. *Young Frankenstein*, which he brought in to Fox, helped elevate him and put him in a position to green-light over three hundred films during his illustrious career, including *High Anxiety* (1977), *Star Wars* (1977), *Alien* (1979), *Blade Runner* (1982), *A Fish Called Wanda* (1988), and *Thelma and Louise* (1991).

So looking back at that fateful year of 1974, which started with *Blazing Saddles* in February and ended with *Young Frankenstein* in December, I can honestly say, it was a *great* year.

And I can also honestly say that 1974 was a much better year for Mel Brooks than it was for Richard Nixon.

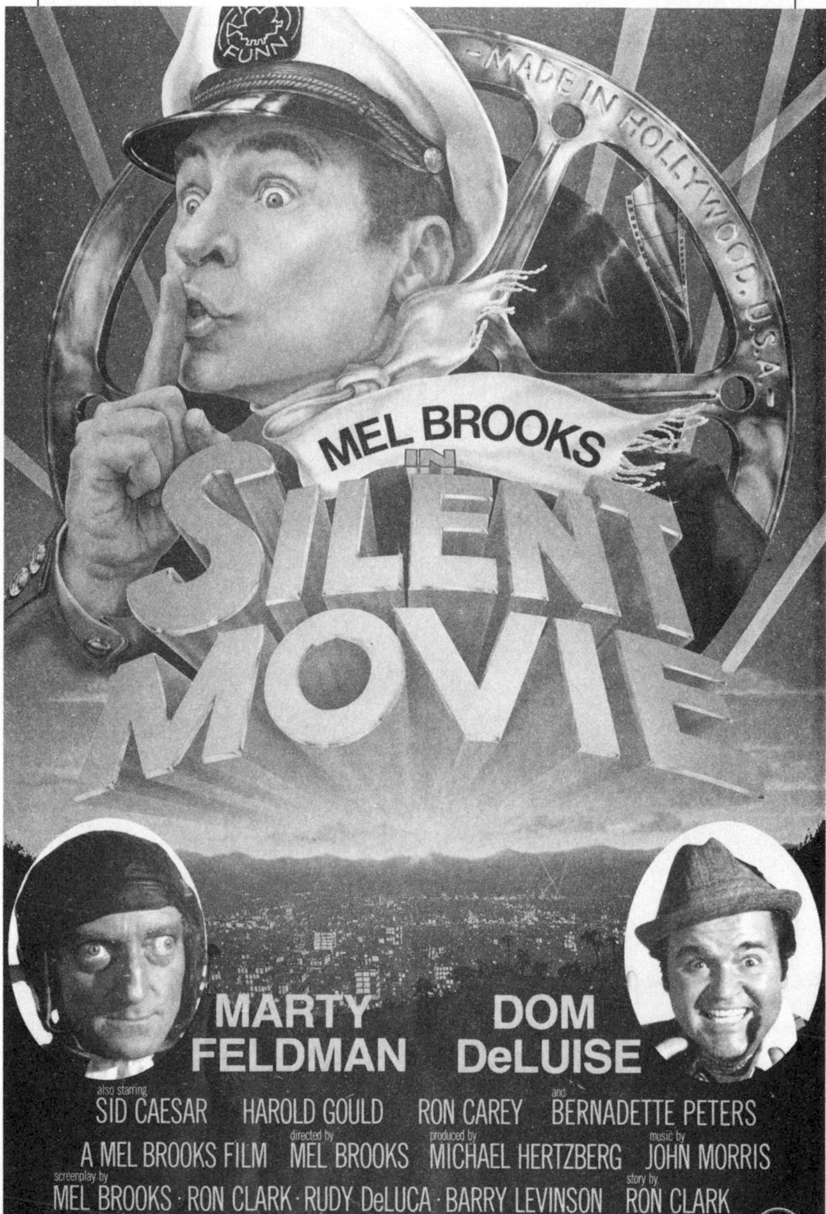

FUNN
-MADE IN HOLLYWOOD. U.S.A.-
MEL BROOKS
IN
SILENT MOVIE
MARTY FELDMAN
DOM DeLUISE
also starring
SID CAESAR
HAROLD GOULD
RON CAREY
and
BERNADETTE PETERS
A MEL BROOKS FILM
directed by
MEL BROOKS
produced by
MICHAEL HERTZBERG
music by
JOHN MORRIS
screenplay by
MEL BROOKS · RON CLARK · RUDY DeLUCA · BARRY LEVINSON
story by
RON CLARK
COLOR BY DELUXE®

Chapter 14

Silent Movie

After *Young Frankenstein* was launched and became a certified hit, both critically and financially, I went in search of my next movie. As luck would have it, I got a call from Ron Clark, a dear friend. Ron was a terrific comedy writer who had written for the famous Jackie Gleason TV show and also wrote a play with Sam Bobrick called *Norman, Is That You?*, which has become a comedy classic.

Ron had a crazy idea for a movie and wanted to talk to me about it.

I invited him to come to the Fox commissary. It turned out to be a most fruitful lunch. Not only did I enjoy my cottage cheese with fruit on top, but Ron's idea was bold and dangerous—I loved it.

He proposed that I make an old-fashioned silent movie in the year 1975.

Even though, like I said, it was a dangerous and iffy idea, I couldn't get it out of my head. It appealed to me on many levels. One, it was wild and different. Nobody had made a silent movie for god knows how long. So in that regard, it was in keeping with Mel Brooks breaking cinematic celluloid ground. I had taken the Western apart in *Blazing Saddles*, and in *Young Frankenstein* I had a party with black-and-white classic horror films. I was satirizing specific genres, but I was also paying tribute to them at the same time. Here was another genre that I dearly loved, and I knew I could have so much fun both satirizing and saluting it at the same time.

When I was a little kid, my older brothers would take me to see Charlie Chaplin, Buster Keaton, and Harold Lloyd in those zany slapstick silent movies. They would have to drag me home. I loved them so much I wouldn't leave the theater.

To this day I remember clearly how much I laughed when Charlie Chaplin was eating his shoe in *The Gold Rush* or brilliantly dancing behind the referee in a boxing match or getting caught up in the huge wheels of machinery in *Modern Times*. Chaplin was truly an amazing all-around cinematic artist. Like Andreas Voutsinas used to say: "Or you got it or you ain't."

Well, in the case of Charlie Chaplin, he certainly got it.

And then there was the angelic face of Buster Keaton, who in *Steamboat Bill, Jr.* (1928) had an entire house fall on him but somehow was standing in the doorway unhurt. And Harold Lloyd famously dangling in midair from one of the hands on a clock face in *Safety Last!* (1923).

I knew it would be a great challenge, but that was also part of its appeal. I loved a good challenge. My first hurdle was selling the idea of making a modern-day silent movie in the year 1975 to Laddie, who was then running Twentieth Century Fox.

"Really? A silent movie?" he said incredulously.

I said, "Yes. Nobody talks. The only dialogue is on title cards, which can be very funny. It's a salute, like what we did with James Whale. This will be a tribute to Charlie Chaplin, Buster Keaton, Harold Lloyd, Mabel Normand, Fatty Arbuckle, Mack Sennett, and the Keystone Kops. All the great stars of silent movies. But it will be funny. Just like *Young Frankenstein* was funny. I won't do anything that's just a salute. It will always be funny."

Laddie said, "So with *Young Frankenstein* you take away color and now you're coming to me and you say you want to make a movie that takes away sound? What else are you gonna take away? If I let you go unrestrained, you're liable to turn Twentieth Century Fox into a vaudeville house!"

I said, "I promise this is the end of my bizarre fight against real films. It will just be *Silent Movie*. It will be the end. After that, I promise I will make regular movies like everybody else."

And so, Laddie agreed.

"Okay, I'm going to finance a script and if I like the script, we'll make the movie."

"Deal!" I said.

Now I had promised Laddie a script. And it had to be a really good script or there would be no money to make the film. Ron Clark came through again and introduced me to two writers from *The Carol Burnett Show* that he thought would be perfect for our *Silent Movie* writing team. They were Rudy De Luca and Barry Levinson.

Rudy was downright funny. Everything he did was funny. Even when he was being serious, he didn't realize he was still being funny. He became a writing fixture in my organization from that point until today, along with performing comedy acting roles in several of my later movies, and he is still a good friend.

Barry was another gift. He had a great movie mind. He had a talent for both character and story and later became an amazingly successful writer/director in his own right. He would tell me wonderfully funny stories about growing up with his friends in Baltimore. I took him to see *I Vitelloni* (1953), Fellini's first film, which is about a group of friends who grow up together in Italy. He wrote the script to *Diner*, his first film, in no time at all and I'm sure *I Vitelloni* helped inspire some of it.

Ron, Rudy, Barry, and I all sat down together to decide what our silent movie was going to be about. I told them that somehow, we should get an engine that pulled our picture along. Something underneath the fun and frolic that drove our movie forward. We came up with a great engine: Money versus Art.

Big commercial companies that had nothing to do with the art of entertainment but were loaded with money were gobbling up old traditional movie studios just for their financial value. I pointed out that Coca-Cola was buying Columbia Pictures, Transamerica now owned United Artists, and Gulf + Western had "engulfed and devoured" Paramount. The bottom line was they had no regard for what kind of movies they were making as long as they brought in money. That would be our premise. Our film would be about an old-fashioned silent movie studio that was in danger of going bankrupt and being taken over by "Engulf and Devour," a huge monolithic commercial company and a sly (or not so sly) reference to Gulf + Western.

Our heroes' mission would be to make a movie that would save their studio, Big Pictures. Their motto was "If it's a big picture, it was made here."

So who would be in it? Fortunately for Gene Wilder but unfortunately for me, Gene decided to do what he had learned from me—writing and directing his own movies. He was busy writing and making his directorial debut in a movie called *The Adventure of Sherlock Holmes' Smarter Brother* (1975). So I couldn't use Gene to be my leading man. Who could I get?

Ron, Rudy, and Barry said, "We found who should be playing the lead in *Silent Movie*."

"Who's that?" I said.

"You!" they answered. "It's about time you used your own god-given gifts as a born comedian."

"I don't know, maybe . . ." I thought about it for a while and then said, "Yes. I'm living with the script every day, and I know just how it should be performed and I know I can do it. But would Laddie buy me as the star who's gonna carry the movie?"

They said, "You won't be the only star. We have an idea."

The idea was to cast the movie with big stars that would guarantee box office by gathering a huge audience. It was a great idea; we could write brilliant comic cameos tailored to their screen profiles.

In addition to that, I would have two really funny comedy buddies along for the ride. I decided on the always hysterically funny Dom DeLuise and the soulful and bizarrely comedic Marty Feld-

Dom, Marty, and me jammed into our little yellow Morgan sports car.

man. They played my sidekicks named Dom Bell and Marty Eggs, who were crammed with me into a tiny convertible yellow Morgan sports car cruising around Hollywood.

Marty's eyes and face and his wiry build made him perfect for a silent movie. Marty was a walking sight gag. In the silent era, Ben Turpin's crossed eyes made him immediately recognizable and put him on the cover of *Life* magazine. I thought Marty with his big protruding hard-boiled-egg eyes was in a way paying homage to Ben Turpin.

Dom DeLuise had the greatest reaction takes in the world. Any time something crazy happened, I just cut to Dom's face, and it told you to laugh. It always worked.

The plot was simple: The three of us as a director and his two sidekicks would go on a quest to convince big stars to be in a picture that would save the studio.

We described my character, Mel Funn, on a title card that read:

Mel Funn, once Hollywood's greatest director, till drinking destroyed his career, is trying to make a comeback. He has a brilliant idea for a new movie.

For my love interest we decided on Bernadette Peters, a multitalented Broadway star. With a brushstroke of serendipity, I had just seen her perform on Broadway as Mabel Normand, the great silent movie star in *Mack & Mabel,* and she was terrific. What could be more perfect? She hadn't yet broken into film, so she was in keeping with my talent for discovering new faces. She was a triple threat and was born to be in movies.

To play the head of Big Picture Studios I turned to my mentor and still one of the funniest actors in the world—the incomparable Sid Caesar. There was something very fulfilling about having Sid

With Bernadette Peters in a classic Silent Movie *pose.*

play the studio chief. It was an important part; the actor playing the head of Big Picture Studios had to be as funny or maybe funnier than anybody else in the movie. The role fit Sid like a glove. Not only was I sure he would nail it, but I also felt that I had found a way to pay him back for all he had done for me and his faith in me when I was an unknown kid from Brooklyn who was just starting out.

Our script was kind of a real-life script:

MEL

Don't worry, Chief, I'll save the studio!
I've got your next hit picture right here!

CHIEF

What is it? . . . A Musical? A Love Story? A Western?

MEL

It's a SILENT MOVIE!

It can't miss; it's a silent movie!

Sid's studio chief was just like Laddie, who nearly collapses with disappointment when he's told that the movie we're going to make to save the studio is a silent picture. When our characters tell him they are going to get big stars to ensure an audience, he is dubious (again just like Laddie!) but bravely goes along with it. And just like Laddie, he tells us that if we get the stars, it's a go picture.

So it's either art imitating life or life imitating art. I'm not sure which but I knew one thing: We had to get big stars or it was a no go.

The first one was easy: I asked my wife, Anne Bancroft, to play herself.

. . . At first she frightened me by saying, "Let me think about it."

When she saw my expression, she broke into laughter and said, "Of course!"

We wrote a musical number for Anne based on the ever-popular Spanish song "Jealousy." It was a crazy number in which Dom DeLuise does a furious flamenco tap dance on a tabletop, driving it into the floor. With Marty, Anne did an amazing thing with her eyes where she moved the right one to the center and back and then with the left one did the same. Marty followed suit with his own wild eyes. The bit really worked.

Anne Bancroft and Marty Feldman in Silent Movie. *The eyes have it.*

The next star was James Caan, the unforgettable Sonny Corleone in Francis Ford Coppola's *The Godfather* (1972), who at the time, happened to live only a block away. I would often run into him on our morning runs.

(I was actually running in those days!)

When I told Jimmy about *Silent Movie,* he thought it was a great idea and immediately said, "Count me in."

He also told me that his dog had just given birth to five new pups and said, "If you need or want a dog, come over and pick one out."

Anne and I took him up on that. We went to his house and one of the pups left the pack and made his way over to us. So instead of picking out a pup, he picked us!

We called him Pongo, after Pongo the main dog in Disney's *One Hundred and One Dalmatians* (1961). He was tan with a white chest and two white front paws. We had no idea that we were getting a pit bull terrier. We just thought he was beautiful. Later we were worried that he would do what pit bulls are stereotyped for doing, but he never ever bit anyone and was a sweetheart of a dog.

Enid, our housekeeper who would sometimes walk him, had an extra-long leash because when he saw other dogs, he wanted to know them in a hurry. So she'd quickly wrap the long leash around a sturdy palm tree so she wouldn't go sailing after him.

Our son, Max, was a toddler then and he absolutely loved Pongo. He'd often thrust the end of a beach towel into Pongo's mouth and then hang on for dear life, screaming with laughter at the top of his lungs while Pongo dragged him across the living room's shiny wooden floors at sixty miles an hour.

Pongo had one habit that used to drive me crazy. When we lived just north of Sunset Boulevard in Beverly Hills, the roof of our living room was close to a hill. Pongo would climb up the hill and jump onto the roof! No matter what I did, no matter how much I begged and pleaded, he wouldn't come down. But Anne had a magic secret. Cheerios! He loved Cheerios. She'd shake a box of Cheerios and he'd come flying down.

Pongo lived with us for a long, long time—almost fifteen years. And I still miss him.

Back to *Silent Movie*, the next star we went after was Burt Reynolds. I knew that he was good friends with Dom DeLuise so I asked Dom to make the pitch to Burt. And it worked! Burt came over to talk about what he would do in the picture.

I proposed a few things, but he cut me off and said, "Why don't I play myself? A big egotistical movie star!"

I loved the idea.

We talked about the fact that he actually had BR monogrammed on everything in his house—shirts, ashtrays, towels, even his door handles. I suggested, in keeping with his ego, we put his name in two-foot-tall letters right on top of his house—movie fans couldn't miss it! He loved the idea. We also added a bit about him not being able to pass a mirror without stopping and adoring his own wonderful face.

In Burt's scene, we see him in his stall shower happily soaping himself up. When suddenly, Dom, Marty, and I rise from the bottom of the frame and appear right next to him. We take over the job of soaping him up and scare the hell out of him! But in the end, he falls hook, line, and sinker for starring as Burt Reynolds in the movie within the movie. He was terrific.

Our next star happened to be eating in the commissary at the table right next to us at Fox. I was having lunch with the writers, Barry, Rudy, and Ron.

Rudy kept saying, "Look! Look!"

"What? What?" I said.

Rudy cupped his hand and whispered, "There! Sitting right there at the next table is Liza Minnelli!"

Talk about good luck! Without being invited, we all moved to her table and never stopped talking about our crazy silent movie until she broke into laughter and said yes.

In the movie we decided to do the same thing, except that Dom, Marty, and I would be in suits of armor as Knights of the Round Table, but still eating in the commissary. We spot Liza Minnelli and try to get to her table to ask her . . . but it's not an easy thing to do in armor and chain mail.

The scene was hysterical. Liza kept breaking up in the scene by laughing every time one of us fell down, and we kept that in the final cut of the movie. Having her in the movie was wonderful.

Our final star cameo was really a huge star at that time—the great Paul Newman. I found out that he loved a beer called St. Pauli Girl. So I sent him ten cases of it, together with a letter that explained why I wanted him to guest star in our film. We knew that Paul was an avid racing fan, and even drove his own race car in real high-speed races.

We explained that we wanted to do a wheelchair chase, and we would find him as he sat in a wheelchair recovering from a racing-car mishap. We had motorized wheelchairs and it was ambitious and a little crazy if not actually dangerous. But he went for it! He loved the idea of speeding ahead of us in his motorized wheelchair. In a P.S. response he explained that I didn't have to send him those ten cases of St. Pauli Girl beer to get him to say yes—but he wasn't going to send them back, just in case my check bounced.

Shooting the Paul Newman wheelchair chase scene was one of the happiest on-set movie experiences of my life. We actually sped flat out doing our best to catch him in his chair, but we never could. Really! He was too damn good.

Every once in a while, I would hear a crash of wheelchairs followed by Marty Feldman's cockney-accented voice shouting, "I'm all right, love!"

Silent Movie also gave me an opportunity to work with enduring comedy icons that I had loved all my life. There were a number of classic bits that were even funnier in the silent format.

Fritz Feld was the ever-present headwaiter in every fancy dining room scene ever filmed. In order to summon another waiter, he would make a popping sound by slapping his hand against his open mouth.

So in *Silent Movie* when he did that, we gave him a title card that said just one word:

POP.

For Fritz Feld aficionados it was spot-on.

We did another version of a classic burlesque bit with Henny Youngman, known for his ever-popular groan-worthy one-liners. We see a van speeding along which reads ACNE PEST CONTROL and on top of which is their logo, a huge plastic fly. As the van approaches a corner it nearly collides with a passing truck. The driver hits the brakes, and the van with the fly on top comes to a screeching stop just in time. But it completely unhinges the huge fly, which sails through the air and lands at an outdoor café table where Henny Youngman is having lunch.

The giant fly almost hits Henny, but lands on his table. He shouts to the waiter via title card:

Waiter, there's a fly in my soup.

There was another bit starring Harry Ritz of the Ritz Brothers, one of my comedy idols. The godfather of physical comedy. You could see where Danny Kaye, Jerry Lewis, and Sid Caesar all got their wacky faces and funny moves from. When I called Harry, he was actually flattered, and thrilled to be a part of our movie. In his scene we see a custom-made tailor shop window with a brown-paper-and-cardboard-stitched cutout of a tuxedo showing us how exquisitely their tailor-made suits are constructed. From the doorway exits Harry Ritz, doing his famous Ritz Brothers crazy walk and proudly wearing the same cutout paper-and-cardboard-stitched suit that we saw in the window.

My last stroke of genius was actually getting the world-famous mime Marcel Marceau to utter the only word we would hear in *Silent Movie*.

In a title card Dom, Marty, and I are on the telephone. On the other end is Marcel Marceau.

Our title card reads:

Monsieur Marceau, we're begging you!
Would you please be in our silent movie?

We cut to Marcel Marceau, who utters the only real line of dialogue in the entire film: *"NON!"*

NON!

The best thing about directing actors in a silent film is that you could shout directions as they were acting, and it wouldn't ruin the shot. We weren't recording any sound. The same way I didn't shoot *Young Frankenstein* in color out of an abundance of caution, here we had no sound-recording devices whatsoever. The crew could laugh as loud as they wanted to! No white handkerchiefs this time around.

I even directed the film with a megaphone to my mouth like they really did in silent movies. I'd shout, "Wave your arms! Bigger gestures! C'mon! We're in a close-up, widen your eyes! Bernadette, show us you're really in love! Give us more!"

I had a ball. It was the most fun I ever had directing a movie. I loved working with my crews and had developed a reputation of having a joyful set and this was no exception.

The final script of *Silent Movie* was the film the public saw, except for a brief sequence that never made it into the film. It was called

Here I am on a camera boom directing a movie starring me as a movie director.

"Lobsters in New York," and it starts with a restaurant sign that reads CHEZ LOBSTER. Inside, a huge lobster in a maître d's tuxedo is greeting two very well-dressed lobsters in evening dress and leading them to a table.

(Already we thought this was hysterical.)

Then a waiter lobster in a white jacket shows them a menu that says "Flown in Fresh from New York." They get up and follow the waiter lobster to an enormous tank, where a lot of little human beings are swimming nervously around. The diner lobsters point to a tasty-looking middle-aged man. The waiter's claw reaches into the tank. It picks up the man, who is going bananas, and that was the end of the scene.

We loved it; we thought it was an inspired turn-about-is-fair-play concept. But when we screened it, it didn't get a single laugh. An absurdly funny almost genius idea, but no laughs. So out it went! Because the final judgment was always left up to the audience, no matter how I felt about it. If it was supposed to be funny and it didn't get laughs, it went the way of all the misfires that preceded it, onto the cutting-room floor.

Since there was no dialogue in *Silent Movie*, music was even more important than in any of my other films. The music became the rhythm of the picture. There was no verbal rhythm to play against or into. John Morris once again rose to the occasion. In our now fifth collaboration, John composed more original music than for any other Mel Brooks movie. It was all big orchestra in big combinations. We were trying to resurrect an old genre without falling back into old clichés. John was very careful not to use a single note of the inevitable silent movie piano in any of the score. His exuberant, upbeat score complemented the naïve good cheer and good hearts of the three protagonists: Mel, Marty, and Dom, three unstoppable innocents in pursuit of a vision of making a silent movie and the box office stars with which to populate it. From the upbeat "Silent Movie March" to the narcissistic, lush Hollywood theme "At Burt Reynolds's House," John Morris was never better.

Silent Movie was released on June 17, 1976, and did surprisingly well at the box office. Roger Ebert, the well-known film critic of the *Chicago Sun-Times,* wrote:

> There's a moment very early in "Silent Movie" (before the opening credits, in fact) when Mel Brooks, Marty Feldman, and Dom DeLuise are tooling through Los Angeles in a tiny sports car. They pass a pregnant lady at a bus stop. "That's a very pregnant lady!" Brooks says (on a title card, of course, since this is a silent movie). "Let's give her a lift!" The lady gets into the back of the car, which tilts back onto its rear wheels. Mel drives off with the front wheels in the air.
>
> This is far from being the funniest scene in a very funny movie, but it helps to illustrate my point, which is that Mel Brooks will do anything for a laugh. Anything. He has no

> shame. He's an anarchist; his movies inhabit a universe in which everything is possible and the outrageous is probable, and *Silent Movie,* where Brooks has taken a considerable stylistic risk and pulled it off triumphantly, made me laugh a lot.

Privately I was very worried about the effrontery to do a silent movie in 1976, but that review calmed all my fears.

In December 1976, the Exhibitors of America had placed me fifth on their annual list of the twenty-five stars that exert the greatest box-office appeal. I was very proud of that, especially since this was my first starring role and one where I didn't even speak!

Burt Reynolds was rated sixth that year. He had to put up with picking up the phone at his home and hearing me announce, "Hello, Six. This is Five speaking."

So in the end, this crazy idea of doing a silent movie was a success and I could look our studio head Laddie in the eye and not be the object of an "I told you so."

Many years later in 2011, the silent movie *The Artist* won a well-deserved Oscar for Best Picture. When I met Michel Hazanavicius, the brilliant French director who made the film, I praised his movie, and then I teased him with, "It's in black and white *and* it's silent; who knows, I might have unconsciously shown you the way with *Young Frankenstein* in black and white and then with my own *Silent Movie.*"

With your permission, let me digress. I had that conversation with Michel Hazanavicius at one of my regular Friday lunches, which started around 1999. *Young Frankenstein* producer Michael Gruskoff and I had lunch on the outdoor patio of a now closed famous restaurant in Beverly Hills called Orso, where a lot of celebrities gathered to dine. We were reminiscing about our wonderful years on the third floor in the executive building at Twentieth Century Fox. Mike had a beautiful dog back then that used to come to work with him, an Irish setter called Lightning. Also on the third floor with us was a talented producer named Marvin Worth, who made some terrific films like *Lenny* (1974), *Malcolm X* (1992), and Carl Reiner's unforgettable *Where's Poppa?* (1970). Marvin was a sharp dresser and always sported a lot of gold chains. I used to joke that when I heard a lot of jangling chains in the hallway, I never knew whether it was Gruskoff's dog Lightning or Marvin Worth. They both jingled and jangled all the way up the stairs!

We had such a good time remembering those days that I suggested that Mike call all the Fox alumni that were still with us and try to set up a weekly lunch at Orso. So Michael went to work and at our next lunch we were joined by our beloved former leader, our studio chief Alan Ladd Jr. (whom we still called Laddie) together with his trusted right-hand man from those Fox days, Jay Kanter.

I've told you a little about Laddie, now let me tell you a little bit about Jay. Jay Kanter was an important decision maker at Fox, but he was also one of the greatest agents ever. In his heyday, he represented Marlon Brando, Grace Kelly, and Marilyn Monroe. A show business trifecta that no one would ever match. But it never went to his head. He is the sweetest, most self-effacing, humble guy that ever lived. At every lunch we would all bombard him with questions about Marilyn Monroe's private life, but Jay would *never* spill the beans.

Soon our Friday lunch table grew to include another notable former resident of the third floor at Fox, the gifted writer/director Paul Mazursky. I first met Paul when we both had offices opposite each other at Fox and he was working on *An Unmarried Woman* (1978). He was an incredibly good neighbor because he would come over and spill his troubles and worries to me, and I would spill all my doubts and fears to him. We would buoy each other up with false statements and lies. He would just walk into my office, sit down on my desk, and say things like, "So what's it all about,

Alfie?" He was worldly like that. The only criminal activity I could accuse him of was when he sat on my desk he could somehow read all my private correspondence, even though from his point of view it was upside down. One of the great things about all of Paul's movies is that they never seem to be written or made up. They felt like they sprang from real life. Films like *Next Stop, Greenwich Village* (1976), *Blume in Love* (1973), and especially *Bob & Carol & Ted & Alice* (1969), where the dialogue flowed so naturally. Paul was a terrific filmmaker. His films were so earthy and rich in human nature that I used to call him our American Fellini. But Paul had his quirks and peccadillos; he was given to bouts of angry contretemps. If I ever mentioned that I won an award like the Screen Laurel Award, which the Writers Guild bestows on writers for advancing the art of the screenplay, he would go bananas. He'd scream, "Why not me! Why the heck did they give it to you?" So at our Friday lunch I was careful to tell everybody not to mention any current award I was being given, or Paul would blow his top and maybe even grab a knife off the table and kill me.

Lunch after lunch the table grew; old industry vets who have since passed on, like the wonderfully hands-on and supportive Fox executive Gareth Wigan and super agent Freddie Fields, began to join us. A word about Freddie Fields—he was the most incredibly persuasive talent agent that ever lived. At his funeral I said, "If Freddie Fields couldn't talk Death out of doing him in, what chance do we have?"

For some reason I decided to pick up the check for lunch that first time, and I just continued to do that for every lunch thereafter. I felt that since I started this thing, I might as well pay for this thing. The only rub in this routine was Mazursky; he was the only one who always ordered a dessert—and an expensive dessert at that—key lime pie, baked Alaska, or even a flaming bananas Foster! But you know I'm kidding; he passed away in 2014 and I miss him and his expensive desserts to this day.

As the years went on, we added more wonderful people to our table. Like Fred Specktor, a CAA agent who filled us with fabulous stories about how crazy deals got made and the nutty behavior he experienced at the hands of studio execs on power trips. But that was not the only thing he filled us with; his wife, Nancy, is an incredible baker and supplied the table with truly magical homemade chocolate chip cookies to have with our coffee. He has often asked us if he would still be invited if Nancy didn't supply those great cookies. To which we all lied, "Of course!"

Another luncheon attendee is my music lawyer, Jay Cooper, perhaps the smartest musical legal mind in the business. Before Jay was a lawyer, he was also one of the best alto sax players in the music business, playing behind famous superstars like Bobby Darin, Nat King Cole, and the one and only Frank Sinatra. He'd often regale us with stories about the trials and tribulations and laughs he had making records with those legends. When my beloved lawyer Alan U. Schwartz retired, Jay took over all of my legal needs. (I paid him back with lunch!)

Also at the Friday lunch table for many years was famous veteran movie director Richard Donner, Dick to his friends. Unfortunately, he passed away recently and has left a real gap at the lunch table. We all miss his buoyant and mischievous spirit. I actually met Dick before he started directing movies when he directed an episode of *Get Smart* that I wrote way back in 1965. Since then, Dick directed such exciting blockbuster movies as *Superman* (1978), *The Omen* (1976), four *Lethal Weapons*, and the cult classic comedy adventure film *The Goonies* (1985). Years after Dick started coming to lunch, one of the kid actors that he cast in *The Goonies*, Jeff Cohen, graduated from law school and ended up becoming an entertainment lawyer. Fans of the movie would remember him as that cute heavyset little guy called "Chunk." So when Dick asked if "Chunk" could be a regular member of the table we said, "Let's give him a try!" Needless to say, we all liked him, and he passed the test.

Jeff isn't the only "younger" lunch attendee; another great addition to the luncheon conversation is a familiar face to all of you who watch Turner Classic Movies—their talented TV host, Ben Mankiewicz. Ben had interviewed me many times for Turner Classic Movies events, and his love and knowledge of movies was absolutely contagious. So it was a no-brainer to ask him to be part of our lunchtime showbiz roundtable soiree. He is a great contributor.

Every once in a while, we have a special guest, like the aforementioned Michel Hazanavicius and his lovely actress wife and star of *The Artist*, Bérénice Bejo. When *My Favorite Year* star Peter O'Toole was in town, he would also join us. Mike Gruskoff had produced a French movie called *Quest for Fire* (1981) that was directed by Jean-Jacques Annaud, so whenever Jean-Jacques was in town he was always invited. The same went for Bernardo Bertolucci, the famous Italian director of such films as *1900* (1976) and *Last Tango in Paris* (1972).

One of our semi-regular guest diners was Norman Lloyd, who believe it or not, lived to the remarkable age of one hundred and six years old! Norman had a storied acting career doing theater with Orson Welles, and then maybe being best known for his role as the evil villain in Alfred Hitchcock's famous black-and-white classic *Saboteur* (1942).

If you saw the movie, you would remember the scene: Robert Cummings, our hero, is gripping the sleeve of Norman's tweed jacket as Norman's body dangles from the top of the Statue of Liberty, a hundred feet above the ground. The camera slowly moves along his arm and comes in for an extreme close-up at the jacket's armpit. One after another we see the stitches holding the jacket together start to *pop . . . pop . . . pop!* After a tense twenty seconds the sleeve separates from the armpit and Norman's agonized face breaks into a howl of despair as he disappears down out of frame. Oh, that Hitchcock! Oh, poor Norman.

Anyway, thank god it was only a movie and Norman went on to not only act for Hitchcock but to later become a director for Hitchcock on his classic TV series *Alfred Hitchcock Presents*. When Norman ate with us, he would casually throw out names like "my friend Charlie" that was his doubles partner for tennis. Unbelievably, he was talking about Charlie Chaplin! And he and Charlie were playing doubles against United Artists founders Douglas Fairbanks and D. W. Griffith. Norman was always good for a remarkable story. On his last visit he told us a story of watching a ballgame featuring Babe Ruth, who tore his pants sliding into second base and the fans had to wait twenty minutes while they sewed his pants up right there on the spot.

Okay, digression over! Let's get back to where I was.

Chapter 15

High Anxiety

The writers of *Silent Movie,* Ron Clark, Barry Levinson, Rudy De Luca, and I, were still all hanging out together and having fun. So I said, "Let's just do another one."

I had paid homage to the Western, the horror picture, and silent movies. They said, "Let's do another genre movie."

I don't know who came up with it, but someone suggested Hitchcock.

"Yes! Hitchcock!" I said. "Alfred Hitchcock. He *is* a genre. Don't we refer to all his movies as Hitchcock films? He's even coined a term describing his cinematic style: Hitchcockian!"

I was a fierce devotee of Alfred Hitchcock. He could do anything—drama, comedy, tension, suspense, excitement, and beauty. He had the amazing ability to cut the film in his mind. He didn't waste time shooting a lot of film and then choosing the right takes. His movie-editing mind was like a Moviola, Avid, and computer combined. He saw the movie as it progressed scene after scene until it arrived at one of his climactic endings. He was, film for film, probably the best movie director that ever lived.

"Let's look at all his films and create a crazy story in which we incorporate every memorable scene from his movies we've ever enjoyed with our own comedy twist," I said.

They all agreed, and we were off to the races.

When we had a rough draft of the script, I decided to make my momentous call to Alfred Hitchcock. If he didn't like the idea, if he said no, I probably would have abandoned the whole notion. His secretary answered and I said, "Could you tell Mr. Hitchcock this is Mel Brooks? I make movies and I'd just love to talk to him."

He gets on the phone. I don't know what to say. I just start babbling, "Hello, Mr. Hitchcock? This is Mel Brooks."

And before I could say another word, he cuts me off, "Is this really Mel Brooks? I love your films. I loved *Blazing Saddles*. It's absolutely miraculously funny."

"Coming from you that really means more than I can say." And then I said, "I have to ask you something really important to both of us, but mostly to me. My last film was a genre film, *Silent Movie,* and before that I did a genre film all about the West, *Blazing Saddles,* and a horror genre film, *Young Frankenstein*. And for my next genre film, I want to do Hitchcock. You, sir, are an entire genre. You are the Hitchcock genre. And I'll say it till the day I die: You're the most talented and the best director who ever lived. And I want to salute you with a comedy that includes a faithful but satiric look at some of your most memorable scenes from your films."

He said, "Well, why don't you come to my office at Universal on Friday at twelve forty-five? I'm having roast beef with Yorkshire pudding for lunch. I'd love it if you could join me."

"Yes, sir, I'll be there with bells on."

When I came into his office on Friday, I had bells hanging around my ankles and shook them. He laughed out loud. I brought him what we had outlined of the script, and he looked through it and said, "Interesting. Very interesting. I think this will work."

As he continued reading, he gave me some wonderful pointers on what he thought was more important, and then not so important. The things he thought would work, and stuff he thought was not worth exploring. Then he said, "Come over every Friday. I'll make time for you and take a look at where you are in the script."

Wow, I couldn't believe it! Dutifully, I was there every Friday for pointers from the great Alfred Hitchcock . . . as well as a free lunch!

On one of those occasions he said, "I've got a joke for you. Maybe you could use it?"

And then he told me the following: "Our hero is running from someone who's trying to kill him. He's running full tilt, full speed. The killer is right behind him and closing in. He comes to a dock and sees a ferry. The space between the ferry and the dock is about eight feet. He leaps with all his might and comes crashing to the deck of the ferry. He just makes it. But unfortunately, instead of going out, the ferry is coming in."

It was really funny, but I could not find a place in the script to use it. (And I never told him it was much too expensive to shoot.)

Over the weeks we became pretty good chums. He was just wonderful. He was like a silent partner. He would give me notes on the script and what he thought I should push. We would eat lunch after, which was set up in the next room. It was always a beautifully prepared meal. I could smell the roast beef and the roast potatoes, the succulent aromas emanating from the adjoining dining room. At that point in his life, Hitch had arthritis and problems with his knees. So unfortunately, one day he was in the doorway between his office and the luncheon room and got kind of stuck there. I don't know what possessed me, but I had a crazy comedy urge and I acted on it. I banged my knee into his tush and said, "Come on, Al. Get moving. We're hungry!"

I immediately realized, *What have I done?*

And then he just broke out into a big laugh. He said, "You naughty boy."

He loved it. I think he enjoyed my basically crude Brooklyn humor. He liked the juxtaposition of it against his proper English background.

Hitch was also very funny. His films used a lot of dark humor to heighten the tension. In *North by Northwest* (1959), when Cary Grant's Roger Thornhill is being led away by the two enemy agents, no one believes he is being threatened. His mother asks the agents, "You gentlemen aren't *really* trying to kill my son, are you?"

Out to dinner with Alfred Hitchcock at the famous Chasen's restaurant in Los Angeles. (Hitch paid.)

Everyone starts laughing and the joke is on his mother.

In *Rear Window* (1954), Jimmy Stewart asks his editor, "Gunnison, how did you get to be such a big editor with such a small memory?"

And the editor comes back with, "Thrift, industry, and hard work, and also catching the publisher with his secretary."

I think he understood that I wasn't going to make fun of him. If the picture is a send-up, it's also an act of homage to a great artist. Hitchcock could really manipulate an audience's emotions; he could go from light comedy to stark drama. I was inspired by his genius. As a matter of fact, I dedicated the film to him.

It read like this:

This film is dedicated
to the Master of Suspense
Alfred Hitchcock

For the basic movie that would house all his unforgettable scenes, we decided on a takeoff of a wonderful Hitchcock thriller *Vertigo* (1958). In particular, we borrowed scenes from Hitchcock's *Spellbound* (1945), *Psycho* (1960), *The Birds* (1963), and *North by Northwest* (1959). But we were careful to structure the script in a way that would make narrative sense even to an audience entirely ignorant of Hitchcock's work. It had to work on its own as a good, funny comedy.

We called our picture *High Anxiety,* and I would be playing the new head psychiatrist of a place we called "the Institute for the Very Very Nervous." My character was called Dr. Richard H. Thorndyke and in the movie when he's asked what the H stands for he says, "Harpo, my mother was a big fan of the Marx Brothers. She loved Harpo."

As the *High Anxiety* script took shape, we also thought a lot about casting. For the main villains of the piece, I hired two inspired comic talents, Harvey Korman and Cloris Leachman. Harvey had done such a terrific job in *Blazing Saddles;* I was always looking for how I could use him again. The same goes for Cloris, who was the iconic Frau Blücher in *Young Frankenstein*. As Dr. Charles Montague and Nurse Diesel, they were stuffing the institute with perfectly sane people that they were making crazy and turning it into an enormous cash cow for themselves.

In one scene with Harvey as Dr. Montague, Harvey's line and his timing were so brilliant that I nearly broke up and ruined the take. It goes like this: I ask Harvey, "Can you tell me the rate of patient recovery here at the institute?"

Harvey replies, "Rate of patient recovery? I'll have that for you in a moment." He reaches into his pocket and whips out a small handheld calculator. He taps it once or twice and then says, "Once in a blue moon."

I don't know how I held it together.

When Cloris showed up to shoot her first scene as Nurse Diesel, she was wearing a nurse's uniform with two large, pointed breasts like a Teutonic Valkyrie in Wagner's "Ride of the Valkyries." At first, I thought that was going overboard, but then I realized she was doing a take on Nurse Ratched from *One Flew Over the Cuckoo's Nest* (1975), which was really perfect. And then I noticed what I thought was a faint mustache under her nose.

When I said, "Cloris, do you realize that in a close-up we can see that you have a mustache?"

She said, "Yes, I know. I put it there."

"Fine," I said. (Who was I to argue with the great Cloris Leachman?)

Dick Van Patten played an innocent and hapless psychologist, Dr. Wentworth, who is going to spill the beans, but before he can, Montague and Nurse Diesel get rid of him in a horrific scene in which he's trapped in his car as the radio (which he can't turn off) plays a loud rock song called "If You Love Me Baby Tell Me Loud" which gets louder and louder until his eardrums burst. It was a very scary scene, which Dick pulled off perfectly.

I met Dick when the two of us played tennis at Merv Griffin's ex-wife Julann Griffin's home. We went on to become close friends. One of the most interesting stories about our friendship involved an emergency call I got from him. Dick was in his home in Sherman Oaks when he became dizzy and unstable. He thought he was having a stroke. He managed to fumble his way to his telephone. His first instinct was not to call a doctor, but to call a comedian. He dialed my number. I picked up the phone.

Dick said, "I've got a problem."

I said, "What's the matter?"

He said, "I think I'm having a stroke. My whole arm is tingling, and now it's going to my leg."

I started yelling at him, "Get to an emergency room! Call the emergency room!"

It turned out it wasn't a stroke, but just a passing seizure. When people would later ask him, "Why on earth would you call Mel Brooks when you think you're having a stroke?"

He responded, "Maybe I was just looking for one last laugh on the way out."

My old friend and colleague from *Your Show of Shows*, our third banana Howie Morris, played my mentor, who I named Dr. Lilloman, which was just a funny shortening of his description "little old man." Like having Sid Caesar in *Silent Movie*, having Howie Morris in *High Anxiety* gave me a nice feeling of repaying old friends for helping me get to where I was.

Directing the opening airport sequence of High Anxiety.

Another wonderful comic actor was Ron Carey, who played Brophy, my sidekick in the film. Edward Brophy was a character actor in the 1930s and '40s. He always played a sidekick or henchman against William Powell or Edward G. Robinson in a lot of Warner Bros. and MGM movies. His character would say things like, "Gee, boss, I couldn't find a cab anywhere."

The brim of his hat was always up. As opposed to Lee Tracy and Warner Baxter, other actors of that time, whose brims were always down. (You have to know who wore hats with the brim up or the brim down.)

Ron was laugh-out-loud funny in the opening scene when he meets me, his new boss, at the airport. He grabs my large trunk and begins to lift it to get it into the back of the car. In the famous scene he says, "I got it! I got it! I got it! . . . I ain't got it."

It crashes to the ground. He does it again and then again, always with "I got it! I got it! I got it! . . . I ain't got it."

Finally, after the third "I ain't got it," I pick it up and put it in the car. Lots of people have told me they quote the "I got it! I got it! I got it! . . . I ain't got it" line from the film in their own lives whenever they have to pick up something heavy.

Ron Carey as my sidekick, Brophy:
"I got it! I got it! I got it! . . . I ain't got it."

For the love interest I naturally once again turned to the marvelous Madeline Kahn, who did a great takeoff of Kim Novak, one of the well-known "Hitchcock Blondes." Madeline came up with a brilliant idea; not only would she be carrying an expensive Louis Vuitton handbag, but she would be dressed in a jumpsuit made of matching Louis Vuitton material, and to top it all off, she would arrive in a Cadillac Seville that was entirely covered in the Louis Vuitton design. It tickled me no end! Her character was called Victoria Brisbane, whose father was Arthur Brisbane, a patient held captive by our money-hungry villains. Which brings me to an interesting story. Albert Whitlock, who had never been an actor, played Madeline's father, Arthur.

I met Albert Whitlock in Hitchcock's office when Hitch suggested that Whitlock could do for me what he did for him. He could create wonderful "matte paintings." They are panes of glass on which scenery and settings are painted, leaving the center of the glass free for the camera to shoot through. So when the film was put together our heroes were surrounded by what looked like a beautiful pictorial setting that would have cost a fortune to actually go on location to get. But through the talents of Albert Whitlock and his magic paintbrush, we could go or be anywhere and save a fortune! Albert painted "the Institute for the Very, Very Nervous" and put it on a big cliff overlooking the ocean. We were actually shooting at Mount St. Mary's College, which was nowhere near the ocean, but in the opening shots of the movie it looked spectacular.

Upon meeting Whitlock, I liked his look and his mild English accent. So I cast him as Madeline's rich father, who was trapped in the institute.

At first, he said, "No, no. Out of the question. I'm not an actor. I can't do that."

But I eventually wore him down. I explained that he only had ten or twelve lines to say in the whole movie, and that afterward, he'd have something to show his grandchildren. I also thought it was a good inside joke that I could spring on Hitchcock.

As the script came along, we also found natural parts for my fellow writers, Ron Clark, Barry Levinson, and Rudy De Luca. Ron Clark played Mr. Zachary Cartwright, a recovering patient due to soon be released from the institute. He comes to my office for a final checkup. With me was Harvey Korman as the wicked Dr. Montague. In the scene, a seemingly recovered Cartwright turns insane again before my very eyes because unseen behind my back is the devious Harvey Korman, scaring the hell out of him with fake vampire teeth and a rubber band shooting paper clips into his neck. I was so alarmed by his loud screams every time a paper clip hit him from Harvey's rubber band, that I immediately sent him back to his room. Ron, who was a wonderful writer but certainly not an actor, actually pulled it off!

Barry Levinson, on the other hand, was not only a terrific comedy writer, but also a pretty good actor. He took to the part of Dennis the high-strung bellboy as if he'd been acting all his life. I named him Dennis after Dennis Day, who was a regular on the Jack Benny radio show. Jack Benny had a running bit where he would call for Dennis Day to do his song with Jack's famous catchphrase, "Oh, Dennis? It's time for your song."

We cast Jack Riley, who like Dick Van Patten I used in many of my films, to play the front desk manager. Jack Riley (just like Jack Benny) said, "Oh, Dennis? Can you take Dr. Thorndyke to his room, please?"

Barry (as Dennis) collects our bags and dutifully takes Brophy and me to the bank of elevators. The hotel we chose, the Hyatt Regency, had a brand new lobby, replete with perfect glass elevators that would terrify my character, Dr. Thorndyke, because unbeknownst to the other characters, but well knownst to the audience, he has an enormous fear of heights. (Hence the title, *High Anxiety*.) As the elevator rapidly ascends you can see my character having a bad anxiety attack, not helped by Barry as Dennis in his high-pitched voice chanting, "Here we go. Straight to the top! Quite a view, isn't it? Here we are. Top floor. Top of the hotel. You can't get any higher! We're pretty high!"

Somehow, I keep it together. On the way to the room I remind Dennis in an insistent tone, "I want that newspaper. It's very important!"

And he curtly replies in a slightly hysterical voice, "All right. I'll get your paper. I'll get your paper!"

Which leads to one of the most important scenes in the movie. Shot by shot I begin to re-create Hitchcock's famous shower scene from *Psycho*. Instead of Janet Leigh's naked back, you see Mel Brooks's naked back. And just as Hitchcock did in *Psycho,* we cut to the showerhead bursting with hot water. Through clouds of steam, we see past the translucent shower curtain to the bathroom door beginning to open. As the famous Bernard Hermann's memorable score for *Psycho* builds ominously, we see a figure with an arm raised approach the shower. And again, faithfully shot by shot we see the shower curtain ripped open and instead of the wacky mother with a huge knife from *Psycho* we see our wacky bellboy Dennis stabbing me with a rolled-up newspaper and in a crazy high-pitched voice he screams, "Here! Here! Here! Here's your paper! Here's your paper! Here's your paper! Happy now? Happy? Happy now!"

And then as I fall just the same way Janet Leigh did, I pull the curtain and all the little rings that held up the shower curtain pop one by one. Instead of blood, the dark print from the newspaper slowly trickles down the drain.

When I showed Hitchcock this scene, he first corrected me by saying, "You're two rings short on the shower curtain, but you're absolutely remarkable on your using newsprint for blood going down the drain."

High praise indeed, coming from the Master of Suspense himself.

Rudy De Luca turned out to be a marvelous addition to the movie. He asked if he could play the killer, and if he could wear aluminum teeth to make his evil smile and laughter crazier. I agreed; he was an inspired choice. One of the things he did that really tickled me was that as he was ominously stalking me from the end of the hotel bar, he was having a highball topped with a little Japanese umbrella.

Together Rudy and I did a phone booth scene, which was one of the funniest bits in the movie. We built a pay phone booth that overlooked the Golden Gate Bridge, which was a salute to Hitchcock's famous shot of the bridge in *Vertigo*. It starts with me calling Madeline in her hotel room, but when I begin to speak, Rudy smashes the phone booth glass behind me and wraps the telephone cord around my neck. Madeline just hears me making strange sounds and gets the wrong idea. She thinks it's one of those weird, inappropriate phone calls. The strange sounds begin to turn her on and she says, "I am not going to listen to any more of this, I mean, I've had just about enough! . . . What are you wearing?"

As Rudy's still choking me, I manage to squeak out, "Jeee! Jeee!"

And Madeline, obviously excited, responds with, "Jeans? You're wearing jeans? I bet they're tight."

Madeline's sexy enjoyment of the "dirty phone call" made the scene hilarious. When I fight Rudy off and he is unwittingly stabbed by a huge shard of glass I'm finally able to talk.

Rudy De Luca as "Braces" trying to choke me to death. Unfortunately, it was hard to say "Cut!" with the phone cord wrapped around my neck.

When she knows it's me, Madeline quickly switches from heavy breathing to utter reality saying, "Richard! I knew it was you all the time. Did you laugh? I laughed."

Madeline was also wonderful in a scene at the hotel piano bar. Like I have done with most of my movies, I wrote the title song: "High Anxiety." I decided that I would sing it in the movie. I found a perfect spot for it in the hotel's piano bar. The genial piano player asks me to sing something, but I explain I'm a doctor not a singer . . . although I do sing in the shower. Madeline urges me to sing a song. I ask the pianist, played by the wonderful comedian Murphy Dunne, if he knows "High Anxiety."

It's amazing; in a flash I go from being a conservative psychiatrist to Frank Sinatra. Handling the microphone like only Frank would, I flip the mic cord over my shoulder as I sing and move around the crowd like I've done it all my life. When I come to the

Singing the title song, "High Anxiety," and handling the microphone like I think I'm Frank Sinatra.

second chorus, instead of singing *"High anxiety . . ."* I belt out *"Oooh 'ziety . . ."* à la Sinatra. I don't think I've ever had so much fun performing in a film. To this day I often sing it onstage when I'm doing my act. I've always been a closet singer, but with this film I came out of the shower.

As always, I brought John Morris in from the beginning to craft the score, which was a tribute to Bernard Hermann, Miklós Rózsa, and all the other composers in Hitchcock's repertoire. We wanted the audience to recognize the familiar suspenseful terrain and ambience. There was not one piece of music I could refer to from Porter, Gershwin, Bartók, or Berlioz that John Morris didn't know. He loved music as much as I did. As he usually did, John used my title song as a main theme for the score. And when I sang it, he came up with a perfect orchestration; it was pure Nelson Riddle.

Before we started filming, I had watched every Hitchcock film over and over again. And one strange thing occurred to me: In addition to all the great characters that Hitchcock peopled his films with, he also seems to cast the camera as another one of his characters, endowing it with a mind of its own. While filming *High Anxiety* I tried to emulate that as well as the way Hitchcock often moved his camera in slow, stealthy push-ins, and yet still add a satiric Brooksian touch. One good example is a slow camera move from outside into the institute's dining room through a glass door. Slowly but surely, the camera gets closer and closer to the dining room. Unfortunately, it doesn't stop, and crashes through the glass door. Everybody in the dining room—myself, Harvey, Cloris, Dick Van Patten, etc.—all look to where the camera crashed through the glass. The camera guiltily withdraws, absolutely mortified by its mistake. The cast goes back to eating as if nothing happened. It always gets a great laugh.

Another camera twist was a scene where Harvey and Cloris are hatching a plot to destroy Dr. Thorndyke, who's a threat to their evil scheme. It's shot at a Hitchcockian angle from beneath a glass coffee table and the camera again develops its own personality. As Cloris puts her coffee cup on the glass table, temporarily blocking our camera's view of the actors, the camera moves to get a better view of our villains. Now Harvey puts his coffee down and once again the camera, obviously highly annoyed, moves away to see the action. The scene continues for another minute and then finally the camera is completely frustrated when Cloris puts a huge tray of apple strudel down, which completely covers the entire table. The camera quits in disgust. (I think Hitchcock liked that one a lot.)

One of the funniest and most memorable scenes in the whole

film was the *"North by Northwest"* corner of the Golden Gate Park scene in which I flee from a scary attack by *"The Birds."* A group of them gather on the nearby jungle gym and then proceed to chase me and pelt me with droppings. Our prop department found the pigeon wrangler who actually trained the birds for *The Birds*, and they got fifty or sixty trained pigeons to fly on cue. They made a mixture of spinach and mayonnaise to look like bird poop, and then loaded it into squirt guns and shot at me from above the pigeons, out of frame. By the time the scene ended my suit, my hair—everything was completely covered. Unfortunately, it wasn't just mayonnaise and spinach, some of the pigeons decided to contribute to the realism of the scene by unloading on me. Sometimes when a movie is over, I get to keep my wardrobe. Now you can understand why I didn't take any of my wardrobe home from *High Anxiety*.

Strangely enough, the title *High Anxiety,* which I had come up with, went on to become a well-known phrase in our lexicon, as if it was a real medical term. In 1990, years after the movie came out, I saw the term splashed across the cover of *Time* Magazine. It was a story about Wall Street with a photo of Harold Lloyd hanging from the clock in *Safety Last!* (1923). I said to myself, "There is no 'high anxiety.' I made it up. It's not real. It's not a medical term or a psychiatric term. It's not a real condition. It's just anxiety with the word 'high' in front of it!" But I wasn't going to upset the apple cart. If the world thinks "high anxiety" is a real thing, let it be real. Who am I to argue?

High Anxiety premiered on December 25, 1977. At that premiere screening, Hitch sat right next to me. I had my own high anxiety awaiting his reaction. He didn't laugh. He just sat and he watched. He only broke up once. When the birds let go and plastered me with their droppings, then I could see his shoulders shaking. When the film was over, he got up and walked out. He didn't say he liked the picture. He didn't say he hated the picture. He didn't say anything. He just left.

I was devasted. And really worried.

I did not take this suit home for obvious reasons. (The dry cleaning would have been too expensive!)

Not long after, when I came into the office, there on my desk was a huge box covered with silver paper and red ribbon. I tore the paper open and underneath was an impressive wooden case with a label that read: CHATEAU HAUT BRION 1961. I opened it to see six big, beautiful magnums of Chateau Haut Brion 1961. A priceless gift of one of the finest wines ever made.

There was a note:

> My dear Mel,
>
> What a splendid entertainment, one that should give you no anxieties of any kind.
>
> I thank you most humbly for your dedication and I offer you further thanks on behalf of the Golden Gate Bridge.
>
> With kindest regards and again my warmest congratulations.
>
> Hitch

Needless to say, all my worries disappeared. If there was one person in the world I really wanted to like the picture, it was Alfred Hitchcock, and god bless him, he did. And as a thrilling bonus, I could now refer to him as "Hitch."

Hitch knew something not everyone knew—that I had become a devotee of fine wines and had a wine cellar featuring some really classic vintages. I don't know a lot, but I do know a lot about wine. (I'm not bragging. It's just a fact.)

I fell in love with wine when I went to dinner one night at Gene Wilder's house in the Village over fifty years ago. Up until then I thought wine was made by Manischewitz—a sweet wine that Jews drink on Passover. I had no idea what was in my mouth when Gene poured me a glass of wine at that fateful dinner. All I knew was that it was NOT Manischewitz, and that it was sublime.

"What is this wine?" I asked him.

He said it was Nuit-Saint-Georges, a French pinot noir from a sub-region of Burgundy's Côte de Nuits. All I can tell you is that it was a profound taste revelation!

ALFRED HITCHCOCK

March 1, 1978

My dear Mel,

What a splendid entertainment, one that should give you no anxieties of any kind.

I thank you most humbly for your dedication and I offer you further thanks on behalf of the Golden Gate Bridge.

With kindest regards and again my warmest congratulations.

Hitch.

Here is the note that Alfred Hitchcock sent me, along with that beautiful case of wine.

Ever since that night I have loved good red wine. Often French, sometimes Italian, and occasionally something delicious from the Napa Valley. And if I go to a Passover dinner, I bring a bottle of my own wine. No more Manischewitz for this guy!

I never got around to going as far as planting grapes and establishing a Mel Brooks vineyard. But funnily enough a couple of guys who make wine up in Napa Valley named Scotti Stark and Michael DeSantis created a wine they dedicated to a signature phrase from *Blazing Saddles*. In the movie, when making a speech as the governor I expect a very big affirmative response from the audience and when I don't get it I angrily point to a man in the crowd and say, "I didn't get a HARRUMPH out of that guy!"

They seized on that word and with my blessing made a beautiful cabernet sauvignon called Harumph. So if you're disappointed when you don't get a "harrumph" out of your audience, you can always buy a great bottle of Harumph wine instead.

Chapter 16

Brooksfilms

High Anxiety was actually the start of a new chapter in my career. Not only was I writing it with my co-writers, directing it, and starring in it, but for the first time I was also the producer. It was a natural outcome of overseeing my movies at every stage from script to screen. By this time, I was closely following their distribution and taking a hand in advertising, publicity, and where and how the film was being released.

In order to do all this, I needed help. When I told Anne that I needed someone to assist me in this new job of producing she immediately said, "I've got the guy."

Stuart Cornfeld joined me as my assistant producer on *High Anxiety* and became a part of my team. My wife had met Stuart when they worked together at a new program she was involved in called the Directing Workshop for Women at AFI, the American Film Institute. In addition to working with me, Stuart was also helping Anne develop her first film as a writer/director, *Fatso*. Anne was going to write it, star in it, and direct it. It was about an overweight Italian man whose sister is determined to get him to lose weight so he can be healthy. Anne would play the sister and Dom DeLuise would play the brother. Anne wrote the *Fatso* script specifically for Dom, who was a good friend of ours at that point. It was very close to her heart because she was from an Italian family and knew better than anybody how wacky, funny, and touching their behavior could be.

It was a lucky day for both Anne and me when we found Stuart. When Laddie agreed to green-light *Fatso* at Twentieth Century Fox, Anne asked Stuart to produce it. It was to become the first film of my new company, Brooksfilms.

Why Brooksfilms? Well, because I had a problem. If the name Mel Brooks was on a movie screen, the audience would expect to see a Mel Brooks comedy. It was Pavlovian! Ring the bell, and the dog salivates. Put the name Mel Brooks on the screen, and the audience is already laughing.

I remembered a thought that Max Liebman, the producer of *Your Show of Shows,* espoused one day in the writers' room. He said, "Sometimes what makes you breaks you." In a strange way, that thought was coming home to roost. What was helping me gain ascendance in comedy was also limiting me because the name Mel Brooks meant "expect to laugh," which constrained me as far as making films that were not meant to just make you laugh but to make you experience a whole range of thoughts and feelings.

Which brings me back to *Fatso,* which was not only comedic but was sometimes a serious and heartbreaking story. I loved Anne's script and I wanted to get it made, but I had to be careful not to put my name on it because I didn't want to mislead the audience into thinking it was a laugh riot. Or steal undeserved credit for something that belonged solely to Anne. So even though I was the producer of the film, I assiduously kept my name off the screen. Brooksfilms was formed so that I could produce films that were more serious. I didn't want to be trapped into only making comic fare for the rest of my life. I wanted to help produce any and all movies that touched me, inspired me, and deserved to be made. *Fatso* was the first.

I have worked with producers all my life. For the most part, I had great relationships with my producers, starting with Sidney Glazier, through Mike Hertzberg, Michael Gruskoff, and of course my great friendship and partnership with Laddie at Twentieth Century Fox. That certainly prepared me to be a producer myself because I knew every single issue and struggle a writer and a director had to go through to make a film. The challenge for me was to find and nurture talented filmmakers. At this point in my life, I knew real talent when I saw it. The second and most important challenge for me was to hold back. I was so used to managing every aspect of production, from the initial idea, the first time a pencil touched a piece of paper, all the way through to the final cut, what the audience got to see on the screen. I had to figure out a balance, how to help and manage the process, without suppressing anyone else's creative vision. And Brooksfilms was the answer. I helped where help was needed, and was hands off when I realized I might be interfering in the filmmaker's vision. When I first opened Brooksfilms, my motto, my mission statement, was "Give talented people room to express their vision."

Unlike many producers, I tried not to micromanage. As a director, I worked hard to keep producers out of the editing room, because they would want to make changes. As a producer, I wanted to create a space where writers and directors could thrive without the producer's heavy hand. When I directed, my writers were always on the set with me. We wrote something together and rewrote it and I always solicited their opinions. Sometimes I took their advice and sometimes I didn't. But I always encouraged opinions and I always listened to what was offered.

Brooksfilms was a big undertaking and needed to be staffed with smart people who understood what was needed to make a good picture. Before I go further let me tell you about two people who were unsung heroes in Brooksfilms's success. The first was Leah Zappy, who started as Anne's assistant on *Fatso*. Leah was recommended to me by Stuart Cornfeld, and after *Fatso* was finished, she quickly became both my and Brooksfilms's chief cook and bottle washer—managing every aspect of day-to-day production. Who would have dreamed that that would be the beginning of an invaluable twenty-nine-year relationship? Leah later became a post-production supervisor and associate producer on many of my movies and is to this day a wonderful friend.

The other person who came on board around this time was Randy Auerbach, daughter of the famous Boston Celtics coach Red Auerbach. (By the way, she turned us all into Celtics fans.) Randy was recommended by Jonathan Sanger and Mark Johnson, who were my first and second assistant directors on *High Anxiety*. She started as my assistant and later transitioned to developing many successful Brooksfilms pictures—the first of which came to me from the aforementioned Jonathan Sanger.

Hollywood has always worked in mysterious ways. How and why a movie comes to the screen is always a quirk of fate. It seems that Jonathan's babysitter had a boyfriend who was a screenwriter, and his name was Christopher De Vore. And he and his writing partner, Eric Bergren, had written a screenplay called *The Elephant Man*. It is the beautiful and true story of Joseph Merrick, an Englishman born with severe deformities in the 1800s, who uses his disfigurement to earn a living as "the Elephant Man," performing in carnival "freak shows." A sympathetic doctor, Frederick Treves, takes Joseph in and helps him to fit in and become a member of regular society. When I finished reading the screenplay I was deeply moved by the story and told Jonathan that I wanted Brooksfilms to make it.

I had a clear challenge: How does a guy who has gained a reputation as a top comedy filmmaker garnering some of his biggest laughs with cowboys sitting around a campfire and loudly farting go on to make such a serious, dramatic, and touching film as *The Elephant Man*? Again, like with *Fatso*, Brooksfilms was the answer. I knew that if the Mel Brooks name was up there, at the first shot of the Elephant Man, the audience would be ready to laugh, which would've been so very wrong for such a poignant story. So once again not to confuse the audience I carefully kept my name off the screen.

I assembled my team: Jonathan Sanger would join Brooksfilms as the producer, Stuart Cornfeld would be the executive producer, and Randy Auerbach acted as Brooksfilms' researcher and project manager. We had the script and now we needed a really gifted director who could bring it to the screen.

Stuart took me to the Nuart Theatre, a small out-of-the-way movie house on Santa Monica Boulevard known for showing different films like John Waters's *Pink Flamingos* (1972). We went there because Stuart was bugging me to see the work of this guy, a new director on the block called David Lynch, and his new film *Eraserhead* (1977). It was a beautiful film, and like I wanted *The Elephant Man* to be, it was in black and white. It was weird and crazy, but in the end for a novice filmmaker it was a wonderful picture.

I still couldn't really believe that this was the director for *The Elephant Man,* but Stuart was convinced. So I met with David Lynch. He'd only meet at one place, a restaurant called Bob's Big Boy, where they served hamburgers and milkshakes. It was way out in the Valley. When I first saw him I thought, *Am I meeting David Lynch or Charles Lindbergh?* He had on a white shirt buttoned all the way to the top and was wearing a worn leather aviator's jacket. I wasn't expecting David to be so polite, but he wasn't blowing smoke—he was genuine. He was an artist in his own right, and I was impressed with his work. He had read the script and he was very savvy about how he thought it should be directed and about certain changes in the script that he wanted, which all seemed spot-on to me. It was the outsider aspect of the story that appealed to him. And that's where we met mentally and creatively. I've always loved a story where the "against the odds" leading character prevails.

Before I hired him, I wanted to see how he would get along with the writers. The next thing I did was have story conferences with David, Christopher, and Eric. They bonded immediately and quickly accepted David's vision of how the film should progress. Even though he was unknown and that would make raising the money more difficult, I knew he was the perfect choice to be the director of *The Elephant Man*. I can honestly say I'm giving myself a pat on the back for braving the unknown and making the right decision.

But most of the studio heads weren't nearly as brave. I got a resounding barrage of no's from almost every studio in town. The notable exception was Paramount Pictures, run at the time by future Disney chief Michael Eisner. Michael told me that he had read the script overnight, and when he finished it, he was brought to tears. Eisner and Paramount signed on to distribute the film. I will be forever grateful for studio heads like that.

David Lynch's casting choices were superb. The title character, the Elephant Man, was a nearly impossible role to cast. But we found him. Together—David and I and Jonathan and Stuart—all agreed that the brilliant John Hurt was the only actor in the world to play the Elephant Man. I remembered specifically his remarkable performances first in a TV movie called *The Naked Civil Servant* as leading character Quentin Crisp, who was openly gay at a time when that was dangerous behavior in the UK, and then also his unforgettable role as Caligula in the epic miniseries *I, Claudius*. His acting blew me away.

Quickly the rest of the cast came together after that. For Dr. Treves, who saves the Elephant Man from a terrible existence, we got the wonderful Anthony Hopkins, who I remembered being so outstanding as young Prince Richard in *The Lion in Winter* (1968). Wendy Hiller was marvelous as the head nurse who tenderly sees to the needs of the Elephant Man when many others in the hospital are frightened by him. We got the terrific Freddie Jones to play the wickedly brutal Bytes, the keeper of the Elephant Man. For the austere hospital governor Carr Gomm we were lucky to get Sir John Gielgud, who was usually too busy playing parts like King Lear on the Old Vic stage to do anything as lowly and frivolous as a movie.

A fun note . . . almost every day on set at the end of filming the great actor Ralph Richardson (known for his roles in movies like H. G. Wells's *Things to Come* [1936], *The Fallen Idol* [1948], and later unforgettably as Olivia de Havilland's stern father in Henry James's classic *The Heiress* [1949]) would pull up on his big BMW

John Hurt as "the Elephant Man" playing Romeo with Anne Bancroft as elegant British actress Mrs. Kendal playing Juliet. Their scene blew me away.

motorcycle, blow his horn, and shout, "Hey, Johnny! I'm here!" He was referring to Sir John Gielgud, his best pal. Sir John would wave goodbye to us and hop on the back of Ralph's motorcycle and off they sped—two of the best actors that ever lived.

There is a scene in *The Elephant Man* in which an acclaimed British actress comes to visit John Merrick. It is one of the most touching scenes in the film. I donated the services of my Oscar-winning wife, Anne Bancroft, to play the actress who reads Shakespeare with John Hurt as the Elephant Man. Upon first seeing him, the actress is shocked by his disfigured appearance, but quickly and skillfully hides it and takes our breath away when together they read the classic eloquent scene from Shakespeare's *Romeo and Juliet*. Anne's performance was absolutely transcendent.

The first day of shooting with David Lynch was in October 1979 on Butler's Wharf on the South Bank of the Thames River just east of London's Tower Bridge. It was a chilly day, and David Lynch had arrived earlier on the set without a coat. I sent somebody to Harrods department store with David's measurements and bought him a warm, dark blue, brushed woolen English overcoat. He wore it every day—I'm not kidding. Every day! Whether he was indoors or outdoors, every time he directed a scene for *The Elephant Man* he was wearing that blue coat. I think he might have believed it was some kind of good luck charm.

Many years later in 2013, when I was awarded the American Film Institute's prestigious Life Achievement Award, among the celebrated filmmakers that honored me that night was David Lynch. When he told the story of how we had met on *The Elephant Man* he actually brought out onto the stage with him the blue coat that I had bought for him at Harrods, which he had carefully tucked away in his cedar closet all these years. I can't tell you how touched I was at the sight of that coat.

Some highlights from *The Elephant Man* that stay with me are, for one, Freddie Francis's outstanding black-and-white cinematography, and, for another, John Morris's exceptional score. It's one of the most moving film scores that you'll ever hear. He seems to capture the beautiful spirit that lived in the Elephant Man's soul. I think it was one of John Morris's best musical achievements.

The Elephant Man premiered on October 2, 1980, and among the wonderful notices it received was a review in *The New York Times* by one of America's foremost film critics, Vincent Canby. Let me give you a few excerpts from his insightful review:

> The physical production is beautiful, especially Freddie Francis's black-and-white photography. . . .
>
> The chief of his admirers is the actress, Mrs. Kendal, played in her best grand-lady style by Anne Bancroft, in scenes that are surprisingly affecting. . . .
>
> Mr. Hurt is truly remarkable. It can't be easy to act under such a heavy mask. . . .
>
> "The Elephant Man," which opens today at the Coronet, is the first major commercial film to be directed by Mr. Lynch, whose only previous feature is "Eraserhead," a cult movie

> I've not seen but which, apparently, is also about an outsider. The new film was written by Christopher De Vore and Eric Bergren, with the later participation of Mr. Lynch. It's a handsome, eerie, disturbing movie. . . .

The Elephant Man went on to capture eight Academy Award nominations: Patricia Norris for Best Costume Design; Stuart Craig, Robert Cartwright, and Hugh Scaife for Best Art Direction; John Morris for Best Original Score; Anne V. Coates for Best Film Editing; Christopher De Vore, Eric Bergren, and David Lynch for Best Screenplay Based on Material from Another Medium; John Hurt for Best Actor in a Leading Role; David Lynch for Best Director, and producers Brooksfilms and Jonathan Sanger for Best Picture. Of course, I was very disappointed that we didn't win any, but my spirits soared at the BAFTAs (the British Academy Awards) when *The Elephant Man* took home the prized award for the best film of the year and they also recognized John Hurt as the Best Actor in a Leading Role.

I was so successful at keeping my name off of *The Elephant Man* credits that to this day people are astonished to learn that my eponymous film company produced it—but I am happy to tell them all about it because I am still so very proud of it.

Chapter 17

History of the World, Part I

Let me tell you how *History of the World, Part I*, the seventh movie that I wrote and directed, came to be. Because of the sheer genius of Albert Whitlock's skill at painting cinematic backdrops (which I had just used in *High Anxiety*), I began to think I could go anywhere in the world with my movies, all while I stayed right at home. I could tell stories that took place anywhere, in any time period, without ever leaving Hollywood.

Hence, *History of the World, Part I* was born.

I had always wanted to make a grand movie, a spectacle. I thought that the history of the world would be the perfect vehicle and the most colorful backdrop for this particular endeavor. D. W. Griffith and Cecil B. DeMille have always been movie-making giants to me. Griffith's credits go back to 1908. He was a filmmaking pioneer who made great films like *Orphans of the Storm* (1921), *Way Down East* (1920), and of course the classic *The Birth of a Nation* (1915). DeMille made big sprawling historical epics like *Cleopatra* (1934), *The Crusades* (1935), *The Plainsman* (1936), *Union Pacific* (1939), and *The Ten Commandments* (1956). I think I learned more about the events that shaped the world from watching those movies than I ever did in history classes at school. So somewhere in my mind, *History of the World, Part I* was a tribute to their cinematic art.

That said, my first loyalty was always to comedy. Nothing can burst the balloon of pomposity and dictatorial rhetoric better than comedy. Comedy brings religious persecutors, dictators, and tyrants to their knees faster than any other weapon. Since my comedy is serious, I've always needed a serious background to play against. There was nothing more serious than the Spanish Inquisition. Poking fun at the grand inquisitor, Torquemada, is a wonderful counterpoint to the horrors he committed. The Roman Empire was an example of "might makes right," wonderful stuff for my twisted mind to play with. And the French Revolution showed better than any other period the incredible difference between the haves and the have-nots.

We've all been taught history in school by well-meaning teachers using well-meaning textbooks, but we all know a lot more about human nature than history books tell us. So I embellished a little more about these famous people and these famous events and maybe all their untold secrets. I wanted to expose their foibles and to show that they were not really such historical big shots.

At the beginning of my career as a comedy writer, I usually worked with other writers. But with *The Producers* I found my own feet and wrote it all by myself. *The Twelve Chairs* was based on a book, so I didn't need any other writers. But it's very lonely, sitting and writing for months all by yourself. I never got used to that. I was used to *Your Show of Shows*, at least five guys and gals in a room, pitching, running, screaming, fighting, and laughing. So *Blazing Saddles* was like going back to the writers' room on *Your Show of Shows* and *Caesar's Hour*.

But now once again, I trusted myself to write the screenplay without engaging any other writers. I decided to do the job all by myself. Instead of one long plot, *History of the World* would be a series of different scenes from different periods of history. I decided I would start with the dawn of man and go from cavemen to the Bible, to the Roman Empire, to the Inquisition, and end with the French Revolution.

History of the World, Part I begins with the beginning of mankind. I decided to have fun with the caveman. And who could be funnier as a primitive caveman than Sid Caesar? I made him the first caveman to discover art. I thought it was appropriate to have my artistic mentor be the first person to create the first cave painting on a cave wall.

The script reads:

> Even in most primitive man, the need to create was part of his nature. This need, this talent, clearly separated early man from animals who would never know this gift.

So Sid shows his amazing painting to the first caveman critic, who promptly urinates all over it. Sid's expression tells us what the creative artist has suffered to this very day.

Rudy De Luca also played one of the cavemen. Sid tries out a new weapon called "the spear." He hurls it through the air, and it finds its way into Rudy De Luca. It works! Sid celebrates; the whole cave celebrates! Everybody is so happy about the invention of the spear . . . everybody, that is, except Rudy De Luca.

From the caveman period I entered the biblical era. I decided I would play Moses delivering the Ten Commandments to the people of Israel. My take on it was that there were originally Fifteen Commandments housed in three huge stone tablets.

I start the scene by saying, "The Lord, the Lord Jehovah, has given you these Fifteen . . ."

BAM! At that point I drop one of the stone tablets and it comes crashing to the ground at my feet. I quickly cover by saying, ". . . Ten! Ten Commandments!"

It always gets a huge roar of laughter.

Another of my favorites from the biblical period was my recreation of Leonardo da Vinci's famous painting of the Last Supper. I asked John Hurt, who was so wonderful as the Elephant Man, to play Jesus, and without hesitation he flew over to do the part.

I cast myself to play a waiter at the last supper. I gave myself

Me as Moses, going from the original fifteen commandments down to the now popular ten.

some funny lines like addressing the disciples with, "Are you all together, or is it separate checks?"

John Hurt and I developed a wonderful bit together. When things went wrong and I didn't get the order straight, in frustration I would utter, "Jesus!"

And John Hurt as Jesus would respond with, "Yes?"

And I'd say, "Yes? What yes?"

And he'd say, "What?"

We had to do it several times because the actors playing the disciples would always break up and ruin the take. But we finally got a good one.

Our set photographer captured the scene beautifully. It looked exactly like Da Vinci's *The Last Supper* except for me holding a big silver serving platter (which looked like a huge halo) behind John Hurt's head. It so happened that at this time my wife Anne's parents, Millie and Mike Italiano, had come to visit and were staying with us in California. I put a copy of that set photo of *The Last Supper* in their guest bedroom. They were both good Catholics and loved the picture—never noticing me as the waiter holding the silver platter!

The Roman Empire section of the movie was filled with very talented actors like Dom DeLuise as Emperor Nero, Madeline Kahn as Empress Nympho, Shecky Greene as Marcus Vindictus, Rudy De Luca as Captain Mucus, Bea Arthur as the unemployment office clerk, Henny Youngman as a pharmacist, Howard Morris as the court spokesman, and Ron Clark and Jack Riley as Roman soldiers. Overall, I think I had more comics in *History of the World, Part I* than maybe any other movie ever made. Needless to say, they were all wonderful in their roles.

I played Comicus, a stand-up philosopher at Caesars Palace. For the exterior of the palace, I indulged myself in a private joke and used the hotel exterior of Caesars Palace in Las Vegas. Richard Pryor was signed to play Josephus, the palace wine steward and my sidekick and buddy. Next to me it was the biggest part in the

And here's me as a waiter at the Last Supper, right behind John Hurt as Jesus. I'm no art critic, but I kind of like this version better than Da Vinci's.

Roman Empire section. We were supposed to shoot on a Monday, and the Friday before, we got terrible news. Richard was suddenly taken to the burn center at Sherman Oaks hospital after he had a bad accident at home. I rushed over to the hospital to see him. He was in sad shape. The doctor assured me he would recover, but it would be in a few months. I was so relieved to know he would eventually be okay.

But what to do, what to do? No Richard Pryor for Monday's shooting.

I called in the cast of the Roman Empire and explained the situation. There would be no shooting on Monday. We were all depressed, but Madeline Kahn saved the day. She told me all about this actor she'd recently worked with in New York. His name was Gregory Hines, and he had just gone solo after working with his dad and brother in their act "Hines, Hines and Dad." She raved about his dancing and his winning personality. She thought he could step right in and play the Richard Pryor role, Josephus.

I immediately called Gregory and he was on a plane the next day. It was an amazing turn of fate, just like the Gig Young episode where Gene Wilder flew out to save me in *Blazing Saddles*. Madeline wasn't wrong—Gregory Hines was sensational. When Gregory as Josephus the wine steward begins to pour a decanter of wine into Empress Nympho's (Madeline Kahn's) wine goblet he says, "Say when."

She immediately responds with, "Eight-thirty."

Gregory's take brought down the house. We even opened the role to include a part where he could show his wonderful dancing. Another great bounce!

Albert Whitlock not only created magnificent matte paintings for the Roman Empire with backgrounds like the Roman Senate and the Colosseum, he also once again did a bit part for me in the role of a used-chariot salesman. Kicking the tires of a chariot, he shouts, "Chariots! Used chariots! Low mileage. They're great!"

There were moments in the Roman Empire that tickle me to

this day. One of them is Bea Arthur as the unemployment office clerk. We see a line of ancient Roman unemployment benefit seekers. Here's how she addresses the guy in line just before me:

CLERK (BEA ARTHUR): Occupation?

MAN: Gladiator

CLERK: Did you kill last week?

MAN: No

CLERK: Did you try to kill last week?

MAN: Yeah.

CLERK: Now, listen; this is your last week of unemployment insurance. Either you kill somebody next week or we're going to have to change your status. You got it?

MAN: Yeah.

And then it's my turn.

CLERK (BEA ARTHUR): Next! Occupation?

COMICUS (ME): Stand-up philosopher.

CLERK: What?

COMICUS: Stand-up philosopher. I coalesce the vapor of human experience into a viable and logical comprehension.

CLERK: Oh, a bullshit artist!

Bea was great.

Another laugh that I remember was Ron Carey as my agent, Swiftus Lazarus, who calls me nuts. He says, "You are nuts! N-V-T-S, nuts!"

The audience also got a big kick out of my depiction of the Roman Senate. The leader of the Senate, played wonderfully by John Myhers, addresses the Roman forum with:

LEADER OF SENATE: O fellow members of the Roman Senate hear me. Shall we continue to build palace after palace for the rich? Or shall we aspire to a more noble purpose and build decent housing for the poor? How does the Senate vote?

The funny and talented cast of "The Roman Empire" in History of the World, Part I. *Left to right: Gregory Hines as Josephus, Mary-Margaret Humes as Miriam, Howie Morris as the court spokesman, Dom DeLuise as Emperor Nero, me as Comicus, Ron Carey as Swiftus, Madeline Kahn as Empress Nympho, Shecky Greene as Marcus Vindictus, and Rudy De Luca as Captain Mucus.*

The entire Senate rises to its feet and shouts:

ENTIRE SENATE: F**K THE POOR!

I also remember two Roman senators speaking on their way to the forum. One of the senators was played by my lawyer Alan U. Schwartz, and the other by Jay Burton, who was a dear friend and one of Bob Hope's top comedy writers.

Alan as the first senator says, "*Sic transit gloria.*"

And Jay replies, "I didn't know Gloria was sick?" A cheap laugh, but a laugh's a laugh.

When the idea to do a musical version of the Spanish Inquisition hit me, I thought it might be too much of a risk. Was I sticking my chin

Me as Torquemada, leading a chorus of inquisitors singing, "We know you're wishin' that we'd go away, but the Inquisition's here, and it's here to stay!"

out a little too far? I mean after all, the Spanish Inquisition was a terrible period of persecution and horror for the Jews of that time. But the challenge of taking big risks and pulling it off was always kind of thrilling. I couldn't resist. I immediately called Ronny Graham, my musical partner in crime. In less than two weeks we came up with a terrific and dangerous song called "The Inquisition."

A short example, here's how it starts:

CHIEF MONK (PHIL LEEDS): [spoken]
All pay heed! Now enters his holiness Torquemada, the Grand Inquisitor of the Spanish Inquisition!
Torquemada; do not employ him for compassion
Torquemada; do not beg him for forgiveness
Torquemada; do not ask him for mercy
. . . Let's face it, you can't Torquemada anything!

Then as Torquemada I enter, sliding down a circular slide into view and begin to sing:

TORQUEMADA: [singing]
The Inquisition, let's begin
The Inquisition, look out sin
We have a mission
to convert the Jews

CHORUS: *Jew-ja-Jew-ja-Jew-ja-Jews*

TORQUEMADA:
We're gonna teach them wrong from right
We're gonna help them see the light
And make an offer that they can't refuse

CHORUS: *That the Jews just can't refuse!*

TORQUEMADA:
Confess
Don't be boring
Say yes
Don't be dull
A fact you're ignoring
It's better to lose your skullcap than your skull!

During the number, I actually had Ronny Graham and Jackie Mason hanging in chains from the dungeon walls. This is what they said:

FIRST JEW (RONNY GRAHAM): [spoken]
I was sitting in a temple
I was minding my own business
I was listening to a lovely Hebrew mass
Then these papist persons plunge in
And they throw me in a dungeon
And they shove a red-hot poker up my ass!
Is that considerate?
Is that polite?
And not a tube of Preparation H in sight!

SECOND JEW (JACKIE MASON): [spoken]
I'm sittin', flickin' chickens
and I'm looking through the pickin's
and suddenly these goys break down my walls
I didn't even know them
and they grabbed me by the scrotum
and they started playing ping-pong with my balls
Oy, the agony!
Ooh, the shame!
To make my privates public for a game!

For my idea of ending the song in a big old-fashioned Hollywood spectacle, we needed a swimming pool in a big soundstage. There was only one and it was at Paramount Studios. So we moved to Paramount to film "The Inquisition." In my mind I saw the famous MGM Esther Williams production numbers in which a line of beautiful dancers in bathing suits dive into the water one after the other. In "The Inquisition" I saw a line of nuns who drop their habits to reveal they're all in tight-fitting bathing suits, and like in

Getting the shot of the chorus of nuns turned into Esther Williams–esque bathing beauties risen from the waters and smiling atop a giant menorah.

the Esther Williams production numbers, they peel off and one by one dive into the pool. To end the number in spectacular fashion, they rise again on the top of a huge menorah with sparks flying off their heads as human candles. Filming it was thrilling as well as hilarious.

The last section of history that I had a lot of fun with was the French Revolution. France, prior to 1789, was a progression of intolerable and despotic kings who became increasingly more remote from the people they were intended to govern. They constantly deferred to their "Divine Right" as rulers to keep their place on the throne. But history shows that there is no "Divine Right." Being king came from being the biggest and the toughest guy on the block. God didn't touch any of the Louises and say, "Rule France!"

The monarchy was a family-owned business. They owned France and they passed it from father to son. I played one of the last of these Louises, the sixteenth, who was a dull, dim-witted despot who led France to the edge of disaster. As Dickens says so brilliantly in his opening sentence of *A Tale of Two Cities*: "It was the best of times. It was the worst of times."

But let's face it, folks, it was mostly the worst of times.

To show the state of abject poverty I hired two wonderful comics: Jan Murray and Jack Carter. Jack is a rat vendor. He shouts about his wares: "Rats. Rats. Nice dead rats for sale. Perfect for rat stew, rat soup, rat pie, and the ever-popular ratatouille."

He's followed by Jan Murray, rolling an empty pushcart. Jan says, "Nothing. Nothing. I got absolutely nothing for sale. If you want nothing—we've got it right here."

In addition to playing King Louis the Sixteenth I played his look-alike double, the Piss Boy. I carried a bucket at outdoor royal events and was at the disposal of the noblemen who summoned me when they needed to relieve themselves.

Playing one of the king's courtiers was the brilliant and always dependable for a big laugh Harvey Korman. Harvey played the

Count de Monet, and I as King Louis always called him "Count de Money." When he corrected me, I always put him in his place by reminding him that I was the king—and the king is never wrong. Harvey, who prided himself on never spoiling a take by laughing, as he often did on *The Carol Burnett Show*, said to me, "I may laugh in a TV show, but I would never ever break up in a movie."

I was secretly determined to prove him wrong.

So upon seeing my resemblance to the servant holding the bucket, Harvey's character says, "Your Majesty, you look like the Piss Boy."

I saw my chance and ad-libbed, shouting back, "And you look like a bucket of shit!"

That did it! He was gone. He laughed so hard he couldn't catch his breath. It cost me some money to shoot the scene over again, but it was worth it.

Another dependable Mel Brooks team player was the always wonderful Cloris Leachman. She played the infamous revolution-

Pamela Stephenson as Mademoiselle Rimbaud with me as the lascivious King Louis XVI.

ary Madame Defarge. All this misfortune was not going by unnoticed. The populace was disgruntled and disgusted, but they were also disorganized. They had a cause but lacked a leader to rally behind. But from every little movement springs a leader all its own. The true leader of the French Revolution was not Danton, or Robespierre, but a wild-eyed commoner who lived in the gutter with the wretched masses and knew their torment. The Revolution was born when the infamous Madame Defarge stepped before the people of Paris and incited them to action:

MADAME DEFARGE (CLORIS LEACHMAN): Fellow wretches. I don't have to tell you that poverty stalks the streets of Paris. Families don't even have enough money for bread. We are down to almost nothing. . . . We have no rights. We have no say. We have no dignity! We are so poor, we do not even have a language! Just this stupid accent!

FELLOW REVOLUTIONIST: She's right, she's right! We all talk like Maurice Chevalier!

MADAME DEFARGE: And now, let's end this meeting on a high note.

She bursts into song, and everybody joins her in hitting a long high note.

More than any other, there is one line from *History of the World, Part I* that people will shout at me when they recognize me on the street: "It's good to be the king." For some reason that line really resonated with the audience. I don't think any of the shouters were actually kings, but they loved the idea regardless.

It was so popular that together with the talented Pete Wingfield I created a rap song with that title as promotion for the film. It was actually a big hit in France!

Here are some of the lyrics:

Well while Paris was rioting we were doing it good
When we heard there was some trouble in the neighborhood

I wasn't too worried, no big deal
You step out of line, Jack, you're in the Bastille
The party kept swinging all day and all night
The champagne was flowing we were feeling all right
They were screaming for bread, things started to shake
But Marie-Antoinette said: Well let 'em eat cake!

Even though we had Albert Whitlock to paint most of our historical settings, we decided that for the French Revolution we would use Blenheim Palace in Oxford, England, to be the backdrop for the Palace of Versailles. While we were shooting at Blenheim Palace, which was the ancestral home of the Dukes of Marlborough, we were visited by the current Duke of Marlborough. When I addressed him as "Your Grace," which I found out was the proper manner when addressing a duke, he said, "Please, please. Call me Sonny." Which was the nickname that he asked most friends to call him. He asked me if I would have dinner with him at his club in London. Since he was kind enough to lend us Blenheim Palace, the least I could do to repay him was to have dinner with him.

It turned out that his club was named "Brooks's Club" and that it was one of the oldest (established in 1762) and most well-known exclusive gentlemen's clubs in all of London. Before dinner we had a glass of wine together and then we were greeted by the austere, handsomely attired maître d' of the club. He said, "What a wonderful occasion, that Brooks's Club should be visited by such an accomplished film director with the same surname! Like yourself, Mel Brooks dining at Brooks's."

Throwing caution to the wind, I went for a laugh.

"To tell you the truth, I actually changed my name to Brooks," I said. "My real name is Melvin Kaminsky. What was the club's name before it was changed to Brooks?"

For a moment, there was dead silence and then the maître d' cracked up with a burst of laughter that shook the room. Sonny joined in the laugh, and it turned out to be one of the best nights out I ever enjoyed in England. To top it off, the wine we had with dinner was Chateau Lafite 1970. (Thank god, Sonny picked up the check.)

When I saw the first assemblage of the rough cut of the movie, I said to myself, "Something's missing. What's missing? I know, coming attractions!"

So I cheekily made some coming attractions for my imaginary next movie, *History of the World, Part II*. The first was "Hitler on Ice," which was a downright terrific title. I hired a great ice skater, slapped on a Hitler mustache and a swastika armband, played some waltzy Germanic music, and had him do beautiful jumps and loops around the ice.

At one screening I actually heard somebody whisper, "Wow! I had no idea that Hitler was such a great skater."

I finished with a coming attraction entitled *Jews in Space*. We see a huge spaceship shaped like the Star of David fighting off dozens of enemy fighters. We cut to inside the spaceship and we see the rabbinical attired Jewish pilots linking arms and dancing a victorious hora. Crazy, but it worked. I got so many letters from fans telling me how much they loved the coming attractions.

To tie all the sections of the movie together I needed a great narrator. I immediately thought of Orson Welles. There was simply no voice as majestic, that would resonate so thrillingly, like the voice of Orson Welles. I knew that words emanating from his mouth would immediately lend stature to the narration. I called my dear friend Alan Yentob in London. Alan was the creative director at the BBC and I also knew he was a good friend of Orson's. Alan put me in touch with Orson, and when Orson read the narration, he called me and said, "It's wonderful, count me in."

It was a thrill to meet Orson Welles. He was so generous with his compliments of my movies. I returned the favor and told him how much I loved *Citizen Kane*, *The Magnificent Ambersons*, and not to mention the brilliant *Touch of Evil*. Orson had some strange requests: First, he wanted his fee in cash, and second, he wanted to have equal say as to what takes of his narration would be used in the final cut. Of course, I trusted his judgment and dutifully met both requests. I got Fox to give me his fee of twenty-five thousand dollars in cash. I put it in a paper bag and gave it to him on the first day of recording.

"Orson, you don't have to tell me, but I'm so curious," I said. "What are you going to do with that twenty-five thousand dollars in cash?"

He said, "I am going to spend it all on fine Cuban cigars and the best Beluga caviar."

(This is entirely true—you couldn't make it up!)

Orson Welles was going to record the voiceover narration between nine A.M. and four P.M. every day for five days. He started Monday morning at nine A.M., and by three o'clock, with a half hour break for lunch, he had recorded the entire narration of *History of the World, Part I.* Twice. Perfectly. He asked if he had to come in again, and I said, "No, we got it!"

Every word of every line exactly as it was needed. His magnificent voice lent a wonderful sense of grandeur to the ambitious title, *History of the World, Part I.* It was a dream come true.

I thanked him and saw him on his way. I then called Alan in London and woke him up to tell him all about Cuban cigars, Beluga caviar, five days of work done in five hours, and again thanked him profusely for connecting me to the incomparable Orson Welles.

By this point, I had reached a level in my filmmaking career where I felt I deserved a fifty-fifty split with the studio, in this case, Twentieth Century Fox. As the studio chief, I asked Laddie to make the following agreement: Fox would spend a modest amount of money on the film and own the domestic distribution, and Brooksfilms would put in half the budget and receive all of the foreign distribution rights.

One of the reasons I wanted this arrangement with the studio was my relationship with Emile Buyse. Emile Buyse was the president of foreign distribution for Fox, and also had become a close friend. He always did a superb job of making my movies popular throughout the world. It seems that Emile had a falling-out with the new head of distribution at the studio, who wanted not only to be head of domestic distribution but also to control foreign—making Emile Buyse's superb gift for foreign distribution redundant. Emile promptly handed in his resignation and was no longer working for Fox.

I was appalled. It upset me to no end. And then in a brilliant stroke, I asked Emile to work for me and to be Brooksfilms' foreign distributor of all future films. He immediately agreed, and it was his strong suggestion that made me ask Laddie for this new arrangement, where Brooksfilms would own foreign distribution on *History of the World, Part I*.

Laddie said, "I agree that you certainly deserve to have such a deal, but as chief of the studio I could be setting a dangerous precedent. Let me think about it."

He didn't think about it for long. The next day he called me and said, "Okay. You've got a deal."

Now here's where the story gets interesting. Even though he told me we had a deal, it was strictly verbal. Nothing was signed. Who could have imagined the following series of events?

Laddie had a big fight with the controlling interests of Twentieth Century Fox. Laddie had chosen to make *Star Wars* (1977), which made many millions for Fox. In return, Laddie wanted to reward the heads of the different departments with a big bonus. The people in New York who held Fox's purse strings gave him an absolute "NO." Instead of being grateful to Laddie for fattening the coffers of Fox, they seriously offended him. He threatened to leave if they didn't say yes, and they didn't believe him and came back with another resounding "NO." So Laddie quit Fox at the peak of success, after a big string of hits, and eventually took over the helm of MGM.

I was flabbergasted. I didn't know what to do. Not only was I heartbroken to lose Laddie as studio chief, but I also had this incredibly great deal for my next movie at Fox, *History of the World, Part I*, and nothing was signed.

But the good news was that Sandy Lieberson, who was in charge of the UK for Fox, was coming into the studio as president pro tem (the temporary president) of Fox until they found a new studio chief. I liked Sandy a lot, I knew him well, and I told him all about my arrangement with Fox and Laddie's verbal agreement. I got my lawyer, the always-dependable Alan U. Schwartz, to quickly finish the contract on *History of the World, Part I* and brought it down to Sandy's office for him to sign.

"Before I sign," Sandy said, "I want to talk to Laddie to make sure that he agreed to this deal."

He picked up the phone, spoke to Laddie, and after a few minutes he smiled and said, "You're absolutely right. Laddie gave you his word. As far as I'm concerned you have a bona fide deal."

And with a quick flourish of his fountain pen, he immediately signed the agreement with Brooksfilms on behalf of Fox. What a relief! So I continued making the necessary preparations to begin production on *History of the World, Part I*.

Then the ceiling fell in.

The new studio chief who replaced Sandy informed my attorneys that in no way would he agree to the deal. He said, "You can take me to court, but no judge would ever find against me for tearing up a contract that was such a bad deal for Fox."

What to do, what to do? Again, Emile Buyse comes to the rescue. Emile says, "Invite him to the press conference you are going to have next week."

I said, "What press conference?"

He said, "You're going to tell them that you're having a press conference next Tuesday with *The Wall Street Journal*."

"What am I going to tell *The Wall Street Journal*?" I said.

"You're not going to tell *them* anything. But you're going to tell *him* that you're going to tell *The Wall Street Journal* the following:

You and your company, Brooksfilms, are leaving Twentieth Century Fox and you're selling all your stock in the company."

"Why am I leaving Twentieth Century Fox?" I said.

"You are leaving because you have no faith in the new administration, and you are worried about their ability to successfully distribute your films. And you're selling all your stock because you are afraid the company is heading in the wrong direction."

"But, Emile, I have no stock in Twentieth Century Fox."

He said, "Only you know that!" Then he said, "Believe me, it's the last thing any new administration of a movie studio wants to see in the financial section of the newspapers."

So scrupulously listening to Emile, I made the call. I invited the new heads of the studio to this mythical press conference with *The Wall Street Journal*. When they asked why and I explained my reasons, the shit hit the fan. In no time, they were all up in my office—the new studio chief, the new head of business affairs, the new head of distribution, and a whole herd of lawyers.

They screamed, "We can sue you for blackmail!"

I countered with, "Sue me! Sue me! Shoot bullets through me!" from Abe Burrows and Frank Loesser's *Guys & Dolls*. (It was wasted on them.)

Anyway, to make a long story short, they argued amongst themselves for a few minutes and came to the realization that publicity like that would doom not only the studio's stock price, but also their own personal career reputations. So like Emile Buyse wisely predicted, they caved in and honored the contract. And thanks to Emile, Brooksfilms won the foreign distribution rights to *History of the World, Part I*.

Let me tell you a little bonus story vis-à-vis *History of the World, Part I*. I was in Europe with Emile Buyse doing publicity for the now Brooksfilms-owned foreign release of the film. When we came to Italy, I was scheduled to appear on a very popular TV show hosted by the Italian Johnny Carson, Ezio Greggio, who hosts the now-long-running program *Striscia la Notizia* which in English means something like "The Snakey News." I loved working with Ezio from the first moment that I met him. I spoke a little Italian, he spoke a lot of heavily Italian-accented English, and we hit it off immediately. That was quite a while ago, and we've remained great friends to this day.

On that show, I did a comedy bit about the sound of various languages. Ezio would give me a word in English and ask me how it was pronounced in Italian, Spanish, French, and finally in German. Whatever the word was, it always sounded lovely in Italian, Spanish, and French. But when it came to German, I went crazy. For instance, Ezio would give me the word "handkerchief." It sounded beautiful in Italian, *fazzoletto*, in Spanish, *pañuelo*, and in French, *mouchoir*. But when it came to German, I left reality behind and went into a Hitlerian rage punctuated with a torrent of guttural explosions. My fake German translation of "handkerchief," complete with gobs of spittle flying from my mouth sounded something like: *"ARRANGA SCHUTZEN PLOTZIN KNOCK FLUGEN SCHNITTZZEL-BLOGENBOMB!"* The audience roared with laughter! It brought down the house.

Chapter 18

Brooksfilms, Part II

In 1982 Eric Bergren and Christopher De Vore, the gifted screenwriters of *The Elephant Man*, came to me with an idea for another film. They wanted to do the life story of Frances Farmer, the beautiful actress who rose to fame in the 1930s and then suffered a nervous collapse and was in serious emotional distress. She was hospitalized in a psychiatric institution against her will, which only worsened her condition. It's a tragic story that once again Christopher and Eric captured in a moving and unforgettable screenplay. Aiding Christopher and Eric in fashioning the script was the son of famed director Elia Kazan, Nicholas Kazan. I really loved their script and wanted Brooksfilms to make it.

Jonathan Sanger came on as producer for Brooksfilms and Randy Auerbach acted as his assistant. For the director of the film, Jonathan found Graeme Clifford, an accomplished film editor who would be directing his first feature film. So once again Brooksfilms was rolling the dice with a relatively unknown filmmaker.

But we weren't taking chances with who would play the lead role. We got one of the best actresses ever to walk in front of a camera: the beautiful and gifted Jessica Lange. Her performance as Frances Farmer was absolutely unforgettable. It earned her an Oscar nomination for Best Actress in a Leading Role. Sadly, she didn't win. But strangely enough, Jessica still won an Oscar that year. She was also nominated and won for Best Actress in a Supporting Role for the movie *Tootsie*, starring my old pal Dustin Hoffman. (I think unconsciously the members of the Academy were giving it to her for *Frances*, but that's my own private opinion.) Anyway, I am very proud that *Frances* is one of the special films in our Brooksfilms library.

One of the few comedies that Brooksfilms made was also released in 1982. *My Favorite Year* is a movie that recalls my early days as a comedy writer in television. A screenwriter named Dennis Palumbo wrote an early draft of the movie for Mike Gruskoff, my producer from *Young Frankenstein*. Mike thought it needed a lot more work before it was up to snuff. He told me it had real potential, and of course I was interested because of my fond memories of working with Sid Caesar on *Your Show of Shows*. We both decided to hire Norman Steinberg, who had worked with me on *Blazing Saddles*, and he took Dennis's first draft of the script and did a truly wonderful job rewriting it into the movie that we hoped to make. It was my love letter to Sid Caesar and the early days of television, and it was also a damn good story.

During *Your Show of Shows*, Max Liebman usually assigned me to assist our guest star celebrities and make sure they were familiar with the workings of TV and specifically that they showed up to rehearsal and learned their lines. Often when making their movies, they would only have to learn a few lines of dialogue before the director said cut. On live television, it was very different. There was no room for mistakes, and they had to memorize the entire script.

The concept for *My Favorite Year* revolved around a big Hollywood actor who is a guest star on a weekly live TV comedy variety show, much like *Your Show of Shows*, and the young writer assigned to "ride herd" on him. In Norman's script, with a little help from me, this particular guest star, Alan Swann, turns out to be more than just a handful to manage. He is full of unpredictable behavior and crazy antics that drive Benjy, the young writer inspired by me and played so wonderfully by Mark Linn-Baker, up the wall.

Once again, as was my dangerous habit, together with our producer Mike Gruskoff, I hired a director who had never directed a motion picture before. Richard Benjamin was a well-known actor who I felt was ready to make the move to the other side of the camera. I wasn't wrong; Richard was absolutely up to the task.

Richard, together with Mike and me, decided on Peter O'Toole to play the "you never know what he'll do next" guest star, Alan Swann. At that point in his career Peter O'Toole had already garnered six Oscar nominations, among them for his performances in *Lawrence of Arabia* (1962), *The Lion in Winter* (1968), *Becket* (1964), and *The Ruling Class* (1972). And he was nominated once again for his magnificent turn in our film, *My Favorite Year*, which he would have and should have won for if he hadn't been up against Ben Kingsley as Gandhi. (Let's face it—anytime you play Gandhi, you have a good chance of winning an Academy Award.)

There were some wonderful back-and-forths between Benjy and Peter O'Toole's Alan Swann:

BENJY STONE: Our audiences are great.

ALAN SWANN: Audience? What audience? Audience?

BENJY STONE: You knew there was an audience. What did you think those seats were for?

ALAN SWANN: I haven't performed in front of an audience for twenty-eight years! Audience? I played a butler. I had one line! I forgot it.

BENJY STONE: Don't worry, this is gonna be easy.

ALAN SWANN: For you, maybe. Not for me. I'm not an actor, I'm a movie star!

Another one of my favorite bits from Peter O'Toole's dialogue was:

ALAN SWANN: Comedy is such a mystery to me. I feel the way Edmund Kean did.

BENJY STONE: The great English actor?

ALAN SWANN: Mmm, yes. On his deathbed, Kean was asked how he felt. He answered, "Dying is easy. Comedy is hard."

Also notable in the cast, playing the "Sid Caesar" role of King Kaiser, was Joe Bologna, who did a remarkable job of capturing the larger-than-life behavior of Caesar. Norman filled the script with wonderful lines for King Kaiser like when thinking about a present for a valued associate, he tells his assistant, Casey, "I think I went a little too far with Sy just now. I really hurt his feelings. I gotta get him something. Here's a hundred bucks. Get him something. Tires are nice. Get him a set of tires. Call my brother in the Bronx. He'll tell you where. Casey, whitewalls."

Another scene that Norman wrote that I really enjoyed was when Benjy takes Alan Swann all the way to Brooklyn to meet his mother, played perfectly by Lainie Kazan, and his aunt Sadie (named after my own aunt Sadie), played by Annette Robyns. This big Hollywood star warmly greets them and couldn't have been nicer, especially complimenting Aunt Sadie on her beautiful white wedding dress, replete with veil and train.

Aunt Sadie responds with, "You like it? I only wore it once."

Another wonderful thing that helped set the mood for *My Favorite Year* was the music under the opening credits. We decided that we would open with "Stardust," the great Hoagy Carmichael song with lyrics by Mitchell Parish, only we wouldn't go into the song itself but instead use just the intro or the verse that precedes the song. It's a haunting and beautiful refrain that captures the feeling of that period perfectly. It's sung by the incomparable Nat King Cole and it definitely creates the magical feeling that surrounds the movie's story, which takes place in 1954.

There's a cute story that occurred in the middle of making *My Favorite Year*. It so happened that Richard Benjamin came to me and said, "I'm running short of money. I'll need about another two hundred thousand dollars to finish the film." He added, "We should go to David Begelman's office together and ask him for the additional funds."

David Begelman, once my agent and still a good friend, had now risen to the rank of studio chief and he was the president of MGM at the time, which was financing *My Favorite Year*.

"No, no!" I exclaimed to Richard. "Bad move. Any time you go to a studio executive's office and ask for money they'll invariably say no."

"Why?" he asked.

"Once they sit behind that big desk in their grand office they are puffed up and feel like kings. And kings are wont to say no. What we have to do is run into him in the hallway either going to or coming back from lunch or even better—catch him in the men's room."

(Where nobody feels like a king.)

We didn't catch him in the men's room, but we slyly followed him back from lunch and caught him in the hallway. I casually said, "David! I'm so glad I ran into you. We're gonna need another couple of hundred thousand to finish the picture. Can I count on you?"

And being my old agent, dear friend, and caught off guard, he said, "No problem. You got it."

Richard Benjamin, jumping for joy said, "I can't believe it. You're a goddamn magician."

Studio executives are funny people. If you need something from them it's always good to find out what kind of a mood they're in first. Check with their secretary or fellow filmmakers who've recently dealt with them. They can be wonderful, friendly, and supportive like Laddie, or they can behave like downright tyrants. It depends on their personality and their mood.

Rumor has it that Frank Yablans, who together with Robert Evans was running Paramount during the *Godfather* movies period, was not an easy executive to deal with. When he left Paramount and moved his production company to Fox, he had a big office on the third floor—not far from mine. So occasionally, I would see him in the hallway, and we'd exchange greetings. One day when I was pulling up to my parking space in the executive building's parking area, Yablans, who had an adjoining space, pulled up next to me. At the time I was driving a beat-up silver metallic Honda Civic. Yablans pulled up in a big black shiny Rolls-Royce, replete with a lush red leather interior. He got out of his car and looked at my car, which next to his looked like a dented tin can with wheels.

He said, "Mel . . . I'll never be big enough to drive a car like that."

Surprisingly funny line from an exec with a reputation for being a tough guy.

MEL BROOKS (ANNE BANCROFT)

TO BE OR NOT TO BE

That is the movie!

BROOKSFILMS PRESENTS MEL BROOKS · ANNE BANCROFT in "TO BE OR NOT TO BE" Starring TIM MATHESON

CHARLES DURNING · JOSE FERRER · GEORGE GAYNES · CHRISTOPHER LLOYD · GEORGE WYNER · LEWIS J. STADLEN · JACK RILEY Music by JOHN MORRIS

Production Design by TERENCE MARSH Director of Photography GERALD HIRSCHFELD A.S.C. Associate Producer IRENE WALZER Screenplay by THOMAS MEEHAN & RONNY GRAHAM Executive Producer HOWARD JEFFREY

PG PARENTAL GUIDANCE SUGGESTED

SOUNDTRACK AVAILABLE ON ISLAND RECORDS & CASSETTES

LIGHTFLEX SYSTEM BY LIGHTFLEX AMERICA INC.

Produced by MEL BROOKS Directed by ALAN JOHNSON

DISTRIBUTED BY TWENTIETH CENTURY-FOX FILM ASSOCIATES

Color by DELUXE

DOLBY STEREO IN SELECTED THEATRES

Chapter 19

To Be or Not to Be

By 1983, I had made a lot of movies but, except for her brief cameo in *Silent Movie*, I had never made one where I co-starred with my beautiful and talented wife, Anne Bancroft. And then it hit me—a wonderful movie that could be a perfect picture for Anne and me to co-star in would be a remake of *To Be or Not to Be* (1942). It was a favorite of both of ours, one of the best films made by the great director Ernst Lubitsch. And it would also reconnect me with one of my tried-and-true sources of dangerous comedy: Adolf Hitler.

Lubitsch was a cinematic hero of mine. He made what I always aimed for—a serious comedy. A lot of laughs, but always driven by something important underneath it. One of his best films was *Ninotchka* (1939) starring Greta Garbo, co-written by Billy Wilder. I never met Lubitsch, but I got to know Billy Wilder. My *Young Frankenstein* and *My Favorite Year* producer Mike Gruskoff and I would often take Billy to lunch.

Billy would always tell us wonderful stories, including the following: One day his secretary brought him some papers to sign and caught him staring out his office window. Her body language and facial expression told him she thought he was goofing off instead of writing.

He quickly corrected her with, "Listen, I want you to know something: When I'm looking out the window—I'm working."

Another thing Billy told us was that at Lubitsch's funeral he was talking with William Wyler (another great director) and Billy said, "Oh my. How sad, no more Lubitsch."

Wyler added, "Worse than that, no more Lubitsch pictures."

Maybe it was Wilder's stories of Lubitsch that made me think about doing *To Be or Not to Be*. In the original, Carole Lombard and Jack Benny played Maria and Joseph Tura, the heads of an acting troupe during the Nazi occupation of Poland who outwit the Nazis. The bravery of Lubitsch was that he made this movie in 1941 and it was very dangerous because Hitler had actually invaded Poland. We had the benefit of hindsight. We could talk about the war and what happened. And Poland! We knew about the Polish resistance, and we knew about the underground. We knew things that Lubitsch had no idea about at the time. We had the template, the blueprint, and also the hindsight.

I put together a wonderful team to write the screenplay. Once again, I leaned on the talents of Ronny Graham, who along with Thomas Meehan rewrote and updated the original script, which was written by Edwin Justus Mayer, from a story by Hungarian journalist Melchior Lengyel, who was friends with Lubitsch.

Tom Meehan had co-written a TV special for Anne, called *Annie, the Women in the Life of a Man* (1970). Tom wrote a tongue-twisting sketch, which had originally appeared in *The New Yorker,* that was one of the best things in the show. It had Anne telling her psychoanalyst, played by Lee J. Cobb, about a dream she'd had. She dreams that she is throwing a party for Yma Sumac, the famous Peruvian singer. The secret of the comedy is that Anne introduces all of the guests to one another by their first names when they enter the party.

Here is what she said:

The doorbell rings.

I open the door, and there to my delight is Ava Gardner.

"Darling!" she says. "How wonderful of you to have asked me."

Funny, I don't know Ava Gardner either.
But in the dream, all of my guests know me very well.
Oddly though, none of them seem to know each other.

Anyhow, "Ava Gardner," I say. "I'd like you to meet Yma Sumac."
"Ahh, please," says Miss Sumac. "Let us not be so formal, *por favor*. Introduce each guest only by their first names so that we may become . . . how shall I say? *Amigos*."
"Fine with me," I say, and introduce the two again, "Ava, Yma."

The doorbell rings.
The second guest is Abba Eban, the Israeli foreign minister.
I make the introductions and as Miss Sumac asked, I keep things on a first name basis.
"Abba, Yma. Abba, Ava."
I start to grin, but no one else finds anything amusing in what I've said.

The doorbell.
It's Oona O'Neill, Charlie Chaplin's wife. I bring her into the room.
"Oona, Yma. Oona, Ava. Oona, Abba."
We are standing in a circle smiling brightly at each other, but nobody is talking very much.

The bell again!
It's Ugo Betti, the Italian playwright. I introduce him.
"Ugo, Yma. Ugo, Ava. Ugo, Oona. Ugo, Abba."

The doorbell rings again.
It's Ida Lupino, the actress, with Ulu Grosbard, the movie director.
"Ida and Ulu, surely you know Yma and Ava. Ida, Ulu; Oona, Abba. Ida, Ulu; Ugo."
"Please . . . there can be no more guests," I whisper to myself.

The doorbell rings again, and everyone stands stony-faced as I usher in the new arrival: the Aga Khan.

"Folks, I guess you all know the Aga Khan."

There is a dead silence, and I must introduce him.

"Aga; Yma, Ava, Ida, Ulu, Abba, Ugo."

I begin to wish that I'd never given the party.

But new guests keep arriving.

Two more at the door: Mia Farrow and Gia Scala.

"Mia, Gia; Yma, Ava, Oona. Mia, Gia; Ida, Abba, Ugo, Aga, Ulu."

And that's only half of it! It's a never-ending comic explosion of crazy first names. It was absolutely hilarious.

Tom Meehan was also an accomplished Broadway book writer, having just written the book for the hit musical *Annie* based on the comic strip *Little Orphan Annie*. (Later he also co-wrote the books with me for both of my Broadway shows, *The Producers* and

Anne and me taking a bow onstage after singing "Sweet Georgia Brown" (in Polish!).

Young Frankenstein—but more on that later.) *To Be or Not to Be* was the first time Tom and I worked together on a movie and the beginning of a long and wonderful collaboration and friendship. He had a delicious wit, and I enjoyed his company to no end. I remember one night, after having dinner with us at our house, Anne and I were going to drive him back to the hotel where he was staying. He jumped into the backseat of the car, slammed the door, and said something straight out of a 1920s movie: "The Century Plaza Hotel! And step on it!"

He loved martinis with extra olives and did the Sunday *New York Times* crossword puzzles only one way—either across or down. Tom passed away in 2017 and I still miss him dearly and think of him often.

To Be or Not to Be was the first adaptation I had done since *The Twelve Chairs*. I worked with Ronny and Tom on the script, but I didn't take any credit for either writing or later for directing because I didn't want any comparisons with Lubitsch and me. To be

Anne and me co-starring as Anna and Frederick Bronski. We didn't have to do much acting to pretend that we were in love.

the film's director I got Alan Johnson, my wonderful choreographer whom I first worked with way back on *The Producers* when we created the marvelous "Springtime for Hitler" production number.

Here's how Roger Ebert described the plot in his review:

> The movie co-stars Brooks and his wife, Anne Bancroft, working together for the first time on screen as Frederick and (Anna) Bronski, the impresarios of a brave little theatrical troupe in a Warsaw on the brink of war. (Anna) Bronski, whose name is in parentheses because her husband has such a big ego, is a femme fatale with an eye for the handsome young servicemen that worship her nightly in the theater. Bronski is an all-over-the-map guy who does Hamlet's soliloquy and stars in a revue called "Naughty Nazis" in the same night and on the same stage. Then the Nazis march into Poland. What can a humble troupe of actors do to stop them? "Nothing!" Bronski declares—but then the troupe gets involved in an elaborate masquerade, pretending to be real Nazis in order to throw Hitler's men off course and prevent the success of the German plans.

Benny and Lombard were wonderful in the original. But Anne and I could sing and dance, and if we were going to remake the movie, it was incumbent on us to add something new. I came up with a crazy idea. I decided we should open the movie with Anne and I as married performers Frederick and Anna Bronski onstage at the Bronski Theatre in Warsaw singing "Sweet Georgia Brown" . . . in Polish. Anne and I found a Polish tutor at UCLA who with great patience taught us all of the brain-breaking translated song lyrics. Together with Alan Johnson's nifty choreography, it was a spectacular and really different and funny way to open the film.

I got Terry Marsh, one of the best production designers in the business, to do the sets. Earlier in his career he had worked on such great films as *Lawrence of Arabia* (1962) and *Doctor Zhivago*

(1965), and more recently he had designed Gene Wilder's *The Adventure of Sherlock Holmes' Smarter Brother* (1975). Gene introduced us, and after seeing his work I grabbed him immediately for *To Be or Not to Be*. It was a stroke of luck; he did a truly remarkable job. He built the entire Bronski Theatre on Stage Five at Fox. It consisted of the box office in the lobby, all the orchestra seating as well as the orchestra pit, and the mezzanine first and second balconies—all with cutouts to stand in for the audience. He also built a wonderful stage with a huge proscenium arch, behind which were the actors' dressing rooms, and to top it off, a backstage alley leading from the street to the back of the theater. It was an incredible feat of stagecraft wizardry. And that wasn't all! His genius didn't stop there. He built a 1939 vision of Warsaw on the back lot of Warner Bros. He took a mile of asphalt and stamped it into cobblestones. It was period perfect right up to the facade of the Bronksi Theatre replete with a beautiful marquee and front entrance. It really worked in an emotional scene where Nazi soldiers marched past the cast lined up in front of the theater, their eyes filled with tears and their hearts breaking at the sight. I can honestly say Terry Marsh gave the movie a truly unforgettable and evocative realism.

In addition to me and Anne, the movie was cast with wonderful actors like José Ferrer, Christopher Lloyd, Tim Matheson, and Charles Durning, who was nominated for an Oscar for his hilarious turn as "Concentration Camp Erhardt," the funny villain of the film. We also had a few first-timers, like Estelle Reiner (Carl Reiner's wife), who played our wonderful wardrobe mistress. Estelle went on to gain movie fame for her unforgettable delivery of the line "I'll have what she's having" in her son Rob Reiner's movie *When Harry Met Sally . . .* (1989).

Also making his film debut was our son Maximillian Michael Brooks. He was nine years old, and he played one of the Jewish children hiding together with their families in the theater's cellar. He was really good and liked doing it . . . for a while. But being only

On the set of To Be or Not to Be *with my son, nine-year-old Max Brooks, in costume for his first acting job.*

nine, he didn't understand doing reshoots from different angles. Then came the clown makeup, for the part of the movie where the Jews escape dressed as clowns. He hated that. He hated the heavy clown makeup being smeared all over his face. I think he decided then and there: *No more acting. I'll do something else.*

(But thank heaven he did do something else. When he grew up, he began writing and was truly meant for it. He eventually became a *New York Times* top-ten bestselling author! More on that later.)

Playing Anne's dresser was James Haake, also known as Gypsy. He was the MC and star of La Cage aux Folles, a well-known Los Angeles drag queen nightclub revue.

Here's how Gypsy described our meeting in an interview:

> By 1983, famous stars like Lucille Ball and Lana Turner had already had their own tables at our club. On Christmas Eve that year, Mel Brooks and his wife Anne Bancroft came to see the show.
>
> Mel said, "How old are you, Gypsy?"
>
> I joked, "Oh, I'm a baby. I'm fifty-one years old."
>
> He said, "You're never too old to become a movie star, and I'm going to make you one."
>
> And he did. Mel Brooks signed me to co-star with him and Anne in the movie *To Be or Not to Be*. I played Anne's dresser, and she coached me every single day for six months during filming. They could've hired a coach, but instead she did it personally. We were in lots of scenes together, and I had a big dance number in drag with Mel. My name was submitted by the head of the studio to the Academy for a Best Supporting Actor Oscar. I didn't get it, of course; I didn't even get the nomination. But my name was submitted. Since that movie, I have done 20-something films and about 100-some television episodes.

Gypsy was a wonderful addition to the cast as well as a never-ending reservoir of good humor and fantastic stories. He helped make the set a happy place to be.

I am so pleased to say that the movie was successful. It did well at the box office and garnered some great reviews, including Vincent Canby's stellar review for *The New York Times*:

> EVERYBODY can relax. Mel Brooks's remake of Ernst Lubitsch's 1942 classic, "To Be or Not to Be," is smashingly funny. . . .
>
> Mr. Brooks and Miss Bancroft played together once before, in his "Silent Movie" in which she had a cameo role, but this is their first co-starring romp. It's one in which we are allowed to discover for ourselves what they seem to have known all along—they were made for each other. . . .
>
> It's no news that Mr. Brooks is one of our national treasures. The revelation for film audiences is that Miss Bancroft is such a wildly gifted comedienne. She is not a foil, but an equal partner, who never fails to meet Mr. Brooks's comic challenges and who, I suspect, provides him with the sort of solid presence that allows him to reach the heights he does. Performing singly or in tandem, they are terrific.

Hard to beat that review!

I was thinking that as part of Fox's publicity campaign for *To Be or Not to Be*, I would do something I had done successfully on *History of the World, Part I*—a rap song. "It's Good to Be the King" made a little history of its own, so I thought why not call Pete Wingfield (my collaborator on "It's Good to Be the King") and make another rap?

I called it "The Hitler Rap."

Here's a little of the opening:

Well hi there people
You know me
I used to run a little joint called Germany.
I was number one
The people's choice
And everybody listened to my mighty voice
My name is Adolf
I'm on the mic
I'm gonna hip you to the story of the New Third Reich.

It all began down in Munich town and pretty soon
The word started gettin' around.
So I said to Martin Boorman I said "Hey Marty . . ."
". . . why don't we throw a little Nazi party?"

The song was really successful; it shook things up, to say the least. Fox even gave us the money to make a "Hitler Rap" music video. I played Hitler singing and dancing with beautiful chorus girls. Once again Alan Johnson created some daring and funny choreography for the backup dancers, and I even hit the floor and did some break dancing. (Which I must confess . . . wasn't always me.)

Me as Adolf, once again slapping on the most infamous mustache in history.

That was the last time I put on my mustache and played Hitler, but there was one other time before that which is worth mentioning. In 1978 Rudy De Luca and Barry Levinson, who did such a wonderful job as writers on *Silent Movie* and *High Anxiety*, created a really funny TV show called *Peeping Times*. It was a send-up of news shows like *60 Minutes*. They wrote a sketch about Hitler and Eva having lunch together at Berchtesgaden, and of course they asked me to play Adolf. It really was hysterically funny and goes a little like this: As they are having lunch Eva swats a fly on the table and my version of Hitler is horrified.

"You killed it!" I say.

She says, "Adolf darling, why are you so upset? It was just a fly!"

Then I reply (mimicking her voice), "It was just a fly! It was just a fly! Tell that to the fly's family, see how *they* feel about it!"

Anyway, the sketch was hilarious.

All in all, I have many fond memories of making *To Be or Not to Be*, it was so much fun. Especially singing and dancing with my gorgeous and sensationally talented wife. Anne really understood me, or at least enough to tolerate me, especially when I was being myself. I truly believe that when you're with the right person, they love you not in spite of your flaws, but because of them. Anne once told a reporter that after meeting me she told her shrink, "Let's speed this process up. I've met the right man."

During an interview with both of us on the *Today* show, Gene Shalit asked Anne whether she was content in her marriage. She stared at him, surprised at the question. Then she said, "I'm more than content! When I hear his key in the lock at night my heart starts to beat faster. I'm just so happy he's coming home. We have so much fun."

In addition to being a wonderful wife and partner, Anne was a truly great mother. Max was diagnosed with dyslexia at a time when it was relatively unheard of. They didn't even call it a learning disability back then. It was dismissed as just laziness, goofing off, or "you're not trying hard enough." So my Annie, one of the greatest, most successful actresses of her day, set aside her career to raise Max and become his educational advocate. She taught herself all about dyslexia and developed coping mechanisms for Max. She met with all of his teachers and made sure that they understood what he was going through. She found ways Max could learn in a nontraditional format. Every year she took all of his schoolbooks to the Braille Institute and had them all read onto audiocassettes so that Max could listen to all of his reading assignments. Had she not done that, it would have been difficult, if not impossible, for Max to have graduated from high school.

If that wasn't enough, Annie was figuring out how technology could help Max. When he was in eighth grade, she forced him to take a typing class. He hated it. She said, "Technology and computers are the way of the future. You're gonna be a writer. This is a writer's tool. You are gonna learn how to type so you can be a writer. You will never have to dictate and you will never have to be dependent on anyone else."

She knew Max's gifts even before he did. He developed a wonderful narrative skill. His images are beautiful, and you always know just where you are and what's happening. As I mentioned earlier in the book, Max grew up to be a brilliant and successful writer—in no small part thanks to the efforts of his wonderful mother.

Anne had amazing range as an actress. She was equally convincing as the first female prime minister of Israel, Golda Meir, or as a mother superior in *Agnes of God*. Anne made acting sound deceptively easy: "It's getting up early and putting on wigs now and learning lines. And, you know, most of it is that very few moments in the day when you're really expressing yourself. It's kind of like giving birth. It's fairly painful and hard work. And yet, isn't it worth it?"

She could be the leading lady or an aide-de-camp, helping people, being quietly on their side pushing them, or she could just be onstage with the spotlight and star in something. She was equally comfortable and easily transitioned between theater, movies, and television. She had several TV specials, which all led to her signature performance as Mrs. Robinson in *The Graduate*, the woman who seduces her friend's college graduate son, played by Dustin Hoffman (who was actually only a few years younger than she was at the time). After decades and many other brilliant performances, it is still the one she is most remembered for. She was a little dismayed that it overshadowed her other impressive work like *The Miracle Worker*. Mike Nichols, one of the great directors that she worked with, said, "Her combination of brains, humor, frankness, and sense were unlike any other artist. Her beauty was constantly uplifting with her roles and because she was a consummate actress, she changed radically for every part."

Anne always pushed me. She has always been an inspiration. She always thought I was talented. She believed in me right from the beginning, as a songwriter as well as a screenplay writer or whatever it was I wanted to do.

Anne, who nicknamed me Mibby (a conflation of Mel and Brooks), always said, "You can do it." She was a gift from God.

I know that my intention in writing this book was mainly to share my adventures in show business, and not to indulge in too many stories of my private life . . . but I've been thinking that every once in a while, I would like to share some of the fun that happened in my other life, the life I lived along the way.

Anne and I were lucky to have great friends. We formed a somewhat exclusive daffy club called "Yenemvelt" which is a Yiddish term meaning "other world." Yenemvelt was the brainchild of the incredibly talented and prolific writer and producer Norman Lear.

The Yenemvelt club (left to right): Carol and Dom DeLuise, Norman Lear, Pat Gelbart, Estelle and Carl Reiner, Lyn Lear, Larry Gelbart, Anne Bancroft, and me.

Back then he had access to a vacation house near Palm Springs. The Yenemvelt group that would gather there for a long weekend were me and Anne, Norman and his wife, Carl and Estelle Reiner, Dom DeLuise and his wife, Carol, Larry and Pat Gelbart, and sometimes Ron and Sheila Clark. We'd stay in our pajamas all day and from sunrise to sunset we'd never stop laughing.

On one of those weekends, I thought I had a great idea. Half of the group was going to have to actually get out of their pajamas to go out shopping, the other half were lucky enough to stay at the house in their bedclothes. Anne and I were in the group that got to stay at home. So I proposed an outrageous practical joke. I said, "Let's make believe that while they were out shopping someone came to the house and murdered us all. We can lay on the floor and cover ourselves in ketchup, but from a distance it'll look like blood."

Everyone was immediately on board. We all lay on the floor and Dom DeLuise assumed the task of ketchup dispenser and doused us all with a liberal coating of ketchup—faces, arms, chests, everything! The works! For about ten minutes we all just lay there awaiting the shoppers return and suppressing our laughter. I shouted, "When you hear the key in the door don't make a sound!"

When the door finally opened they came in talking to each other and then for moment—utter silence. We knew we had them. They were in shock! . . . until somebody smelled the ketchup, and then the jig was up. You never in your life heard such an explosion of laughter.

At this writing Yenemvelt founder Norman Lear is almost one hundred years old, as sharp as ever, and he is still a dear and cherished friend.

Let me tell you some of the other stories from our travels. Sometime in the early sixties, Anne and I made friends with Harry Lorayne and his wife, Reneé. We had met them at Marty and Genii Charnin's home, where once a week we'd all have dinner and play word games. Marty was a songwriter and TV producer. He produced two wonderful Anne Bancroft television specials; that's how we initially met. We all lived in the Village, so it was easygoing. Harry and Reneé became good friends of ours and we would often share summer vacations together.

Harry was a memory expert and wrote a big bestselling book called *The Memory Book*. He went on *The Johnny Carson Show* and memorized the whole audience. Johnny would tell them to stand—almost five hundred people—and believe it or not, Harry could remember all of their names. It was truly amazing! In addition to that Harry was a bit of a genius when it came to close-up magic tricks. He would wow us because no matter how we shuffled and cut the deck of cards, we always wound up with the ace of spades. They were really a fun couple, and Anne and I so enjoyed our two or three weeks traveling with them every summer.

One summer sometime in the mid-seventies Carl Reiner and his wife, Estelle, bought a little house in a fake seventeenth century village called "Castellaras" that was actually built in the sixties somewhere in the south of France near the city of Mougins—Harry pronounced it "Muggins."

We traveled there on the Concorde. The supersonic airliner got us from New York to London in three and a half hours. To say it was fast would be a bit of an understatement, especially in comparison to the eleven days I spent in stormy seas when I was a soldier heading for Europe; it was pretty darn fast and much more enjoyable.

In those days when we were in London we usually stayed at a beautiful hotel on Mount Street called the Connaught. We enjoyed having a late dinner after seeing a show in the West End. We dined at famous eateries like the Ivy, which is right across the street from St. Martin's Theatre, where Agatha Christie's *The Mousetrap* has been playing for a record-breaking sixty-five years.

After about a week in London we headed to Nice, in the south of France. We stayed in Cannes at the Majestic Hotel, which was a lovely hotel with big balconies overlooking the Mediterranean Sea. I stocked our little hotel fridge with delicious, locally made yogurt

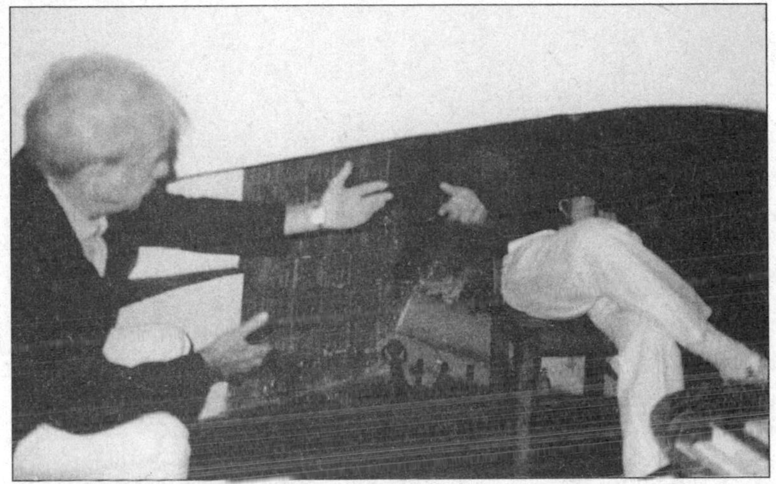

Harry Lorayne and me sitting in Carl and Estelle's living room in the south of France. For some reason, I liked sitting in the fireplace (but only when there was no fire).

and succulent fresh peaches. Every morning on our balcony we'd have peaches and yogurt with a croissant and café au lait. Then we'd hit the beach and swim in the warm waters of the Mediterranean.

At night, in our rented French sedan, Anne and I together with Harry and Renée would drive up to Castellaras to meet Carl and Estelle for dinner. Their house was a stone's throw from the famous Moulin de Mougins restaurant, whose founding chef was the world-famous Roger Vergé. It was expensive, but well worth it. But we actually had more fun finding little out-of-the-way outdoor cafés and restaurants nestled in the surrounding villages. It was a good life, to say the least.

After spending a glorious two weeks in the south of France with Carl and Estelle, we all got into our car early one morning and drove a little past Monte Carlo to the French border town of Menton. The French customs agents scrupulously studied our faces against our passports and finally relented and let us drive on to Italy. A half hour later we were greeted by the Italian customs of-

Me, Anne, Estelle, and Carl (and a lot of pigeons) in our beloved Venice.

ficials in Ventimiglia. It was completely opposite the French. The stern looks we'd received from the French customs officials were replaced with huge smiles and happy, singsong *buongiornos*! from the welcoming, good-natured Italians.

Then began our six-hour wonderful drive through Italy on our way to Venice. We stopped for lunch in Bologna for, of course, their world-famous spaghetti bolognese. We were toasted with an Italian dessert wine called *limoncello*. It was kind of a lemon liqueur. We only had a small glass because we still had a ways to drive.

We arrived in Venice just before sunset. We drove our car onto the ferry that would take us to the Lido, an island a few miles outside of Venice on the Adriatic Sea. As the ferry passed the Doge's Palace at Piazza San Marco we were greeted with an incredible and moving view of the sun setting over the famous Venetian Grand Canal. We finally arrived at our hotel on the Lido, the Excelsior. We checked in and had dinner on their beautiful dining terrace overlooking the sea. Even though we were tired, it was heavenly.

The next morning, we went to our rented cabana #14 on the sparkling Lido beach. We met our neighbors at #15, Edward Lee and his wife, Agnes. He was English, she was French, and they both lived in London. We fell in love with them, they fell in love with us, and we often had lunch with them at the beach dining room.

After reading, talking, singing, sunbathing, swimming, and napping all day we would shower, dress, and board the Ciga boat to Venice for dinner. Ciga was the name of the hotel chain that ran the Excelsior. Their boat was a big beautiful motorboat seating about a dozen people. The sun was setting as our boat swept along the waters to its dock at the Hotel Danieli in Venice. We then grabbed a water bus, or *vaporetto,* to take us to our restaurant, usually some splendid outdoor terrace overlooking the Grand Canal. One of our favorite places was the Gritti Palace. The food and wine were always wonderful and the view was spectacular. After dinner we would wander through the narrow streets of Venice, crossing many bridges, and often finding a little out-of-the-way place for dessert and coffee. Then we'd grab the late Ciga boat back to the Excelsior. We returned many times, and when the time came to leave Venice, I often booked us for another few days because it was so hard to tear myself away from that magical place.

At this point, with your kind permission, let me indulge in a small anecdotal aside: Many years later in 2017, my musical version of *Young Frankenstein* was leaving our very successful out-of-town tryout in the city of Newcastle, England, on its way to the Garrick Theatre in London's West End. It was going to be about ten days before the load in of scenery and rehearsals was ready for the London opening.

I called my dear British BBC pal Alan Yentob and said, "Alan, I've got a week on my hands before *Young Frankenstein* opens at the Garrick. Why don't we go to Venice?"

He happily agreed and the next day we were on our way. Of course, I had us booked at that great hotel on the Lido, the Excelsior, where I had such fond memories of staying so long ago. When we checked in, they graciously gave me a grand suite with a large sitting room overlooking the water, and a smaller room for Alan.

After enjoying the view of the Adriatic from the grand suite's balcony I said, "Alan, let's take a look at your room."

We walked down a flight of stairs, went to the end of the hall, and opened Alan's door. As I entered the room I broke into tears. Alan asked me what was wrong, and I explained.

"Could we switch rooms? Because this is the very same room that Anne and I stayed in so many years ago."

Alan said, "Okay. I guess I'll have to rough it up in the grand suite."

Chapter 20

Brooksfilms, Part III

So sometime in 1984 or early 1985, Stuart Cornfeld came to me with an idea. He said, "I've just read a great script. There's a movie that Fox owns that we should remake . . . it's called *The Fly*."

I remembered that movie. It was about tele-transportation and the scientist who's in the teleporter doesn't realize there's a fly in the chamber with him. He ends up becoming a grotesque hybrid of human and fly.

"As I remember, there was nothing special about it. Why are you suggesting it?"

Stuart replied, "This script I read by a writer called Charles Pogue has a different take on it that I think would turn it into a really good horror movie. You see in the original, the event turning the scientist into the fly happens so quickly that it's not horrific. It's almost funny. But why not take our time with the process? Actually have the scientist very slowly become the fly."

"Go on . . ." I said.

He said, "Well, in this version he thinks the experiment is a failure. He doesn't realize that he has absorbed the genes of the fly and is slowly but surely becoming this horrible creature."

"Ahh! Like a metamorphosis!"

"Right!" he said. "For instance, he's putting six or seven teaspoons of sugar in his coffee and he doesn't notice it. So like in every good horror movie, the audience knows what's happening but not the leading character."

"Okay! Sounds good. Let's get the rights from Fox."

We did, and Stuart began developing the film. His choice for director was the super talented Canadian David Cronenberg, who had made a reputation for himself as a top horror film director. I had seen some of his movies, including *Scanners* (1981), *Videodrome* (1983), and *The Dead Zone* (1983), and thought they were terrific. I agreed with Stuart that he was the guy.

David read Charles Pogue's screenplay and liked it very much but would only sign on to direct if he got carte blanche on rewriting the script.

I said, "Stuart, let's take a chance."

So we signed Cronenberg. After a long back-and-forth in casting choices to play the lead we all decided on a brilliant actor Jeff Goldblum. I remembered seeing him in *The Big Chill* (1983) and thought he was wonderful.

Fox, our distributor, said, "No. Goldblum is good, but he's not a star. We need a big star."

I said, "No, we don't need a big star. We need the right guy for the role, and that guy is Jeff Goldblum."

Finally, they gave in.

In a lucky break for us, Jeff had a girlfriend who was an actress. He asked us to screen-test her for the female lead in *The Fly*. We tested her, and we loved her. Her name was Geena Davis. It was her first real starring role. She was marvelous in the part, especially in a scene where Jeff as Seth Brundle brings a new girlfriend to his laboratory.

When she's a little frightened by the explanation of the teleporting chamber, he calms her with, "It's okay, don't be afraid."

Geena steps out of the shadows where she has been hiding and says, "No, be afraid. Be very afraid."

The phrase jumped out at me and I thought it would be perfect for the lead line in our advertising campaign. As a matter of fact, we made it the most important phrase right underneath the title, reading: THE FLY—BE AFRAID. BE VERY AFRAID.

It was a dynamite tagline, capturing the imagination of the public.

Cronenberg did a sensational job both in writing with Pogue and in directing the film. He was aided by a team of wonderful makeup artists, Chris Walas and Stephen Dupuis, who won the Academy Award for Best Makeup that year for their hideous and genius creation of "the Fly." And composer Howard Shore did a magnificent job with the score of the film.

The Fly did very well, making almost five times its budget in box office. It was also a critical success. Patrick Goldstein wrote in the *Los Angeles Times*:

> . . . Artfully constructed by Cronenberg and co-screenwriter Charles Edward Pogue, "The Fly" is as much a romantic tragedy as a black-humored horror film, but it unfolds with such eerie grandeur that it will leave you stoked with a creepy high for hours after you've left the theater. . . .
>
> One reason the film exercises such a potent grip on our emotions is that it's as much a tragic love story as a chilling spectacle. While much of the credit should go to the sensitive script, the film is graced with a pair of wonderful performances by Goldblum and Davis that bring out the film's underlying compassion and its edgy, ironic spirit.

Our faith in Jeff Goldblum's and Geena Davis's wonderful talent was not misplaced. We didn't have to eat humble pie for the Fox executives. As a matter of fact, in a rare display of studio bigwigs admitting when they are wrong, we were drenched with hearty congratulations from the top brass.

Once again leaning on Dickens's opening sentence in *A Tale of Two Cities*: For Brooksfilms, 1986 was the best of times and also the worst of times. It was the best of times with the success of *The Fly*, and the worst of times with a film called *Solarbabies*.

Let me tell you the saga of *Solarbabies* . . .

The idea for the movie was brought to me by Jonathan Sanger, who had done a great job producing *The Elephant Man*. He had read an outline of the script for *Solarbabies* by Walon Green and Doug Metrov, and he thought it was an interesting sci-fi story. It was about a bunch of roller-skating orphans on a distant future Earth that's starved for water. They find a magical alien orb from another galaxy that is able to restore the Earth's water in an apocalyptic scene where they experience their first thrilling thunderstorm. It was an exciting and heartwarming tale. And since the *Star Wars* trilogy's huge success, sci-fi was a very hot film genre.

Jonathan Sanger was too busy to do it, but Irene Walzer, who was doing a great job in publicity for Brooksfilms at the time, also read the script and thought it could be a winner, plus her enthusiasm for the project was contagious. She wanted to move up to producing, and since Jonathan thought the film could be made for at most five million dollars, Irene joined forces with another producer called Jack Frost Sanders (no pun intended, that was his real name!). He had produced low-budget films before and had some modest success, so even though Irene was a newcomer to producing I felt that the two of them as a team could do the job.

To really keep the budget down they would shoot it in Spain. So with my blessings, they went off to Spain to scout production sites. Like I said before, they thought five million was the most it would cost (which is a pretty low-budget movie for those times), and since I wanted to build up a film library for Brooksfilms it seemed like a good prospect.

I got my former choreographer, Alan Johnson, who had directed *To Be or Not to Be*, to direct the film. He put together an exciting cast of mostly young actors. It had some future stars like Jason Patric, Jami Gertz, Lucas Haas, Peter DeLuise, Adrian Pasdar, James Le Gros, Richard Jordan as the bad guy, and a meaty role for the always wonderful Charles Durning.

I had chosen to fund the production of *Solarbabies* myself. They needed a million dollars to start production, which I dutifully provided. In a very short time, they needed another million . . . and not one foot of the movie had been filmed yet.

Most of the outdoor shooting was set to be done in an area around a city called Almeria. They chose Almeria because, like Southern California, it was mostly dry and the weather was consistently good. But that year, unlike the wonderful Alan J. Lerner lyrics in *My Fair Lady*, the rains in Spain *did not* fall mainly on the plains . . . they fell mainly on Almeria. So there goes the main story line of a planet in drought!

But that was only the first of the many things that went wrong with the production. I'll spare you the details, but the bad news had only just begun and by the time they had shot the first twenty minutes of film they had run through the entire original five-million-dollar budget. I had depleted my own money, and now went to a bank and got a three-million-dollar loan to complete principal photography.

And then, I woke up one morning and said, "Wait a minute, there's a thing called post-production."

I went back to the bank and explained to them that I needed more money to complete the film, and if they didn't give me the money it would be very difficult for me to repay their initial three-million-dollar loan with only half a picture to sell. So they kindly gave me another two million. But I was wrong. Post-production ended up costing a lot more than I had imagined. It was a sci-fi film and required a lot more special effects than an ordinary movie.

So this five-million-dollar, low-budget quickie was going to cost twelve or thirteen million dollars after all was said and done. I was in financial quicksand, and the sand was approaching my mouth and my nose. I needed more money. What to do, what to do?

So I went to my dear old friend Laddie and told him my tale of woe. Laddie, who was now running MGM, came up with a great idea. He said to me, "The executives running UPM are coming for their annual visit to L.A."

UPM was a foreign distribution company, and they distributed the films of Universal, Paramount, and MGM abroad. Laddie thought if I could come up with an exciting trailer for *Solarbabies* and show it to them, together with my promise that I would personally visit every country in the world and sell it, they might give me the monies that I needed to finish the film in exchange for the foreign distribution rights.

So I took all the footage, put it in the hopper, and came up with a trailer for *Solarbabies* that looked and sounded like another *Star Wars*. Miracle of miracles—Laddie was right. It worked. When I showed the trailer to the UPM executives they loved it. Together with my promise to personally go out and sell it they thought it was a good bet and gave me all the money I needed. They gave me enough money to finish post-production, pay back the bank, and make me whole once again. Thank god for Laddie!

Somewhere around 1985, my wife, Anne, had read a book by Helene Hanff called *84, Charing Cross Road*. It's about the long correspondence between an author in New York and the owner of a bookstore in London, who both adored great works of literature. Anne thought it might make a wonderful film and brought it to the aforementioned Randy Auerbach, who was still busy working in development for Brooksfilms. Randy had also read the book and agreed with Anne that it would make a lovely movie. They sought out the rights, but they weren't available. But Anne and Randy didn't give up. A year later when the rights did become available, they grabbed them for Brooksfilms. And so, a wonderful journey to make *84 Charing Cross Road* was begun.

Anne of course took on the author's role of Helene Hanff, the New York writer, and Anthony Hopkins, whom she had shared the screen with in *Young Winston* (1972) and *The Elephant Man*, was secured to play Frank P. Doel, the owner of the London bookstore at 84, Charing Cross Road. Interestingly enough, the two leading players of the film, Anne and Anthony, never actually are onscreen together. Because of the story's geographical structure, all of Anne Bancroft's scenes were shot in New York and all of Anthony Hopkins's scenes were shot in London.

The film suffered one near tragic setback. Just before shooting was to begin, the line producer suffered a heart attack. The production had to be put on hold, and it was touch-and-go whether it would be canceled altogether. But luck was with us, the producer thankfully recovered, and a few months later production finally began. It was a true salute to everybody connected with the film that they were able to adjust their schedules so that they could make the movie.

And make the movie they did! The talented director David Jones shot the entire film in only six weeks of filming—three in New York and three in London. And after about six months of post-production, he delivered an eloquent salute to those special devotees of enduring literature. As a bonus, for Anne's warm and moving performance in the movie she won the prestigious BAFTA award for Best Leading Actress.

The Brooksfilms library of special and unique movies that I have produced over the years is something that I am very proud of. Yes, even the ones that caused me great headaches were worth it in the end. Strangely enough, many years later even though *Solarbabies* hadn't made much of a splash when it was originally released in 1986, that wayward orphan of a movie eventually not only got even but went into profit! Which sounds like a modest achievement but is a minor miracle because actually getting your money back in the movie business is a great victory.

I learned my lesson about investing my own money in my projects, and the experience inspired me to write these words in my musical version of *The Producers,* which together with Tom Meehan I would write a few years later. Nathan Lane as Max Bialystock and Matthew Broderick as Leo Bloom have the following exchange:

MAX: . . . now that we've got our surefire flop, it's gonna be our job to fill that safe with two million dollars.

LEO: Two million. Gee. How much do we put in?

MAX: How much do we put in? Bloom, the two cardinal rules of being a Broadway producer are, one, never put your own money in the show.

LEO: And two?

MAX: *[up close in Leo's face, shouting]* NEVER PUT YOUR OWN MONEY IN THE SHOW! Get it?

LEO: Got it.

MAX: Good.

Chapter 21

Spaceballs

My son Max loved the *Star Wars* movies. I would take him to various showings of them. And for his tenth birthday, he had a *Star Wars*–themed birthday party. And boy, did those kids love it! So I thought, *Science fiction! Now there's a genre I haven't wrecked yet. . . .*

I destroyed the Western in *Blazing Saddles*. I savaged classic horror films in *Young Frankenstein*. I sent up silent films in *Silent Movie*, and I had fun with Hitchcock in *High Anxiety*. Of course, even though I poked fun at all of these genres, in truth I dearly loved them. Cowboy pictures and horror films made my childhood so much more enjoyable. But there were not many genres left for me to satirize, so I eagerly attacked science fiction. There was *Star Wars*, *Star Trek*, *Battlestar Galactica*, and, reaching back for more fun, the unique and campy director Ed Wood's *Plan 9 from Outer Space*. It was a genre rich with opportunities for devastating satire.

I called my trusty writing sidekicks Ronny Graham and Tom Meehan, who had served me so well on *To Be or Not to Be*. They agreed with me that we could have a ball writing our space spoof *Spaceballs*—a title I came up with that immediately clicked with both of them.

The first thing that popped into my mind was the familiar opening crawl of every *Star Wars* movie in which they tell their galactic

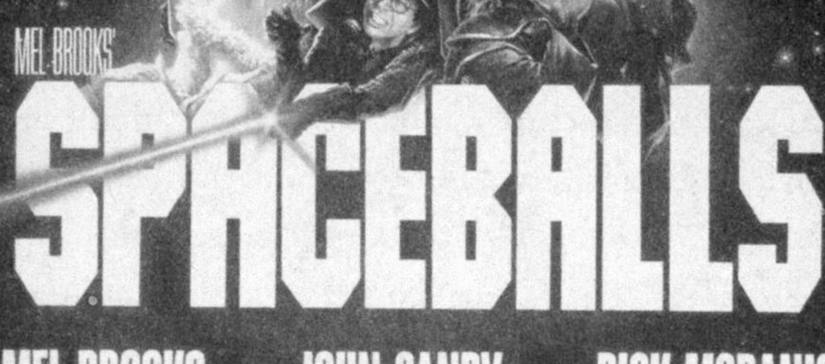
MEL BROOKS'
SPACEBALLS
MEL BROOKS JOHN CANDY RICK MORANIS
A BROOKSFILMS Presentation MEL BROOKS' SPACEBALLS Also Starring BILL PULLMAN DAPHNE ZUNIGA
DICK VAN PATTEN GEORGE WYNER JOAN RIVERS as the voice of Dot Matrix Costumes Designed by DONFELD Music by JOHN MORRIS Production Designed by TERENCE MARSH Director of Photography NICK McLEAN
Co-Producer EZRA SWERDLOW Written by MEL BROOKS & THOMAS MEEHAN & RONNY GRAHAM Produced and Directed by MEL BROOKS
PG PARENTAL GUIDANCE SUGGESTED
SOME MATERIAL MAY NOT BE SUITABLE FOR CHILDREN
Original Motion Picture Soundtrack Available on Atlantic Records, Cassettes and Compact Discs.
DOLBY STEREO
IN SELECTED THEATRES
© 1987 METRO-GOLDWYN-MAYER PICTURES, INC.

story. If I was going to do a satire of space movies, I would definitely need to have some fun with that opening crawl. We copied their visual format of a receding scroll of information, but put our own twist on it:

Once upon a time warp . . .
In a galaxy very, very, very, very far away there lived a ruthless race of beings known as . . . Spaceballs.
Chapter Eleven.
The evil leaders of planet Spaceball, having foolishly squandered their precious atmosphere, have devised a secret plan to take every breath of air from their peace-loving neighbor, Planet Druidia.
Today is Princess Vespa's wedding day. Unbeknownst to the princess but knownst to us, danger lurks in the stars above . . .

And then in smaller print we wrote:

If you can read this, you don't need glasses.

We cut from the crawl to our needlessly enormous, outsized spaceship. The Spaceballs' super galactic ship is so big it takes nearly two minutes to make its way across the screen (which is almost an eternity in movie time!). Finally, at the tail end we see its bumper sticker, it reads: WE BRAKE FOR NOBODY.

The plot of *Spaceballs* was inspired by Frank Capra's 1934 classic *It Happened One Night*. Frank Capra was a groundbreaking pioneer in filmmaking. He was the first director to get his name above the title of a picture, and together with sharp and witty screenwriter Robert Riskin, they made a formidable creative team. *It Happened One Night* was the first film to sweep the Oscars, winning all five top categories—Best Picture, Best Director, Best Adapted Screenplay, Best Actor, and Best Actress. It is the story of a runaway heiress (Claudette Colbert) who escapes her marriage by fleeing on her wedding day from a very, very rich but very, very dull groom and then she subsequently falls in love with an attractive wise-guy commoner (Clark Gable).

We took that same basic plot and shoved it into space! Instead of a Princess Leia we had a Princess Vespa of Planet Druidia. She flees from her wedding to the aptly named Prince Valium and instead she falls for Lone Starr, a good-looking vagabond space bum in the vein of Han Solo. For Princess Vespa we got Daphne Zuniga, who had recently starred in Rob Reiner's film *The Sure Thing*.

When I first offered her the role she said, "I don't know. I haven't done much comedy."

I said, "That could be a plus!" And I explained to her that part of good comedy is playing it very seriously.

For Lone Starr, I found another newcomer, Bill Pullman. He had only done one picture before. I had seen him in an Off Broadway play, and he had charm, presence, and I knew he was the right guy for the part. He proved me right and he delivered Lone Starr lock, stock, and barrel.

In place of Han Solo's co-pilot, Chewbacca, we created a half-man, half-dog character named Barf, who would play Lone Starr's furry sidekick. He was played by the big, warm, lovable John Candy. We outfitted him with doggy ears and a swishing tail that sometimes had a mind of its own. Twisting an old cliché, we wrote a great line for Barf, "I'm a 'mawg'—I'm half-man, half-dog . . . I'm my *own* best friend."

Instead of a futuristic spacecraft, we decided to put our heroes in a Winnebago RV. Of course, it was decked out with ramjet engines and some space bells and whistles, but in the end, it was a strange but wonderful salute to what you'd see on any highway in America. A good old-fashioned Winnebago!

When the Winnebago crash-lands in the desert, John Candy adlibbed one of the big laughs in the movie. As he undoes his seatbelt after the crash he quips: "Well, that's going to leave a mark."

Lone Starr and Barf had the task of rescuing the runaway princess from the clutches of the Spaceballs, whose monster ship was quickly catching up to her. They reach her in the nick of time and get her aboard their Winnebago.

She imperiously announces herself when she enters their ship:

PRINCESS VESPA: I am Princess Vespa, daughter of Roland, King of the Druids.

LONE STARR: Oh great. That's all we needed. A Druish princess.

BARF: Funny, she doesn't look Druish.

Another brilliant casting choice, who happened to be a former co-star of John Candy's from the great *Second City* TV series, was the uniquely gifted and hilarious Rick Moranis. Rick played our comic take on the villainous, evil Darth Vader. We called him Dark Helmet, and because Rick was short, we decided to literally encase him in a huge black helmet. The giant helmet is a sight gag that works every time. It was a big, dumb, funny idea. It was the kind of cartoonish joke that worked for adults as well as kids. Rick was hysterically funny in the role. He cost me a lot of money because I ruined so many takes he was in by helplessly breaking into loud laughter. He brilliantly improvised one of his most famous scenes in the movie, the one in which he gets caught playing with little action-figure versions of Lone Starr, Princess Vespa, and himself.

Enjoying a break on set hugging the lovable John Candy as Barf.

When Colonel Sandurz, played by the ever-reliable George Wyner, breaks into his private sanctum unannounced, Rick screams:

DARK HELMET: Knock on my door! Knock next time!

COLONEL SANDURZ: Yes, sir!

DARK HELMET: Did you see anything?

COLONEL SANDURZ: No, sir, I didn't see you playing with your dolls again!

DARK HELMET: Good!

Speaking of action figures . . . the same way I called Alfred Hitchcock to get his blessings on *High Anxiety*; I sent the *Spaceballs* script to *Star Wars* creator George Lucas. If not to get his blessing, then certainly to give him a heads-up on what I was doing vis-à-vis *Star Wars*. He was kind enough to read it and respond.

He said he had seen *Blazing Saddles* and *Young Frankenstein* and was a big fan. He enjoyed the script, and only had one real caveat for me: no action figures. He explained that if I made toys of my *Spaceballs* characters they would look a lot like *Star Wars* action figures. And that would be a no-no for his lawyers and his studio's business affairs department. So he gave his blessing to make my funny satiric takeoff of *Star Wars* as long as I promised that we would not sell any action figures.

Me as our version of Star Wars' Yoda—"just plain Yogurt."

I said, "You're absolutely right." And that was one of the rules we didn't break.

So even though in the movie itself we have Dark Helmet playing with action figures . . . we never sold any.

The exchange with George Lucas also triggered a beloved comedy scene in which a character that I played, Yogurt, a takeoff on Yoda, responds to Lone Starr's question of "What is this place? What is it that you do here?" with a whole exposé of the movie business:

> YOGURT: Merchandising! Merchandising is where the real money from the movie is made. *Spaceballs* the T-shirt! *Spaceballs* the coloring book! *Spaceballs* the lunchbox! *Spaceballs* the breakfast cereal! *Spaceballs* the flamethrower! (The kids really love that one.)

So even though we didn't actually do any commercial merchandising, we still had a lot of fun with the scene. And over the years *Spaceballs* movie fans have sent me more than one mockup of "*Spaceballs*: The Breakfast Cereal."

In addition to playing Yogurt (not Yogurt the Mighty, not Yogurt the Magnificent, not Yogurt the All Powerful—but just plain Yogurt), I also play another character: President Skroob. He's the president of Planet Spaceball. I was trying to spell Brooks backward but missed by a letter. I wanted to make fun of presidents, because presidents were not always the smartest people to lead a country:

> PRESIDENT SKROOB: Sandurz, Sandurz. You got to help me. I don't know what to do. I can't make decisions. I'm a president!

It was a joy to come to the set on *Spaceballs*. In addition to the fun I had with John Candy and Rick Moranis I got to once again work with my friend Dom DeLuise. Instead of Jabba the Hut, he did the voice for "Pizza the Hut"—a mountainous living pizza complete with bubbling cheese and studded with slices of pepperoni. Also in the scene with Pizza the Hut was my old pal Rudy De Luca, who played a robotic space mobster named Vinnie, who worked for Pizza the Hut and delivered a threat to Lone Starr, telling him to pay up a million space bucks "or else Pizza is gonna send out for *you*!"

George Wyner as Colonel Sandurz, Rick Moranis as Dark Helmet, and me as President Skroob in a scary moment in Spaceballs.

We had another wonderful robot character in *Spaceballs*, Dot Matrix. She's the princess's female version of C-3PO. Professional mime Lorene Yarnell was in the Dot Matrix outfit on set and was terrific. She was a real trooper while encased in her metallic shell when we were shooting on location in Yuma, Arizona, re-creating the desert scene in *Star Wars*. Sometimes the temperature got up to 110 degrees. But Yarnell came through every time. The problem with shooting in the Yuma desert was that if you do more than one take in sand, you've ruined the pristine quality of the sand. It would drive us nuts. We had to get a blower or a sand broom out there to make sure that the sand was ready for the next take.

To voice Dot Matrix, I reached out to the incomparable Joan Rivers. The character acts as kind of a governess to Princess Vespa and safeguards her chastity at all costs. Joan made it so memorable and delivered some of the funniest moments in the movie. I love her delivery when Princess Vespa and Lone Starr are finally about to kiss and suddenly the air is filled with a loud alarm:

Me as President Skroob chuckling with Rick Moranis as Dark Helmet. (I'm pretty sure that's him in there.)

LONE STARR: What the hell was that noise?

DOT MATRIX: That was my virgin-alarm. It's programmed to go off before you do!

As a special treat, I got John Hurt to reprise his role from *Alien* (1979) in which a terrifying creature horrifically bursts out of his chest. We had our own version of the creature once more burst out of John's chest and he got a great laugh when he said: "Oh no . . . not again!" But I couldn't stop there, so I had the creature go on to sing and dance "Hello My Baby" complete with waving a straw hat and a cane!

One of the most memorable lines in the movie is Dark Helmet's order to Colonel Sandurz as they chase after the princess:

COLONEL SANDURZ: Prepare the ship for light speed.

DARK HELMET: No, no, no, light speed is too slow!

Literally "combing the desert" in Spaceballs.

COLONEL SANDURZ: Light speed, too slow?

DARK HELMET: Yes, we're gonna have to go right to ludicrous speed.

Even though we invented ludicrous speed, somehow it caught on! Obviously famous Tesla automaker Elon Musk is a fan of *Spaceballs*. His cars feature a ludicrous mode and he's even announced that for a future model they'll be "going to plaid." Which happens later in *Spaceballs* when, in a twist on *Star Trek*'s warp-speed visual effect, the *Spaceballs One* ship actually goes to "plaid."

Another of my favorite running bits in *Spaceballs* was inspired by *Blazing Saddles*, in which I had the entire town of Rock Ridge all have the last name Johnson.

I did the same thing in *Spaceballs*, it goes like this:

DARK HELMET: Careful, you idiot! I said across her nose, not up it!

LASER GUNNER: [*turns to Dark Helmet, revealing he is incredibly cross-eyed*] Sorry, sir! I'm doing my best!

DARK HELMET: Who made that man a gunner?

SPACEBALLS OFFICER: I did, sir. He's my cousin.

DARK HELMET: Who is he?

COLONEL SANDURZ: He's an asshole, sir.

DARK HELMET: I know that! What's his name?

COLONEL SANDURZ: That is his name, sir. Asshole, Major Asshole!

DARK HELMET: And his cousin?

COLONEL SANDURZ: He's an asshole too, sir. Gunner's Mate First Class Philip Asshole!

DARK HELMET: How many assholes do we have on this ship, anyway?

[The entire bridge crew stands up and raises their hands.]

ENTIRE BRIDGE CREW: Yo!

DARK HELMET: I knew it. I'm surrounded by assholes!

Terry Marsh, my friend and the brilliant production designer who did such a great job on *To Be or Not to Be,* also did a spectacular job on *Spaceballs*. In a strange way he brought space down to earth, with exaggerated visual space clichés like the super white vast interiors of the Spaceballs' ship and the warm, homey looking inside of the Winnebago. To do his wizardry, Terry took over Studio 15 at MGM. He kept reminding me that this was where they filmed the famous *The Wizard of Oz*. Sometimes when I was directing, I would imagine seeing Judy Garland, Ray Bolger, Jack Haley, and Bert Lahr all cavorting around the same stage.

Instead of the famous signature line from *Star Wars*, "May the Force be with you," Ronny, Tom, and I came up with our own version:

YOGURT: I am the keeper of a greater magic, a power known throughout the universe . . . as the . . .

BARF: . . . the Force?

YOGURT: No, the Schwartz!

With my Lone Starr and Princess Vespa, Bill Pullman and Daphne Zuniga, posing in front of the big statue of just plain Yogurt.

Sometimes when people recognize me in a restaurant or just walking down the street, I'll know they've seen *Spaceballs* because they'll shout, "Hey, Mel! May the Schwartz be with you!"

(I think the person who enjoyed it the most was my lawyer Alan U. Schwartz!)

Spaceballs went on to become one of the biggest hits in the Mel Brooks cinematic universe. I think I've autographed more *Spaceballs* posters than for any other Mel Brooks film. I've even gotten some letters from young fans that saw *Spaceballs* before they saw *Star Wars*. They would often ask me why *Star Wars* wasn't so funny.

Tom Meehan, bless his soul, came up with a classic line near the end of the film. It's when our heroes say a heartfelt and teary goodbye to Yogurt:

LONE STARR: I wonder, will we ever see each other again?
YOGURT: Who knows? God willing, we'll all meet again in *Spaceballs 2: The Search for More Money*.

It's over thirty years later, but I'm still not ruling it out!

ERATO
IG

Chapter 22

Life Stinks

The country was going through some hard economic times in 1991. To reflect what was going on at the time, I decided to make the film *Life Stinks*, where I played Goddard Bolt, a billionaire who bets another billionaire that he can live on the streets for thirty days without money. (Never imagining that these many years later, the homeless situation in the country would be even more dire.) When we sat down to talk about it I said, "This is the time for a movie like this."

And I was taking a big chance because while it was very funny, it wasn't a laugh riot. The fun comes from my playing a billionaire who is used to living in luxury but now because of his own hubris he is sleeping in a cardboard box. But it was also depicting the stories of real people wondering where their next meal was coming from. Not many movies talked about hard times in America like John Ford's *The Grapes of Wrath* (1940) and Preston Sturges's screwball comedy *Sullivan's Travels* (1941). Like I've said before, I've always liked a real engine to unconsciously be there to drive my comedy. I thought that making *Life Stinks* could be funny but have that message about how the homeless are neglected underneath it. A crazy comedy that's supported by the good bones of a story that rings true.

I set out to explore three things: What happened to society? What happened to brotherly love? And what happened to caring about your fellow human being?

Life Stinks was all of that, and I wanted to make it. I laid the story out, along with Ron Clark, Rudy De Luca, and Steve Haberman. Steve had been introduced to me by Rudy and was a newcomer to my writing team. They had worked together on *Transylvania 6-5000* (1985), a movie that Rudy wrote and directed, and Rudy had a lot of faith in Steve's creative ability. He wasn't wrong—Steve was a terrific addition to the writing team.

The story was simple. Two billionaires, both vying for the same slum property in L.A. that could be developed into a multimillion-dollar area, make a bet. My character, Goddard Bolt, bets that he can survive without a penny in his pocket for thirty days in that very same slum property. And if he can do it, his rival will have to sign over his half of the property to Goddard. It was a daring and foolish bet, but his billionaire's ego told him that he could do it. And so begins a series of adventures in which Goddard Bolt learns the hard truth about what being poor and homeless really entails.

But who would put up the money for a comedy that featured so many bleak truths?

Jeffrey Tambor and me as rival egomaniacal billionaires making the big bet in Life Stinks.

I went to Laddie and told him that I knew this film was risky, but if we didn't spend too much money we could surely break even, and maybe in the long run, with ancillary markets, perhaps make a real profit. I knew box office would be smaller because the title alone is going to keep people away: *Life Stinks*. And I didn't want to fake out people by saying "life is beautiful" or "life is worth living." I wanted to tell the truth, as life does stink for the disenfranchised. Laddie once again trusted me and agreed to put up the money on behalf of MGM.

We cast the multitalented Jeffrey Tambor to play the role of Vance Crasswell, the other billionaire who was vying for the property my character wanted. I remembered him from a film that my friend and co-writer Barry Levinson co-wrote starring Al Pacino and directed by Norman Jewison called . . . *And Justice for All* (1979). Jeffrey could play both mean and funny—perfect for the villain in *Life Stinks*.

In addition to the comedy and drama, *Life Stinks* also has a touching love story. Goddard Bolt realizes that living on the streets is a lot more challenging than he imagined, and that he has bitten off more than he can chew. Goddard is getting desperate when he runs into a slightly dotty homeless young woman, Molly, who takes pity on him and teaches him some of the rudiments of how to survive in the streets and filthy alleys of the slums. Slowly but surely, he recognizes that underneath her dirty exterior is a beautiful soul that he begins to fall in love with.

He steals a bottle of wine to share with her, toasting to her happiness. Molly responds with, "No, I don't like happy. Happy is no good. Happy doesn't last. I like depressed. Depressed stays with you for a while."

So he says, "Okay, here's to depressed!"

To play this love interest I cast the beautiful and talented Lesley Ann Warren, who began her career as a ballet dancer. In a funny and enchanting sequence, we dance together in a rag factory to Cole Porter's "Easy to Love." Lesley's dancing was absolutely wonderful. She was ethereal.

Having fun during filming with the lovely Lesley Ann Warren.

One of the funniest moments in the film is when we realize at the end of the dance that we love each other and begin to make passionate love. I start to undress her and it gets funnier and funnier as I take one garment off only to reveal another and another underneath. Because out of necessity people who live on the streets often wear every piece of clothing they own all at once. It took a long time to get to the romance as the parade of clothes never ended.

I cast my old friend Howie Morris from *Your Show of Shows* to play another character I meet on the street, and I based his character Sailor's funeral on the real-life story of Howie's father. Howie's father, Hugo, dies, and Howie goes to the funeral home and pays for all of the burial expenses.

The funeral home director says, "There's one more charge for a hundred and twenty-five dollars."

Howie says, "No. I paid for everything."

The director replies, "You had your father cremated. The urn for his ashes is one hundred and twenty-five dollars."

Howie says, "I won't need an urn. We're going to scatter his ashes in the Hudson River."

Which was Howie's father Hugo's final request.

Lesley Ann Warren as Molly and me as the homeless billionaire Goddard Bolt, falling in love as we dance together in a rag factory.

So the director says, "Well, do you have a container for the loved one's ashes?"

Howie said, "Can you find a paper bag?"

The director replied, "I'm sorry, we don't use anything like a paper bag for the loved one's ashes."

Howie says, "Okay, wait here. I'll be right back."

He runs across the street and buys a can of Medaglia d'Oro coffee. He opens it up and he dumps the coffee in the gutter. He said the grocery store owner came out and watched him dump the coffee and was puzzled by what Howie was doing. Howie runs back to the funeral home with the empty coffee can.

He gives it to the director and says, "Put Hugo's ashes in here."

The haughty director of the funeral home says, "Sir, you don't want your father's ashes in there—it absolutely reeks of espresso."

And Howie says, "Never mind, put the ashes in there. Soon it will reek of the Hudson River!"

So they put the ashes of Howie's father, Hugo, in the coffee can.

Howie and his mother take the can of ashes and they drive down the West Side Highway searching for a spot where they could scatter the ashes in the river. But they can't find an easy place to get close to the river itself. Finally, around Seventy-ninth Street he gets off the highway and makes his way down to the riverbank.

Howie climbs up on a rock and looks out on the river with tears in his eyes. He says, "Goodbye, Dad. Rest peacefully in your wonderful Hudson River." With that he opens the coffee can and hurls the ashes toward the river.

. . . But the blustery December wind has other ideas.

It takes the ashes and blows most of them right back into Howie's overcoat. Unfortunately, it is a dark blue double-breasted coat with a belt in the back. (It looked like cashmere but it wasn't.)

So for the next half hour Howie smacks his overcoat like he's beating a rug to get some of the ashes into the river. All the while repeating, "Goodbye, Dad! Love you, Dad! Rest in Peace!" etc.

So I asked him, "Howie, where do you think your father's final resting place is? In the river? On the banks of the river? Where?"

And he says, "I don't know for sure, but I'll tell you this—every time I pass Rand Cleaners on Seventy-ninth Street I break into tears!"

So that bizarre but true story worked perfectly in the goodbye-to-Sailor scene in *Life Stinks*.

The aforementioned Rudy De Luca, one of the writers, played a homeless guy who was delusional in *Life Stinks*. He thought he was actually billionaire J. Paul Getty, and when my character tells him he's a real billionaire living in the slums on a bet, Rudy's character becomes incensed and insists he's much richer. So we begin to fight. We get into a Three Stooges–type slapping scene. It's funny as hell, but unfortunately in order to make it work we really slapped each other senseless. Talk about slapstick—we turned it into slap*schtick* and really went to town.

That's one of the key things I keep in mind when making a movie: You must always strive to create an illusion of reality. Hence, the real slaps. While the actor in me was unhappy with the pain, the director in me, after looking at the monitor after the last take, was happy with the utter crazy reality of the scene.

It wasn't easy directing myself as an actor. I always demanded the best from my actors, and I didn't stop when I demanded it of myself. After all, this was the first and only picture that I made in which I carried the whole film as the lead. Its success hinged on my performance. Normally, in other movies, I'd nail a scene in three or four takes, but in *Life Stinks* sometimes I'd do up to sixteen takes to make sure that I wasn't just phoning it in.

There was another scene that I really thought was telling in the film. It concerns the fact that even though my character lived on the streets for thirty days and had won the bet—my lawyers sell me out to my rival. I tell them, "You've been with me ten years. How could you turn on me? Where's your sense of loyalty, honesty, decency?"

They respond: "Mr. Bolt . . . we're lawyers."

(I'm sure that didn't sit well with some of the lawyers of the world!)

Near the end of the movie, Lesley Ann Warren's character, Molly, has a wonderful speech, where she's trying to motivate my character in the hospital as my health is touch-and-go:

> MOLLY: I know you wanna give up, but you're wrong. Even without money, life is good. No? What about when—when you didn't eat for two days and then you had your first big meal at the mission? Wasn't that good? Remember the other night? When we drank champagne and danced . . . and rolled around in rags? I know they're only moments, but that's all life is: just a bunch of moments. Most of them are lousy . . . but once in a while, you steal a good one. Come on. Come on back to me. Don't be such a selfish bastard. You're the only person I can stand!

By the end of it she's crying and begs, "Don't leave me. I love you. Please. Don't leave me."

Somehow the speech gets to me and I open my eyes and say, "Molly, you're crying. What happened? Did somebody die?"

And through her tears she smiles and says, "No, somebody lived."

I loved making *Life Stinks.* Every minute of it: living down in the slums, the rats, and the unrelenting smell of urine. I loved saying what I had to say about these courageous people who lived in alleys, in the gutter, who went to the mission for their dinner, and despite all of their adversity they were kind to one another. There was a sweetness about it. I felt it was a testament to the enduring human spirit.

I believe *Life Stinks* was also the best work I have ever done as an actor. One of my personal favorite moments of all my movies is in this one: I'm on the roof of an old warehouse in the slums. I've done thirty days' living in garbage and filth. I've been a billionaire for the last twenty years, and now here I am penniless.

I go up to the roof and I say, "God, thirty days. A month." And I began to cry. I'm just so happy and relieved that I did it.

And I say, "Thank you. Thank you, God." And then I take a pause and I say, "I'm sorry I didn't believe in you when I was rich."

And then I just leave. It's my favorite line because it's both funny and touching.

It was a foolish and brave movie to make, and I'm lucky that even with the title *Life Stinks,* it actually broke even. Not only did it get its money back, but also, interestingly, foreign sales did very well—especially in Italy, where it was actually a big hit. Number one for six weeks running! Unbeknownst to me, but knownst to the Italians, I made a kind of Italian movie. I guess I joined De Sica and Fellini as a fellow filmmaker in speaking to the human condition.

Chapter 23

Robin Hood: Men in Tights

Not many people know this, but *Robin Hood: Men in Tights* was not the first time I had fun with the legend of Robin Hood. In the mid-seventies, Norman Steinberg (who was one of the writers on *Blazing Saddles*) and two other writers, Norman Stiles and John Boni, came to me with an idea of a parody of Robin Hood. I liked the idea, so we turned it into a half-hour television comedy called *When Things Were Rotten*.

Dick Gautier played Robin Hood. I had seen him on the Broadway stage in *Bye Bye Birdie* as Conrad Birdie and he brought his wonderfully comic talent to the role. We rounded out the cast with Dick Van Patten, Bernie Kopell (the evil Siegfried from *Get Smart*), Henry Polic, II, Richard Dimitri, and our Maid Marian was played by the lovely and talented Misty Rowe. The first season ran for thirteen episodes in 1975. We shot the episodes like we were making a film, as opposed to the three-camera sitcoms, which were much less expensive but didn't have the same quality. The best one we did was with Sid Caesar as a guest star, playing the French ambassador. Our ratings weren't bad, and we got some nice notices, so I thought the series was going to go places. And then, *BANG!* ABC decided it was too expensive to make and pulled the plug. The cancellation was sudden and unexpected.

I thought, *They're standing in line to see Mel Brooks movies, and I'm giving them free Mel Brooks on television and ABC just*

cancels it? Well, that's show business. Ups and downs. We can only hope we get more ups than downs.

But little did I know that Robin Hood was still in my future . . .

Sometime in 1992, a talented young writer by the name of J. D. Shapiro came to me with a wonderful new take on the classic Robin Hood story. He was a pleasure to work with and in no time, we had a script worth making.

I stole my Robin Hood once again from Rob Reiner, from whom I had earlier stolen Daphne Zuniga for *Spaceballs*. In Rob's magical picture *The Princess Bride* (1987) I found my perfect Robin Hood: Cary Elwes. He had the look, the voice, and the charm. I thought he could possibly be the next Errol Flynn! Cary was a delight to

Cary Elwes as Robin Hood using half a dozen arrows to make sure he hits his target.

work with; we got along really well on the set and to this day we are still good friends.

One scene from the movie I particularly love is the exchange between Cary and Mark Blankfield, who played Blinkin. Upon

Robin's return from the crusades, Blinkin catches him up on what's happened to his family during his absence:

BLINKIN: . . . this never would have happened if your father was alive.
ROBIN HOOD: He's dead?
BLINKIN: Yes . . .
ROBIN HOOD: And my mother?
BLINKIN: She died of pneumonia while . . . Oh, you were away!
ROBIN HOOD: My brothers?
BLINKIN: They were all killed by the plague.
ROBIN HOOD: My dog, Pongo?
BLINKIN: Run over by a carriage.
ROBIN HOOD: My goldfish, Goldie?
BLINKIN: Eaten by the cat.
ROBIN HOOD: [*on the verge of tears*] My cat?
BLINKIN: Choked on the goldfish.
. . . Oh, it's good to be home, ain't it, Master Robin?

The bewitching, beautiful, and downright funny Amy Yasbeck became our Maid Marian. She had gorgeous flaming red hair and her comic timing was perfect. She was all in on our running gag where she wore a heavy iron chastity belt that clanked every time she sat down.

We got the talented Roger Rees to play our renamed sheriff of "Rottingham," and Dick Van Patten (the only actor to appear in both of my Robin Hoods) played "the Abbot," so named so that I could steal the "Hey, Abbott!" catchphrase from Abbott and Costello.

One of my favorite comedians, Richard Lewis, was cast as the evil Prince John. He was the most unlikely, against-type Prince John that ever lived. We gave him a big mole on his cheek, and in every scene, it moved to another place on his face.

We were lucky enough to get Tracey Ullman to play Madame Latrine. I don't use the G-word very often because it's so overused.

But as far as genius is concerned, I know only two for sure—Orson Welles and Tracey Ullman. She can do so many characters with such perfection. She can be poignant. She can be bizarre. And she is always hysterically funny.

She and Richard Lewis have one of my favorite exchanges in the movie:

> PRINCE JOHN: Such an unusual name, "Latrine." How did your family come by it?
>
> MADAME LATRINE: We changed it in the ninth century.
>
> PRINCE JOHN: You mean you changed it *to* "Latrine"?
>
> MADAME LATRINE: Yeah. Used to be "Shithouse."
>
> PRINCE JOHN: . . . It's a good change. That's a good change!

I looked everywhere for a good sidekick for Robin Hood. I saw forty or fifty different people for the role of Ahchoo, and none of them really clicked. And then there was this skinny little kid. He came up and began reading the lines in a very simple and funny way. His name was Dave Chappelle and he was relatively unknown.

Cary Elwes as Robin Hood and funnyman Dave Chappelle as his sidekick, Ahchoo.

Here I am as Rabbi Tuckman, marrying Amy Yasbeck as Maid Marian and Cary Elwes as Robin Hood.

But nevertheless, I fell madly in love with him. I knew he would make the perfect buddy. Dave was wonderful. He came through one hundred percent.

He scores with a great line after Robin appoints him to be the new sheriff and the puzzled crowd yells back, "A black sheriff?"

Dave responds with: "And why not? It worked in *Blazing Saddles*."

Coming off of *Life Stinks*, I was really enjoying wearing my actor's hat in my own movies. At first, I couldn't find a part for me to play in Robin Hood. Then it occurred to me—of course! Instead of Friar Tuck, I could play "Rabbi Tuckman."

We wrote some funny dialogue between the rabbi and Robin Hood:

RABBI TUCKMAN: And who might you be, with the exceptionally long feather in your hat?

ROBIN HOOD: I am Robin of Loxley.

Switching roles from actor to director on Robin Hood: Men in Tights.

RABBI TUCKMAN: Robin of Loxley? I've just come from Maid Marian, the lady whose heart you've stolen, you prince of thieves, you! I knew her mother and father before they were taken by the plague, Lord and Lady Bagelle. You know, you two were made for each other, you and Maid Marian. What a combination. Loxley and Bagelle! It can't miss!

I could go on and on about our wonderful cast for *Robin Hood: Men in Tights*. We were so lucky to get Eric Allan Kramer as Little John, Matthew Porretta as Will Scarlet O'Hara, the great soul singer Isaac Hayes as Asneeze, and Robert Ridgely, who reprised his role in *Blazing Saddles* as the hangman once again. For my friend the ever-hilarious Dom DeLuise, we invented a Mafia-type don who employs a bow-and-arrow-slinging archer whose job it is to wipe out Robin Hood. At the end of the picture, we got *Star Trek*'s Patrick Stewart to play our beloved King Richard, who returns from the Crusades. He got a big laugh in his scene with Prince John, his evil brother:

KING RICHARD: Brother, you have surrounded your given name with a foul stench! From this day forth, all the toilets in the kingdom shall be known as . . . johns!

PRINCE JOHN: NOOOOOOOOOOO!

KING RICHARD: Take him away! Put him in the Tower of London! Make him part of the tour.

In order to make *Robin Hood: Men in Tights* not just another Robin Hood story but a Mel Brooks movie, it had to break away a little.

So I had some fun writing a theme song for Robin's Merry Men. It went like this:

We're men, we're men in tights.
We roam around the forest looking for fights.
We're men, we're men in tights.
We rob from the rich and give to the poor, that's right!
We may look like sissies, but watch what you say or else we'll put out your lights!
We're men, we're men in tights,
Always on guard defending the people's rights!

I lined up the Merry Men and had them do a cancan-style kick line in the middle of the song. It got a huge laugh.

One of the craziest ideas that I ever had for a film was when an army of knights in suits of armor guard Prince John's castle. They're lined up one after the other, barely a foot apart. That's when we thought, *What would happen if you pushed one of those knights?* So during the fight at the castle, Robin swings from a chandelier and kicks the last knight in line. One after another, they all come crashing down like a never-ending row of dominoes. It was a spectacular scene. (I keep one of those suits of armor that were made for that scene in my office to this day to remind me of it!)

Among the strange happenstances that occurred while filming *Robin Hood: Men in Tights* was when we were a little while away from shooting on a castle site we had built in Santa Clarita, California. The surrounding grounds were parched by a drought, all yellow and brown. It looked nothing like a castle and grounds would look in England. I was thinking of actually painting the dry ground green so exterior shots of the castle would look more like it should in Nottingham. But suddenly, it started to rain! And Roy Forge Smith, our gifted production designer, sent a crew out with a ton of grass seed, which they quickly planted all around the castle. It rained nonstop for three or four days, and when we were finally ready to shoot, all the fields around the castle were covered in lush green grass. A minor miracle! Michael O'Shea, our cinematographer, captured it all in brilliant sparkling color.

I had a bunch of great people helping me make the movie behind the scenes. I got some terrific assistance from Peter Schindler, who wore two hats as executive producer and as my second unit director. In another stroke of good fortune our young editor was Stephen E. Rivkin, who later became one of the most sought-after editors in all of Hollywood. (You might have heard of a couple little movies he did called *Pirates of the Caribbean* and *Avatar*.) He was invaluable in putting the picture together, and still remains to this day one of my dearest friends.

Leah Zappy, who had been with Brooksfilms from its very beginning, was now a production executive and took care of all the complicated aspects of shepherding the film through post-production and delivery. She did such a terrific job that we were both on time and slightly under budget.

Robin Hood: Men in Tights did pretty well at the box office and went on to become quite the cult favorite. Parents often tell me that they introduce Mel Brooks pictures to their kids by starting with *Robin Hood*.

(I imagine it takes a while longer before they let them see *Blazing Saddles*.)

Chapter 24

Dracula: Dead and Loving It

To me, the best cinema spoofs are made by directors who love the subject they are satirizing. I've never poked fun at any genre that I didn't absolutely love. Not since *Young Frankenstein* had I toyed with the idea of doing another horror spoof. There were other famous monsters. Just as Boris Karloff in his portrayal of Frankenstein's monster made *Frankenstein* unforgettable, so Bela Lugosi did the same for Count Dracula, king of the vampires, in Tod Browning's 1931 Universal black-and-white film *Dracula*.

It all came together in my head when I saw Leslie Nielsen in the *Naked Gun* series and was tickled by his deadpan portrayal of his character in the midst of comedy chaos. Then and there, I knew he would make a perfect Count Dracula. That was the spark that eventually became *Dracula: Dead and Loving It*.

I met with Rudy De Luca and Steve Haberman, just recently my co-writers on *Life Stinks*, and they both agreed. Steve Haberman was a true horror-film aficionado, and actually later went on to get a doctorate in film studies. His encyclopedic knowledge of classic horror films from the silent *Nosferatu* (1922) through Tod Browning's *Dracula* and on through the Hammer Dracula films was invaluable in putting together our story and screenplay. We took inspiration from all of them, but the one we stayed closest to for the look was the classic Tod Browning *Dracula* film from 1931. Even though *Dracula* was shot in black and white, I decided to shoot our film in color. I was probably influenced by the classic Hammer horror films' memorable use of buckets of blood. Blood doesn't work unless it's all over the place in bright vibrant color. And boy, did we use it! (More on that later.)

But we did parody some details from other famous Dracula films. We used the ludicrous hairdo of Gary Oldman's Count Dracula from Francis Ford Coppola's 1991 film *Bram Stoker's Dracula*. It featured two big white buns on either side of his head, but instead of using it as a hairdo we just turned it into his big crazy hat. Later in that same film, Dracula's shadow plays a prominent part. For our version, we made his shadow show the audience Dracula's real feelings. For example, after he falls down the stairs, even though Dracula doesn't portray any aftereffects, his shadow limps after him obviously in pain.

In addition to casting the very funny Leslie Nielsen as Count Dracula, I decided that I would play his mortal enemy Professor Van Helsing. I based my character on the Edward Van Sloan version of Van Helsing, but I based my accent on the Albert Bassermann character Van Meer from Hitchcock's classic *Foreign Correspondent* (1940). He spoke in a crazy, loopy German accent. I remember Steve saying to me about Bassermann, "Maybe English was his second language, but he spoke it as if it was his fourteenth."

We were lucky that once again my Academy Award–winning wife had the time to lend us her talents to play a small cameo as a gypsy woman who warns us against the strange count who lives in the castle above the village. Anne would take her fingers and shake her throat while delivering the lines in a salute to famous Russian actress Maria Ouspenskaya's signature shaky delivery.

For the female lead we once again got our talented and beautiful flaming redhead Amy Yasbeck, who was so terrific as Maid Marian in *Robin Hood: Men in Tights*. Her character, Mina, was our damsel in distress, who was at risk of being turned into a vampire by Count Dracula. Her fiancé, the very proper Victorian Englishman Jonathan Harker, was played by the talented Steven Weber, who was starring at the time on the hit comedy TV show *Wings*.

A good clue to his character is in the dialogue between him and Mina:

> MINA: Oh, it makes me so happy to be at the opera! I love this palace of art and beauty!
>
> JONATHAN: Oh yes, my dear, the opera is astonishing! The music is fraught with love, hate, sensuality, and unbridled passion! . . . All the things in my life I've managed to suppress so far.

Steven's line reading was absolutely exquisite. The character of Renfield, who becomes Dracula's devoted servant, was brilliantly played by Peter MacNicol, who was responsible for so many of the funniest scenes in the movie. I remembered him from his very humorous performances in *Addams Family Values* and *Ghost Busters II*. The Renfield character was played by Dwight Frye in the 1931 Dracula film, and Peter delivered a perfect imitation of his somewhat nutty mannerisms. Good old reliable Harvey Korman was cast as Dr. Seward, a bumbling British physician which he

Setting a scene with the wonderful Leslie Nielsen while directing Dracula: Dead and Loving It.

Harvey Korman as Dr. Seward, me as Professor Van Helsing, and Steven Weber as Jonathan Harker in Dracula: Dead and Loving It.

played in the manner of Nigel Bruce's Dr. Watson from the famous Sherlock Holmes series.

He and Peter had a hilarious breakfast scene together. It went like this: We see Peter MacNicol's Renfield and Harvey's Dr. Seward eating outside in a garden. MacNicol is trying to convince the doctor that he is perfectly normal, but Harvey suspects that he is crazy. Instead of eating the food, MacNicol snatches a bug crawling across the table and surreptitiously shoves it into his mouth.

Dr. Seward sees him out of the corner of his eye:

DR. SEWARD: You just grabbed something from the table.

RENFIELD: I did not.

DR. SEWARD: Yes, you did, I saw you, you put it in your mouth. I think it was an insect.

RENFIELD: [*quickly covering up*] Oh, that was a raspberry.

DR. SEWARD: Raspberry? We're not serving raspberries.

RENFIELD: Then it must have been a raisin. I guess it fell off the muffin. [*He picks up a muffin and points to it.*] There. Seems to be one missing.

Then Renfield sees a grasshopper on the ground and purposely drops his fork so he can bend down to get it. After some scrambling around under the table he returns to his seat with the grasshopper's leg still sticking out of the corner of his mouth.

DR. SEWARD: My god, man! You're eating insects right from the ground!

RENFIELD: What makes you say that?

DR. SEWARD: Because I can see one trying to get out of your mouth!

RENFIELD: [*speaking around the grasshopper leg*] Out of my mouth?

DR. SEWARD: Yes, out of your mouth! Your very own mouth—it's wriggling about!

RENFIELD: Don't be ridiculous. Wriggling?

DR. SEWARD: I'm not ridiculous at all! It's wriggling all over the place; the poor thing is fighting for its life!

It was one of the wackiest scenes in the whole movie, topped only by Lucy's staking scene. Lucy, best friend to Mina, played by the lovely Lysette Anthony, was bitten by Count Dracula and thus becomes a vampire. My character Van Helsing knows she needs to be destroyed, so accompanied by Steven Weber's Jonathan Harker, we sneak into her mausoleum at midnight to do the dirty terrible job.

JONATHAN HARKER: [*looking at Lucy in her coffin*] My god . . . now she's dead.

VAN HELSING: No she's not.

JONATHAN HARKER: She's alive?

VAN HELSING: She's Nosferatu.

JONATHAN HARKER: She's Italian?

VAN HELSING: . . . No. It means the undead. She's cursed to spend eternity in misery. Hunting the living like a wild animal.

JONATHAN HARKER: What should we do?

VAN HELSING: For the sake of her eternal soul we must destroy her. The only way is to drive a wooden stake through her heart.

JONATHAN HARKER: Oh, that's horrible. Is there no other way?

VAN HELSING: One other. We could cut off her head, stuff her mouth with garlic, and tear off her ears!

JONATHAN HARKER: [*after a moment's thought*] . . . Give me the stake. [*He pauses again.*] No. No, I can't do it . . . You do it!

VAN HELSING: No, it must be done by one who loved her in life!

JONATHAN HARKER: I only liked her!

VAN HELSING: Close enough! Here—

He hands him a pointed wooden stake and a huge mallet.

VAN HELSING: . . . Now place the point of the stake directly over her heart and hit as hard as you can.

Harker raises the mallet high in preparation, and before he can bring it down Van Helsing shouts, "Wait!" stopping him. Van Helsing then runs and hides behind a huge pillar in the mausoleum. Once his body is totally shielded, he shouts, "NOW!" Harker smashes the stake into Lucy with the mallet and an enormous geyser of blood gushes up from the coffin and completely soaks him from head to toe.

JONATHAN HARKER: Oh . . . my . . . GOD! There's so much blood!

VAN HELSING: [*from behind the pillar*] She just ate!

JONATHAN HARKER: [*peering into the coffin*] Oh! She's still alive!

VAN HELSING: Hit her again!

JONATHAN HARKER: No, no, I can't.

VAN HELSING: How much blood can she have left?

Harker sighs in resignation and with all his might once again brings the mallet down onto the stake. Unbelievably, an even larger fountain of blood erupts from the coffin, drenching Harker in a shower of blood for the second time. He throws up his hands in exasperation and mutters in disgust. Van Helsing creeps out from behind the pillar and peeks into Lucy's coffin.

VAN HELSING: She's almost dead.

JONATHAN HARKER: [after a long pause] . . . She's dead enough.

Harker throws down the mallet and tries desperately to wipe the blood off his face.

JONATHAN HARKER: Oh! This is—this is ghastly!

VAN HELSING: Yes, you're right. We should have put newspapers down!

JONATHAN HARKER: Oh, what have I done? What have I done to poor Lucy?

VAN HELSING: You have released her, my boy. Now she sleeps in peace. Forever. Here—

He reaches into his pocket and pulls out a small white handkerchief.

VAN HELSING: Clean yourself up.

JONATHAN HARKER: [*taking the handkerchief*] Thank you. Oh, poor Lucy! Poor poor Lucy! Here—

He goes to hand the handkerchief back to Van Helsing. Van Helsing looks at the now completely blood-soaked handkerchief and says:

VAN HELSING: . . . Keep it.

When I said "cut," I never heard such a loud laugh in my life. The entire crew collapsed in laughter. We could only shoot that scene four times, because our costumer only had four white period shirts for Steven Weber to wear. After each take, the entire set was cleaned up and Steve showered off the fake blood and put on a new white shirt. With each successive take we used bigger and bigger fountains of blood. So of course we ended up using the fourth take, which was practically visual pandemonium. Every inch of that set was drenched in a deluge of bright red blood. It might not have appeared realistic, but like they say in comedy: Bigger is better.

For our ending we took a page from Bram Stoker's book that Dracula must never be seen in daylight. He can only roam the earth in darkness. In Hammer's 1958 film *Horror of Dracula*, Van Helsing rips the curtains from a window before Dracula can get safely back into his coffin, flooding the room with sunlight and immediately reducing Dracula to ashes. For our film we had it be Dracula's own devoted minion Renfield who attempts to save him by opening a trapdoor in the attic to let him escape his pursuers. Unfortunately, Renfield fails to realize it is daytime and so the trapdoor lets in a huge beam of sunlight, which instantaneously starts to destroy Dracula.

As he turns to dust, he screams angrily, "Renfield, you asshole!"

Trying to make the best of a bad situation, Renfield draws a little smiley face with his finger in the mound of dust that used to be his master.

We had so much fun working on the movie that even after it was finished and released, Rudy De Luca, Steve Haberman, and myself kept up our habit of having lunch together in my office about once a week. Those luncheons with Rudy and Steve went on for quite a while, but they don't win the award for my longest running meal companion . . .

That award goes to Alfa-Betty Olsen, who I first met way back on *Get Smart* and who was also invaluable to me in many roles, especially as casting director while I was making my first movie, *The Producers* (1968). Alfa-Betty still lives in New York, but she frequently comes out to California for a visit. It all started with dinner with just me, Alfa-Betty, and her longtime writing partner and close friend Marshall Efron. Marshall was a brilliant comic, writer, and actor, best known for his performances on the PBS series

The Great American Dream Machine. We'd all have Chinese food, and just like with Mario Puzo, there were never leftovers to take home because Marshall took care of that—he was a Chinese-food vacuum cleaner, and never let a stray noodle go unslurped.

It was somewhere around this time, I forget exactly when, but one summer when Anne and I were in London, my British BBC pal Alan Yentob introduced me to a prominent literary agent by the name of Ed Victor. I really liked Ed, he was a bright snazzy dresser and genuine bon vivant. Even though he was an American, he chose to make his business and home in London. At any party he was always a standout—wearing a double-breasted chalk stripe suit replete with a yellow flowered boutonniere in his lapel. And in his right hand a beautiful crystal glass of expensive French Bordeaux. He became so damn British that eventually he earned a CBE, a "Commander of the Most Excellent Order of the British Empire." We had two important things in common: good books and good wine. Ed and I became good friends, and it was fortuitous that, like Anne and I, Ed also had a summer house in the same little town in the Hamptons called Water Mill. We'd often go to dinner with Ed and his lovely wife, Carol, when we were both in the Hamptons during the summers.

When my son Max showed me a rough draft for what would become his first book, *The Zombie Survival Guide*, I thought it was so unique and original. It was a completely serious look at something totally unreal: a step-by-step guide on how to survive a zombie apocalypse. And we happened to be in the Hamptons at the time, so naturally, the first person I shared it with was my literary agent friend, Ed Victor. After reading it, Ed agreed that the book was completely different, quirky, and really entertaining. He immediately told Max he wanted to represent it. And represent it he did! He made a great deal for Max at the Crown Publishing division of Random House. The only thing that slowed up its sales at the beginning was that because Max had been an Emmy-winning writer at *Saturday Night Live*, the book was put in the humor section of bookstores instead of where it eventually found a home, and its huge readership, in the self-help and reference section. Like Max explains, "I can't think of anything less funny than dying in a zombie attack."

The book eventually ran for many, many weeks on *The New York Times* bestseller list and sold over a million copies. I'll never forget the thrill that Anne and I felt when we saw Max's book featured in the windows of bookstores all over Manhattan. His next book, *World War Z*, was not only another big bestseller, but was also made into a hit major motion picture starring Brad Pitt.

So like Hitler and the Nazis were pretty good for me, zombies turned out to be pretty good for Max Brooks.

Chapter 25

The Producers on Broadway

It all began with a nonstop series of phone calls from David Geffen. The founder of Geffen Records is a bit of a genius. He came from humble beginnings, but because he has a gift for discovering musical talent and he found great artists he became very successful. He released hit albums from singers like Elton John, Joni Mitchell, Donna Summer, Cher, and many more. Geffen Records, which was eventually sold to Universal in a significant deal, made him a true music mogul.

So when he called, I listened.

"Mel, I think *The Producers* would make a great Broadway show," he said. And he knew what he was talking about. David was one of the producers of a very successful Broadway musical called *Dreamgirls*. It won six Tony Awards and ran for close to four years.

"It would be the funniest show ever done on Broadway."

It was an interesting idea, but I was too busy with Brooksfilms at the time, so I said, "David, it's a perfectly good little movie. I won an Academy Award for the screenplay! Let's leave it at that."

. . . But he wouldn't leave it at that. David is a guy who won't easily take no for an answer. He called me nearly every week for a few months explaining why we had to make it. He was relentless and finally he wore me down. I agreed to meet with him. He lectured me, chapter and verse, about why he was sure a Broadway version of *The Producers* would be so successful.

716
NATHAN
LANE
MATTHEW
BRODERICK
THE
PRODUCERS
the new
MEL BROOKS
musical

I finally caved in and said, "Okay, let's do it."

David had some stipulations. One of which was to get somebody like Jerry Herman, who did *Hello Dolly!, Mame*, *La Cage aux Folles,* and *Mack & Mabel*, to write the music. Even though David was comfortable with me writing the book, he wanted a great, well-known Broadway composer to write the score. Jerry Herman was among the few who could write both music and lyrics. He was in that elite musical club with Broadway greats like Irving Berlin, Cole Porter, and Frank Loesser.

. . . But I am fortunate that I am able to do that too. And I secretly wanted to write the score myself, but I didn't bring it up then. I dutifully went off to meet with Jerry Herman. The first thing Jerry said when we met was, "*The Producers* is one of my favorite movies of all time." The second thing he said was, "David's crazy. I can't do it."

"Why not?" I said.

"Because there's another guy who's perfect for it."

Jerry goes over to the piano, sits down, and he plays "Springtime for Hitler." He turns to me and says, "That's a great song. That's your centerpiece. That's your second act's climax!"

And then he played "Prisoners of Love." He said, "You have two great songs already. Write half a dozen more and you've got a perfect Broadway show. You're a natural-born songwriter. You should write the score. You write music, you write lyrics, and you know *The Producers* inside out."

He then picked up the phone and called David Geffen.

"David, it's Jerry. I've just sat at the piano. I've played Mel's music. I've sung his lyrics. You're crazy! You've got a diamond in the rough. Nobody knows that he's a wonderful lyricist and composer, and you've got to use him for *The Producers* as a musical."

So Jerry Herman got me the job.

I was going to create the score of a new Broadway show. Every note of every song was going to be written by me. I only had one small question: *Could I do it?* Once again, I confessed all my worries and doubts to Anne. And once again, she dispelled them immediately with, "Of course you can do it. You were meant to do it. So go write your score!"

Writing all the songs for *The Producers* musical would be a challenge, but I wanted to do it. What's life without a challenge?

However, turning the screenplay of the movie into the libretto of a Broadway show, what we called "the book," was a different thing altogether. I knew I needed help. So I called Tom Meehan, who in addition to working with me on *To Be or Not to Be* and *Spaceballs* also had written the book for *Annie*, one of the biggest hits ever on Broadway, for which he won the 1977 Tony Award for Best Book of a Musical. Tom loved the idea; he thought *The Producers* was a natural to become a big, bold, brassy Broadway musical. We started work right away.

"What we've got to do," he said, "is to take the screenplay of *The Producers* entirely apart, as if we were dissecting the works of a finely crafted Swiss watch, and then put it back together again, adding new pieces called the songs where necessary, and hope that when we are finished it's still ticking."

My first vision of it before Tom got involved was basically what David Geffen had envisioned. That it was *The Producers*, the movie onstage as basically a play, where people sang once in a while. But if there were only one or two more songs besides "Springtime for Hitler" and "Prisoners of Love," it wouldn't have been a musical, but rather just a play with music.

Tom said, "No. A musical is a musical, not a play with music. A full-blown musical has many more songs covering many more emotions and plot twists. It's a grand celebration."

I realized I had my work cut out for me. I naïvely asked Tom, "How does one know where to stop the show and start a song?"

Tom said simply, "When you are so overcome with emotion that you can't talk anymore . . . you start singing."

I knew then that I had found a gem in Tom Meehan.

Tom suggested a British guy by the name of Mike Ockrent for

our director. He was well known in the London theater scene and Tom had met him there and was really taken by him. Having seen his 1992 production on Broadway of *Crazy for You*, I thoroughly agreed. It was a wonderful conglomeration of George and Ira Gershwin's standards with a bright, funny book by Ken Ludwig. Mike's wife, Susan Stroman (who everyone calls Stro), won the Tony for *Crazy for You*'s fabulous choreography. They made a great team.

Tom had set a meeting with Mike and Stro for the afternoon after I was scheduled to arrive in New York. But I got to New York earlier than I expected, so I did something a little crazy. I went to Mike and Stro's penthouse apartment, unannounced and unexpected. When they opened the door, I didn't say hello, I burst into song! I started singing a song I had just written for the show, called "That Face." A paean of praise to Bialystock and Bloom's beautiful secretary, Ulla. I sang the song all the way down Mike and Stro's long New York apartment hallway then jumped up on their sofa, finished the song like Al Jolson, and then said, "Hello. I'm Mel Brooks!"

They laughed their heads off and embraced me. They loved my crazy entrance, but more important—they liked the song. It was a match made in heaven. I knew Tom and I had found the right Broadway partners in crime.

The next day we met with Mike at a rehearsal hall where Stro and Mike were rehearsing for the musical version of *A Christmas Carol,* which they presented every Christmas at Madison Square Garden. Tom and I laid out our idea of how the book should go, and Mike stopped us and added wonderful thoughts along the way. Mike immediately saw ways to restructure the story of the film to turn it into a musical.

He said, "You've got to open with a curtain raiser."

I said, "What's that?"

"That's a little number at the top of the show that says hello to the audience. And then you have to end the first act with a great big production number."

I said, "Oh, I get it."

Let me tell you, there's a big difference between writing a screenplay and writing a musical. I learned that unlike any other form of entertainment a Broadway musical is a bunch of small fragments that come together. Book, music, staging, and so many other things have to be nurtured and developed over weeks and months by very talented people, otherwise it will never all gloriously work together onstage.

Tom and I decided that our opener would be an introduction of Max Bialystock, who used to be called "the King of Broadway" but has fallen on hard times and is now cursed with producing flop after flop. It would tell the audience right away that this is not going to be a simple re-creation of the movie, but its own unique entity.

MAX BIALYSTOCK:

I used to be the king, the king of old Broadway
The best of everything was mine to have each day
I always had the biggest hits
The biggest bathrooms at the Ritz
My showgirls had the biggest tits
I never was the pits in any way!

Max is a villain, but a lovable villain. When you write a song for a Broadway musical, the song not only has to work as a song but also has to move the story forward. We start with Max's lament, and immediately enlist the audience's sympathy.

During that period when Tom and I were writing the book, I couldn't wait to meet him at noon each day at Madame Romaine de Lyon's restaurant on Sixty-first Street. Who was Madame Romaine de Lyon? She was the best omelet maker in the world. Her omelets were always perfect—slightly browned on the outside and soft and runny in the middle (as the French say *baveuse*). Her menu was a thin book of one hundred omelets. Our favorite was *jambon, tomate, et fromage* (ham, tomato, and cheese) and once in a while we'd ask her to throw in some truffles.

That reminds me of a great joke Carl Reiner made on eating truffles in a French restaurant. He said to the waiter in perfect French: "*Mes compliments au cochon qui a trouvé ces truffles.*" (My compliments to the pig who found these truffles!)

So every day, Tom and I would meet there at noon and sit in a quiet corner. We'd order our Madame Romaine omelets—one each. Because Madame Romaine said, "You can split a steak. But never split an omelet—it doesn't work."

So we'd eat our omelets, we'd drink our coffee, and we'd write our musical. We finished working each day either at Tom's place or mine. Looking back at those Madame Romaine days, I can honestly say they were some of the best times of my life. It was nice being back in New York, the town I grew up in. My biggest journey in those early days was going across the Williamsburg Bridge from Brooklyn to New York. We Brooklynites never called it Manhattan; we always called it New York. It was vital, throbbing, and always exciting. The great pulse of the city to me was always Broadway, and now I was finally writing my big Broadway show.

So our audience had met Max, and now they needed to meet his future partner, Leo Bloom. In less than a week, I wrote a song that totally explains who Leo Bloom is and what makes him tick. It's called "I Wanna Be a Producer."

LEO BLOOM:

I wanna be a producer
With a hit show on Broadway
I wanna be a producer
Lunch at Sardi's every day
I wanna be a producer
Sport a top hat and a cane
I wanna be a producer
And drive those chorus girls insane!

I thought that song was finished until I met Glen Kelly. Mike Ockrent suggested that we hire Glen Kelly, who did such a great job for him on *Crazy for You,* to do our musical arrangements. Glen Kelly was invaluable in fashioning the score. With his skillful talent he takes a song and turns it into an event. From a lead sheet on a piano to a full-blown musical arrangement. Glen took my song "I Wanna Be a Producer" and wrote a terrific intro to it that sets the mood perfectly. We see Bloom in the middle of a bevy of accountants in the accounting office of Whitehall and Marks. They all begin to sing:

ACCOUNTANTS:

Unhappy . . . unhappy . . . very unhappy
Unhappy . . . unhappy . . .
Very very very very very
Very very unhappy

It was a marvelous setting for Leo to begin his soul-searching song.

LEO BLOOM:

I spend my life accounting
With figures and such

ACCOUNTANTS:

Unhappy . . .

LEO BLOOM:

To what is my life amounting?
It figures, not much.

ACCOUNTANTS:

Unhappy . . .

LEO BLOOM:

I have a secret desire
Hiding deep in my soul
It sets my heart afire
To see me in this role

It then segues into the main chorus of "I Wanna Be a Producer." So you don't know what's missing until it's there. And then you realize it was missing all along. That's the genius of Glen Kelly. He knows what's missing and how to fill it.

By the way, another person needs credit for helping me with the lyrics of that song: my old friend Ronny Graham. When I said to him, "Ronny, I'm stuck. I can't find anything that rhymes with '*figures and such*.'"

Ronny brilliantly said, "How about: '*It figures, not much*.'"

God bless Ronny Graham!

There were other important roles in fashioning the music of our musical. There was Patrick Brady, who not only did our vocal arrangements, but also later became our masterful conductor. Then we got Doug Besterman, who is in my opinion the best orchestrator on Broadway. The first time I heard the full orchestra playing my score I broke into tears.

The development of our book and the songs I was writing were going along at a good pace when heartbreaking disaster struck. Tragically, our director, Mike Ockrent, who we had grown to love and respect, had developed leukemia. He was managing it well with treatment and still working, but unfortunately in December of 1999 it took a turn for the worse and he tragically passed away at the age of fifty-three. We were all shattered by his death, but Stro was absolutely devastated. They had just gotten married in 1996, and now, only three years later, he was gone. We did our best to console her, but let me tell you, it was a very rough time in all of our lives.

David Geffen came up with some good suggestions as to who could take over the reins of the show and continue to direct it, but Tom and I had a better idea. The answer of who should take over directing the show was right under our noses: the supremely gifted Susan Stroman. In addition to being an award-winning choreographer, Stro had just staged her first big show as a director at Lincoln Center. It was called *Contact*. Tom and I had of course been there on opening night and we were both really impressed by her work. She would go on to get a Tony nomination for Best Director and then the show went on to win the Tony for Best Musical. We knew nobody else could complete the job of directing *The Producers* as well as Stro.

Even though it was only a few months after Mike's passing, Tom and I went to her and said, "We want you to continue Mike's work and direct the show."

She turned us down; she said she just wasn't up to it.

Undaunted, Tom and I went to her apartment every day and we'd sit with her. Finally, one day I grabbed her by the shoulders and said, "You just can't cry all day. Cry in the morning before you come to the rehearsal hall. Do your work. Then go home and cry at night. But in between you are going to take over and direct *The Producers*. It's not only good for us, and good for the show, but it's good for you."

She couldn't answer. The next day, we got a call. Stro said, "Okay. I finished crying in the morning. I'm ready."

She came in, directed *The Producers*, and then went home to cry again. And she bravely did that every day until the job was done.

We started having weekend bagel meetings. We'd all meet at Stro's penthouse, and she'd order in from Zabar's on Broadway. There were bagels, cream cheese, smoked salmon, tuna salad, egg salad, and green and black olives. All topped off beautifully with Zabar's great coffee. I was in charge of the bagels. They liked the way I cut them into three thin slices instead of two thick ones and toasted them to perfection. We'd eat our bagels and drink our coffee and then Glen Kelly would sit at the piano and we'd work on the show. We would change and edit and revise, and once in a while I'd introduce a new idea for a song that I wanted to get everybody's agreement on. Those were wonderful fun-filled hardworking sessions that really polished the show into a gem.

For instance, in one of our early sessions Glen said, "Mel, you've written a wonderful song called 'We Can Do It' but it needs a beginning, a verse. Something that introduces it."

Left to right: Stro, Glen, me, and Tom at one of our bagels-and-coffee weekend creative sessions.

So for our next session I came back with a new intro for the song; it went like this:

MAX BIALYSTOCK:

What did Lewis say to Clark when everything looked bleak?
What did Sir Edmund say to Tenzing as they struggled toward Everest's peak?
What did Washington say to his troops as they crossed the Delaware?
I'm sure you're well aware!

LEO BLOOM:

What'd they say?

Max then launches into the song:

MAX BIALYSTOCK:

We can do it, We can do it
We can do it, me and you
We can do it, We can do it

We can make our dreams come true
Everything you've ever wanted, is just waiting to be had
Beautiful girls wearing nothing but pearls
Caressing you, undressing you, and driving you mad

We can do it, We can do it
This is not the time to shirk!
We can do it, You won't rue it
Say goodbye to petty clerk
Hi, Producer
Yes, Producer!
I mean you, sir, go berserk!
We can do it, We can do it
And I know it's gonna work!

The song was uplifting and exciting and it moved the story forward. By the way, I got a wonderful compliment on one of those lyrics from one of the greatest Broadway lyricists of all time: Stephen Sondheim. He said, "Mel, I really enjoyed your rhyming '*Delaware*' with '*well aware*.' "

The next big step was casting, but Tom, Stro, and I had decided way in advance that there was only one person who could fill Zero Mostel's shoes on Broadway . . .

Nathan Lane was at the Ritz Hotel in Paris in 1998. When he came down to go swimming, there were only two other people in the pool: Anne and me.

He said, "Hi, kids."

Talk about things being meant to be! After the three of us chatted, Anne went up to our room and I immediately talked to Nathan about playing the Zero Mostel role of Max Bialystock on Broadway. It turns out that *The Producers* was one of his favorite movies, and the idea of playing Max Bialystock really appealed to him. Just like with me offering Gene Wilder the role of Leo Bloom for the movie, a couple of years after that first lucky conversation with me offering Nathan the role of Max Bialystock, we were in rehearsals with Nathan Lane in the lead.

We had scheduled a backers' audition reading for April 9. The backers' audition is where you play a staged piano reading of the show in order to get the money people interested in investing in it. We went full steam like a runaway train developing the script right up until April 9. Everything was going well and then a week before we were hit with bad news.

David Geffen had to bow out as our producer. I think he must have been much too busy running his new film company, DreamWorks. But I shall be forever grateful to him for being the spark that ignited the whole show.

Stro, Tom, Glen, and I were considering canceling the backers' audition, but since we had everything lined up except for now needing producers, we went ahead. We got on the phone and called every producer, theater owner, and theatrical investor we knew. Believe it or not they all showed up. So there at Nola Studios on Fifty-fourth Street on Sunday April 9 we gave the world its first glimpse of a brand-new Broadway musical comedy, *The Producers*.

When we arrived at Nola Studios I looked out through the window and saw huge white snowflakes. Wow, how unusual. It was snowing in New York in April! I didn't know if it was a good omen or a bad omen or maybe no omen. It didn't last long; the big white snowflakes melted as soon as they hit the ground. Anyway, everything on that fateful day stuck in my head, even the snow in April. So I thought I'd mention it.

For the reading we assembled a cast that included Nathan Lane, Gary Beach, Cady Huffman, Mario Cantone, John Schuck, Nick Wyman, and Evan Pappas. The backers' audition went beyond our wildest dreams. At the end of the first act our audience broke into cheers and applause. Before we could start the second act, we were besieged by an avalanche of Broadway producers who all wanted to be involved in the show.

The most exciting offer was from Rocco Landesman, who since 1967 was the president of the Jujamcyn Theater Group. He was so excited at the end of act I, he said, "If I can be one of your producers, you have the St. James Theatre if you want it."

Wow, the St. James! One of the most sought-after theaters on Broadway. So many memorable Broadway musicals had played there like *Oklahoma!*, *Hello Dolly*, *The King and I*, *The Pajama Game*—just to name a few.

I said, "It's too good to be true!"

Then Tom brought me down to earth. He said, "Never go by the reaction of audiences that consist of family and friends, and especially people that haven't paid to get in. That is one of the most important rules of the theater."

But still, the St. James Theatre! My spirits were soaring. We were on our way.

In addition to getting our producers and our backers, the reading also showed us where the show needed tightening up. Stro was really invaluable in that. I had created these characters, but she knew there was more about them in my head that I hadn't revealed yet. The big lesson I learned was that Max and Leo have to sing and dance about their wants, needs, and dreams rather than do it just through dialogue. The music drives the emotion. That was a huge revelation. And in the musical more than the movie, you root for their friendship and their success as failed producers because the emotions are being heightened by the music. Stro showed me what the audience wants from a musical comedy on Broadway. It has to sing. It has to dance. It has to have beautiful girls. It has to look splendid. It has to be funny. It has to be rich. And always entertaining. She showed me all of that. It has to really thrill the audience for two hours. So together we worked toward thrilling the audience.

For example, I wasn't so sure about a tune I wrote called "Along Came Bialy." It's about how much Bialystock meant to his bevy of little old lady show backers. I told Stro that I really wasn't happy with it and I wanted to throw it out and start from scratch with another tune.

Stro said, "No, no, no! I have a good idea for that song."

"A good idea" was putting it mildly. She had a *brilliant* idea. She put the little old ladies in walkers, and they did an amazing tap-dancing routine with them singing their hearts out with love for Max Bialystock. A song I was going to throw out became one of the real high points of the show.

Another time, I confessed to Stro that I was very unhappy that we couldn't show the audience that great overhead shot from the movie of the dancers in Alan Johnson's amazing original "Springtime for Hitler" choreography rotating in the shape of a swastika. I knew it was impossible onstage. Two days later Stro came back with a perfect solution. She got a huge mirror and tilted it at a forty-five-degree angle above the stage and presto! Now the audience would get to see that incredible overhead shot of the dancing swastika.

So you might say I was taking a crash course in musical theater at Susan Stroman University. We were all working to make sure that the musical was at least just as good as the movie and, if possible, even better.

Tom and I came up with a great idea for the book. In the musical we would take the character of Roger De Bris, our flamboyant director, and because of an accident on opening night Roger has to step in and play the role of Adolf Hitler in the show within the show. I came up with a song for Hitler's big Broadway entrance that really stopped the show. It was called, "Heil Myself."

It went like this:

Heil Myself
Heil to Me
I'm the Kraut who's out to change our history
Heil Myself
Raise your hand
There's no greater Dictator in the Land
Everything I do, I do for you
If you're looking for a war, here's World War Two!

In the second chorus I wrote this lyric:

Heil Myself
Watch my show
I'm the German Ethel Merman
Dontcha know

That was a little salute from me to Ethel Merman, who starred in the first musical I'd ever seen—Cole Porter's *Anything Goes*.

Another big step we took for the musical was the addition of a new love story we didn't have in the movie between Bloom and our beautiful Swedish secretary who introduces herself as Ulla Inga Hansen Bensen Yonsen Tallen-Hallen Svaden-Svanson—but we just called her Ulla.

Tom said, "You can't do a musical on Broadway without a love song."

And he was right. I wrote "That Face" to celebrate the love that Ulla inspired in Leo Bloom.

LEO BLOOM:

That face, that face
That dangerous face
I mustn't be unwise
Those lips, that nose, those eyes
Could lead to my demise
That face, that face
That marvelous face
I never should begin
Those cheeks, that neck, that chin
Will surely do me in

I must be smart
And hide my heart
If she's within a mile
If I don't duck
I'm out of luck
She'd kill me with her smile

To play that tall blond statuesque beauty with the killer smile we just had to look back at our cast from the backers' audition. The magnificent Cady Huffman really knocked 'em dead.

I'll never forget after the backers' audition my cousin and close friend Howard Kaminsky, who was well known in publishing circles for then being the president of the prestigious Random House, who was always a wonderfully witty guy and even shorter than me, said, "Mel, first thing tomorrow morning I'm going to Abercrombie and Fitch and buying a pickax, pitons, and a thousand feet of very strong rope."

"Whatever for?" I said.

He said, "I'm going to climb Cady Huffman."

As I said before, every important character in the show needs an introductory song, and I wrote a real knockout for Ulla. It was called "When You Got It, Flaunt It."

ULLA:

When you got it, flaunt it
Step right up and strut your stuff
People tell you modesty's a virtue
But in the theater modesty can hurt you
When you got it, flaunt it
Show your assets, let them know you're proud
Your goodies you must push
Stick out your chest, shake your tush
When you got it, shout it out loud

[spoken] Now Ulla dance!

And with Stro's magical choreography she moved her tall, beautiful body in a way that absolutely hypnotized Max and Leo—and not to mention later the entire audience at the St. James Theatre. Talk about talent! We were so lucky to get Cady; she was a real find.

But Cady Huffman wasn't the only great find from our reading, Stro had previously worked with Gary Beach and told us how he was not only flat-out funny, but he could also thrill the audience with his amazing voice. She wasn't wrong, at the backers' audition his performances as the colorfully theatrical Roger De Bris and then later as Roger De Bris playing Adolf Hitler were both just sensational. Later on in previews when he made his entrance wearing an evening gown that looked not unlike the Chrysler Building he got a roaring ovation.

The person we cast to play De Bris's comedy partner, his "roommate" Carmen Ghia, actually didn't originally audition for that role. Roger Bart originally auditioned for Franz Liebkind, the crazy Nazi playwright. To put it succinctly, he was utterly wrong for the part. He was physically too small to be the menacing crazy Nazi hulk that we needed to scare Bialystock and Bloom.

But Stro, who had asked him to audition, said, "He's so talented. I'm so disappointed . . ." Then she stopped short and said, "Wait! I have an idea!"

Roger had already left but she ran after him. She came back and explained to Tom and myself that she had given him the lines in the script for him to come back in and read for Carmen Ghia, Roger De Bris's over-the-top common-law boyfriend. So an hour later Roger Bart came back to the audition room and flattened us all with his incredibly on-the-nose perfect rendition of Carmen Ghia. Stro was so happy that her faith in Roger wasn't misplaced.

We still needed a Franz Liebkind, our crazy Nazi playwright. We found him in Ron Orbach, who I had seen playing . . . me! He was in Neil Simon's *Laughter on the 23rd Floor*, a salute to Sid Caesar's writers, and Ron's character was based on me. And I thought he did me just fine! (As a matter of fact, a little better than I could do me myself!)

Anyway, Ron was a wonderful Franz Liebkind—big, Teutonic, nutsy, and scary. Unfortunately, he never made it to Broadway because in out-of-town rehearsals he injured his knee. He valiantly went onstage for a few performances, but the knee wouldn't let him continue.

What to do, what to do? In a movie you don't have anybody to replace an actor who is hurt waiting in the wings—in a movie, there are no wings. But in the cast of a Broadway musical there is always somebody ready to step in if one of the principals can't do it. And lucky for us, we had Brad Oscar, who not only filled in, but made the part his own. Let me tell you, Brad was so damn good that when Nathan Lane finally had to leave the show after his long run, the inevitable choice to replace him as Max Bialystock was never-let-you-down, always-keep-the-show-running, the infallible Brad Oscar.

Stro had the best eye on Broadway for casting the ensemble dancers in a show. She called them her "Beautiful Broadway Babes" and she was spot-on. They were absolutely gorgeous. All of our principal roles were really funny, so therefore when Stro hired our chorus (who would also serve as understudies for some of the leads) she made sure they not only were terrific singers and dancers but also could step in and handle the comedy as well.

One of the toughest minor roles to cast was Hold Me Touch Me, one of the old ladies that dallies with Max on his couch. In the movie, we had Estelle Winwood, one of the grand old dames of the theater, who had been in her eighties when she had done the part. But we couldn't hire a real old lady, because in addition to playing Hold Me Touch Me she'd be in the chorus for the rest of the show singing and dancing her feet off. We needed somebody from our ensemble that with a little hair and makeup could pass as an old lady. After seeing a few pretty good candidates, we were blown away when a woman who appeared to be in her seventies or maybe even in her eighties came in. In a cracked, elderly voice she asked for an audition. We didn't want to be disrespectful or tell her that we couldn't use her, so we allowed her in. She was terrific! When we started to tell her that we couldn't give her the demanding role, she threw away her cane, took off her granny glasses and wig to reveal herself as a young and vibrant Madeleine Doherty. What a great surprise! She got the part.

So we were still missing one major player: our Leo Bloom. And into the spotlight, at I think the suggestion of Nathan Lane, stepped Matthew Broderick. When he appeared on stage, he was actually our leading man, and the character the story was all about. A caterpillar who dreams of one day becoming a butterfly, or in this case, a little accountant who dreams of one day becoming a Broadway producer. Most of America knew Matthew from his breakthrough movie *Ferris Bueller's Day Off*, but he had actually scored on Broadway. We all agreed with Nathan that he'd be great for the part because we'd seen him as J. Pierrepont Finch in *How to Succeed in Business Without Really Trying*, for which he won the Tony Award for Best Actor in a Musical.

Matthew is really funny. After we made him the offer, and he accepted, I said to him, "I was so afraid you were going to turn us down."

He said, "Turn you down? There was only one thing you had to do for me to take this part."

I said, "What was that?"

"You just had to ask me."

Matthew's chemistry with Nathan was magical. They were the beautiful Broadway musical equivalent of Zero Mostel and Gene Wilder. Right from their very first rehearsal together we knew we had the right duo.

Tom and I were happy with the way the rehearsals were going. The show was in pretty good shape. But one day Nathan came to us with a complaint, and he wasn't wrong. He said that "Springtime for Hitler" was the big second-act climax of the show, but he wasn't in it. He thought his character needed a final second-act star turn for the audience to remember him as the star of the show. He didn't want to take second place to "Springtime for Hitler." He was right. The only thing missing to make the show a perfect musical was an eleven o'clock spot for its star, Nathan Lane. That is the last spot before the ending of the show and the final curtain.

What to do, what to do? Necessity really is the mother of invention, and we came up with a bit of a miracle. Since at that point in the show Max was sitting alone in jail feeling betrayed by his partner who has absconded to Rio with Ulla and the money, I wrote a number that would cover the story and also provide that star turn that Nathan was talking about. It was aptly called "Betrayed." Alone and abandoned in his cell, Max goes into a five-minute-long raving nervous breakdown of a number that gave Nathan full leeway to go screamingly over the top and stop the show:

MAX BIALYSTOCK:

Just like Cain and Abel, you pulled a sneak attach
I thought that we were brothers, then you stabbed me in the back
Betrayed! Oh boy, I'm so betrayed!

Like Samson and Delilah, your love began to fade
I'm crying in the hoosegow, you're in Rio getting laid!
Betrayed! Let's face it, I'm betrayed!

Boy, have I been taken! Oy, I'm so forsaken!
I should have seen what came to pass
I should have known to watch my ass!

I feel like Othello, everything is lost
Leo is Iago, Max is double-crossed!
I'm so dismayed. Did I mention, I'm betrayed?

The number worked and would eventually bring down the house. The show was now firmly in Max Bialystock's hands and Nathan was the star.

It takes a village to make a musical, but you need very specific villagers. You need a villager who is a set designer, somebody to design and build the sets. We were so fortunate to get scenic designer Robin Wagner, who had worked with Stro on *Crazy for You*. What

Stro liked more than anything were quick set changes that were fluid and moved the show along at a brisk pace. She knew Robin could deliver that in spades. Not only did he deliver a great office set that harkened back to the cinematic look of the movie right down to Bialystock's huge half-moon office window overlooking Forty-eighth Street on Broadway, but his "Springtime for Hitler" set took what was onscreen in the movie and blew it up to a bigger and better glorious cascade of beautiful descending stairs with inventive Third Reich regalia. And lighting those sets exquisitely every night was the work of our next talented villager, lighting designer Peter Kaczorowski. He was brilliant; in an instant he could go from a solo follow spot to completely flooding the stage for our big production numbers with rich, elegant lighting. Then came our next really important villager, William Ivey Long, our gifted costume designer who had also worked with Stro before on *Crazy for You*. William really had his work cut out for him. We had only twenty-three people in the cast but because the ensemble played multiple roles, we had something like three hundred and twenty costumes. Everything from men playing little old ladies to women playing Nazi storm troopers. Not to mention the hundreds of shoes, boots, hats, and helmets that went along with them. That's just part of why a big Broadway musical can cost over ten million dollars—and that was then! Who knows what it would cost today!

Speaking of costs, we had a big decisive meeting with the producers. They thought the show was in good enough shape to skip going out of town and, to save the million dollars it would have cost, they wanted to just go straight to Broadway.

Both Stro and Tom adamantly said, "No, spend the money!"

Stro vehemently added, "Out of town is critical—it will tell us what we have and what we don't have."

Stro wasn't wrong. Out-of-town audiences are usually kinder to a new show than the tough, show-me Broadway audiences. When a show goes out of town it gives the actors a chance to play for a crowd of non–New Yorkers who will not boo or walk out while a show is breaking in. Giving the cast, especially a comedy, a chance to fine-tune their performances in front of sympathetic audiences. Playing first to out-of-town audiences is critical to the success of a Broadway show, but it can also be a difficult, heartbreaking experience. Sometimes things you wrote that were wonderful in rehearsal just don't land out of town and you start to wonder, *Could your big hit possibly be a big flop?*

My old friend Larry Gelbart from *Caesar's Hour* once said, "If Hitler was still alive, the worst thing I could wish him was to be out of town with a musical."

So we went out of town and we took Hitler with us!

The Producers made its out-of-town debut at Chicago's big, beautiful Cadillac Palace Theatre on February 1, 2001. Inside the theater, life was good but let me tell you something about Chicago in February. Calling it the Windy City was not a mistake. It lived up to "windy" in spades. It would have been cold enough without the wind, but with the cold blasts of wind at freezing temperatures I was the coldest I've ever been in my life. Yes, even colder than being a soldier in Germany during World War II in the late winter of 1945. It was just freezing! Absolutely freezing, I had to wrap a scarf around my face and pull my woolen hat down so that I could just about peer through the tiny space between my hat and my scarf to see where I was going. I was so happy to get to the Cadillac Palace Theatre, which was always warm and filled with music, laughter, and, not to mention, beautiful showgirls.

The entire run was almost completely sold out. We had our ups and downs, but generally the Chicago audiences were generous with their laughter and their applause. But Tom kept reminding me: "Out of town is out of town. It is not Broadway."

And to be truthful, we felt the show was running a little too long. Instead of watching what was happening onstage all the time, sometimes Tom and I would watch the audience. We were afraid of what's called "audience fatigue." No matter how good the show is, after about two and a half hours the audience simply gets too tired of sitting in a theater to enjoy it anymore. So we trimmed jokes that got some laughs but the laughs weren't surefire. We cut things that could have worked but weren't worth the time when we knew we needed to make the show shorter.

When I was asked by a cast member who got a laugh on reading his line, "How could you cut my line? I got a laugh!"

I said, "Yeah . . . but the laugh wasn't big enough." So as far as jokes were concerned, it was survival of the funniest.

But you learn a lot out of town; sometimes instead of cutting you need to add a bit. It can be as small as needing an extra minute for a scene change. I remember one instance where Stro asked me to extend Matthew's exit from the accounting office to cover the time necessary to make a smooth scene change. I went upstairs to my hotel room and came back down with this exchange between Leo Bloom and his boss, Mr. Marks:

MR. MARKS: Bloom, where do you think you're going? You already had your toilet break!

LEO BLOOM: I'm not going into the toilet! I'm going into show business! Mr. Marks, I got news for you: I quit! And you're right about one thing: You are a C.P.A.—a Certified Public ASSHOLE!

So not only did we adequately cover our scene change, but we got a big laugh. That joke survived all the way to New York, but many fell along the way.

Our producers' worries about the cost of going out of town were happily unfounded. We didn't lose a penny by going to Chicago, but we gained something more valuable. When you go out of town, not only do you work out the kinks, but the actors get to bond with one another. Going out of town gives everybody working on a show away from their home an opportunity to become a happy family all pulling together for the same goal: a big fat smash hit. They even kind of grow to love one another, and by the time they get to New York they come in as a unit, as opposed to a disparate bunch of actors with egos who might fight with one another. And somehow, I think that love makes its way across the footlights to the audience.

We left Chicago with a show that we felt had a good chance to make it on Broadway. We made a lot of little changes, but the most important addition was a "goodbye song." You remember I told you that in the Borscht Belt we all had "hello songs" to greet the audience? Hence my crazy "*Here I am, I'm Melvin Brooks. I've come to stop the show.*"

A "goodbye song" would be the other side of that coin. I said to Stro, "I feel that we should somehow blow a kiss goodbye to the audience to thank them for laughing and applauding all night."

She agreed a hundred percent. The idea really excited her. As a matter of fact, she said, "I'm going to stage it right at the end of the curtain calls!"

And here's the "Goodbye Song" that I wrote; I tried to make it touching but still funny:

Thanks for coming to see our show
Sad to tell you we got to go
Grab your hat and head for the door
In case you didn't notice, there ain't any more!
If you like our show tell ev'ryone but . . .
If you think it stinks, keep your big mouth shut!
We're glad you came but we have to shout
Adios, au revoir, wiedersehen, ta-ta-ta
Goodbye . . . get lost . . . get out!

It was a huge success, the cherry on top of the cake.

The Producers began previews on Wednesday, March 21, 2001, at the St. James Theatre. Before you open on Broadway you have a thing called previews. It's a week or two of performances in front of audiences without critics to trim the fat off the show, hoping to get a lean, mean successful machine. The whole team was there every night, and after the show we'd have a note session for trimming, tweaking, polishing, and, last but not least, praying.

Things didn't always go swimmingly with the audience during our previews. At one of them, during "Springtime for Hitler" an irate member of the audience came storming up the aisle yelling, "Where is Mel Brooks? This is an outrage! You're celebrating Adolf Hitler?"

I said, "Let me handle this." I ran and met him at the top of the aisle. I said, "I'm Mel Brooks. What's your problem?"

He said, "This show is a disgrace. How could you sing about Hitler! I was a soldier. I fought in World War II!"

I said, "I also fought in World War II. I don't remember seeing you there." That kind of took the wind out of his sails. I said, "It's all in fun, please take it that way." Believe it or not, he actually calmed down and went back to his seat.

And now it was April 19, 2001, opening night at the St. James Theatre, where 1,706 people (not counting critics) would tell us whether *The Producers* was a hit or a flop. I think most of you reading this know what happened next. It was an explosion of some of the greatest reviews of my career, and for that matter the greatest reviews of any show ever on Broadway.

The first review anybody ever reads the morning after opening night is *The New York Times*. Ben Brantley, the theater critic at the *Times* at the time, who was usually pretty stingy with his praise or accolades, wrote in his review of *The Producers*:

> How do you single out the highlights in a bonfire? Everybody who sees *The Producers*—and that should be everyone the Saint James Theatre allows—is going to be hard pressed to choose one favorite bit from the sublimely ridiculous spectacle that opened last night . . . It is, to put it simply, the real thing: a big Broadway book musical that is so ecstatically drunk on its own powers to entertain that it leaves you delirious, too.

He ended by calling the show, "fast, fierce, shameless, vulgar and altogether blissful." Remember how I told you about Renata Adler's scathing review of *The Producers* movie in *The New York Times*, one which I never forgot?

Brantley wasn't alone in his praise for the show. Review after review, each better than the last, shouted to the rooftops what a sensational Broadway hit they had seen at the St. James that night. You couldn't get better reviews if you wrote them yourself. *The Producers* went on to become a bona fide Broadway phenomenon. Ninety percent of my phone calls were from people begging me for tickets. As they used to say in thirties songs, I was "ridin' high."

Less than a month later the nominations for the Tony Awards were announced. It was almost too good to be true. In total *The Producers* was nominated for, believe it or not, fifteen Tony Awards. I would have been very happy to have gotten half of that number, because as they say, it's a pleasure just to be nominated. (But that's not completely true. It's so much nicer to win one than just be nominated for one.)

The 55th Annual Tony Awards were held that year on June 3 at Radio City Music Hall. Radio City can actually seat over six thousand people; it is so big you could almost call it a cinematic cathedral. Two of those seats, in the fifth row on the aisle, were occupied by Mel Brooks and his wife, Anne Bancroft. We were trembling with excitement. When they announced the winners for Best Book of a Musical, Tom Meehan, who was sitting on the aisle right across from me, stood up and together we both joyfully marched up onto the stage to the microphone. I can't honestly remember what we said, but somebody wrote it down. Here's a brief version of my acceptance speech:

> "So I'm going to have to do the hardest thing I've ever done in my life: Act humble. I want to thank the guy to my right, Tom Meehan. I could have done it without him, but it wouldn't have been half as good. I want to thank Susan Stroman. I love her, she blessed our show with such magical talent. And

> I would also like to thank her late husband, Mike Ockrent, who was there at the beginning, who put our feet in the right direction, showed us where to go, and we went there. I want to thank my wife for sticking with me through this. I want to thank everybody. I want to thank my kids, Stefanie, Nicholas, Edward, and Max. I also would like to thank my mother and father but they're dead. So nice working with you!"

I was brought back onstage just a few moments later by the great Lily Tomlin, who presented the Tony Award for Best Original Score—the music and lyrics of the show. Once again, I don't know what I said, but here's some of what was recorded:

> "I want to thank Stephen Sondheim for not writing a show this year. Thanks, Steve!"

That got a big laugh.

> "Sometime around 1966, my wife said you can write the score of your movie *The Producers*. You can write those songs. Go to your room. So I went to my room. My wife is Anne Bancroft. She's beautiful. She's sitting right there. And she said, you come out in one hour with your score. And I came out in one hour and four months later and I had 'Springtime for Hitler' under my belt. And from then on, it was a pleasure."

There were more awards to come and I was drunk with hubris and joy on our momentum, so I ended my second acceptance speech with:

> ". . . I'll see you in a couple of minutes."

That got another big laugh, but I wasn't far off the mark.

There was a veritable deluge of Tony Awards raining down on *The Producers* that night. Peter Kaczorowski won for Best Lighting Design, Robin Wagner won for Best Scenic Design, William Ivey Long won for Best Costume Design, and Doug Besterman won for Best Orchestrations. Susan Stroman won two Tonys that night—one for Best Choreography and the other for Best Direction. Cady Huffman won Best Featured Actress in a Musical for her knockout performance as our blond bombshell Ulla. Gary Beach won the Tony for Best Featured Actor in a Musical for his incredible twin performances as director Roger De Bris and then later as Roger playing a larger-than-life Adolf Hitler. He actually beat out two of his co-stars, Roger Bart as the fabulous Carmen Ghia and Brad Oscar as the hilariously insane Franz Liebkind. That happened again when Nathan Lane won a well-deserved Tony for Best Actor in a Musical, beating out his equally deserving but unfortunately not awarded co-star Matthew Broderick. It's too bad Matthew couldn't share the award with him, but the award says Best Actor not *Best Actors*.

And then at the end of the ceremonies, Glenn Close took the stage and announced that "the 2001 Tony Award for Best New Musical goes to—they've broken the record! *The Producers*."

And indeed—we had! All in all, *The Producers* won more Tonys that night than any other musical in the history of Broadway. And we hold that record to this day! Other shows threatened to knock us out of the winner's circle, most recently Lin Manuel Miranda's *Hamilton*, which I loved, but secretly hoped didn't surpass us. It ended up winning a well-deserved eleven Tonys, but with twelve Tony Awards, *The Producers* still held the crown.

When I got back onstage for the third time to accept that final award of the night, I started by thanking the most important person in our show:

"Well, I want to thank Hitler. For being such a funny guy onstage."

It got a roar of laughter. I went on to thank the American Theatre Wing, which presents the Tonys, everyone who helped me make the original movie, and everyone who helped me make the Broadway show, especially Tom and Stro. Then I couldn't leave the stage without thanking our dynamic duo:

"Nathan Lane and Matthew Broderick are just a gift from the gods. I mean, those guys are tops in taps. They're better than eating pizza and watching *Top Hat*."

And last but not least, I had to thank all of the producers of *The Producers*.

"Behind me you see a phalanx, an avalanche of Jews who have come with their talent and their money. But most of all, their spirit and their love for the theater. And that's what brings us all together tonight. We all love this thing called the theater. And I'm so proud to be a part of it. I'm not choking up. I'm just dry. But I just want to thank everybody behind me. It would be foolish of me to try and name them all. You should've worn signs . . . God bless you all. It's been wonderful working with you. See you next year!"

There are certain nights in your life that you would call "a night to remember." For me, that was certainly one of them.

On a New Year's Eve during the run of *The Producers* on Broadway I decided to surprise Nathan and Matthew by sneaking in and appearing onstage as the judge in the courtroom scene. The judge's lines went like this:

JUDGE:

Gentlemen, it breaks my heart to break up such a beautiful friendship. So I won't.

[*Slamming down his gavel.*]

Five years in the state penitentiary at Sing Sing! Court adjourned!

So unbeknownst to Matthew and Nathan, but knownst to some sharp members of the audience, I donned the judge's robes and took my place onstage at the judge's bench. Whispers and murmurs began to spread throughout the audience and there was a definite buzz in the courtroom. Obviously, a few people in the audience had spotted me. Matthew and Nathan were puzzled and looked around, not knowing what was happening. It all became clear, shocking, and funny when I read the judge's lines with my own twist on the dialogue:

ME AS JUDGE:

Gentlemen, it breaks my heart to break up such a beautiful friendship. So I won't.

[*Slamming down his gavel.*]

TWENTY-FIVE YEARS in the state penitentiary at Sing Sing! Court adjourned!

When they heard "TWENTY-FIVE YEARS" they were shocked! They looked up, saw me, and burst into laughter. I'm happy to say I got a small ovation for my one and only acting turn in *The Producers*.

The Producers musical is a gift that keeps on giving. Since its birth on Broadway, it has played in many languages in many cities and countries all over the world. One of the most exciting runs was at the Theatre Royal, Drury Lane—one of the most historic and beautiful theaters right in the very heart of London's West End. The Drury Lane traces its history all the way back to 1663; it was closed for the plague, burnt down, rebuilt, and rebuilt again in 1812 where it still stands today as a splendid monument to British theater. Somewhere hidden behind the second balcony is a special toilet, just for the use of the queen. (I must confess that on an emergency occasion—I used it. But please don't tell anyone!)

Stro put an incredible cast together for the London production. Leading them was the wonderful British comic and actor Lee Evans as Leo Bloom and as Max Bialystock the talented American actor Richard Dreyfus, best known for his roles in movies like *American Graffiti* (1973), *The Goodbye Girl* (1977), *Close Encounters of the Third Kind* (1977), and *Jaws* (1975). At one of the early rehearsals in London, Richard threw his back out—badly. He valiantly struggled to carry on and promised Stro that he'd be ready on opening night, but Tom and I could see that it would take more time than we had for him to be fit to perform by opening night. So we asked Stro to call Nathan Lane and beg him to come over and save the show.

When Stro called Nathan I put my ear next to the phone, praying that Nathan would say yes. I grew desperate when I heard Nathan say, "No, not in a million years. I need a break from Max Bialystock. I can no longer do that part."

I didn't know what to do; I was panicking. Then it came to me and I whispered in Stro's ear: "Cry."

She held her hand over the phone and said to me, "What?"

I said, "Start crying! He's a softie! He won't turn you down."

She said, "I can't."

I said, "You must! Cry, cry!"

So Stro said in a tearful voice, "All right, Nathan, I understand. I don't blame you. I still love you." Her cries growing with each word.

There was a long pause on the phone. And then finally I heard Nathan angrily shout, "All right, dammit. I'll be there on the weekend."

Stro said a brief thank you and hung up and then Tom, Stro, and I held one another and both laughed and cried joyously. Nathan was coming to save the show!

And boy, save the show he did! *The Producers* opening night at the Drury Lane on November 9, 2004, was a triumph for the ages. A lot of the audience were standing on their seats and screaming bravos to the rafters. We all had to make speeches, and I got a big laugh when I said, "So much for British reserve!"

If possible, the London notices for *The Producers* were even better than the New York ones. *The Independent* called it "an epidemic of bliss" and *The Guardian* said, "What is its secret? At its simplest, it puts the comedy back into musical comedy."

So in the end, it was worth it for Nathan to come over to Lon-

Stro and me, showing off two of the twelve Tonys that The Producers *won that night—the most Tony Awards ever won by a musical in Broadway history.*

don. He not only got standing ovations every night and great reviews, but he went on to win the coveted Olivier Award for Best Actor in a Musical and our show was honored as the Best New Musical of the year.

Another truly memorable production of *The Producers* was at the world-famous Hollywood Bowl. It was the biggest theater that we had ever played, and I knew that we needed one of the biggest Max Bialystocks who ever played the part in order to have an actor who could reach the back row. There was only one name on my list—the multitalented, hilarious, and very loud Richard Kind. And what a great job he did! The Hollywood Bowl was packed for three nights under the stars with, believe it or not, seventeen thousand people in the audience. The laughs were so tremendous that they actually shook the stage. What an event! After the curtain call, I came up onstage to take a bow and say a few words. I got a standing ovation topped by a roar of approval from all seventeen thousand people. I secretly said to myself, "Maybe I should run for president? Seventeen thousand votes! That's a good beginning."

The Producers was the most wonderful and at the same time the most challenging thing that ever happened to me. It reached such great heights that it would seem impossible to write anything else that would ever come near it—but eventually I tried. It happened just after I lost Anne. She had struggled with cancer for several years, but in 2005 she lost her battle. For a long time, I was inconsolable. It was hard to wake up and live through the day.

Tom Meehan and Susan Stroman pulled me out of my depression with the same advice I had given to Stro when her husband, Mike, passed away.

Stro said, "Remember, the only way to climb out of grief is to work."

So Stro and Tom pulled me out of my abyss of despair, and we went to work on our next musical together. But what would it be? It came about when Tom said that just the other night he had been watching *Young Frankenstein* on TV. Frau Blücher's hilarious line, "He vas my boyfriend!" stuck in his head.

He said, "That's not just a funny line—that could be a whole funny song."

I said, "You're right. I can already hear it in my head . . ."

That was the beginning of another wonderful Broadway adventure with Tom and Stro, and many of the other talents from our great *Producers* team. *Young Frankenstein* the musical got standing ovations all through its previews in New York, so I foolishly thought we had another big hit. But I was treated to a rude awakening, and the mixed reviews proved me wrong. I then began to realize that the wild success of *The Producers* was much too big to duplicate. Although audiences were laughing and applauding, we couldn't match the incredible phenomenon that *The Producers* had created. By no means was *Young Frankenstein* a failure, it was a successful show, but it never could reach the impossible heights of its forerunner.

Nevertheless, I loved the show, and when asked several years later if I would be interested in a new production of it in London's West End at the Garrick Theatre I jumped at the chance. It gave me another opportunity to work on it and to do things that I had realized it had always needed. I knew it needed to be cut in places; the show wanted to be shorter and happier. That's the wonderful thing about the theater. Unlike in the movies where once a movie is finished and released you can't change it, in the theater a show is a living thing. When you realize something is wrong you can actually fix it and mount a new production.

And mount a new production we did! The London run of *Young Frankenstein* was an unqualified success. No mixed reviews here! Both the critics and the audiences loved it. It did my heart good to read those five-star reviews. I went to the theater almost every night just to sit and bathe in the laughter and applause from the wonderfully enthusiastic audiences that packed the Garrick Theatre.

While I was in London I stayed at the Savoy Hotel, a storied landmark dating all the way back to 1889 when it was built by Richard D'Oyly Carte with the money he earned from producing all of those wonderful Gilbert and Sullivan operettas like *H.M.S. Pinafore, The Mikado,* and *The Pirates of Penzance*. It's located on the Strand overlooking Waterloo Bridge and the Houses of Parliament on the Thames River. There were suites named after famous guests who had stayed there like Maria Callas, Winston Churchill, Charlie Chaplin, and Katharine Hepburn. When they asked me toward the end of my stay if they could put my name above the door of the suite I had been staying in, I said "Absolutely! I'd be honored."

With my three Tony awards for *The Producers* on Broadway, I became an EGOT—someone who has won an Emmy, Grammy, Oscar, and Tony Award. At the time, in 2001, I was only the eighth person in history to do so. I joined Richard Rodgers, Helen Hayes, Rita Moreno, John Gielgud, Audrey Hepburn, Marvin Hamlisch, and Jonathan Tunick, and I was immediately followed by Mike Nichols.

As important and as meaningful as all of these awards were and still are, *The Producers* on Broadway was my life as a writer, composer, producer, actor, and director coming full circle. It was my happiest professional experience because I felt that I was truly paid for my creative work. But I'm not talking about the money. It's a different kind of payment. It's *emotional* currency. It's audiences laughing their heads off, applauding, and at the end of the show giving you a standing ovation.

My god! This is what I was always meant to do.

Chapter 26

My Third Act

So while I've been lucky enough to receive many awards and honors throughout my career, and while each one is important to me, a few really stand out.

In 2009 I was chosen as one of the recipients of the Kennedy Center Honors. Since 1978 the awards have been presented annually at the Kennedy Center in Washington, D.C., to recognize individuals who have made significant and lasting contributions to American culture.

It actually wasn't the first time I was selected to be one of the honorees. A year or so before that, when George W. Bush was president, they called me to tell me I had been chosen.

"Thanks, but no thanks," I said.

I didn't want to be honored by Bush because as a veteran I was very unhappy about Americans being sent to war in Iraq. But in 2009, when Barack Obama was in the White House, I was delighted to once again be offered the Kennedy Center Honors. I immediately accepted and asked them whether I could get two, because I had turned down the first one. They were nice about it, explaining that they only give one to a customer.

Anyway, all kidding aside I really enjoyed that visit to Washington, D.C. My co-honorees that year were iconic musician Bruce Springsteen, the truly great actor Robert De Niro, jazz pianist virtuoso Dave Brubeck, and the talented opera star Grace Bumbry.

President Obama and First Lady Michelle Obama hosted a reception for the honorees at the White House. It was quite a gala occasion, and I got to bring my whole family with me: my daughter, Stefanie; my son Nicholas; my son Eddie and his wife, Sarah, and their daughter (my granddaughter), Samantha; and my son Max and his wife, Michelle, and their son (my grandson), Henry. We all got a wonderful tour of the White House capped off by being able to take beautiful pictures in the Blue Room with the president and First Lady. (I never realized how short my whole family is until we took pictures beside the Obamas. They were like redwood trees next to us!)

Me and the entire Brooks family flanked by the president and the First Lady at the White House for the Kennedy Center Honors in 2009. Left to right: First Lady Michelle Obama; my daughter, Stefanie; my daughter-in-law Michelle with my grandson, Henry; my son Nicholas; my son Max; me; my son Edward; my daughter-in-law Sarah; my granddaughter, Samantha; and President Barack Obama.

Later on, the president turned to each of the honorees to say a few words about their contributions to the arts. Dave Brubeck was before me, and Obama said very complimentary things about Brubeck and his musical genius. When he was finished and it was my turn, I interrupted him with an ad-lib about Brubeck. I said, "He never understood 4/4 time."

That got a big laugh, especially from Brubeck. And Obama retorted with, "Mel, I'm trying to say something nice about you, now. Please don't upstage me!"

That kept me quiet! Now I'm going to take this opportunity to shamelessly share with you the praise that the president of the United States heaped upon me.

> "By the time he was nine, this boy from Brooklyn had seen his first musical and dreamed of becoming 'the King of Broadway.' But World War II meant service in the Army—or, as he put it, 'the European Theater of Operations' with 'lots of operations' and 'very little theater.' Returning home, he found success cranking out quips for Sid Caesar—or as Mel described his reaction to success—'panic, hysteria, insomnia . . . and years of psychoanalysis.'
>
> "That's right, we're reading back all your golden moments here, Mel. Unfortunately, many of the punch lines that have defined Mel Brooks' success cannot be repeated here. I was telling him that I went to see *Blazing Saddles* when I was ten. And he pointed out that I think, according to the ratings, I should not have been allowed in the theater. That's true. I think I had a fake ID. But the statute of limitations has passed.
>
> "Suffice it to say, in his satires and parodies, no cow is sacred, no genre is safe. He mocked the musical—and Hitler—in *The Producers,* the Western in *Blazing Saddles,* and the horror film in *Young Frankenstein.*
>
> "But behind all the insanity and absurdity, there's been a

> method to Mel's madness. He's described his work as 'unearthing the truth that is all around us.' And by illuminating uncomfortable truths—about racism and sexism and anti-Semitism—he's been called 'our jester, asking us to see ourselves as we really are, determined that we laugh ourselves sane.' "

I hope he didn't get in trouble for revealing that he had snuck into *Blazing Saddles*!

Later on, when I was talking to the president alone, he put his arm around my shoulders and asked me how I was getting along having recently lost Anne after our forty-five years together. There is no good answer to that question, but I told him how much I appreciated that he was so caring.

The part of the Kennedy Center Honors that you see on TV happened later that night. It was a veritable explosion of talented people saluting talented people. Someone wisely asked Susan Stroman to be the one to put together a little show for my section of the gala. One of the funniest moments was Harry Connick, Jr., singing my song "High Anxiety." After the first few notes the little section of the stage he was standing on started to rise. By the time he finished the song he must have been forty or fifty feet in the air and was clearly feeling the anxiety in "High Anxiety." He got a roar of laughter when right before the final note he said, "Can someone get me down from here PLEASE?"

An unexpected laugh at my expense came when Ben Stiller took the stage to salute Robert De Niro. He looked up at the balcony where we were seated and decided to have some fun with the other honorees. He called me, "A pioneer. A trailblazer. He's like the Barack Obama for short funny Jews."

That got a big laugh out of both me *and* the president. It was all kind of surreal. It's hard to really explain how many different things I felt coursing through me that night, but suffice to say, it was another night to remember.

Me and the prez, laughing it up.

The Kennedy Center Honors was not the last time I would visit the White House. In 2015 I was named as a recipient of the National Medal of Arts, the highest honor given to artists by the United States government. (Up until then, the highest honor that had been bestowed on me by the government was making me a corporal in the U.S. Army.) So the following year I went back to Washington, D.C., to receive the medal from someone who now I considered my old pal, President Barack Obama.

I was filled with emotion by the president's speech:

> "We are here today to honor the very best of their fields, creators who give every piece of themselves to their craft. As Mel Brooks once said to his writers on *Blazing Saddles,* which is a great film: 'Write anything you want, because we'll never be heard from again. We will all be arrested for

> this movie.' Now, to be fair, Mel also said, a little more eloquently, that, 'Every human being has hundreds of separate people living inside his skin. And the talent of a writer is his ability to give them their separate names, identities, personalities and have them relate to other characters living within him.' And that, I think, is what the arts and the humanities do—they lift up our identities, and make us see ourselves in each other. And today's honorees each possess a gift for this kind of creative empathy—a gift that allows us to exchange a sense of what's most important and most profound in us, and to identify with our collective experience as Americans."

When he put the big, beautiful medal around my neck he said, "to Mel Brooks, for a lifetime of making the world laugh."

. . . And I made believe the medal was so heavy that I was falling! I grabbed the president to steady myself, and everybody cracked up—including the president! He warned me that he would catch me if I tried to sell the medal on eBay. So I promised to keep it, but said that I might use it as a coaster when I drink my iced tea.

I was lucky to have another honor bestowed upon me in 2013, the prestigious American Film Institute Life Achievement Award. AFI president Bob Gazzale, who since then has become a good friend, described the event as somewhat of a "roast"—but a clean roast, without all the usual insults fraught with dirty words. So it's a roast, but classier. It was a really fun occasion that I was able to celebrate with my entire family by my side. Especially my grandchildren, Samantha and Henry, who were both a little older by that time and able to have fun sharing the red carpet with me.

The whole evening was joyously emceed by the hilariously brilliant Martin Short. I had the joy and pleasure of getting to know Marty pretty well a few years earlier when he played Leo Bloom opposite Jason Alexander as Max Bialystock for the Los Angeles run of *The Producers* at the Hollywood Pantages Theatre. Even though

I'd seen the show a hundred times, I often went back just to enjoy Marty's particular brand of rib-cracking comedy, especially in the "blue blanket" sequence.

That night at the AFI gala I was absolutely thrilled to be saluted by some of the biggest filmmakers in Hollywood, but I wasn't expecting them to bitterly complain about what I had done to their beloved film genres. Clint Eastwood was the first to take me to task. He said, "The Western is one of the great genres of American film. Since the early days, Westerns have given us indelible images—the grandeur of endless landscapes, the intimacy of coffee at the campfire, men that do the right thing. I guess you could say the Western embodies the spirit of America . . . and this is what Mel Brooks did to it."

They cut directly to my famous campfire scene from *Blazing Saddles* where after eating mounds of beans and drinking gallons of black coffee, the cowhands let loose with loud explosions of wind across the prairie. I'm happy to report that the sounds of farting were outdone by the roars of laughter.

Next up was George Lucas. He said, "Early on in my career I set off on a bold adventure to see if I could take mythological motifs and turn them into a contemporary movie, and I called this adventure *Star Wars* . . . and this is what Mel Brooks did to it."

Once again, they cut directly to a hilarious scene in my movie *Spaceballs,* where Rick Moranis, encased in his huge dark helmet, says to Bill Pullman as Lone Starr during a clash of light sabers, "I see your Schwartz is as big as mine."

That double entendre was a little risqué with my grandchildren there, but I'm not going to take the rap for that—it was AFI's call and considering the big laugh it got it was worth it.

Next on the screen was the familiar face of the great film director Steven Spielberg. He said, "Movies bring history to life. They allow us to see, to experience great moments of the past as if we were there living it. From the dawn of man to the eternal stories of the Bible, to the epic tales of the Roman Empire—film's ability to help us understand where we came from is a proud and important tradition . . . and this is what Mel Brooks did to it."

There on the screen was my famous scene from *History of the World, Part I* with me playing Moses coming down from the mountain carrying three large stone tablets. In a commanding tone I utter these sacred words, "The Lord, the Lord Jehovah, has given you these Fifteen—" *Crash!* I drop one of the stone tablets and it smashes to pieces on the rocks below. So after a slight, embarrassing pause I continue with, "Ten! Ten Commandments!"

Which of course got one of the biggest laughs of the night. And then one after another a slew of top-drawer personalities came onstage and reduced me to tears of laughter with a barrage of comic barbs and insights that were just a little too true. There was Billy Crystal, Whoopi Goldberg, Robert De Niro, Sarah Silverman, Amy Poehler, Cloris Leachman, David Lynch, Jimmy Kimmel, Conan O'Brien, Nathan Lane, Matthew Broderick, Larry David, Jerry Seinfeld, and Carl Reiner. You couldn't hope to be insulted by more delightfully talented people!

They were all great, but one was particularly funny, stinging, and equally extravagant with praise and insults. That was Larry David. I had done a season of his very funny show *Curb Your Enthusiasm* and made a lot of jokes at his expense. He got even that night at the AFI.

Here is what he said:

> "Lavishing praise on people does not come easy to me. In fact, I find it quite distasteful. Let's just say it's not my cup of tea. Usually I have to wait for somebody to die to do it, and even then, I have to give it a couple of years. But not so tonight. When I first heard the 2000 Year Old Man, I was laughing so hard my father came into the room and turned off the record player. 'What the hell's going on in here, Larry?' See, my parents didn't mind me chuckling at a comedy album, or a TV show. A little chuckle was fine. But this was something

> else entirely. This was disturbing. So out of the ordinary. I never knew a person could be that funny. And from the very first time I heard that album, from that moment on, I said to myself, I can never ever be a comedian. What is the point? So Mel Brooks didn't get me into comedy. He kept me away from it. I wasted years doing nothing because of him. No job, living at home, lying on the couch watching *Shindig*. My parents were beside themselves. They cried themselves to sleep every night. He killed them. He killed my parents that little Jew bastard. Working with Mel on my show was one of the great thrills of my life. And that season was inspired by what was possibly the greatest comedic premise that anyone has ever dreamed up. *The Producers*."

When the camera cut to my reaction everybody was puzzled—I wasn't there! I had slipped under the table, unable to speak and laughing my brains out.

Earlier the AFI had asked me to choose from a list of previous recipients who I wanted to actually present the award to me at the end of the night. The minute I saw Marty Scorsese's name on the list I said, "See if you can get him."

When Bob Gazzale called me back to say that Scorsese was honored to be chosen and more than happy to do it, I was absolutely thrilled.

Here is what Martin Scorsese said that night when he handed me the award:

> "You know, there is a lot we take for granted but we shouldn't. And one of them is the treasured tradition of classic American film comedy. That's what we're celebrating here and honoring tonight. Because in Mel's films, all bets are off. The boundaries between what's funny and what isn't kind of fade away or tumble like that sheet falling in *It Happened*

> *One Night*. Mel breaks these boundaries with laughter. These boundaries actually disintegrate before your eyes at the end of *Blazing Saddles*. Telling a joke is one thing, making it part of a cohesive whole is something else again. And that's where the filmmaking comes in, his mastery of filmmaking. Mel has an anarchic spirit but a loving heart, and his films come from a profound fondness for classic cinema and a deep understanding of it. His uniquely manic sensibility is hardwired to something that is so easy to miss because we are laughing so hard, and that is his extremely disciplined mastery of the vocabulary of film. Mel has made his own comedy his own way and reminded us yet again what it's all too easy to forget: You could be a great filmmaker, just for laughs.
>
> "Ladies and gentlemen, the recipient of the AFI 41st Life Achievement Award, Mel Brooks."

Needless to say, I was humbled and flattered by Scorsese's beautiful and eloquent tribute. But now it was time for me to say good night and give my acceptance speech.

Here is how I began: From inside my tuxedo pocket, I pulled out a stack of notecards. I said, "So here are my notes."

I picked up the first one and read:

> "Thank AFI, friends, family, and colleagues for coming—try to be sincere."

I set that card aside to a nice bit of laughter and picked up the next card:

> "This says I grew up in a tenement at 365 South Third Street and everyone there was either working or destined to end up working in the Garment Center. But I took a road less traveled: movies. And they saved me. Movies saved my life. They rescued my soul. No matter what was bad or wrong it could be wiped out on Saturday morning."

Now let me interrupt here to explain something. I'm gonna tell you the god's honest truth. I realized that the recipient of the AFI award, if they are still alive, usually comes back to say some nice words the following year about the new AFI honoree. I just didn't want to do that. I didn't want to have to come back here, wear a tuxedo and tight shiny patent leather shoes, eat that dry chicken washed down with not the very best wine, and—no offense—make believe I was enjoying the evening. So instead, I devised a plan to both do the job and not have to come back.

This is what I said:

> ". . . with your permission I'd like to *preemptively* toast next year's honoree. So I don't have to come back, okay? Listen, he or she is a remarkable creative force who has had a *huge* impact on my life and career. I've known him or her for over twenty years and can honestly say that he or she is the only person that I've never been jealous of, because when somebody is truly talented you just have to salute it! So here's to you for a well-deserved award, and to the AFI—you finally got it right!"

I got a standing ovation. I picked up my award, said good night, blew some kisses, and made my way offstage.

. . . But a year later, my escape plan was ruined! I got a call from the next recipient of the AFI Life Achievement Award, the one and only Jane Fonda. She had heard my not coming back speech but begged me to please attend. Who could say no to Jane Fonda? I was there.

If that wasn't enough, the following year the AFI recipient was Steve Martin, who chose me from the list of previous winners to present the award to him. Once again I just couldn't say no. I was always a big fan of Steve's incredibly funny and insightful comedy. So I suffered the dry chicken, the tight shoes, the bad wine, and went to give a much-deserved honor to the gifted and brilliant Steve Martin.

Even at an age where many people are retired I am always looking for new projects to exercise my mind and engage my creativity. Because in my experience if you're not working, you're not really alive. In 2010 Dick Cavett, who I had done so many interviews with on TV through the years and who is also a good friend, asked me to join him for a live event onstage to promote his new book: *Brief Encounters: Conversations, Magic Moments, and Assorted Hijinks*. Dick, just like Johnny Carson, had a knack for getting the crazy best out of me. The back and forth was always hilarious. So knowing that, I decided to get a camera crew to tape the evening. I wanted to have a record of what he called the "hijinks." I turned it into a special that premiered on HBO with a new title: *Mel Brooks and Dick Cavett Together Again*.

I had so much fun making that show that I just kept doing it. My second special for HBO was *Mel Brooks Strikes Back!* With my old friend Alan Yentob from the BBC interviewing me onstage. For my third special I wanted to do something that was not an interview, something that was closer to a one-man show on Broadway. So I booked the Geffen Playhouse in Westwood and said, "Get me my tux and roll out a piano!"

I extolled the highlights of my adventures in show business from the Borscht Belt to Broadway and then I picked up a microphone and sang my heart out. May I say immodestly that the show was a resounding success. I think I enjoyed it as much as the audience.

Just recently I worked with HBO again to bring my old friend Alan Yentob's unusual and amazing documentary covering our long working friendship to American audiences. *Mel Brooks: Unwrapped* spans from his first interview with me at Twentieth Century Fox when I was directing *History of the World, Part I* all the way through present day with the two of us still hanging out and having laughs together.

It was around this time that I decided that I missed the sound of laughter emanating from a live audience. There is just nothing

Taking a well-deserved bow onstage at the Geffen Playhouse. (Forgive the immodesty.)

like it! So I started traveling around to different places, different theaters in different cities, and I'd get onstage and tell them a lot of what I've told you in the book: how I came to be Mel Brooks. I was lucky to have a great accomplice in Kevin Salter, my producer from *Mel Brooks Live at the Geffen*. Kevin would bring me onstage and ask me just the right questions that would always bring forth answers that would spark explosions of laughter. They were great nights, filling me with the joy of thousands of people all laughing together. I played such storied venues as the Prince of Wales Theatre in London, the Kennedy Center for the Performing Arts in D.C., the Lunt-Fontanne Theatre on Broadway, twice at the Chicago Theatre, twice at the Wynn in Las Vegas, and what a thrill it was to see my name on the marquee of Radio City Music Hall with a wonderful SOLD OUT next to it.

I'd usually start the evening by playing one of my movies before I took the stage, most often *Blazing Saddles*. It was so enjoyable standing offstage in the wings and listening to the audience crack up at some of those dangerous gags in the film. Today my movies are usually played on small TV sets in people's homes. But there is

Pretty thrilling for a kid from Brooklyn to be headlining at Radio City Music Hall.

nothing like seeing your movie on that incredibly huge silver screen and getting the fantastic communal laughter that it was meant for. Talk about an opening act—you couldn't beat *Blazing Saddles*.

Toward the end of the evening Kevin would ask the audience for questions and sometimes I would get really lucky with an answer that would bring down the house.

For instance, I remember one night an audience member shouted out: "Mel! What do you wear—boxers or briefs?"

I shouted back: "DEPENDS!"

I've gotta say, the theater shook with a veritable earthquake of laughter in response. (Actually, I don't wear Depends . . . but as I get on in years I *might* not just be telling a joke.)

Another common question was: "Mel, what's your secret to a long life?"

I always replied: "Don't die."

Boy, that really landed. I still think that the best thing in the world is saying something funny, and then having an audience explode with laughter. I will never grow tired of that. It's magical.

The famous author of *The Great Gatsby,* F. Scott Fitzgerald, once said, "There are no second acts."

Well, I've been lucky enough to prove him wrong. I have had a great second act and I'm enjoying a pretty good third act too. If I were a Shakespearean play, I'd be rooting for five acts!

I'm also proud to say that I have made people laugh for a living, and whether or not you'll allow me to, I'm going to brag—I can honestly say, I've done it as well as anybody. I started in 1938 as a street-corner comic in Brooklyn, and I'm still doing it . . . just on more well-known street corners. Comedy is a weird but very beautiful thing. Even though it seems foolish and silly and crazy, comedy has the most to say about the human condition. Because if you can laugh, you can get by. You can survive when things are bad if you have a sense of humor.

I started writing this book because, like everyone else in 2020, I was stuck at home. So I figured, why not? My son Max encouraged me. He said, "Just tell all the stories you told me when I was growing up and you'll already have a big fat book."

It's been a lot of fun writing this memoir, and I'm sorry I have to bring it to a close. But who knows, maybe we'll meet again in another chapter called:

The History of Mel Brooks, Part II.

"Where you headed, cowboy?"
"Nowhere special."
"Nowhere special . . . I've always wanted to go there."

—THE WACO KID AND SHERIFF BART,
Blazing Saddles

Acknowledgments

I hope I have remembered things as they happened so many years ago. If any of you who know me well remember them differently—keep it to yourself.

It's not easy to write a book, especially an autobiography. There are so many things to remember and so many ways to say those things. It's almost impossible if you don't have the right people to help you accomplish this mighty task. First and foremost, people like Shelby Van Vliet. There are words to describe her that simply can't say enough about who she is and what she's done for me in fashioning this book. Words like "indefatigable"—to wit, untiring, incapable of being fatigued—hardly describe her monumental feat in getting this book out of me every day in every way. Encouraging me to go on when I was stumbling, bumbling, and sometimes ready to quit. Her tireless optimism and good nature filled me with the courage and energy to go forth and continue on. So thank you, Shelby, for your gracious good humor and for suffering my explosions of despair and being the sturdy guardrails that always kept me on track. The truth is I could never have written this book without your help.

To my literary agent, Jonny Geller, for fighting my initial resistance and talking me into this incredible undertaking. Thank you, Jonny.

To my editor, Pamela Cannon, for her never-flagging enthusiasm and great support at every twist and turn all along the way. Without you and the whole wonderful team at Ballantine Books I don't think I could have done it (at least not nearly as well!).

To Eddy Friedfeld, without whom I would still be lost in the wilderness of almost a century of memories. Eddy, thank you for your boundless resourcefulness in helping me put together a fabulous road map of everything I've ever said or done. You're a lot more than just a researcher and archivist, you're a bit of a genius.

To Leah Zappy, Randy Auerbach, Michael Gruskoff, Alan Yentob, Steve Haberman, and all the other friends and colleagues I leaned on to help me remember the where and when of what happened behind the scenes as I went from movie to movie on my way to Broadway.

To Kevin Salter, for helping me take the stage for my third act, and always being there to make everything I do so fulfilling and enjoyable.

To Dave Rodgers, my right hand and my right arm, for keeping me upright every time I faltered and for always being there any and every time I needed you.

And last but not least a great big thank-you to my wonderful family. My children, Stefanie, Nicky, Eddie, and Max, and my remarkable grandchildren, Samantha and Henry—I could not have gotten through the marathon of writing this book without you all being there right through to the finish line, rallying me on with your faith in me. You are my never-ending source of strength and hope. I love you all.

Image Credits

PAGE

iii From the author's collection
15 Courtesy of Mel Brooks
28 Courtesy of Mel Brooks
37 Courtesy of Mel Brooks
46 Courtesy of Mel Brooks
50 (left and right) Courtesy of Mel Brooks
56 Courtesy of Mel Brooks
57 Courtesy of Mel Brooks
58 Courtesy of Mel Brooks
61 Courtesy of Mel Brooks
62 Courtesy of Mel Brooks
70 From the author's collection, originally appearing in *Stars and Stripes* military newspaper
72 Courtesy of Mel Brooks
82 NBCUniversal via Getty Images
98 Courtesy of the Sid Caesar estate
102 CBS Photo Archive via Getty Images
110 NBCUniversal via Getty Images
113 Courtesy of the Sid Caesar estate
114 Courtesy of Mel Brooks
117 Courtesy of MGM Media Licensing
120 Courtesy of Mel Brooks and the estate of Carl Reiner
125 Gerald Smith/NBCU Photo Bank via Getty Images
131 Michael Ochs Archives via Getty Images
136 NBCUniversal via Getty Images
142 ScreenProd/Photononstop/Alamy Stock Photo
145 Courtesy of Mel Brooks

156 Courtesy of Mel Brooks
168 PictureLux/The Hollywood Archive/Alamy Stock Photo
172 Entertainment Pictures/Alamy Stock Photo
186 PictureLux/The Hollywood Archive/Alamy Stock Photo
194 (top and bottom) Courtesy of Brooksfilms Limited
196 (left and right) Courtesy of Brooksfilms Limited
204 PictureLux/The Hollywood Archive/Alamy Stock Photo
209 PictureLux/The Hollywood Archive/Alamy Stock Photo
212 WARNER BROS/Ronald Grant Archive/Alamy Stock Photo
213 Photo 12/Alamy Stock Photo
219 Allstar Picture Library Ltd./Alamy Stock Photo
222 Courtesy of Brooksfilms Limited
228 YOUNG FRANKENSTEIN © 1974 Twentieth Century Fox. All rights reserved. Poster design by John Alvin.
238 PictureLux/The Hollywood Archive/Alamy Stock Photo
240 YOUNG FRANKENSTEIN © 1974 Twentieth Century Fox. All rights reserved.
245 PictureLux/The Hollywood Archive/Alamy Stock Photo
246 Collection Christophel/Alamy Stock Photo
247 Ronald Grant Archive/Alamy Stock Photo
252 Hulton Archive via Getty Images
254 SILENT MOVIE © 1976 Twentieth Century Fox. All rights reserved.
259 SILENT MOVIE © 1976 Twentieth Century Fox. All rights reserved.
260 SILENT MOVIE © 1976 Twentieth Century Fox. All rights reserved.
262 Pictorial Press Ltd./Alamy Stock Photo
267 Moviestore Collection Ltd./Alamy Stock Photo
268 SILENT MOVIE © 1976 Twentieth Century Fox. All rights reserved.
279 © 1976 Twentieth Century Fox. All rights reserved.
282 HIGH ANXIETY © 1977 Twentieth Century Fox. All rights reserved. Photo by Elliott Marks.
283 HIGH ANXIETY © 1977 Twentieth Century Fox. All rights reserved. Photo by Elliott Marks.
287 HIGH ANXIETY © 1977 Twentieth Century Fox. All rights reserved.
288 HIGH ANXIETY © 1977 Twentieth Century Fox. All rights reserved. Photo by Elliott Marks.
291 HIGH ANXIETY © 1977 Twentieth Century Fox. All rights reserved. Photo by Elliott Marks.
293 Courtesy of the Estate of Alfred Hitchcock c/o Reeder Brand Management
300 Pictorial Press Ltd./Alamy Stock Photo
306 HISTORY OF THE WORLD PART I © 1981 Twentieth Century Fox. All rights reserved.

307 AF archive/Alamy Stock Photo
310 HISTORY OF THE WORLD PART I © 1981 Twentieth Century Fox. All rights reserved.
311 HISTORY OF THE WORLD PART I © 1981 Twentieth Century Fox. All rights reserved.
313 HISTORY OF THE WORLD PART I © 1981 Twentieth Century Fox. All rights reserved. Photo by Elliott Marks.
315 HISTORY OF THE WORLD PART I © 1981 Twentieth Century Fox. All rights reserved. Photo by Bert Cann.
330 TO BE OR NOT TO BE © 1983 Twentieth Century Fox. All rights reserved.
334 TO BE OR NOT TO BE © 1983 Twentieth Century Fox. All rights reserved. Photo by Stephen Vaughan.
335 TO BE OR NOT TO BE © 1983 Twentieth Century Fox. All rights reserved.
338 TO BE OR NOT TO BE © 1983 Twentieth Century Fox. All rights reserved. Photo by Stephen Vaughan.
341 AF archive/Alamy Stock Photo
344 Courtesy of Mel Brooks
347 Courtesy of Mel Brooks
348 Courtesy of Mel Brooks
360 Courtesy of MGM Media Licensing
363 Courtesy of MGM Media Licensing
364 Courtesy of MGM Media Licensing
366 Courtesy of MGM Media Licensing
367 Courtesy of MGM Media Licensing
368 Courtesy of MGM Media Licensing
370 Courtesy of MGM Media Licensing
372 Courtesy of MGM Media Licensing
374 Courtesy of MGM Media Licensing
376 Courtesy of MGM Media Licensing
377 Courtesy of MGM Media Licensing
382 Courtesy of Mel Brooks
383 ROBIN HOOD: MEN IN TIGHTS © 1993 Twentieth Century Fox. All rights reserved. Photo by Robert Isenberg.
385 ROBIN HOOD: MEN IN TIGHTS © 1993 Twentieth Century Fox. All rights reserved. Photo by Robert Isenberg.
386 ROBIN HOOD: MEN IN TIGHTS © 1993 Twentieth Century Fox. All rights reserved. Photo by Robert Isenberg.
387 ROBIN HOOD: MEN IN TIGHTS © 1993 Twentieth Century Fox. All rights reserved. Photo by Robert Isenberg.
390 United Archives GmbH/Alamy Stock Photo

393 RGR Collection/Alamy Stock Photo
394 United Archives GmbH/Alamy Stock Photo
402 Courtesy of Brooksfilms Limited
411 Courtesy of Scott Bishop
433 ZUMA Press, Inc./Alamy Stock Photo
438 Courtesy Barack Obama Presidential Library
441 Courtesy Barack Obama Presidential Library
449 Courtesy of Michael Lamont
450 Courtesy of Brooksfilms Limited

PHOTO: © STEVEN R. STACK

Mel Brooks, director, producer, writer, and actor, is an EGOT—one of the few entertainers in an elite group to earn all four major entertainment prizes: the Emmy, the Grammy, the Oscar, and the Tony. His career began in television writing for *Your Show of Shows,* after which he helped create the TV series *Get Smart.* He and Carl Reiner wrote and performed the 2000 Year Old Man Grammy-winning comedy albums. Brooks won the Oscar for Best Original Screenplay for his first feature film, *The Producers.* Many hit comedy films followed, including *The Twelve Chairs; Blazing Saddles; Young Frankenstein; Silent Movie; High Anxiety; History of the World, Part I; To Be or Not to Be; Spaceballs; Robin Hood: Men in Tights;* and *Dracula: Dead and Loving It.* His film company, Brooksfilms Limited, produced critically acclaimed films such as *The Elephant Man, Frances, My Favorite Year,* and *84 Charing Cross Road.* In 2009 Mel Brooks was a Kennedy Center Honoree, recognized for a lifetime of extraordinary contributions to American culture. In 2013 he was the forty-first recipient of the AFI Life Achievement Award. In 2016 Mr. Brooks was presented with the National Medal of Arts by President Obama.

ABOUT THE TYPE

This book was set in Sabon, a typeface designed by the well-known German typographer Jan Tschichold (1902–74). Sabon's design is based upon the original letter forms of sixteenth-century French type designer Claude Garamond and was created specifically to be used for three sources: foundry type for hand composition, Linotype, and Monotype. Tschichold named his typeface for the famous Frankfurt typefounder Jacques Sabon (c. 1520–80).